# STATES
versus
# MARKETS

History, Geography, and the
Development of the International
Political Economy

# STATES
## versus
# MARKETS

History, Geography, and the
Development of the International
Political Economy

## Herman M. Schwartz
*University of Virginia*

St. Martin's Press

*New York*

*Executive editor:* Don Reisman
*Managing editor:* Patricia Mansfield-Phelan
*Project editor:* Talvi Laev
*Production supervisor:* Elizabeth Mosimann/Joe Ford
*Art director:* Sheree Goodman
*Graphics:* Maryland CartoGraphics
*Cover design:* Marek Antoniak

Library of Congress Catalog Card Number: 92-62749

8 7 6 5 4
f e d c b a

For information, write:

St. Martin's Press, Inc.
175 Fifth Avenue
New York, NY 10010

ISBN: 0-312-06594-9

Published and distributed outside North America by
THE MACMILLAN PRESS LTD
Houndmills, Basingstoke, Hampshire RG21 2XS
and London
Companies and representatives throughout the world

ISBN 0-333-61852-1

A catalogue record for this book is available from the British Library.

For CMS and MDS
*Brief candles*

# Preface

*States versus Markets* is about the interaction of states and markets in the international economy. Markets constantly, impartially, and unconsciously change the distribution of production in geographic space. States intervene to help or hinder this market-driven redistribution, but on an intermittent and self-interested basis, and often with unintended results. States experienced their greatest successes in controlling international and domestic markets during the period commonly referred to as the postwar era. (The very perception of a division between the two markets is a measure of their success.) From roughly 1945 to 1973, states used the institutions built during the Great Depression and World War II to regulate their domestic economies and to shelter domestic markets from pressures emanating from the international market. Beginning in 1973, however, their ability to do so eroded. Markets became increasingly unstable. Productive and financial capital that had once been well rooted seemed to whiz uncontrollably around the globe seeking out profitable opportunities. New competitors emerged in distant countries. Industrialization seemed all too easy for some poor countries and a distant dream for others.

Most books about the international political economy tend to look at these trends as deviations from the normal pattern of the postwar period. Consequently, they cannot give an adequate picture of the present-day situation. Far from being normal, that is, typical, the stability and successful state intervention of the postwar period represented a dramatic departure from the typical processes of the global economy. The global economy is in fact moving *back to the future*, resembling more and more the global economy of the nineteenth century.

This book examines the international political economy in a self-consciously geographical and historical way. It explains the typical processes of the prewar global economy in order to see how the postwar period deviated from those processes and to provide an understanding of the probable future. Much of what is happening now becomes intelligible if we look at the basic processes of the prewar economy. Several tensions shaped the prewar economy. The intertwined emergence of the modern state and the modern world economy from medieval Europe meant that states existed not only at the interface between domestic society and the international arena for politico-military purposes, but also at the interface between emerging domestic and existing world markets. States could not exist without revenue, and international market outcomes strongly influenced revenue streams. Because states had only limited abilities to control international market pressures, they could not prevent enormous and wrenching shifts in the location of global agricultural production (and agriculture constituted much of the economy then). This situation created ongoing social tensions as peasants, landlords, and small-holders tried to cope with increased competition and falling prices. It also threatened the states' major sources of revenue. And while the evolving inter-national division of labor in agriculture meant new opportunities for industri-alization in some places, that industrialization in turn created a threat of deindustrialization elsewhere. States thus faced a continuing problem of main-taining industrial competitiveness in a global economy.

The first half of the book describes these key tensions between markets and states in the prewar period. The second half shows how the postwar economy temporarily departed from the patterns these tensions had created, but argues that many of the older patterns are now reasserting themselves. States' revenue bases and their ability to borrow are once more hostage to international market outcomes. The shifting pattern of both industrial and agricultural activity has seemingly mired entire regions in unemployment and zero growth while others are booming. A cursory scan of any newspaper on any given day yields many articles on deindustrialization and demands for state intervention to promote competitiveness.

## Caveat Emptor

This book does not pretend to be either a comprehensive survey of all current issues in the international political economy or a detailed description of the post–World War II period. Coverage of the postwar period was deliberately pared down to include material from preceding periods, and in particular to give some attention to the pre-twentieth-century agricultural economy. Cover-age of the postwar period has also been designed to elucidate, where possible, trends that have continued from the previous period as well as breaks with those trends. Furthermore, any synoptic review that covers a long period of time and a large number of countries while devoting the necessary depth of coverage to production as well as exchange is necessarily stylized. A good empirical overview is both a useful corrective and a supplement to this kind of enterprise. Fortunately, St. Martin's Press also publishes the best empirical survey of the post–World War II period: Joan Edelman Spero's *The Politics of International Economic Relations*. Detailed coverage of major alternative view-points on the international political economy has also been omitted in favor of lower-level theories about production and the (re-)distribution of production in space. But, to steal language from the software world, this treatment is upwardly compatible with many of those theoretical visions.

# Acknowledgments

Isaac Newton once said that he was able to see so far because he was standing on the shoulders of giants. Somewhat shorter than Newton, I am perched precariously on ladders resting on the shoulders of a number of giants. Part of this book's purpose is to make the work of such giants available for a more general audience. I also saw as far as I did because some people provided or held the ladders on which I stood. Richard Rosecrance stayed polite through several excited arguments about Jane Jacobs, cities, and trade a very long time ago while I was at Cornell University. More important, Rosecrance introduced me to Edward Fox at Cornell, whose influence on this book can be seen in the application of Johann von Thünen's location theories to the prewar economy. My former colleagues and students at the New School for Social Research gave me a chance to work out many of the ideas presented here. In particular, I wish to thank Janet Abu-Lughod, who broadened my geographic and historical horizons while we co-taught a seminar on the making of the "Third World," and Ari Zolberg, who forced me to read Charles Tilly closely while we co-taught a seminar on national security. Despite discouraging me from doing this project (now), Richard Bensel suffered through my ramblings on what eventually became Chapters 8 and 15.

At the University of Virginia, Jeremiah Reilly, John Duffield, and Aida Hozic each read the entire manuscript, and Aida in particular helped to focus many arguments. John Echeverri-Gent, Len Schoppa, John Blakeman, Jason Hubbard, Jim Hunter, and Lorna McDaniel also helped. At St. Martin's Press, Don Reisman and the perpetually good-humored Talvi Laev helped to shepherd the book to completion. The following reviewers for St. Martin's Press also provided useful comments: Edward Friedman, University of Wisconsin at Madison; Stephan Haggard, Harvard University; Glenn Hayslett, University of North Carolina at Chapel Hill; Timothy McKeown, University of North Carolina at Chapel Hill; Eduardo M. Ochoa, California State University at Los Angeles; Brian Pollins, Ohio State University; Neil Richardson, University of Wisconsin at Madison; and Beth Simmons, Duke University. Most important of all, Eve Schwartz, my wife, provided incredible emotional support during an otherwise very difficult time in our lives.

*Herman M. Schwartz*

# Contents

## PART II

## Back to the Future:
## The Reemergence of a Global Economy

# List of Figures and Tables

## FIGURES

## TABLES

# PART I

# States, Agriculture, and Space

# Introduction

Tom Peters, a management guru popular in the 1980s, used to tell a story about his experiences as an engineer. In 1972 the company he worked for asked him to work up cost figures for a new petrochemical plant they were building. Since oil is the basic input for petrochemicals, he sat down to project the cost of oil over the 20-year working life of the plant. He put his ruler down on a graph of the nominal cost of oil per barrel for the last 20 years — basically a straight line — and then drew a line that continued out another 20 years. Surprise! By early 1974 the nominal price of oil had quadrupled, and over the next 20 years the price of oil fluctuated between $10 and $40 per barrel, rarely resting at any one price.

Meanwhile, most people would probably like to find some way to sort out the order within the apparent chaos of world markets. Unfortunately, the certainties that misguided Peters in 1972 no longer exist, nor do the institutions and dynamics that characterized the international economy from roughly 1948 to the mid-1970s. However, the end to the certainties characterizing the immediate past does not mean an end to patterns in the global economy altogether. The global economy is returning to even older patterns that characterized the prewar global economy.

# The Problem

At its most basic level, the international political economy is about how market pressures cause a constant relocation of productive activities in a global space, and how states try to bend those market forces when it hurts them and allow them to work when it helps. Markets constantly change the distribution of production in geographic space. States intervene to help or hinder this market-driven redistribution, but often with unintended results. Because states were able to control or contain markets during most of the postwar period, most people assume they will be able to continue to do so in the future. This foreshortening of historical vision makes it difficult to understand what is most essential about the modern world economy, because that economy is going *back to the future*. In its most fundamental respects, it is becoming much more like the kind of world economy that existed in the late nineteenth century than that of the mid-twentieth century. During the earlier period two market forces typically overwhelmed state policies.

The first was a secular trend toward greater movement of people, capital, commodities, and firms internationally. Entering the market before 1914 meant entering the world market. Before 1914 trade grew rapidly, based on complementary flows of goods between exporters of agricultural goods and exporters of manufactured goods. Roughly 120 million people moved overseas either voluntarily or involuntarily. European settlers and colonial governments transformed the ecology of entire continents in their search for more food and raw materials. Market forces dictated the general location of these new agricultural zones. Competent or lucky states seized the opportunities before them; incompetent ones fumbled the future. At the same time, the British industrial revolution threatened to displace industrial production from continental Europe and turn much of Europe into an agricultural supply region for Great Britain. Again, competent or lucky states blocked this threat and helped local firms defend themselves from the British; incompetent ones found themselves relegated to being suppliers of raw materials for Britain. Yet, in all this activity states rarely blocked the effects of market forces. Instead, they deflected market pressures in the directions they preferred.

The postwar international economy differed because it came after a long period in which trade and other flows actually shrank. The period 1914 to 1948 thus represented a great rupture with past centuries. As a proportion of total economic activity, global trade did not regain its 1914 levels until roughly 1980. The diminished importance of world trade created a space in which states could impose a remarkable stability on their economies. Postwar stability was a temporary outgrowth of the relatively small part international trade played in most economies during and after the Great Depression.

So states actually dominated markets for a time after the 1930s. This may seem a peculiar statement, since the 1930s are generally regarded as a period in which markets ran wild, harming many people. However, precisely in reaction to the calamities of the 1930s, states gained the legal and institutional power to try to control markets. States imposed controls over capital movements, foreign exchange, labor markets, agricultural prices and output, sometimes industrial prices and output, and interest rates. In short, they invaded and regulated local markets to a considerable extent, while sheltering those markets from the international economy.

The international market cooperated in this effort at local control, because reduction in international trade and capital flows in the 1930s meant that international market forces were small in comparison to the relatively tamed local market forces. The immediate postwar period also saw substantial degrees of formal cooperation between long-established states. Most important, it saw very little — relatively speaking — international movement of capital, industry, and people.

But the world of today is becoming more like the world of the nineteenth century, when international market forces impelled capital movements, trade, and migration, and when states at best coped with the consequences of those market forces and at worst collapsed before them. Fearing the efforts of the state to regulate the market, firms have been and are continuing to do an end-run around regulation and to position themselves in their major markets through either investment or strategic alliances. With 100 times the amount of foreign exchange needed to finance all global trade in one year passing from one gambler to another *daily*, even states ruling the largest economies find it difficult or impossible to maintain a fixed exchange rate or to try to conduct an independent monetary policy.

The second trend appears to involve the recurrence of economic cycles. There are constant — but not automatic — upswings and downswings in the economy. New innovations, what Joseph Schumpeter called "gales of creative destruction," threaten industrial dinosaurs with extinction. These innovations usually combine different kinds of scientific/engineering technologies with new management technologies. In today's economy, this means energy saved by using electronic rather than physical processes to move information, like faxing; smart machines that transform energy into work more efficiently, like computer-controlled machine tools, electronic ignition, or biotechnologies; and, of course, new products, like PCs, automatic coffee makers, and VCRs. Simply using these new tools or making these new products is no guarantee of success, however; they also have to be used more efficiently. "Soft" management technologies like team work, total quality management, just-in-time inventory systems, and giving workers more responsibility, combined with new organizational structures such as so-called virtual or networked corporations, matter just as much as and perhaps more than the hard scientific technologies themselves.

These hard and soft innovations have tended to cluster in time and in space. Because they cluster in space, the core of industrial activity has shifted, much to the chagrin of formerly dominant states. For example, Britain's nineteenth-century industrial supremacy wilted before challenges from the United States and Germany, and U.S. postwar industrial supremacy has been ground down by Japan and Germany—though not as much as many think.

## What This Book Is About

This book looks at how markets created distinct spatial patterns in what was produced and at how states attempted to influence that distribution of production. It thus examines domestic as well as international institutions from a long-term perspective. I hope to provide a better guide to the future of the international political economy.

Chapters 1 and 2 describe the coincident emergence of a world economy and the modern state. The modern state emerged at a time when the international economy was the only real market economy. Use of "international" here is actually an abuse of the term, for nations did not exist; a waterborne economy is perhaps closer to the truth. National economies did not exist as such, for the interior of what became most nations was composed of a set of largely self-sufficient microeconomies in which exchange occurred, but not via markets with self-regulating prices. In the guise of mercantilism, the state sponsored a "marketization" of those microeconomies, bringing the global economy inward. This action created an enduring set of problems for the state. At first, it involved the creation of a homogeneous internal legal space in which self-regulating markets could function. Later, state-sponsored railroad building opened up the interior physically, creating national markets. In this process, the state sought stable internal sources of revenue, which it obtained. Ironically, however, it also exposed the internal market, and thus its revenue sources, to enormous external competitive and monetary pressures. By World War I railroads—often state-sponsored—had opened up the interior of most states' territory. But the vast pool of international money held as overseas assets and the weakness of central banking meant that any independent monetary policy was impossible. The rise of new manufacturing and agricultural economies also exposed established producers to extreme competitive pressures. Thus, the current preoccupation with competitiveness has antecedents, as does the constant oscillation in state policy between more and less openness to world markets.

Chapter 3 examines the recurrent emergence of new paradigms for manufacturing, and thus the constant relocation of core manufacturing activities. It also discusses the emergence of new paradigms for organizing the world economy politically, that is, the creation of hegemony. Chapters 4 through 6 expand on this discussion by looking at the symbiotic expansion of European industry and agriculture globally in the nineteenth century. Chapter 4 starts with a discussion of the British industrial revolution. Britain's extraordinary, if temporary, industrial competitiveness threatened continental European states with deindustrialization. British industry's appetite for agricultural raw materials and foods induced or forced most of the world to begin supplying it with those things.

States responded to the British industrial revolution with a combination of two strategies. *Ricardian* strategies used exports of raw materials to generate economic growth. These strategies were based on comparative advantage. *Kaldorian* strategies tried to use verdoorn effects—the increased rates of productivity growth created by increasing rates of output, increasing returns to scale, learning by doing, and rapid technological innovation—to generate economic growth and ultimately *competitive* advantage. The Ricardian strategy predominated in the nineteenth century, because it was easier to accomplish. Although Kaldorian strategies are at the heart of successful industrialization, they were much more difficult to pull off.

One of the most important points made in Chapter 4, therefore, is that European states could not take industrialization for granted. Britain's new paradigm for "best practice manufacturing"—the application of mechanical power to the production of household goods in factories by full-time wage laborers—threatened to sweep away those states' own industrial bases. Industrialization in Western Europe was just as problematical as industrialization is in the periphery or Third World today. Industrialization in Europe was neither an automatic nor a fully spontaneous process. Like today's late industrializers in the Third World, European states systematically intervened in the market, sheltering local industry from hypercompetitive producers elsewhere and cultivating leading sectors to pull the rest of the economy forward.

Fears that external competition might sweep away local industry were not confined to the nineteenth century. Early (or earlier) industrialization did not guarantee continued competitiveness for European economies. Every few generations a cluster of new innovations threatened established producers with Schumpeter's creative destruction. Thus, the current mortality and morbidity among U.S. and European firms as Asian producers invade their markets are nothing new. The same thing happened when U.S. firms invaded Europe and when Britain exported to the world. Chapters 8, 11, and 14 look at this process of competition among developed industrial economies. Later, Chapters 12 and 13 pick up the discussion of late industrialization begun in Chapter 4 and extend it to the modern Third World.

Chapters 5 and 6 discuss the consequences of British industrialization for the parts of the world inside and outside Europe that opted for Ricardian strategies. Industrialization in Western Europe both depended on and energized a vast ecological transformation inside and outside Europe. Millions of acres of forest and plain were turned into fields for production of grain, fibers, stimulants, and sugar, and millions of foreign animals spread into empty ecological niches in the Southern Hemisphere. If kangaroos could pass immigration laws, there would not be over 100 million sheep in Australia today. Food and agriculturally derived raw materials accounted for over half of international trade as late as 1929. Transportation costs and the availability of land ruled the global dispersion of European agriculture, which deserves an explanation based on those dynamics.

Most international capital movements in the nineteenth century financed this transformation. Any discussion of the international political economy that ignores agriculture minimizes the forces that created today's periphery. Chapters 6 and 7 focus on the creation of these agricultural supply regions and the methods used to finance Ricardian development.

This ecological transformation also caused a vast demographic transformation. Traditionally, the international political economy's holy trinity has been money, trade, and investment. A better trinity might be commodities, capital, and people. Over the centuries people have also entered into international exchange as commodities — slaves — and as willing migrants. Slavery is largely a thing of the past now, but the reasons why Salvadorans migrate today are fairly similar to the reasons why the Irish migrated in the nineteenth century. Chapter 5 considers migration and the role of political force in creating labor supplies in the world economy.

The first half of the book comes to a close with a consideration of the international monetary and trade systems. Here, too, looking at the past is a good guide to the future. The international monetary system today increasingly resembles the securities (stocks and bonds) -based money system of the late nineteenth century. The only major difference is the absence of gold backing for money, which predisposes the system to inflation. The end of Chapter 7 focuses on these issues. The international trading system has also been drifting away from the guarded liberalism of the Bretton Woods era to the more extensive and eclectic kind of protectionism present in the nineteenth century. This protection mixed a concern for noncompetitive sectors with a desire to promote leading sectors. Nineteenth-century trade was not "managed," but that reflected a paucity of instruments, not of desire. Chapter 8 looks at those issues by focusing on the decline of British competitiveness as the United States and Germany pursued successful Kaldorian industrialization strategies. Chapter 8 closes with a discussion of declining British hegemony and the origins of the Great Depression.

The second half of the book continues these themes but is careful to contrast what is truly new with continuities from the past and with the reemergence of older patterns. Chapter 9 discusses the rise of a new paradigm for best practice manufacturing based on the production of consumer durables on assembly lines by semiskilled, unionized workers in the United States. Much like the earlier British industrial revolution, this development threatened to displace producers elsewhere. It shows how U.S. domestic politics contributed to the creation of multilateral institutions to regulate the world economy after World War II. It also shows how states were able temporarily to control their economies.

Chapter 10 discusses the international monetary system. Unlike in the first half of the book, which subordinates its discussion of money to deeper processes, money deserves a full and early chapter here because states' (temporary) postwar control over monetary flows constrained the market flow of goods and capital. These constraints in turn generated an enormous surge of investment by mostly U.S. transnational corporations. Chapters 11 and 12, looking, respectively, at the developed and underdeveloped countries, pick up the discussion of late industrialization started in Chapter 4, but add to it issues related to transnationals.

Chapter 13 continues discussions started in Chapters 6 and 8. It adapts arguments about the rise of new agricultural supply regions to the rise of low-wage labor zones for the manufacture of simple commodities. It shows how trade continues largely to be regionalized, and it reveals how trade frictions are related to the adoption of Kaldorian strategies by late industrializers.

Chapters 14 and 15 continue the discussions started in Chapter 8, explaining how successful Kaldorian industrialization strategies in Japan have undermined U.S. competitiveness and thus U.S. hegemony. Chapter 15 closes with a discussion of the relative positions of the three major economic blocs, the United States, Japan, and the European Community.

# CHAPTER 1

# The Rise of the Modern State:
# From Street Gangs to Mafias

The territorial state . . . [was] the instrument of the "nationalization" of the market and the creator of internal commerce.

*Karl Polanyi*

The power to tax is the power to destroy.

*John Marshall, Chief Justice*

## States and Markets in the 1500s

States and markets, power and plenty, are inextricably intertwined in the international economy, because the modern state and the modern international economy emerged together. Indeed, in some ways neither the modern state nor the international market could have emerged without the other. Thus, the international political economy can be approached by examining either the origins of the European state and state system at about the fifteenth century or the international markets of the time. Neither can be understood without looking at agriculture and at the limits placed on the division of labor by the miserable transportation systems of the time. I will start by looking at states. One of the great peculiarities of history is that an economically marginal, technologically backward set of religiously fractionalized and fanatic peoples "governed" by elites with virtually no administrative apparatus managed to conquer most of the world in about 300 years.

European states were able to achieve this success because they combined "lawyers, guns, and money" in a particularly potent and violent way that made it possible for them to subdue or subordinate much larger economies and empires.[1] Europe's peculiar states emerged from a three-sided conflict among kings, nobles, and merchants for control of the resources that could be extracted from the agricultural economy of fifteenth-century Europe. States where one side won completely tended to have long-run weaknesses relative to states in which the three sides worked out durable compromises that constituted and funded well-armed states.

The modern national state is a well-defined organization with a legitimate and continuous monopoly of violence over a defined territory. This monopoly of violence gives the state its ability to subordinate other organizations and groups within that territory to its rules, its laws. Creating and maintaining a monopoly of violence requires resources. In the short run, states can steal from outside their territory. In the long run, however, perpetuating that monopoly requires a stable supply of resources from within. This in turn requires a limited degree of legitimacy. Frederic Lane describes the process of legitimation nicely: "A plunderer could become in effect the chief of police as soon as he regularized his 'take,' adapted it to the capacity to pay, defended his preserve against other plunderers, and maintained his territorial monopoly long enough for custom to make it legitimate."[2] Because agriculture constituted about 80 percent of economic activity, it ultimately provided the resources supporting all states at that time. However, the nature of that agriculture limited the amount of surplus available for extraction, and the poor transport of the time meant that even if surplus could be extracted it was hard to concentrate in the hands of the state. The nature of agriculture thus set limits on the forms state organization potentially could take in the fifteenth century.

Because of the difficulties involved in extracting resources from agriculture, most states pursued a policy known as mercantilism. Mercantilism is usually described as an externally oriented policy through which states tried to create inflows of bullion (specie or metallic money). Actually, mercantilism's external policy was a means to an internal end: the creation of a homogeneous internal legal space, dominated by central authority. This homogeneous space makes it possible for states to stop relying on external resources and to use more stable internal resources to fund themselves. Reciprocally, greater funds mean a more stable internal administration and thus more homogeneous law. Thus, the distinctive compromise worked out in successful European states between lawyers, guns, and money also emerged from struggles over the implementation of mercantilist policies.

This chapter first examines the nature of fifteenth-century agriculture, the limits it imposed on European state-building, and the ways agriculture shaped the social groups contending for power in Europe. Next, the trajectory of state-building in three European states is discussed to show how conflicts within and among those states forced them to make a compromise between lawyers, guns, and money. Mercantilism, with its sometimes complementary and sometimes conflicting goals, is a key part of that story. Finally, the chapter surveys the early period of European expansion to show how a handful of fairly small European states began to dominate the entire world, reshaping ecologies and economies as they went. The patterns and problems established in this early period persist today, even though some of these processes have run their course. States' relative power continues to rest on their ability to extract resources from society without damaging long-term growth in the economy, to transform those resources into organized violence, and to manage the interface between their internal economy and the world economy.[3] Meanwhile, the diffusion of the institutional outcomes of the European compromise —

professional militaries, extensive systems for taxation, and regularized justice — to the rest of the world has steadily eroded European dominance of the world economy.

## Agricultural Limits on State Formation

From the fifteenth to the end of the nineteenth century, agriculture lay at the heart of the international economy (and for that matter most "local" economies as well). As late as 1929, some kind of primary product, mostly agricultural goods, made up three-fifths of internationally traded goods. Even fifteenth-century luxury goods like silk, saffron, and spices tended to be agriculturally derived. For most states agriculture was the resource base. All efforts to construct states were shaped by the common challenge of extracting resources from agriculture. And all those efforts ran into one overwhelming difficulty: before mechanically powered transport, hardly anyone ever transported grain overland for more than 20 miles.

This key fact dominated agricultural production and trade up until the railroad, and it constrained various efforts to construct states. All economies involve the transformation of energy into life and production. In pre-railroad agricultural economies, virtually all energy came from grain, and for grain to be turned into work, it had to be processed through muscle power. The reliance on grain as a source of energy set the outer limits of exchange through both barter and, to a certain extent, even monetized markets. For humans — in this case the peasants who made up about 80 to 90 percent of the population in the world in the fifteenth century — 20 miles represented about the longest possible one-day walk to a market. Practically, however, because most peasants could not afford to linger in town, 10 miles was the outer limit, particularly if the peasant was hauling a sack of grain or other food on his or her back.[4] But what if our peasant had some horses and a wagon?

As it turns out, one of the greatest but least-known German economists, Johann von Thünen, conducted an experiment on this question. He loaded a standard wagon with a standard load of grain, hitched up two horses, and had two farm workers drive the wagon as far as they could go, feeding themselves and the horses on the grain. Theoretically, the wagon could go about 230 miles on a road running through a flat plain before the humans and animals consumed all the grain, which was their only source of energy.[5] In practice, the real limit to overland transport by wagon approximated transport on someone's back: 20 miles. First, anyone shipping grain would want to get his wagon, horses, and farmhands back, so even when the wagon arrived, not all the grain could be sold. Some grain had to be reserved as "fuel" for the trip back to the farm. (Alternatively, the entire load could be sold and part of the money used to buy grain on the return trip. Either way, however, roughly the same amount of cash came home.) Second, roads were scarce, and most of Europe was not particularly flat, which increased the amount of grain consumed on the trip to the market. Finally, once the wagon reached its destination, it had to have enough grain left to sell to make it economically worthwhile to ship grain in the first place.

Consequently, virtually all economic, social, and political life took place in *microeconomies* centered in market towns surrounded by an agricultural hinterland of about 20 miles. Adam Smith argued that the greater the division of labor, the greater productivity and thus incomes. The fact that nearly all economic life took place in a relatively small area with a relatively small population meant that the Smithian division of labor was quite low, because few people could afford to specialize even if they had the capital to do so. In the microeconomies a vicious cycle limited economic growth and income: a small division of labor limited productivity; low productivity limited economic growth; and low economic growth kept the division of labor low.

This 20-mile limit persisted well into the modern period. As late as 1835, France produced or imported about 173 million tons of goods, of which 15 million moved by some form of water transport. Of the total, about 127 million tons, or 75 percent, were consumed at the place of production. The remaining 46 million tons were consumed an average of 37 miles away, indicating that only about 13 percent of production was consumed more than 20 miles from its production site. The 15 million tons moved by water transport probably made up the bulk of long-distance consumption.[6]

Although microeconomies all lay nestled together, they had very little contact with each other, trading only a little with neighboring microeconomies and virtually nothing with more distant ones. (The obvious exceptions, microeconomies with access to water transport, are dealt with later in this chapter.) *Until the era of canals and railroads — and indeed well into that era — no such thing as a "national economy" existed.* An international economy — that is, a complex division of labor linking economic areas located in different political units — existed long before transportation improvements brought all microeconomies into close economic contact within most political units.

Since virtually all forms of social organization larger than a village need to extract surplus energy (meaning money or food) from the agricultural economy, the 20-mile limit on overland transport of grain meant that it was hard, but not impossible, to construct "states" on a large geographical or administrative scale. Armies and bureaucrats have to be fed and paid. The difficulty in moving bulk goods overland obstructed any attempt to extract and move more than a minimal amount of revenue from these microeconomies. Peasant economies usually do produce a surplus well above their subsistence needs. However, even if the agents or builders of a would-be state could take that surplus away from those peasants, they could not move it very far in the form of physical grain. Any effort to build a social or political network or system larger than the microeconomy had to contend with this harsh, energy-defined 20-mile limit. Charles Tilly has noted that in about 1490 the average radius of a European political unit was about 50 miles, meaning about two microeconomies in any given direction, or the distance a band of men on horse could travel in one day in order to supervise a noble's peasants or to patrol "borders."[7] These average figures conceal the fact that large social organizations and states did exist, because the overland transport of grain was not the only way to get or move energy.

The three exceptions to this limit on overland exchange and extraction defined both the possibilities for building larger social organizations and the three groups that ultimately contended for control of the European state in the fifteenth century. Each of these groups tried to construct a different network to mobilize and move surplus food/energy. The melding of these groups in uneven ways created variations on the distinctive European state. First, water and wind power could be directly harnessed through mills. Second, grain and other commodities could be transported not only overland but also by water. The wind provided free energy for transport over water, although capturing this energy required a large fixed investment in ships. Finally, money and other precious items (i.e., goods with a very high value-to-weight ratio) could be moved long distances. Money represented a kind of movable energy. It could be used to buy energy — that is, grain — where it was produced, and thus it freed travelers or shippers from hauling their food/energy with them. Information, the classic high-value but low-volume, low-weight commodity, could also be transported easily, provided enough grain or money came along or that the information could be exchanged for such things.

Each of the three social groups contending for control of territory and economic activity in Europe more or less controlled one of these exceptions. Although these groups differed in how they extracted resources from the microeconomies and how they organized the society built on those resources, they all overlapped and came into conflict in the market town at the heart of each microeconomy.

## The Nobility and the Acceptance of Limits

Nobles controlled the first exception, wind and water mills. They solved the problem of resource extraction by moving themselves, not grain; they went to where the grain was, and they used direct coercion to extract surplus grain. In most of premodern Europe, a collection of brigands turned nobles controlled the local economy. These nobles were a kind of dispersed biker gang: armor, horses, and their propensity to resort to violence elevated them above the rest of the population in the same way that leather and Harleys elevate movie bikers in situations where state authority is absent. Nobles had made themselves into the state when the Roman empire collapsed, removing most legal constraints on the behavior of people who happened to have weapons, and when Charlemagne deliberately dispersed his soldiers across the countryside so they could find grain to feed their horses.

Through a mixture of custom and coercion, nobles extracted a surplus from peasants in two ways. They took rents in kind, directly appropriating grain and other products, including payments for the use of mills where peasants ground grain for bread. They also directly appropriated labor from their serfs, forcing them to work on their land. Nobles had little need directly to monetize their local economy, that is, to shift from a barter economy with the direct exchange of goods to a commercial economy in which money served as a universal medium of exchange. Virtually everything they needed was at hand through direct exchange or as rents in kind. Nobles and peasants lived in a delicate balance of terror, with the peasantry's propensity and ability to revolt setting limits on how much nobles could extract.

The nobility constructed a society based on mobile people controlling an immobile surplus. Nobles linked themselves together through a network of hospitality that allowed nobles to travel without carrying grain, since invariably another manor was located one day's horse ride away from their own. Once they arrived they could "refuel" their horses and themselves, gossip, annoy each other, and then move on to the next manor. Nobles moved themselves, and through marriage their children, rather than the economic surplus.

What nobles lacked was anything that could not be locally produced. So, by definition, they lacked luxuries. These luxuries were generally commodities with a high value-to-volume/weight ratio, or they could not be moved. Nobles could buy these luxuries from merchants if they had either money or commodities that the merchants wanted. Inland nobles usually had to exchange money, while nobles on coasts or navigable rivers often could exchange bulk commodities directly for luxury goods. Nobles resisted the monetization of their local economies above and beyond this minimum amount of money. Although monetization might help them attack and conquer their neighbors, it exposed them to the possibility that the rents they charged peasants could be fixed in money terms. Then inflation might erode the real value of those rents. Inflation was a real problem for the nobility after 1500, because the great inflow of silver and gold from the newly conquered Americas increased the European money supply by about half.[8]

The reluctance of the nobles to monetize the economy beyond the point needed for them to acquire luxuries brought them into conflict with kings, the second social force attempting to control the microeconomies. Kings and would-be kings sought to monetize the microeconomies in order to shift part of the peasants' surplus away from nobles and toward themselves. Offsetting this conflict of interests was a common interest in keeping the peasantry under control and fending off other predatory states. During the sixteenth and seventeenth centuries, the nobility faced nearly constant threats from below and from the outside, forcing them to calculate finely how much of the surplus they needed to relinquish to their king in order to get protection from these threats.[9]

## Absolutist Monarchs, Internal Markets, and External Enemies

Kings and would-be kings, in contrast, wanted to connect all the microeconomies via and under an administrative hierarchy best symbolized by the absolutist state. Nobles linked discrete microeconomies through a horizontal, primarily social network of persons engaging in travel, supplemented by a vertical network of reciprocal obligations. Kings wanted to link microeconomies together with a vertical bureaucracy, using flows of information (orders down to bureaucrats and reports back up to the king's cabinet) and money (salaries down to bureaucrats and taxes up to the king). Both money and information were easily transported.

Kings' desire to centralize authority faced an internal and an external obstacle. All the kings of Europe were really "wannabe" kings. De jure, kings had authority over their realms. De facto, nobles' power and the web of mutual obligation linking king to vassal weakened this authority. Because nobles could use violence, they often actively resisted royal authority. Sovereignty—legal authority—was dispersed in feudal society. Each noble had some rights to rule in a given area, had exemptions from various royal laws, and could make claims on the king.

Kings were originally nominated leaders of the bands of brigands from which the nobility emerged, merely princes (*principes*), or first among the equal society of nobles. Having roared into and conquered some region, these princes dispersed their gangs into the countryside, because these bands were too large to be fed off the grain available in any one area. Instead the brigands had to go to the grain. In the fiefs the king granted them, they could find enough peasants whose rents (grain) could support themselves, their horses, and their ancillary thugs. Kings tried to retain control over the nobility by retaining the right to confirm the inheritance of fiefs. Technically, landowner-ship had rested in the king but was granted to the nobility in exchange for their loyal service. Once dispersed, however, the nobles tended to subordinate any loyalties they had to the king to their own interest in extracting rent from their serfs and passing a fief on to their children. Nobles represented the real locus of government, justice, and taxation in each microeconomy, because they were there and the would-be monarch (or the monarch's hired representative) was not. This challenge to the monarchy's internal authority was considerable, for many nobles were strong enough to think about making themselves into kings.

Kings could increase their internal authority only to the extent that they could, first, replace semi-independent nobles' local monopoly of violence with police forces controlled from the center, and second, shift control over law and taxation from the nobility to their own hired hands, that is, bureaucrats who had no independent source of power. They needed to put those bureau-crats into each microeconomy and have those agents take control of law, policing, and resource extraction. This took enormous amounts of money, for kings had to pay their agents enough to prevent them from being suborned by the local nobility. Kings thus had two strong reasons to monetize microecono-mies as much as possible. First, monetization gave them access to a greater volume of resources in any given area. Second, it allowed kings to extract resources without having to go through the nobility. Ideally, the king would use the tolls charged for access to market towns to pay their agents' salaries. By purchasing microeconomy-produced goods to sustain themselves, those agents would then put money back into the local economy, closing the local financial loop.

To monetize the microeconomies over which they sought control, kings also had to find some source of actual money—gold, silver, or copper—to put into circulation in the microeconomies. (Paper money, then and perhaps now, was like an oral contract; it was not really worth the paper it was printed on.) This led them to look to merchants for support against nobles, for merchants, naturally, had money.

The kings' external problem likewise forced them to look to merchants, but, paradoxically, it also forced them to look back to nobles for support. Externally, kings faced a second threat to their authority: other would-be kings. Kings could only increase their wealth (the minimal flow of monetized resources flowing out of the microeconomies and into their hands) by taking away land from other kings and nobles. Therefore, would-be kings were in constant conflict with other would-be kings over turf. Wars with other kings forced kings to deploy increasingly larger and better organized armies, raising the amount of cash needed for success.[10] Most medieval armies started as a reaggregation of the brigand gangs and their ancillary thugs. Their disloyalty, insubordination, and erratic individualism all undermined the kings' ability to fight other kings. In response, kings tried to professionalize their armies, replacing the gang members with hired mercenaries. Unlike the old brigand armies, mercenary armies had to be paid.

Conflict with other kings also forced kings to be cautious in their efforts to subordinate nobles. No king could long risk fighting both internally and externally. Therefore, where kings could not subdue local nobles or the reverse, both often had to enter into some kind of pact in which nobles permitted kings enough revenue to defend everyone against external threats and restive peasants. Since nobles sought to limit a king's ability to project power inward, they were often cheap about funding his ability to project power outward. Armies could be used in either direction. Therefore, the kings' need to pay for war also forced them to borrow from merchants.

## Merchants and the Wider Maritime World

Merchants constitute the last group struggling to control the resources available from the microeconomies. Merchants fall into two categories depending on whether they were oriented more toward long-distance trade, usually over water, or local, usually overland trade. This distinction should not be seen as the traditional one between trade in luxuries and trade in daily necessities. Trade in luxuries inevitably occurred alongside trade in much more mundane commodities like grains and other foodstuffs, wool, timber, and pitch. Merchants often needed these commodities simply to build and to ballast their ships. Trade in mundane commodities also provided a kind of cheap money for merchants involved in the long haul of luxury goods. If they simply loaded their ships with luxuries, they would have to parcel out these goods along the way in order to buy food and water. By ballasting with bulk commodities, they could exploit local differences in prices between points $a$, $b$, and $c$ to earn enough to provision their ships at each of those points. They thus preserved their luxury cargo for resale at the end of their journey, where it would fetch the highest possible price.

One group of merchants controlled inland trade and in particular the trade of the market towns at the center of each microeconomy. To the extent that they dealt in commodities produced outside the microeconomy, they dealt largely in luxuries, for the high cost of transport hindered overland movement of bulk commodities. These merchants eventually did get involved in the production and transportation of bulk goods, but not until kings had reestablished law and order.

The other group of merchants conducted long-distance trade. They constituted a third network, based, not on social obligation or sovereign authority backed by violence, but on contractual obligation (ideally, anyway, as many merchant communities were tied together by ethnicity or religion). Merchants linked communities and cities on the coast and navigable rivers through flows of money and goods; kings linked mostly inland microeconomies through flows of information, money, and violence. Thus, they were not completely in opposition, except where waterborne and inland trade overlapped. This group of merchants benefited from the fact that water transportation undid the limits on the division of labor imposed by local food supplies. To the extent that waterborne food from other microeconomies augmented local supplies, the local population could grow and more labor could be devoted to industrial activities.

These merchants wanted to be left alone to make money unhampered by either nobles or kings, both of whom had an annoying habit of stealing from merchants. The best way to gain this independence was to construct a network of separate trading cities capable of individually deterring attack. Because these cities had much higher productivity and incomes than any given microeconomy, they often could assemble and pay for substantial military forces.

The presence of external and internal threats created overlapping interests between merchants and kings and merchants and nobles. Merchants possessed enormous amounts of money. Kings could try to seize this money, but this typically worked only a few times, for merchants could and always did move elsewhere. After trying erratic ripoffs, kings began borrowing regularly from merchants. Merchants liked this system since it provided an outlet for surplus funds. And since kings in effect used this money to monetize microeconomies, they increased the markets available to merchants by integrating them at least partially into the network of waterborne trade. Similarly, to the extent that nobles' power declined, merchants would be less burdened by the multitude of internal tolls nobles threw up along trade routes. Finally, merchants benefited from the kings' ability to deploy violence on their behalf against competing merchants and predatory nobles and kings. Meanwhile, merchants and the nobility had a common interest in seeing that kings did not become too powerful. Since it was never clear which would-be king would actually triumph, prudence dictated diversifying loans among many different nobles.

## State-Building: Lawyers, Guns, and Money

Kings, nobles, and merchants each would have preferred to pursue their own vision for the world, producing, respectively, absolutist states, hyperfragmented entities like the Holy Roman Empire or Poland, and networks of mercantile cities like the Hanse or Italian city-states. To different degrees, each of the large-scale societies outside of Europe took one of these forms. But in

Europe the respective weaknesses of each group and their mutual vulnerability to external competitors combined with their occasionally overlapping interests to produce the peculiar amalgam of "lawyers, guns, and money" characterizing the modern state. Compromises brokered among all three parties were regularized into constitutions that defined rights and obligations (lawyers). These states rested on territorially defined monopolies over violence, deployed against internal and external threats (guns). The bureaucracy running this monopoly of violence depended on a parallel bureaucracy for revenue extraction (money).

When the conflicting and common interests of the kings and nobles intersected, the result was the development of states' constitutions. The medieval revival of Roman law provided principles to justify, legitimate, and facilitate a deal between nobles and kings. Roman law contained two absolute but conflicting principles. First, it guaranteed an absolute right to private property, in contrast to the parcellized sovereignty and multitude of weak rights and mutual obligations that feudal law placed on property and persons. The nobility seized on this principle as a guarantee of their rights to landownership and the rents thereof, in the face of centralizing kings who might claim ownership of these lands. Second, Roman law seemed to claim that the will of the sovereign was law. Sovereigns had been as bound by feudal obligations as their vassals. Would-be kings seized on this principle to justify imposing taxes and reducing the privileges of the nobles.

The clash of these two principles and the common fear of internal and external enemies led to the formation of parliaments that were designed to regularize the king's ability to raise and finance a central military. In these constitutional compromises, kings reduced the nobility's privileges and power (that is, exemptions from taxation and the right to private armies) but not to the point where nobles would revolt and seek aid from other kings against their own. Although the nobles submitted to regular taxes, they limited the king's ability to impose them without the permission of the assemblies of nobles. They also permitted the king to raise his own army, but only if they were allowed to staff that army. Regular taxes allowed kings to generate the steady flow of money that their new bureaucracies of violence (police and armies) and administration required.

Whereas the kings and nobles' intersection led to constitutions, that between kings and merchants produced the public debt as an institution. Since kings specialized in violence, they enticed merchants to support them in return for protection from other kings and merchants. Merchants supported kings' efforts to build more powerful militaries with loans and, sometimes, taxes. Merchants benefited from this protection insofar as it opened otherwise closed markets and reduced the risk that other merchants (and their king's militaries) would seize assets.[11]

The intersection of nobles' and merchants' conflicting and common interests produced lawyers. Both groups had an interest in absolute private property rights, and both groups had an interest in limiting kings' ability to tax them. At the same time, both had an interest in colonizing the kings' bureaucracy so as to seize control of the revenues it generated. Absolute private property rights and regular taxation created a legal framework in which mercantile activity could flourish.

The intersection of different kings' conflicting and common interests produced formidable armies but also grudging agreement to respect one another's control of specific turfs. In other words, it produced a belief in absolute sovereignty that replaced prior feudal practices of divided and partial sovereignty — a noble could theoretically owe allegiance to multiple lords — with the notion that loyalty had to be undivided.

Charles Tilly has provided the perfect metaphor to describe this process of compromise: state-building was at first a form of organized crime, he says.[12] Just like the modern-day mafias, would-be states, under emerging absolutist monarchs, tried to establish monopolies of violence over specific turfs, promising protection to nobles and especially merchants on that turf. The nobility had been a collection of neighborhood gangs. Kings were would-be godfathers seeking to control a multitude of the turfs by incorporating nobles' small gangs into one larger gang. Merchants benefited from protection, as long as taxes and the occasional defaulted loan were offset by the extra markets acquired through conquest, depredation of competing merchants, and restrictions on competing merchants' access to home markets. The merchants' and nobles' acquiescence gave legitimacy to the violence that states deployed inward; the grudging respect from other, competing godfathers accorded to a powerful godfather secured him from external threats.

## Mercantilism: Internal and External State-Building Projects

The characteristic policy of these "mafias" enroute to statehood was a messy agglomeration of practices later called mercantilism. Mercantilism has traditionally been seen as the use of state power (organized violence) in the pursuit of plenty (economic wealth). Mercantilist states, looking outward, tried to boost their exports and limit their imports. This positive balance of trade let them accumulate specie — metallic money. Most analyses concentrate on this external aspect of the mercantilist project, the better to condemn it as irrational from the point of view of neoclassical theories of comparative advantage and trade.

When we consider mercantilism as a two-sided project with both an external and an internal impulse, a compelling and rational political logic reveals itself: trade surpluses and the accumulation of metallic money were the most practical way for kings to monetize their realms. Because of limits on the overland transport of common agricultural goods, a unified international market emerged far sooner than national markets almost anywhere. The international, waterborne economy contained much more in the way of movable resources than did any given king's collection of microeconomies with a very limited division of labor and a very small economic surplus. Given this situation, states consciously tried to use external resources to expand their internal sources of revenue. In the long run, internal sources were more dependable and consistent.

A trade surplus under mercantilism meant that a king had traded the many diverse commodities created by the labor of his many otherwise worthless subjects in the microeconomies to get the one crucial commodity needed to build a state: money. This money accumulated in the hands of merchants, who then could loan it to kings. Mercantilism's internal impulse was the king's effort to remove barriers to the internal movement of goods imposed by the nobility (there already were enough natural ones) and to make noble wealth taxable by homogenizing the legal status of all of the king's subjects. The elimination of barriers to trade reduced the sources of revenue controlled by the nobility. Thus, the international economy and state systems grew up simultaneously. Mercantilism funded and consolidated some states while impoverishing others; imperialism abroad was simply the logical extension of this policy. The last two sections of this chapter will look at this process for several European states.

Each of the European states that survived and thrived from the fifteenth to the nineteenth century—and over 300 potential states did not—worked out its own version of the lawyers, guns, and money compromise. If, to steal a phrase from Tilly, states made war and war made states, not all states succeeded: as would-be states made war, war *unmade* many states.[13] States that evolved more efficient compromises in terms of their ability to extract revenue and thus also to deploy violence externally were more likely to survive. Meanwhile, European states' constant warfare forced them to devise ever better, ever cleverer, and ever more efficient means for extracting revenue, deploying armies and winning internal consent through submission rather than coercion. Table 1.1 shows the ratcheting-up of war costs for Britain in the 1700s. These advances in the social technologies for funding and deploying organized violence ultimately allowed relatively backward states to invade and transform societies that were often demographically larger and more advanced technologically and administratively. A quick survey of areas outside Europe shows why the absence of the compromise blocked a ratcheting-up of state war-making capacity.

TABLE 1.1

## Warfare Costs for Britain, 1689–1784

| War | Duration (years) | Average annual expenditure (£ million)[a] | Increase in public debt (£ million)[a] |
|---|---|---|---|
| Nine Years' War (1689–97) | 9 | 5.5 | 16.7 |
| War of Spanish Succession (1702–13) | 11 | 7.1 | 22.1 |
| War of Austrian Succession (1739–48) | 9 | 8.8 | 29.2 |
| Seven Years' War (1756–63) | 7 | 18.0 | 48.0 |
| American Revolutionary War (1775–84) | 9 | 20.3 | 115.6 |

[a]£2 would buy a year's supply of grain for one person.

SOURCE: John Brewer, *The Sinews of Power: War, Money and the English State, 1688–1783* (Cambridge, Mass.: Harvard University Press, 1988), p. 30.

## State-Building outside Europe

For a useful comparison with the European experience, we can look briefly at Imperial China, where in effect the "king" completely triumphed over his other two adversaries and created an absolutism more absolute than any found in Europe, and at the Indian Ocean trading economy, where merchants triumphed and created a trade-based world.[14]

China had a highly commercialized (monetized) economy in which kings had reduced the nobility to bureaucrats. Chinese towns tended to fall into one of four categories with a very simple and geographically defined relation to one another.[15] The relationship between these cities can be best visualized as a set of cones, each with a city at its apex, and with the apices of lower cones constituting the bottom of the cone above. At the bottom level were small villages where peasant families lived. Most of their daily life, including a vast range of nonmonetary exchanges, took place in this village, which, not surprisingly, was located close to their fields. Between 6 and 18 of these small villages sat within a half-day's walk from a standard market town. This town contained the area's landlords, a variety of permanent shops selling goods that peasants could not produce for themselves, cultural and religious sites, and, of course, a monetized market where peasants could sell their surplus.

In turn, six standard market towns usually arrayed themselves around an intermediate market town. While the standard market towns usually competed with each other, the intermediate market town provided a wholesale market for the standard markets. Intermediate market towns attracted professional merchants and landlords from standard market towns. Finally, six intermediate market towns ringed an administrative city from which the Imperium ruled the county. Usually walled (indicating their military function), these towns contained both a central wholesale market connecting each county to other counties and the emperor's professional bureaucracy for governing the county.

The walled administrative cities collected rice destined for the capital via one of the great rivers or the Grand Canal connecting them. The emperor used a corps of paid civil servants, selected by examination, to rule each county, rather than delegating authority to nobles as in Western Europe.

As in Europe, external and internal enemies threatened China's central authority. When these enemies triumphed, however, they tended to restore central authority. The very administrative superiority of China's bureaucracies made it easier to restore the old system than to search for newer and better ways to use violence in the pursuit of money. Nor was there any brokering of compromises that might establish the basis for higher levels of taxation, because merchants were unimportant to efforts to seize or maintain central power. Most mercantile activity was inward oriented, focusing on day-to-day life or the network of canals in southern China. China's highly commercialized economy—more advanced than Europe's in the 1400s and 1500s—made it easy for the central authority to gather the resources needed to crush challenges from would-be nobles.

In contrast, the Indian Ocean and its neighboring Southeast Asian archipelagoes harbored a complex network of trading communities whose power and autonomy most European merchants could only envy. These communities were insulated from the various inland empires by the same means that insulated Europe's merchants from would-be kings. Therefore, inland rulers were content to buy what they needed and usually left merchants alone. Among themselves, the different merchant communities had reasonably peaceful relations. Most merchants were small, privately organized traders plying between independent emporium ports.

While piracy did exist, it was not the state-organized, tax-funded piracy of Europe. None of the merchant or pirate communities possessed the capacity for organized conquest at sea. Most of the empires and coastal principalities had coastal defenses, and some freebooting mercantile communities like the Omani pirates had cannon, but none of these amounted to a Spanish Armada. Consequently, no one tried to monopolize the sea-lanes. In contrast to Europe's Mediterranean coasts, where Muslim and Christian fought with considerable hostility, Muslims, Hindus, and a score of other groups cohabited the Indian Ocean's coasts with a minimum of conflict.

These two descriptions reveal extremes that were rare in Europe. China represents the realization of what European kings had in mind: an economy sufficiently monetized to support an extensive bureaucracy controlled by the king and barred from direct landownership, with the king able to extract revenue from an extensive territory.[19] The Southeast Asian archipelago and littoral was the embodiment of a merchant's dream: an economy unfettered by imperial authorities, with a multitude of ports and coastal economies linked by a dense network of financial and commercial ties. Outcomes such as these two were much harder to achieve in Europe for two reasons.

First, the much higher ratio of coast and navigable river to inland microeconomies in Europe than in China (perhaps excepting southeast China) created much greater opportunities for European merchants trading long distance in bulk goods. As a result, Europe's mercantile community was much larger in toto than that in China. The cash held by this community represented the only easily accessible source of finance for centralizing kings and for nobles resisting centralization. Second, European administrative technologies lagged behind those in China, making centralization harder. Where the Chinese emperors could rely on a cadre of mandarins selected from a vast body of literate candidates by a countrywide examination, Europe's kings usually had to rely on a mixture of their few literate household servants and the occasional trustworthy priest. So a Chinese-style absolutism was harder to achieve in Europe.

Among the European states, the centralization achieved in France best approximates that in China. Even there, however, the nobility retained considerable power and privilege, in contrast to the fully bureaucratized administration in China. Furthermore, overseas commerce constantly pulled cities on the periphery of France toward the Mediterranean and Atlantic worlds and provided those cities with the resources to stand away from Paris.[16]

Even if European monarchs could not achieve the central power such as the Chinese emperors had, they made it difficult for European merchants to find safe havens in pure, often insular, city-states as happened in the Indian

Ocean. The vast numbers of city-states in the Rhine corridor and on France's coast that were absorbed into larger, microeconomic-based political units show the fragility of merchant cities that cannot move their capital. In contrast, mercantile states like the United Provinces (Holland), the major Italian city-states, and, to a lesser extent, England were partially insulated from the inland monarchies that threatened to absorb them. These mercantile states contained some kind of hinterland, a zone of microeconomies that could be absorbed into their commercial economy. Thus, they were able to raise formidable enough armies to dissuade their neighbors from attacking and absorbing them.

Those European states that survived essentially constant warfare from 1500 to 1814 developed various uneasy combinations of and equilibria among "lawyers, guns, and money." Europe's peculiar geographic balance of coastal and inland areas combined with its relative backwardness in administrative technologies meant that no one state could establish an exclusive dominance. Continuous war imposed an evolutionary pressure on states to develop better forms of organized violence. Through this evolutionary pressure, the ability of European states to use violence "productively" soon surpassed that of most other states and societies. This is nowhere more evident than in the European incursions into the Indian Ocean littoral. The next two sections first sketch the development of compromises and military ability in Spain, France, and England, and then examine Portuguese, Dutch, and English incursions into the Indian Ocean.

## From Mafias to States: Mercantilism's Internal Project

At present we [Europeans] ceaselessly imitate ourselves. Has Prince Maurice of Orange learned how to lay siege? We will get used to it. Has [the Dutch strategist] Cohorn changed his approach? We will change also. Have some made use of new kinds of weapons? Everyone else soon will try them. Does one state increase its troops? Or levy a new tax? It is an advertisement for the others to do the same.

*Montesquieu*

The 1500s and 1600s in Europe were years of almost constant struggle among kings, nobles, and merchants that produced states out of the existing "mafias." Mirroring state-building in Europe were European efforts to dominate the Indian Ocean economies. Both efforts show a decisive trend toward more bureaucratic forms of control and an oscillation between commercial and state interests. Changes in Western Europe, driven by struggles among states for survival, reflected this trend.[17]

In the sixteenth and seventeenth centuries, Europe's kings made concerted efforts to establish absolutist states, subordinating both nobles and merchants and trying to swallow up competitor states in Europe. Success would have created a dominant land power indifferent to a scattering of mercantile communities on its periphery and fairly immune to any military force their money could buy. Consequently, this period witnessed almost constant warfare among the major powers, accounting for perhaps 96 out of 100 years in the 1500s and 94 in the 1600s.[18] The period culminated in the Thirty Years' War (1618–48), which combined a free-for-all in Central Europe with bitter and localized conflicts on Europe's extended littoral, including some of the new overseas colonies. Spain, France, Sweden, Britain, and the larger German kingdoms were all created in these years by feasting on neighbors; in contrast, Holland and Switzerland created themselves by resisting being eaten.

Expanding conflict meant raising taxes, and thus internally an unusually high number of peasant revolts took place against nobles, and along with noble and mercantile revolts against would-be monarchs. The European states that prospered most in the long run after 1650 survived because they steered a course between the external Charybdis of war and the internal Scylla of revolt. Somewhat accidentally, they generated a law-governed compromise among the king's guns, the nobles' guns, and the merchants' money. Among the European states, England stands out because its peculiar geographical position created a state perfectly suited to the exigencies of an international economy in which the economical use of force (or the forceful use of economic advantages) positioned a state to dominate the emerging European-centered world economy.

English superiority seems predictable only in hindsight, of course. Looking forward from 1500 to 1700, most contemporary observers would probably have said that Spain and the Hapsburgs were more likely to become the dominant continental power, while France was more likely to work out a viable law-governed compromise between king and nobles. Spain had the largest and most potent combination of guns and money. At its zenith the combined Spanish-Hapsburg empire combined all the wealth of the Americas, the Portuguese dominions in the Indian Ocean, the Netherlands (then meaning both Holland and Belgium), much of southern Italy, and Austria's Central European holdings, including mineral-rich Silesia and silver- and food-rich Bohemia (the western part of what is now the Czech Republic). These resources financed armies on a then unprecedented scale. France, meanwhile, had established forms of representation for nobles and towns that should have facilitated a brokered deal between them and the monarchy.

England, in contrast, was a relatively poor, backward economy on the fringe of Europe and had a fairly centralized, powerful monarchy that seemed to preclude any need to deal with noble or mercantile interests. England's geography also seemed to insulate it from the kind of pressures that forced would-be kings to create military and civil bureaucracies. So England seemed to lack both guns and money, as well as any pressure to find some brokered compromise among merchants, nobles, and the monarch.

First Spain and the Hapsburgs and then France made the only serious efforts to eliminate all potential continental rivals. Both of these projects came to grief, however. The Spanish state could not balance the competing claims of "guns and money" through any formal legal deal. The French king brokered deals giving too much away to the nobility. Why did England come to work out a viable compromise and dominate the world economy? In the cases of

Spain and France, initial advantages turned out to be disadvantages. In England, meanwhile, initial disadvantages turned out to be long-term advantages. (The same process occurred in the Indian Ocean.)

## Spain

Spain's very powerful initial financial and military advantages turned out to be long-term disadvantages. Its initial military advantage accrued from the long wars both Castile and Aragon waged against the Muslim Umayyad Caliphate in southern Iberia. At first, the nobility allowed itself to become subordinated to the monarchy's military simply to withstand Muslim expansion and then to grab Muslim land during the Caliphate's long retreat back to Africa. However, the terms by which Castile and Aragon united to fight the Muslims prevented any true center from emerging in Spain. Aragon, Catalonia, and Valencia remained free from central taxation, and the central state did not have the right to send troops into these areas.[19] Therefore, while Castile was "modernized" through the creation of a bureaucratic apparatus for taxation, no such modernization occurred in Aragon. The Spanish crown could offset this gap in its tax capacity with gold and silver flowing out of the newly conquered Americas. The easy availability of this silver deterred the crown from trying to find more durable internal sources of revenue.

The crown actually went out of its way to destroy these sources. Muslims and Jews had controlled most mercantile activity in the Iberian peninsula before 1492, but the reconquest and subsequent Inquisition drove both sets of merchants either out of Spain and Portugal or underground. This one-time-only windfall deprived the crown of access to mercantile wealth on a continuing basis. Meanwhile, the inflow of silver from the Americas actually undercut the remaining local mercantile activity in an early example of the deindustrialization process called "dutch disease." Massive silver inflows led to inflation, which priced Spanish and Portuguese producers first out of export markets and then out of their own domestic markets, reducing the potential mercantile tax base. Finally, American silver freed the crown from the necessity of coming to terms with its own nobility. The seemingly enormous and secure source of American revenue made it irrational for the crown to reduce its power voluntarily in order to convince nobles to agree to taxation.

American silver created a continuing reliance on itself. Silver was, however, vulnerable to piracy, which the English practiced and perfected at Spain's expense. Moreover, it was an inflexible and ultimately inadequate source of revenue. Spain's continental-scale military adventures created a need for continental-scale revenues. Beginning in 1519, Spain and the Hapsburg empire attempted to conquer most of the lands lying between Madrid and Vienna while also holding off Turkish expansion in the Balkans. In that century, Spain's military expanded from about 20,000 to 100,000. Spain's budget grew by 80 percent from 1520 to 1600, with military spending accounting for 80 percent of total spending.[20] Unable to tax its (now nonexistent) domestic merchants or Aragon, the crown declared bankruptcy in 1557. Then it tried to tax the rich Spanish Netherlands, leading nobles there to demand lower taxes and an end to military occupation, and finally to rebel in 1557–58.

Paradoxically, Spanish efforts to raise revenue ended up not only depriving Spain of revenue but also requiring it to find more money to try to retake the Netherlands with an army of 65,000 soldiers. With Spain severed from Hapsburg Austria after the abdication of Charles V (1556), fiscal pressure increased, and the Spanish crown began looking for new sources of revenue. It turned to tax-exempt Portugal and Catalonia, both of which revolted in 1640 rather than bear the cost of Spanish wars. Spain's early military and fiscal advantages preempted the need to forge a balance among lawyers, guns, and money. Spain relied too heavily on parasitic, mafia-style sources of revenue rather than more reliable and sustainable commercial sources. The crown had to repudiate its debts six times between 1557 and 1647. Having lived by the sword, Spain died by the sword when England cut its lifeline to American mines.

## France

France, which launched the second effort to create a dominant inland empire in Europe, seemed better positioned to forge a compromise. First, the king had already won the right to place his administrative agents in each province. However, he had not won the right to impose the king's law in these provinces, and agencies supposedly controlled from the center tended to turn into locally controlled organizations.

Second, a large number of representative institutions already linked the Valois kings and the nobility in France. But this proliferation of regional representative institutions prevented the emergence of any central institution for brokering deals between nobles and king over taxation. Threatened by the rampaging English during the Hundred Years' War (1337–1453), the Valois made one mediocre deal with the nobility and then tried to overcome its consequences. In this relatively early deal, the nobility agreed to a countrywide tax, or *taille royale*, to support a central army. In return, the king exempted the nobility from the tax and accepted limits on the size of the central army, and thus his power.

Lacking Spanish-scale external resources, the king naturally sought to use both merchants and peasants as his tax base. To compensate merchants for increased taxation, the king allowed them to become "tax farmers," creating and selling offices in his fiscal bureaucracy to merchants. Tax-farmers were responsible for collecting taxes from a given region and were allowed to keep a fixed percentage of what they collected. Inland merchants began investing in tax-farming rather than production, essentially shifting the tax burden onto the peasantry and overseas-oriented merchants. Consequently, many coastal mercantile towns remained in overt or covert rebellion through the 1500s and 1600s. Tax-farming was an inefficient, venal, and corrupt form of taxation; why turn over revenues to the central state until it came looking for them?

This weak fiscal and administrative base forced the king to grind peasants and coastal merchants into the ground when he was faced with the multiple threats of the 1500s. The Hapsburgs attacked France from all points of the compass and conquered northern Italy, and religious and regional schisms erupted into a long civil war. The *taille* rose from an estimated 6.5 percent of gross agricultural product in 1515 to 8.0 percent in 1607. Cardinal Richelieu's decision to have France enter the Thirty Years' War, and to expand the army from 15,000 to 100,000 men and thoroughly modernize it, entailed even greater increases in taxation. Taxes rose 250 percent between 1610 and 1640, provoking rebellions in six of France's great port cities and many peasant areas. The *taille* on the peasants rose to 14.6 percent of gross agricultural product by 1641 and then to 19 percent by 1675 as Louis XIV expanded the army to around 400,000.[21] This sharp rise in taxation was accompanied by a sharp rise in peasant resistance: France endured almost constant peasant revolts from 1625 to 1675.

With the peasantry revolting, the king again turned to the expedient of selling offices. This short-run cure for the revenue problem stifled the development of a loyal, professional bureaucracy. Once more the inland mercantile community invested in offices rather than in productive activity. By the 1640s the sale of offices generated about 35 percent of royal revenues. To compensate for this fragmentation of authority (bought offices were only partly loyal to the king, since the buyers saw them as a source of revenue for themselves), the king actually had to construct a parallel system of administration.

Meanwhile subduing the revolting port cities gutted the vitality of that part of France's mercantile community which was oriented toward the dynamic overseas economy. With inland merchants still diverting their investment into offices, the state was forced to create purely state-run commercial operations to compensate for the absence of a dynamic merchant community.

Jean-Baptiste Colbert (1619–83) set up a range of state-run factories and overseas ventures. Then and now these seemed the purest expression of mercantilism, but in fact they express the earlier failure of the emerging French state to come to terms with its mercantile community. The defeated coastal mercantile community could finance ventures in Caribbean sugar and tobacco, the fur trade in Canada, and a limited Indian Ocean operation, but these did not approach the comprehensive and global scale of Dutch and English operations, even though both Holland and England worked from a smaller demographic base.

Just as Spain was fatally hindered by its seeming advantage in centrally controlled revenues from the Americas, France's initial advantage in representative institutions turned into a disadvantage. The very range of institutions cemented regional particularism in place and shielded the nobility from the center. The king debased his own administrative apparatus to raise funds, inventing offices and undoing the centralization and bureaucratization that underpinned an effective absolutism. A truly unified and uniform professional central bureaucracy awaited France's last great king, Napoleon Bonaparte.

## England

In contrast to Spain/Portugal or France, England seemed unlikely to emerge either as a world power or with a viable compromise among merchants, nobles, and kings. It was economically and militarily weak, dwarfed in population terms by both the French and Spanish/Habsburg empires. Even so, it had a number of strengths. Because of the Norman conquest (1066), England's kings had already constructed a central and systematic administrative apparatus free of local particularisms. The Exchequer (Treasury) had a reasonably professional staff for its time, and the king's right to tax was fairly well established.

With only the relatively weak Scotland and Wales as neighbors, the king did not need an expensive army; this also seemed to preclude any need for consultation with either nobility or merchants. Another geographic peculiarity enhanced the relative power of England's mercantile community. Aside from Holland, England alone among the large and medium powers had a very high ratio of coastal and riverine land to inaccessible interior land. This high ratio created a potential for many more trade-oriented towns and nobles to emerge proportionally than in Spain or France. In 1500, 10 percent of the English population was already living in towns with a population of over 400, and by 1700 the figure had risen to 25 percent. London, which could draw on an enormous commercial agriculture through water transport, became the largest city in Europe in 1700.[22]

In 1400, however, the English nobility still resembled a typical brigand gang controlling traditional, and cheap, feudal levies. A series of clever princes had led them on rampages through France for most of the past 100 years, but once France responded to these rampages with a professional army and the *taille*, English military power waned rapidly and France retook England's major continental holdings. Unable to rampage in France, the nobility turned their violence inward and killed one another off in the Wars of the Roses (1455–85), strengthening the monarchy's relative power.

The English state's need for funds was never tested by a real war, despite the crown's seeming administrative centralization. The Tudor monarchs' military ventures were financed on the cheap and by expedients. For example, Henry VIII sold off the church land he had seized to finance his (failed) invasion of France, and both he and Elizabeth I turned to a voracious and vicious pirating of silver from Spanish America to finance naval operations. Compared to those of their European competitors, those operations were also very small. Even under Elizabeth I (1558–1603), England never put together an army of over 10,000 men. England's puny military effort required puny fiscal resources; therefore, unlike France's, its monarchs could resist the temptation to exempt the nobility from taxes or to sell offices on a large scale.

After 1603 the Stuarts continued this pattern of ignoring the nobility and Parliament and, in Charles I's case, alienating them. Charles I (1625–49) seemed to come to an accommodation with the nobility in 1628, when he promised not to levy taxes without parliamentary approval. Thereafter, however, he resorted to forced taxes. As in Spain, this expedient created a crisis for the state when it really needed funds. Revolts in Scotland and Ireland (1639–41) forced Charles to call Parliament, which refused to grant taxes and eventually sponsored a rebellion against him. Unlike noble revolts on the continent, however, which centered around nobles' efforts to win or retain *immunity* from taxes, the English Civil War revolved around efforts to obtain *consent* for taxes, because substantial parts of the rebellious nobility in England had become commercialized. This conflict mostly pitted those nobles within 15 miles of a coast or navigable river (and thus capable of participating in a commercial economy based on water transport) against those more than 15 miles inland (who thus were more oriented toward subsistence and rent in kind from the microeconomy they controlled).[23] By 1640, many landowners produced for the London market and wanted the kind of absolute property rights guaranteed in Roman law. Noble and mercantile interests had partly fused in England, creating a potential community of interests between a commercial nobility interested in "protection" for its overseas ventures and the emerging central state.

England's geographic peculiarities also played their part. Insularity and a naval orientation meant the king had no army to unleash on recalcitrant nobles. Insularity meant that civil war did not invite massive external intervention. The Civil War fatally weakened the ability of the monarchy to rule without consent. The subsequent Glorious Revolution of 1688 confirmed this development when incoming King William III accepted parliamentary control of spending in the Bill of Rights.

Like Spain's monarchs, England's precociously powerful kings and queens tried to rule without forging a durable consensus with the nobility over taxation. Like Spain's monarchs, they found themselves faced with revolt when they did tax nobles. Unlike Spain's nobility, England's commercialized nobility had the financial resources to fund their own army. Unlike France's nobility, England's was gathered in one central parliament. England's nobles could survive their monarch's onslaught and forge a durable compromise over how and from whom to fund the level of military activity England needed to survive in a world of competing powers. And, unlike these three countries, England drew its tax revenue mainly from regularized exactions from a productive base, not a parasitic collection of other people's treasure. Therefore, England alone had the durable fiscal base needed to sustain global operations. This was the domestic counterpart and basis for its successes in the Indian Ocean, to which we now turn.

# Mafias Abroad:
## The External Side of State-Building

It's money that matters, wherever you are.

*Randy Newman*

Money in the necessary quantities [for war] could come only from trade . . . [and] the capacity to sustain war and so maintain political power in Europe became, during the seventeenth century, increasingly dependent on access to wealth either extracted from the extra-European world or created by the commerce ultimately derived from that wealth.

*Michael Howard*[24]

States struggling for survival and mastery in Atlantic Europe used mercantilist policies to acquire metallic money (specie) so as to widen their tax base and pay for loyal military and civil bureaucracies. All of these states faced two problems. First, the isolation of most microeconomies from each other kept the division of labor and thus the potential level of revenue available to each state small. Second, Western Europe consistently ran trade deficits with the Baltic, the Levant, and Asia. (See Table 1.2.) Because the rising European states had few goods that exporters in the Baltic and Asia found desirable, they demanded specie for their exports. The constant drain of money eastward and the need to monetize their internal economies drove the emerging European states to search for metallic money overseas. Their overseas ventures generated specie in four ways. First, Spanish conquest of the Americas and pillage of Spanish specie shipments from the Americas directly provided states with specie. Second, by taking control of trade with the Indian Ocean economy, successful mercantilists could reduce overseas specie shipments. Third, domestically, by controlling and taxing imports of Indian Ocean goods, states could generate enormous amounts of revenue. Fourth, externally, any state that successfully monopolized the flow of goods from the Indian Ocean could reexport those goods to other European states, helping to draw money out of its competitors' economies.

The Spanish and Portuguese conquest of the Americas, running from 1492 until about 1650, ultimately found the most raw specie. According to official figures, the Spanish and Portuguese stole or mined—at an incredible cost to human lives—about 180 tons of gold and 16,000 tons of silver, an amount roughly equal to half of Europe's money stock.[25] The almost purely military enterprises of the Spanish and Portuguese were not self-sustaining, however. Having emptied the hoards of the local civilizations and worked the natives to death in the mines, Europe again faced the problem of specie flowing east. The production of drugs, foods, and raw materials soon replaced mining as the chief activity in the Americas. (See Chapter 5.) In the meantime, real wealth lay eastward, in the Indian Ocean region.

The less-known story of European incursions into the Indian Ocean is more revealing of the inner workings of the new European state than the Iberian conquest of the Americas. Just as Spain's and Portugal's reliance on American silver prevented them from developing the institutional forms needed to compete inside Europe, so a European reliance on American silver

TABLE 1.2

## Specie Outflow from Western Europe, 1600–1750, Selected Years
### (annual average in millions of guilders)[a]

| Region | 1600 | 1650 | 1700 | 1750 |
|--------|------|------|------|------|
| Baltic | 1.85 | 2.65 | 2.65 | 2.65 |
| Levant | 1.0 | 2.0 | 2.0 | 2.0 |
| Asia | 1.0 | 1.7 | 3.3 | 5.7 |
| *Total* | 3.85 | 6.35 | 7.95 | 10.35 |

[a]20 guilders would buy a year's supply of grain for one person.
SOURCE: Hans Christian Johansen, "How to Pay for Baltic Products?" in Fischer et al., eds., *The Emergence of a World Economy 1500–1914* (Wiesbaden: F. Steiner, 1986), p. 127.

to fund its dealings with Asia would have enabled it to have only a glorious period of overconsumption rather than centuries of dominance.

## Three European Powers in the Indian Ocean

Virtually all European states with some maritime capacity eventually entered the Indian Ocean, but only three states dominated the ocean, in succession, from 1500 to 1800: Portugal, Holland, and England. The Indian Ocean region contained a large, sophisticated, and highly articulated maritime economy. (See the map on p. 33.) This economy had three natural circuits of trade, containing a multitude of traders of different religious and ethnic backgrounds.[26] The pattern of wind and water currents defined each circuit, breaking each into a series of natural short coastal hops. The first centered on the western Indian Ocean, linking the Arabian peninsula (and from there the Mediterranean and Europe), the eastern coast of Africa, and the Indian west coast. The second centered on the eastern Indian ocean, linking the Indian east coast and the Southeast Asian peninsula and archipelago. The last centered on the China Sea, linking the Southeast Asian archipelagoes, China, and, occasionally, Japan. These circuits met at choke-points defined by geography and prevailing winds: Hormuz and Aden, which, respectively, controlled trade between the Indian Ocean and the Persian Gulf and Red Sea; Surat, which sat in the middle of the west coast circuit; Jaffna and Colombo, which controlled trade between the eastern and western Indian Ocean; and Malacca, which controlled access from the Indian Ocean to the South China Sea. These cities, all sizable emporia, constantly competed commercially with one another and with nearby cities for dominance of trade routes.

Both bulk and luxury goods entered trade, of which textiles and fine spices were the most important. Each culture and cuisine on the ocean prized goods and spices it could not produce: Hindus and Arabs valued Southeast Asian cinnamon, cloves, and nutmeg; Arabs desired Indian rice and cottons; Chinese wanted Indian pepper; and the archipelagoes favored fine Chinese silks and Indian cottons. Everyone liked Arabian coffee, an addictive drug. Each group of merchants brought one of these goods to the table to be exchanged for the goods desired back home, so all had to coexist.

The Indian Ocean economy had a twofold attraction for the European states. First, its large supply of goods with potentially high levels of price-insensitive demand in Europe meant that control over those goods could be used to generate revenue for the state. The various spices that added variety to an otherwise monotonous diet of bread and porridge were culturally addicting. Sugar, caffeinated drinks like tea and coffee, and, of course, opiates produced actual physical addiction. Like today's mafias, the European states and their merchants found these goods an irresistible temptation. Second, by going directly to the Indian Ocean, the Europeans hoped to be able to stop the drain of specie from Europe.

The Europeans were able to fasten themselves, leechlike, to the Indian Ocean economy because they played the game completely differently than did the Indian Ocean mercantile communities. First, beginning with the Portu-

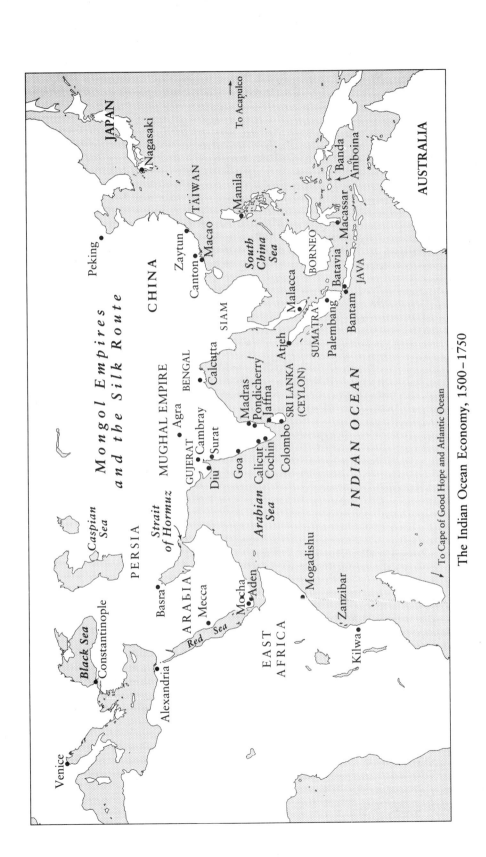

The Indian Ocean Economy, 1500–1750

guese, they claimed exclusive jurisdiction over the entire ocean and attempted to back it up by seizing *all* the important trade choke-points. Second, beginning with the Dutch, they attempted to dominate the actual production of all commodities and thus undo the necessity for cooperation. Finally, beginning with the English, they began to integrate European and Indian Ocean societies through trade in bulk commodities.

## Portugal

The Portuguese were the first Europeans to venture in large numbers into the Indian Ocean propelled by economic motives. They sought gold, and they sought African slaves for the production of sugar and tobacco. They also sought to challenge the Venetian monopoly on Indian Ocean pepper with pepper from West Africa. Having gone down the west coast of Africa, they found it natural to try the east coast.

Once in the Indian Ocean, the Portuguese essentially created a gigantic protection racket. Unlike most traders, the Portuguese were highly militarized, and their comparative advantage was in the deployment of force, not in trading per se. The organizational structure of their venture into the Indian Ocean reflects this military orientation. They traded out of *feitorias*, which combined a fort and trading post and excluded traders other than those associated with their own monopoly. The Carreira da India, a state-owned military organization that monopolized the transport of Indian Ocean goods back to Portugal, and the Estado da India, a military organization running the *feitorias*, were Portugal's instruments for extracting protection money from other traders and for shipping spices back to Portugal. The Portuguese militarized maritime trade, arming ships for defensive and offensive purposes.

Beginning in 1505, the Portuguese systematically set about seizing Diu, Goa, Malacca, Hormuz, and Colombo, which allowed them to blockade the Red Sea and the Persian Gulf, and to control access from the Indian Ocean to the China Sea and shipping from one side of the Indian Ocean to the other. Continuing the *reconquista*'s religious battles, they destroyed their only plausible and mostly Muslim rivals in sea battles in 1509. This also allowed them to defeat their rivals in Europe, for Genoa supported Portugal financially, while Venice's alliance with Muslim Mamluk Egypt meant it relied on passage through the Red Sea and the Persian Gulf for its supplies of pepper and spices. The Portuguese used a divide-and-conquer strategy against the Muslims, for many Hindus were smarting from the recent conquest of inland India by the Muslim Mughals. Only Aden, at the mouth of the Red Sea, escaped Portuguese control.

Portuguese innovations — forts, armed ships, and control of the choke-points — allowed them to force merchants to buy a *cartaze*, a safe-conduct pass. The *cartaze* was purely and simply a form of protection. Passage through the choke-points required a *cartaze*; if a shipper lacked one, the Portuguese would seize the ship and cargo. The Portuguese used *cartaze*-generated revenues to support their network of outposts in the Indian Ocean, to buy pepper for resale in Europe, and to provide revenue for the Portuguese crown. In the years for which data are available, over 80 percent of Portuguese imports from Asia by weight were pepper, and nearly 100 percent were some sort of spice. Only in the seventeenth century did textiles amount to more than 10 percent of Portuguese-controlled imports. Roughly half of the Portuguese crown's revenues in the 1500s came from various imperial sources, of which the Estado da India consistently provided a quarter.[27] In the 1500s Indian Ocean pepper production is estimated to have doubled. This meant steadily rising revenues for the Portuguese crown, whose fiscal foundation otherwise rested on a very small demographic base of about 1.5 to 2 million metropolitan Portuguese.

Through blockade, fort, and *cartaze*, the Portuguese dominated Indian Ocean trading patterns for half a century. Their monopoly began to unravel after 1550, when the Dutch successfully displaced them. Why did the Portuguese dominance fade? Portuguese decline stemmed, first, from that dominance's almost purely military character. What the sword could do, other, better swords surely could also undo. The Portuguese military edge dulled fairly rapidly as local merchants and states adopted European cannon and methods of warfare. One of the major Portuguese technological edges came from its combination of the Arab triangular lateen sail with traditional European square-rigged ships to produce fast, highly maneuverable ships capable of carrying many cannon. This combination of multiple guns and extra maneuverability allowed the Portuguese to destroy much larger fleets. However, both changes were rapidly assimilated by Indian Ocean shipbuilders, who soon proved capable of building ships as big and powerful as those of the Europeans.

Second, the Estado da India was not an efficient revenue extractor. As a purely predatory military operation, it had no way to increase revenues on its own; in fact, the more it extracted from Indian Ocean merchants, the less likely they were to cooperate and pay for "protection." The Portuguese responded to this inefficiency by trying to establish more commercial ventures in the Indian Ocean. In a characteristically absolutist fashion, they did so by either granting or auctioning off the right to organize voyages to well-connected individual nobles and soldiers after 1564. Since these entrepreneurs only completed one voyage, no permanent commercial organization capable of exploiting the Indian Ocean came into being. Indeed, these entrepreneurs had every incentive to underinvest in the forts and ships that were the basis for Portuguese supremacy; they could not take these home with them.

Third, just as the Portuguese did not control the production of spice in the Indian Ocean, they did not control wholesaling in Europe. Antwerp, in the Spanish Netherlands, and Amsterdam, in the United Provinces (Holland), controlled wholesaling. When Spanish depredations of the primarily Jewish merchants led the Antwerp merchant community to flee to Amsterdam, control over the spice trade shifted to merchants who were linked to a state hostile to Portugal.

Portugal's dominance began to unravel almost immediately after its consolidation, as Muslims organized a concerted counterattack. By 1530 the Turks had reappeared in force in the Persian Gulf, challenging Portuguese control of the western side of the Indian Ocean. Meanwhile, Malacca, key to trade between the eastern Indian Ocean and the rich China Sea, remained dependent for food on Muslim sultanates in Java and Sumatra. These sultanates became quite proficient with cannon and began to sail directly across the Indian Ocean to Aden, thus evading the Portuguese. The *cartaze*, estimated to have affected only 20 percent of trade, began to slip, and by 1630 Portugal also controlled only about 20 percent of the pepper coming from the Indian Ocean. The old Muslim-Venetian pepper trade through the Mideast revived after 1560, and about 60 to 80 percent of spices again flowed to Europe through overland routes. As the Portuguese declined, the Dutch entered. Their own temporary supremacy rested on innovations that overcame the deficiencies of the Portuguese military operation.

## Holland

Holland did everything the Portuguese did, but better. Holland used a bureaucratic, commercial organization — at the time the world's largest joint stock corporation — not only to organize trade, but also to control the production and sale of the spices themselves. By controlling spice production, the Dutch directly controlled trade, and did not simply tax it as the Portuguese had done.

Dutch supremacy over the Portuguese rested on five factors. First, the Dutch had more, better, and cheaper ships. Because the Dutch literally lived off grain exports from the Baltic (one-sixth of their grain consumption came from there) and fishing, they pioneered the production of standardized shipping. While these ships were smaller than the Portuguese or Spanish galleon, they also had better designed and controlled sails, and so used a much smaller crew.[28] More and cheaper ships with smaller (and thus cheaper) crews permitted the Dutch to dominate North Sea fishing. About 1,500 ships and 20,000 sailors fished for herring alone. Fish were a concentrated form of energy with a higher protein content than grain. Dutch sailors therefore tended to be less debilitated than their rivals.

Second, cheap fish, cheap ships, and cheap crews lowered the cost of transport, allowing the Dutch to undercut their rivals in trade with the Baltic, which then was the source of most inputs for the production of ships: pitch, timber, linen, hemp, and iron. The Dutch got the first cut at all of these crucial inputs and thus were able to dominate European waters. By 1570 Amsterdam alone could deploy about 232,000 tons of shipping, and a century later about 568,000 tons more ships than all the other Atlantic states combined.

To superior naval might — and thus a much more efficient enforcement of the *cartaze* — the Dutch added a sophisticated private trading corporation, the Dutch East India Company, or VOC (its Dutch initials). The VOC was organized as a joint stock corporation. Its owners' liability was limited to the money that they had invested in the VOC's stock shares, so the company could raise money through impersonal capital markets. The VOC started in 1602 with a capital equivalent to 64 tons of gold, roughly 10 times the size of its closest foreign rival, the English East India Company (EIC). By 1690 the VOC deployed about 100 to 160 ships, 8,000 sailors, and about 10,000 settlers in garrisons in the Indian Ocean area.

Fourth, the whole strategic orientation of the VOC differed from that of the Estado da India. Unlike the Portuguese, who were content merely to skim off the existing trade flows, the VOC attempted to dominate spice production and through that all of Indian Ocean trade. Simultaneously with its efforts to capture or destroy Portuguese *feitorias* at the geographical choke-points, the VOC also captured islands in the Southeast Asian archipelago (modern Indonesia) that produced the four fine spices crucial to Indian Ocean trade patterns: cinnamon, cloves, nutmeg, and mace. Beginning with Amboina in 1605 and ending in the 1660s with the fall of the clove-producing islands and of the pepper-producing coast in India, the VOC systematically eliminated rival producers of spices. It first tried to assure itself a monopoly via exclusive contracts with each island's leadership, but when this approach failed to control trade it turned to violent methods. Starting in 1621 with nutmeg-producing Banda, it began killing and relocating island populations, enslaving deportees on islands where Dutch colonists produced spices.

Finally, by controlling the flow of the four fine spices into Indian Ocean commerce, the Dutch could control both the prices and quantities of goods flowing around all three Indian Ocean trade circuits. By linking the entire coastal trade of Asia under one company, they could systematically exploit opportunities for arbitrage. Arbitrage occurs when a middleman can exploit buyers and sellers who lack knowledge of each other's costs and prices. The Dutch could convert the profits spun out of this arbitrage into goods for export back to Europe.

Whereas the Portuguese exported protection money back to Europe in the form of spices, the Dutch exported their profits in a wider variety of goods: spices (about 60 percent of Dutch exports back to Europe by value in the 1600s, of which about half to two-thirds was pepper), sugar (5 percent), drugs (about 5 percent), and textiles (about 20 percent). By the 1700s trade shifted decisively in favor of tea and coffee (about 25 percent) and textiles (30 percent).[29] The VOC's control of both production and wholesaling in Europe allowed it to shift among goods as demand changed. When demand for pepper leveled off, the VOC could shift to other goods because it was positioned inside rather than primarily outside trade circuits.

Like the Portuguese, however, the Dutch had to yield supremacy in the Indian Ocean to another contender, although the VOC and a Dutch colonial presence in the Indian Ocean managed to survive in various guises until 1947. Holland's weaknesses were much smaller than Portugal's, but in the end they were sufficient to assure a waning of its power. Holland had an even smaller, albeit richer, demographic base than Portugal. In addition, the purely commercial orientation of the VOC and its owners meant that they were loath to engage in military operations and to sustain the levels of violence necessary to control Indian Ocean trade. Indeed, even during the period in which the VOC was consolidating Dutch supremacy in relation to the Portuguese, the VOC's directors in Holland constantly hectored their on-site proconsul to spend less on forts and campaigns. In the same way, the commercialism of the VOC's directors led them to help fund and provision Portuguese campaigns in the 1650s in order to retake Brazil from the VOC's rival, the Dutch West Indies

Company! Dutch purchases of English public debt also served to enhance their competitor's position.

The VOC preserved its position as English strength waxed by cutting a deal with the English, whose East India Company (EIC) had entered the Indian Ocean in the early 1600s. At first, the Dutch tried to use the English against the Portuguese. The English and Dutch cut a deal in which the EIC agreed to help fund part of the cost of maintaining VOC forts in return for a guaranteed quota of spices. When the VOC seemed at the point of dominating the Indian Ocean and used its control of spice prices to rip off the EIC, the EIC became openly hostile. The VOC and EIC struggled from 1650 to 1700, with the VOC eventually ceding hegemony to the English. Nonetheless, the Dutch remained the largest shippers in the Indian Ocean until well into the 1700s.

## England

Like the Dutch before them, the English triumphed because they both assimilated and surpassed all their predecessors' strengths, and because they developed a few institutional innovations of their own. Like the Dutch they excelled in shipbuilding, and like the Portuguese they divided and conquered their enemies. To these methods they added long-distance trade in bulk goods rather than luxuries. In the short run, they probably would have preferred to muscle into the lucrative Dutch spice trade, but in the long run, being forced to take the second-best alternative, textiles, proved more lucrative.

The English state used a variety of judicious industrial policies to propel its merchants into a more competitive position. In 1609 King James I (1603–25) reserved all English fishing grounds to English ships in an effort to displace Dutch fishing fleets. Oliver Cromwell's Navigation Acts in 1651, which restricted all English trade to English ships, created a demand for new ships. English shipwrights rapidly reverse-engineered Dutch ships, assimilated their techniques, and tripled the size of the United Kingdom's fleet during 1600–89. Eventually, they were able to outgun the VOC in the Indian Ocean.

The English also revived Portugal's divide, conquer, and coopt techniques. The EIC's strategy produced two condominia—agreements on shared ownership—in the Indian Ocean, one over trade with the VOC and one inside India with local rulers. The EIC first allied with the Dutch against the Portuguese, and then reversed this alliance, using the shift to consolidate control over Portuguese exports back to Europe. With Portugal coopted and the Dutch weakened, the English then cut a new deal with the VOC in order to be free to confront the French. Under this deal, the VOC retained control both of the production of spices and of the coastal trade. The EIC took over control of long-distance trade in drugs, particularly tea, and, equally important, of bulk goods such as textiles. This arrangement simply reflected the EIC's lack of enough resources to kick out the Dutch.

The EIC's condominium with the VOC dovetailed with its early involvement on the mainland; it helped to push the EIC into a condominium with mainland rulers, particularly in Bengal. The EIC turned to Bengal and the eastern coast in general because the Dutch and Portuguese had ignored this relatively poor area. This move involved the EIC in local politics, however. As it had with the European powers, the EIC played various Indian powers off one another. The Mughal empire's control over southern India, always tenuous, began to disintegrate as a result of internal power struggles after 1707. Coastal and near-coastal principalities started to withhold tax revenue and eject Mughal garrisons. The EIC offered these principalities military advisers and equipment in return for trade concessions; the EIC also wrested from the Mughals the legal right to collect taxes.

These two condominia both permitted and forced the EIC to deal in bulk goods. The EIC had always specialized in the shipment of second-best bulk goods like textiles and tea to Europe. From 1650 to 1700 roughly three-quarters of the EIC's exports to Europe consisted of cotton textiles and silks, compared to the VOC's 20 percent; absolutely, the EIC exported twice as much fabric as the VOC. At first, this distribution reflected necessity: the VOC controlled the lucrative spice trade and the EIC lived at its fringes, making do with less valuable commodities. However, the EIC's onshore condominium eased EIC development of the trade in bulk goods by allowing it unmediated access to local producers; earlier, most European merchants had to deal with powerful Indian middlemen.

As it turned out, the spice trade had inherent limitations: it was geared primarily to a well-to-do but limited continental European market. Pepper sales stagnated at around 7 million pounds annually from the mid-1600s on.[30] In contrast, cotton textiles had a large mass market, and even if the average person could afford to buy only one shirt a year, that still meant millions of potential consumers, especially in England.

To the trade in textiles the EIC added tea and coffee. These mildly addictive substances, along with tobacco, were the crack cocaine of the time. Both proved more durable long-term profitmakers than spices. Tea sales enjoyed explosive rates of growth in the 1700s, doubling from the 1720s to the 1740s, and then nearly doubling again to the 1750s; by then, tea constituted nearly half of all Asian exports to Europe. During the 1800s, when tea production shifted from China to EIC-controlled plantations in India and segments of the British working class experienced rising real incomes, tea sales would rise astronomically, hitting 96,000 tons in 1900.[31] In the 1700s, tea partly displaced coffee, whose control the EIC and VOC shared. Along with sugar and tobacco, American products that other English companies controlled, tea and coffee enjoyed the fantastic sales that addictive substances generate. Equally important, opium and other commodities that were produced for and by the British in Bengal could be sold in China, thus reducing the outflow of specie from European-controlled economies to the east. As late as the mid-1700s, three-fourths of the EIC's exports to Asia were still specie, but by the end of the century only one-fifth were.[32] The English created and dominated a new circuit of intra-Asian trade to which the Dutch could not gain access.

The EIC's condominium with the Dutch therefore gave them the lion's share of the commodities experiencing rapid growth in the 1700s and then in the 1800s. During 1752–54, years for which relatively complete data are available, the EIC exported 17 percent more by value from the Indian Ocean than did the VOC, mostly because larger textile and tea exports offset the VOC's larger spice exports.[33] In the long run, the EIC's involvement on the Indian mainland allowed it to extract enormous revenues from a highly monetized set of microeconomies that it then incorporated into overseas commerce. Before 1800, the EIC took its spoils in money as taxes and land rent; after 1850, the railroad allowed the cheap inland transport of goods taken as taxes in kind. The EIC in effect became the king of the Indian microeconomies, squeezing taxes out of a massive peasant population.

European efforts to extract resources from the Indian Ocean economy both mirrored and enhanced the European states' ability to deploy and use organized violence back in Europe. Overall, the Indian Ocean economy was both larger and perhaps more sophisticated than the European economy, and perhaps even than its rich northwest corner. The relatively small European states that attached themselves to this enormous economy were able to draw enormous resources out of it without "killing the goose that laid the golden eggs." Of the states discussed here, England was the largest, with around 4 to 5 million inhabitants. The Indian Ocean linked Asian economies encompassing perhaps 300 million people in 1650, and those people possessed a per capita income roughly similar to that of the Europeans. So even if the Europeans took only a small percentage of the surplus available from these economies, it would have had a huge impact back in Europe.

As an extension of mercantilist policies, these ventures into the Indian Ocean proved enormously important. Mercantilism and state-building required money. The states that fastened onto the Indian Ocean accumulated specie in two ways. First, by paying for the Indian Ocean commodities their own societies consumed out of the profits of their Indian Ocean mercantile (or protection-racket) activity, they reduced the outward drain of specie. As it was, Europe overall continued to lose specie to the Indian Ocean economies through 1800, a loss offset only by the specie coming out of Latin America. Second, the three most successful dominators of the Indian Ocean were able to reexport Indian Ocean commodities to other states and areas, thus offsetting potential deficits with those areas. For England and Holland, this reexport was particularly important in offsetting imports of otherwise unobtainable commodities, especially strategic naval materials, from the Baltic area. Northwest Europe's deficit with the Baltic almost equaled deficits elsewhere in the world in 1600 and was still significant as late as 1750. Meanwhile, the volume of colonial produce shipped by northwest European countries into the Baltic increased from 3.1 million pounds in 1700 to 33.8 million pounds by 1780.[34]

Domestic and overseas success worked together to create durable states capable of deploying organized violence in a systemic, sustained way. Yet at the same time, the compromises needed to create regular revenue extraction at home, as well as the competitive pressures facing states in their adventures abroad, guaranteed that states would not dominate economic activity. At home, law assured merchants protection in return for specified payments. Abroad, the increasing costs of financing protection rackets in an Indian Ocean full of rapidly arming peoples forced a shift from purely predatory activities to a more business-oriented approach using monopoly control of commodities. States moved from simply threatening to toss rocks through windows to actually having to help run the enterprises. England's and Holland's experiences in the Indian Ocean created enormous institutional centers of financial power, linking the external and the internal world and balancing the state's ability to project violence inward and outward. Both state and economy simultaneously reached inward and outward, and both literally grew up in the interface between the internal, territorial base of the state and the world market based on water transport. The growth of states and the international economy reshaped both their internal economies and those of other states, which is the topic of the next chapter.

# Notes

1. All credit to rock artist Warren Zevon for stating this truth lyrically as well as succinctly.

2. Frederic Lane, "The Economic Consequences of Organized Violence," *Journal of Economic History* 18(1958):403; Margaret Levi, *Of Rule and Revenue* (Berkeley: University of California Press, 1988).

3. Paul Kennedy, *Rise and Fall of the Great Powers* (New York: Random House, 1987).

4. Wilhelm Abel, *Agricultural Fluctuations in Europe: From the Thirteenth to the Twentieth Centuries* (London: Methuen, 1980), trans. Olive Ordisk, p. 7; G. William Skinner, "Marketing and Social Structures in Rural China," *Journal of Asian Studies* 24(1964):3–43.

5. See Johann Heinrich von Thünen, *The Isolated State*, Peter Hall, ed., and Carla M. Wartenberg, trans. (New York: Pergamon Press, 1966), pp. 12–38; Douglas C. North and Robert Thomas, *Rise of the Western World* (Cambridge: Cambridge University Press, 1973).

6. Roger Price, *An Economic History of Modern France 1730–1914* (London: Macmillan, 1981), pp. 19–20.

7. Charles Tilly, *Coercion, Capital, and European States* (Cambridge, Mass.: Basil Blackwell, 1990), p. 45. He notes that the average state occupied about 9,500 square miles, fewer than El Salvador, and contained about 300,000 people, fewer than Wyoming. Abel, *Agricultural Fluctuations in Europe*, p. 5, notes that a town of 3,000 needed about 33 square miles to feed itself, given agricultural yields before the agricultural revolution of the late 1500s. Scaling up to Tilly's 300,000 people gives a land requirement of 3,300 square miles. Since not all land was arable, animals used some land for grazing, and towns required some forest land for fuel and timber, agricultural limits may have set Tilly's average population.

8. Peter Kriedte, *Peasants, Landlords, and Merchant Capitalists: Europe and the World Economy, 1500–1800* (Warwickshire: Berg, 1983), p. 48.

9. See Perry Anderson, *Lineages of the Absolutist State* (London: Verso, 1979) for an argument that the nobility was willing to shift power and sovereignty to absolutist monarchs in order to gain protection from these threats.

10. Michael Howard, *War in European History* (Oxford: Oxford University Press, 1976), pp. 35–48.

11. Lane, "The Economic Consequences of Organized Violence," pp. 401–417; Douglass North, *Structure and Change in Economic History* (New York: Norton,

1981); Niels Steensgaard, *The Asian Trade Revolution of the Seventeenth Century* (Chicago: University of Chicago Press, 1974); and Tilly, *Coercion, Capital, and European States*.

12. Charles Tilly, "War Making and State Making as Organized Crime," in Peter Evans, Dietrich Rueschmeyer, and Theda Skocpol, eds., *Bringing the State Back In* (Cambridge: Cambridge University Press, 1985); see also Tilly, *Coercion, Capital, and European States*.

13. William McNeill, *Pursuit of Power: Technology, Armed Force and Society* (Chicago: University of Chicago Press, 1982); Geoffrey Parker, *The Army of Flanders and the Spanish Road 1567-1659* (Cambridge: Cambridge University Press, 1972); and Geoffrey Parker, *The Military Revolution* (Cambridge: Cambridge University Press, 1988).

14. Janet Abu-Lughod, *Before European Hegemony* (Cambridge: Cambridge University Press, 1990).

15. G. William Skinner, "Marketing and Social Structures in Rural China."

16. Edward W. Fox, *History in Geographic Perspective: The Other France* (New York: Norton, 1966).

17. Joseph Strayer, *On the Medieval Origins of the Modern State* (Princeton, N.J.: Princeton University Press, 1970), Anderson, *Lineages of the Absolutist State*, and Tilly, *Coercion, Capital, and European States*.

18. Tilly, *Coercion, Capital, and European States*, p. 72.

19. Anderson, *Lineages of the Absolutist State*, pp. 64–67.

20. Peter Kriedte, *Peasants, Landlords, and Merchant Capitalists*, p. 47.

21. Peter Kriedte, *Peasants, Landlords, and Merchant Capitalists*, p. 93.

22. Fernand Braudel, *Civilization and Capitalism, Fifteenth-Eighteenth Century*, vol. I (New York: Harper and Row, 1981) (trans. Sian Reynolds), pp. 483–484.

23. Len Hochberg, "The English Civil War in Geographic Perspective," *Journal of Interdisciplinary History* 14, no. 4 (Spring 1984): 729–750.

24. Howard, *War in European History*, pp. 37–38.

25. Braudel, *Civilization and Capitalism*, vol. I, pp. 466–467.

26. K. N. Chaudhuri, *Trade and Civilisation in the Indian Ocean* (Cambridge: Cambridge University Press, 1985); and *Asia before Europe* (Cambridge: Cambridge University Press, 1990).

27. Sanjay Subrahmanyam and Luis Filipe F. R. Thomaz, "Evolution of Empire," in James Tracy, ed., *The Political Economy of Merchant Empires* (Cambridge: Cambridge University Press, 1991), pp. 309 and 328.

28. Braudel, *Capitalism and Civilization*, vol. III, p. 190.

29. Niels Steensgaard, "Trade of England and the Dutch before 1750," in James Tracy, ed., *Political Economy of Merchant Empires*, pp. 114–117.

30. Holden Furber, *Rival Empires of Trade in the Orient* (Minneapolis: University of Minnesota Press, 1976), p. 263.

31. Steensgaard, "Trade of England and the Dutch," in Tracy, ed., *Political Economy of Merchant Empires*, p. 131; L. Stavrianos, *Global Rift* (New York: William Morrow, 1981), p. 250.

32. Kriedte, *Peasants, Landlords, and Merchant Capitalists*, pp. 121–125.

33. Steensgaard, "Trade of England and the Dutch," pp. 148–149.

34. Hans Christian Johansen, "How to Pay for Baltic Products?" in Wolfram Fischer et al., eds., *The Emergence of a World Economy 1500-1914*, vol. II (Wiesbaden: Franz Steiner, 1986), pp. 128–138.

CHAPTER 2

---

# States, Markets, and the Origins of International Inequality

Division of labor is limited by the extent of the market.

*Adam Smith*

A waterway brought animation to the land all around. . . . Without the Seine, Oise, Marne, and Yonne, Paris would have had nothing to eat, drink or keep warm by. Without the Rhine, Cologne would not have been the largest town in Germany even before the 15th century.

*Fernand Braudel*

## The Rise of Spatial Inequality

The last chapter looked at the rise of predatory European states and their expansion into the world. This expansion clearly involved enormous exploitation and created inequality among countries. To what extent did this inequality rest only on political or noneconomic mechanisms of predation? Did the rise of a world economy initially centered on Europe also cause inequality through *economic* mechanisms? Did the market forces unleashed by Europe's internal economic development, first through the agricultural revolutions and then through the industrial revolution, have global consequences? Were these revolutions dependent on the creation of absolute poverty elsewhere, and how did they affect the global distribution of production? These questions have aroused enormous controversy, reflecting the equally enormous issue at stake.

Each question centers on the fact that a novel kind of inequality emerged after 1400, an inequality that had strong *spatial* aspects, which reflected enormous disparities of income across societies. Inequality, after all, had always existed. But the kind of inequality found in premodern Europe and other agrarian societies reflected stratifications *within* societies: peasants versus landlords and warriors; impure versus pure castes; the damned versus the saved; slaves versus the free. What was novel about inequality consequent to the expansion of the northwestern European maritime economy was its *spatial* aspect: inequality existed and persisted not just inside countries but also among regions and nations.

At the beginning of the modern era, per capita incomes in settled societies everywhere were relatively equal. As late as 1800, Asian per capita income was roughly equal to that in Europe and North America as a bloc, with the richest country having no more than twice the per capita income of the poorest.[1] By the end of the 1800s, however, Britain and settler societies like the United States, Australia, Canada, and Argentina had per capita incomes *10 times* those in Asia and India. By the end of the 1900s, on a per capita basis, the developed countries as a whole were about 10 times richer than the Third World.[2]

Do market forces alone explain this new kind of inequality? If the predatory kinds of coercion associated with colonization are more important, then the sovereignty attained by virtually all Third World countries should lead to a lessening of inequality. However, if markets alone can create spatial inequality, what options do states/economies have for altering the global distribution of production in their favor?

Roughly speaking, we can give three possible answers to the question of whether European *economic* growth alone, or the world market alone, caused poverty and backwardness elsewhere: no, yes, and maybe. Theories based in neoclassical economics (NCE) claim that economic growth produced a relative inequality, but that economic growth in one place does not cause poverty elsewhere or require exploitation of those other areas. Participation in the world market should lead to growth. In short, the international market and international trade are benign forces—they affect all economies the same way. A set of quasi-Marxist theories going by the name world systems theory (WST) or dependency theory argue the reverse. European growth created poverty and would not have occurred without economic exploitation of other regions. Participation in the world market *underdevelops* many countries. In short, the international economy and international trade are malign forces. Finally, a group of agnostics argue that the world market alone can only create opportunities or a context in which regions can grow or stagnate and that these outcomes ultimately rest on internal conditions, in particular state institutions understood broadly. This group sees both malign and benign influences in the international market and trade. In short, politics determines which particular outcome will emerge from a set of possibilities revealed by an area's position in the world market.

We will examine each of these three different explanations before turning to Johann von Thünen, who was introduced in Chapter 1. Von Thünen allows us to tie together the important insights of each of these three groups. His explicit analysis of the spatial consequences of market forces creates a basis for understanding the purely economic consequences of the international market. Von Thünen makes a powerful case for a market-driven distribution of production activity that sorts economic regions into regular zones producing goods with varying degrees of value added. As value added varies, so too does the potential for national (or regional) income and thus inequality, and so, too, do the level of resources available to the state, and thus vulnerability to predation. Although market forces create these zones, states can try either to adapt to those forces or to overcome them. This creates two generic strategies, which we can label, respectively, Ricardian and Kaldorian, after the economists most closely associated with the ideas presented under those names. This chapter will focus mostly on a static consideration of the question of inequality (i.e., the spatial distribution of production), and will end with a look at the two different strategies for development. Later chapters provide a dynamic and empirical consideration of the forces described here.

## Neoclassical Economic Explanations

Neoclassical economics (NCE) argues that global economic spatial inequality is inevitable but that wealthier national economies are not wealthy because of their exploitation of poorer ones. It asserts that all backwardness is relative: rising incomes in industrial societies make nonindustrial societies look backward. However, growth in industrialized countries is only hampered by external poverty, and the natural diffusion of production technologies means that backward societies will rarely lose ground absolutely. Similarly, international trade can only help economies, by maximizing allocative efficiency, that is, by allowing them to produce whatever they make most efficiently and to exchange it for goods they are less efficient at producing.

NCE arguments derive from Adam Smith and David Ricardo. Smith argued that economic growth came from an increase in the division of labor. As economic specialization increased, so did the level of productivity and thus income. In Smith's famous example, the output of two people making pins could be increased if one person only drew wire for the bottom of a pin while the second only put heads on pins rather than each one making pins start to finish. Smith assumed that people's natural inclination to barter and truck would create markets, and that markets in turn would force producers to innovate and increase the division of labor. Innovation and increased specialization create a virtuous circle. Thus, international inequality does not surprise NCE, even though it typically ignores geography in its analyses. Because innovation leads to different levels of productivity in different places, it also produces different levels of income. Similarly, as Ricardo argues, because the distribution of factors of production is not even, trade enhances everyone's welfare.

When NCE applies this analysis historically, it claims that northwestern Europe, and in particular Holland and Britain, experienced quite rapid innovation because of these countries' strong institutions protecting property rights, which helped their respective agricultural and industrial revolutions.[3] Consequently, their incomes per capita rose above the level prevailing in the rest of the world, where unmodified forms of agriculture set income levels. As their agricultural and industrial innovations diffused outward, productivity and income rose elsewhere. The major impediments to the adoption of technology are social and political, not economic. Religion or custom may impede technology transfer, while a weak state incapable of enforcing property rights may hinder investment. The diffusion of innovation and of an increasingly complex division of labor thus produces spatial inequality because not all areas take up innovations or continue innovating at the same rate.

NCE argues that the diffusion of innovation produces only *relative* inequality: while laggards may never catch up, they usually do not regress either. Similarly, since innovation is *endogenous*, it obviously cannot be true that development (i.e., rising productivity and incomes) in one place causes regression (not simply a *relative* decline) in another, or that this decline is necessary for innovation to take place in areas with high or rising income. Thus, NCE sees links between rich and poor areas, particularly trade links, as desirable, for these links will speed technological diffusion.

NCE bases this claim on variations of David Ricardo's original insights about static comparative advantage. Obviously, if Country A produces wheat with fewer inputs of capital and labor than Country B, but Country B produces rock videos with fewer inputs than Country A, both countries will gain by exchanging wheat and videos and concentrating on the production of what they do best. This is referred to as absolute advantage, because A is absolutely better at making wheat and B at producing videos. Ricardo's insight was to show that even when absolute advantage did not exist, *comparative advantage* made trade worthwhile. Ricardo showed that the incomes and consumption of countries rose if they specialized in the production of whatever they produced most efficiently and used exports of those goods to purchase imports of goods they were less efficient at producing. Comparative advantage existed when Country A produced both wheat and videos more efficiently than Country B, but A used more inputs to produce videos than wheat when it made both, while B used relatively more inputs to produce wheat than videos when it produced both. In this situation, it made sense for A to shift its resources into the production of wheat and for B to shift resources into the production of videos, and then for A to exchange its wheat for B's videos. Both countries gained from this sort of exchange.

NCE has nothing to say about the *kinds* of production systems that should emerge in any given economy.

## World Systems Theory Explanations

World systems theory (WST) takes a position diametrically opposed to NCE. It argues that the development of capitalism in northwest Europe both required and caused not just relative but also *absolute* backwardness elsewhere. It also contends that trade generally exacerbates spatial inequalities.[4]

WST, like NCE, claims that the world market, in this case a defined subset called a world economy, drives all change. World economies are characterized by a single division of labor but multiple polities; in contrast, in world empires, the division of labor is contained within one political system. For WST, capitalism is unlikely to emerge within a world empire. In our terms, WST argues that in world empires dominant kings tend to squeeze out both nobles and merchants. Because nobles are turned into prebends (salaried officials who can also draw revenue from a defined territory), kings can absorb virtually all of the surplus that peasants produce. Because kings have no (or many fewer) internal and external enemies, merchants do not have the leverage that kings' voracious appetite for funds gave them in Europe. In contrast, competition among states in a world economy creates a space in which accumulation can occur, because kings and/or their states need the cash merchants make available via the public debt. Merchants can then accumulate capital.

For WST, participation in the world economy determines domestic class structures, the structure of export production, and ultimately state power. The spatial expansion of the world economy increases specialization, differentiating national economies into core and periphery areas. In contrast to the NCE view, in which specialization is mutually advantageous, WST claims that specialization benefits only the core areas. Trade between core and periphery condemns peripheral areas to the production of low-value-added goods that do not lead to more economic development. Wages and national income stagnate, while the core benefits from low-cost inputs that raise the rate of capital accumulation.

WST calls this phenomenon the transfer of surplus from (emerging) peripheral areas back to emerging core areas via unequal exchange. Unequal exchange occurs because low wages in peripheral areas mean that peripheral areas in general have to exchange many more hours of labor with core economies to buy goods embodying a given hour of high wage work.[5] Through this surplus transfer core areas experience more growth while peripheral areas slow down. Unequal exchange is a significant part of the WST argument. Mere looting of colonial areas would not necessarily have impeded long-term development. Unequal exchange explains how market pressures *alone* can cause underdevelopment. Because peripheral areas have shallow internal markets, their economies remain "extroverted," that is, oriented toward the world market. This orientation reinforces their low local wages.

WST thus asserts that the impoverishment of the periphery by world market mechanisms is crucial to the development of the core. In this regard, WST is loyal to its Marxist origins: the analysis of core and periphery mirrors Marx's analysis of the dialectical relationship between capital and labor. Core and periphery could not exist without each other. Core implies periphery in the same way that capital—private ownership of the means of production by a limited group of people—implies labor—a larger group separated from the means of production. Moreover, in contrast to NCE, which sees only a relative poverty, WST claims that absolute regression not only can occur but often is also the norm in the periphery, because unequal exchange can cause capital *de*cumulation there.

Because observed reality confronts WST with a gradient of incomes, market power, and state power rather than a sharp polarization, WST inserts an intermediate zone called semiperiphery between core and periphery. Although some WST theorists like Wallerstein have offered political reasons for the existence of the semiperiphery, no WST theorist to date has come up with a convincing explanation of what differentiates this area that does not rest only on a comparison with either extreme. Instead, WST offers a definition of semiperiphery in relation to the core and periphery. The semiperiphery trades high-value-added goods to the periphery and low-value-added goods to the core in exchange for low- and high-value-added goods, respectively. The semiperiphery suffers from unequal exchange with the core but exploits the periphery through unequal exchange.

Unlike NCE, WST asserts that the world market also structures the kinds of classes and production systems in each type of economy. Core economies combine skilled labor and highly capitalized production systems without overt extraeconomic coercion. Peripheral economies, particularly those in the preindustrial era, were typified by unskilled labor and low levels of capitalization, and labor often was coerced through methods ranging from slavery to state-enforced violence. Once more, semiperipheral areas occupy an intermediate position with systems that mix market and political coercion. By shutting their economy off from market pressures emanating from the world economy, states can move their economies up in this hierarchy of economic zones.

## Agnostics, or Explanations Centered in State and Society

Analysts looking at the role of the state and groups within society take an intermediate position, claiming that markets alone determine nothing and that inequality, persistent or transitory, relative or absolute, depends on how the state and social groups react to market opportunities. This heterogeneous group mixes Marxists like Robert Brenner and statists like Alexander Gerschenkron.[6] This group is united by an insistence that internal politics and struggles rather than external market pressures determine outcomes. For Brenner, the balance of power between peasants and noble landlords ultimately determined whether conditions conducive to capitalist development — free markets for labor and land, producers dependent on the market for their survival — emerged. For Gerschenkron, the presence of established producers means that latecomers will have difficulty industrializing unless their state can craft industrial promotion policies (see Chapter 4). Because those political reactions can vary, so can outcomes.

These analysts see considerable room for maneuvering within the confines of the world economy. Brenner and like-minded analysts see development as an outcome of class struggles that permit innovation and force capitalists to invest. Where NCE ignores class and the nature of production systems, and where WST claims both are determined by external market pressures, Brennerites advance the reverse logic. For them, class struggle determines the relative efficiency of an economy and its rate of investment. Brenner looked at struggles between landlords and peasants/serfs in seventeenth-century Poland, England, and France, which WST views, respectively, as peripheral, core, and semiperipheral areas. WST claims that Poland's participation in world grain markets led to the underdevelopment of its economy, whereas England and Holland developed by virtue of manufactured exports to Poland.

In contrast, Brenner argues that the absence of towns in Poland and Eastern Europe in general weakened the position of the peasants relative to landowners. Because many peasant villages in Poland and elsewhere in Eastern Europe had been founded recently, they lacked the internal solidarity necessary to confront and contain rapacious landlords.[7] Landowners deployed state violence to fix peasants in place, making them serfs who worked on nobles' estates. Because this reinforcement or re-creation of feudalism prevented investment, Poland's stagnation is not surprising. In France, meanwhile, peasants had relatively greater power vis-à-vis nobles than did peasants in either England or Poland. They asserted their ownership rights to the land they farmed and restricted nobles' ability to impose various kinds of rents. These peasants could not be cleared off the land, which made it difficult for nobles to assemble the kind of landholdings that would make agricultural investment rational. At the same time, these peasants had no incentive to invest either. They had access to land without having to go through the market. They could ignore market pressures to increase production or productivity continuously; competition did not affect their ability to survive. Only in England, where towns existed but landlords were able to dispossess peasants, did a classic capitalist investment dynamic emerge. There the replacement of peasants by tenant farmers created a group of actors whose long-term survival did depend on their ability to cope with competitive pressures by investing and increasing productivity. Tenants risked losing their lease to higher bidders if they fell behind in the competitive struggle. A crucial part of Brenner's argument is that since trade was a relatively minor part of economic activity in this period, it cannot explain the consequences for which WST gives it credit.

Whereas Brenner looks at the relative balance of power among classes, Gerschenkron focuses on the role of the state and state institutions as the midwife of economic development. Gerschenkron argued that technological diffusion and catchup do not occur automatically. In contrast to both WST and NCE, Gerschenkron maintained that the state played an important role in catchup by creating novel institutional frameworks in which productive investment could occur. Without these new institutions, market forces emanating from existing producers selling world markets would dissuade local entrepreneurs from investing.

Gerschenkron thus invests the state with a much wider role in correcting market failure in backward economies than does NCE. Gerschenkron, like Brenner, argues that local decisions can determine an economy's relative position in the world market, but, unlike Brenner, he locates the source of difference in state policy. Like WST, Gerschenkron argues that the world market sets up substantial obstacles to the emergence of modern industry in backward countries, but, unlike WST, he does not see these as insuperable. Brenner and Gerschenkron come together in their insistence that local institutions have a profound effect on development. Unlike NCE, they do not view state institutions only as enforcing property rights. They understand institutions more broadly, as entities encompassing all state activity in support of the economy, including the institutionalization of class conflict.

## A Von Thünen Perspective on the Division of Labor

All three analyses share a common concern with the consequences of a global division of labor and with how the market defines potential outcomes regarding inequality and growth. This common concern has three axes: how does the division of labor expand? what are the consequences of its expansion? how does an expanding division of labor bear on the (im)possibility of technological diffusion? Von Thünen provides a key to understanding the spatial distribution of production and thus of the emergence of unequal rates of growth, innovation, and technological diffusion.

As Chapter 1 noted, limits on agricultural productivity and the transportation of staple (bulk) agricultural products set profound limits on an increased division of labor in Europe. The division of labor is increased by increasing the proportion of the population in nonagricultural — usually urban — but productive activities. The agricultural surplus left over after peasants, nobles, and their draft animals have been fed determines the size of this population. Low productivity in most premodern European agriculture limited this surplus, and in turn limited the urban population. But the fewer people agriculture could support outside agriculture, the harder it was to increase agricultural productivity. Agriculture in fifteenth-century Europe was caught in a vicious circle in which a limited surplus (often consumed unproductively by the nobility) in turn limited both the ability to invest in agriculture and the utility of investment in agriculture. Until about 1600, between 25 and 33 percent of the grain crop had to be retained as seed for the next year's production; this condition persisted outside northwestern Europe until the 1800s. (Table 2.1 provides data on seed-to-yield ratios, and Table 2.2 provides data on comparative agricultural productivity.)

Von Thünen's observation that grain was rarely transported more than 20 miles overland meant that the division of labor in an ideal typical microeconomy was limited by the population that could be fed on the surplus produced within a 20-mile radius of its market town. In addition, most "manufacturing" involved the transformation of agriculturally derived raw materials, setting yet another limit on expansion of the division of labor inside microeconomies. The production of food and of agricultural raw materials (nonfood agriculturals, or NFAs) competed for land in most microeconomies; the one often could not expand without forcing a decline in the other. Similarly, foods and NFAs also competed because of the interaction between incomes and food consumption. Food consumption increases both absolutely and relatively as income expands, because people eat more and better foods; from 1400 to 1900, "better" meant foods containing more fats and animal protein. Produc-

TABLE 2.1

### Average Harvest-to-Seed Yield Ratios in Europe, 1500–1820

| Years | England/ Netherlands | France/ Spain/Italy | Central Europe | Eastern Europe |
|---|---|---|---|---|
| 1500s | 7.4 | 6.7 | 4.2 | 4.1 |
| 1600s | 8.0 | 6.2 | 4.3 | 3.9 |
| 1700s | 10.1 | 6.7 | 4.6 | 4.1 |
| 1800–20 | 11.1 | 6.2 | 5.4 | — |

SOURCE: Peter Kriedte, *Peasants, Landlords, Merchant Capitalists* (Warwickshire: Berg, 1983), p. 22.

TABLE 2.2

## Agricultural Productivity Index,[a] 1800–1910, Selected Years[a]

| | 1800 | 1830 | 1860 | 1880 | 1900 | 1910 |
|---|---|---|---|---|---|---|
| *High-Productivity Agricultural Exporters* | | | | | | |
| Argentina | — | — | — | — | — | 61.2 |
| Australia | — | — | 20.2 | 31.0 | 32.9 | 50.4 |
| Canada | 8.6 | 9.0 | 11.4 | 15.6 | 32.1 | 33.0 |
| Denmark | 8.0 | 10.9 | 20.0 | 27.4 | 35.0 | 39.8 |
| New Zealand | — | — | 32.9 | 41.3 | 51.0 | 59.4 |
| United States | 20.5 | 20.8 | 26.1 | 35.0 | 40.7 | 47.0 |
| *Average* | 12.3 | 13.6 | 22.1 | 30.1 | 38.3 | 48.4 |
| *Industrial Europe* | | | | | | |
| Britain | 13.2 | 13.5 | 18.0 | 19.2 | 21.3 | 24.1 |
| Belgium | 7.0 | 8.1 | 10.9 | 13.8 | 18.1 | 21.3 |
| France | 6.5 | 7.9 | 12.2 | 13.7 | 16.9 | 17.7 |
| Germany | 6.5 | 7.8 | 12.2 | 16.0 | 25.5 | 30.6 |
| Netherlands | 9.0 | 9.3 | 10.8 | 12.2 | 15.8 | 19.0 |
| Sweden | 4.2 | 6.0 | 8.4 | 10.3 | 12.2 | 15.3 |
| Switzerland | 5.8 | 6.4 | 9.0 | 10.7 | 12.7 | 13.9 |
| *Europe average[b]* | 6.0 | 6.6 | 8.0 | 8.7 | 10.3 | 11.2 |
| *Low-Productivity Agricultural Exporters* | | | | | | |
| Austria-Hungary | 5.0 | 5.0 | 6.2 | 8.6 | 10.3 | 11.3 |
| Greece | — | — | 4.9 | 4.9 | 5.0 | 4.7 |
| Norway | 4.5 | 5.0 | 7.9 | 7.3 | 7.5 | 9.6 |
| Portugal | — | — | 4.1 | 3.5 | 3.5 | 3.7 |
| Romania | — | — | 6.7 | 8.0 | 11.3 | 13.9 |
| Russia | — | 5.6 | 5.9 | 6.0 | 6.7 | 7.4 |
| Spain | 4.3 | 4.9 | 6.1 | 6.2 | 8.1 | 9.1 |

[a]Millions of direct calories produced per male agricultural worker. Note that these are best-guess estimates.
[b]Includes low-productivity exporters, Denmark, and Italy.
SOURCE: Paul Bairoch, "Economic Inequalities between 1800 and 1913," in Jean Batou, ed., *Between Development and Underdevelopment, 1800–1870* (Geneva: Librairie Droz, 1991), p. 12.

tion of animal protein is relatively inefficient, requiring animals to consume about 5 calories in grain to produce 1 calorie of dairy or meat.[8]

Because most towns lived off their microeconomy, the majority of towns in 1500 held between 400 and 1,000 people, and few exceeded 5,000. In Germany towns had an *average* population of 400.[9] As a result, specialization (in a Smithian sense) was kept very low, limiting productivity and income. Emerging centers of manufacturing in the fifteenth through nineteenth centuries required access to extensive supplies of calories and raw materials.

This suggests three alternative paths for "towns" whose population grew to the point where it consumed all the food and NFAs produced within its microeconomy. Fernand Braudel states these succinctly: "Thousands of towns were founded [in the 11th century], but few of them went on to brilliant futures . . . The destinies of these very special cities were linked not only to the progress of the surrounding countryside but [also] to international trade."[10] In the "Malthusian" path, no economical external sources of food or NFAs existed, and agricultural innovation either was not fast enough or did not happen. In this case a town's expansion and development would stop, perhaps after overshooting its natural limits and then starving back down to them.

"The progress of the surrounding countryside" suggests a path around the barriers imposed by overland transportation costs. If more production could be squeezed in a sustainable way from the land in a microeconomy, then the town's population and the division of labor could both grow. This growth did occur in a very gradual way. Both Dutch and English farmers innovated new crop rotations—as part of the agricultural revolution of the 1500s—which increased productivity per acre.[11] The so-called improved husbandry and convertible husbandry increased seed yield and left much less land fallow (unused) than the older two- and three-field systems, which, respectively, left half and one-third of the land fallow each year. Less fallow and higher yields in northwestern Europe allowed farmers to produce much more dairy and meat. Much as NCE expects, Dutch and English techniques did diffuse to the rest of Europe, but slowly. Techniques innovated in 1500 did not reach Poland and Hungary—a distance of only 700 miles, or about the distance from New York to Chicago—until 1825.

The introduction of the potato and maize (corn) from the Americas after 1600 supplemented these new crop rotations. The potato was perhaps the single most important innovation in this respect. It created "new" land because it generated three times as many calories out of a given area as did grain production. Planting potatoes on one-third of a microeconomy potentially freed up the other two-thirds for use in producing animal protein, more urban food, or industrial raw materials. The potato thus liberated inland microeconomies from limits on their division of labor, allowing them to begin growing in advance of the railroad. In highly urban Belgium, by 1800 potatoes provided 40 percent of the calories that had formerly been supplied by grain.[12]

Adopting convertible husbandry was not simple. Convertible husbandry's multiple rotations required relatively large parcels of land and more inputs of labor and manufactured goods (e.g., seed drills). Convertible husbandry was possible only when markets for land and labor already existed or when peasants, for whatever reason, were willing to respond to market signals and had cash to buy inputs. The slow diffusion of convertible husbandry testifies to the absence of these markets. At this minimal level Brenner is correct: capitalist development in Europe occurred only where noble and other landlords eliminated peasants and ownership.

In the final alternative, which we might call the Wallersteinian path because it leads directly to the world market, the extension of agricultural supply zones into new areas via water transport allowed an expansion of the division of labor. It is no surprise that an expanding division of labor grew within and perhaps because of the expanding mercantile economy in northwest Europe. All of the cities in this area had access to huge supply zones because of their littoral location. As they outstripped their own microeconomies, they turned to overseas sources of grain, fish, and NFAs, searching farther and farther away to find more and more littoral areas capable of producing grain and other food. By the 1600s the Baltic was shipping enough grain to feed about 750,000 people yearly. This grain went to food-deficit urban centers, including Holland, which appears to have imported about 15 percent of its food, and, equally important, to the Iberian cities, which otherwise would have been severely hamstrung by their backward agricultures.[13] Industrial Holland and then England also drew their flax, timber, hemp, and wool from new agricultural zones that extended out to the Baltic coast and up its major rivers, as well as up the Rhine River. Without access to these zones, Dutch and, later, English cities would have faced a severe trade-off between raw materials and food production. *The creation and expansion of a capitalist world economy of the sort WST describes thus rests on the core's ability to find and generate an expanded supply of foods and NFAs.* At this minimal level, WST is correct about the reciprocal interaction of core and periphery: because food and NFA production could not be increased within the confines of the microeconomies surrounding most towns, the core could not have developed without the periphery.

Two innovative principles thus underpinned the emergence of a global capitalism based on urban industrial activity, as opposed to the more diffuse mercantile networks that always existed. First, an expanding division of labor requires innovation in the technology of food production itself. Second, better transport, and particularly water transport, could permit a larger division of labor.

## The International Division of Labor and Spatial Inequality

Virtually all the towns that broke the 1,000 population barrier did so because they had access to water transport and so were able to acquire part of their food supply from outside their microeconomy. What did this expanding division of labor around these larger cities look like? Did it generate inequality? Again von Thünen provides a suggestive analytic scheme. His major contribution to economics, *Der isolierte Staat,* or *The Isolated State,* elaborated a location theory for agricultural activity.[14] In a thought experiment, von Thünen posited a flat, featureless plain of uniform fertility with a town at its center. The town provided manufactures for the farms around it while getting its food and fuel from those agricultural areas. Then he asked: how will farming activity distribute itself around town? Von Thünen assumed capitalist markets for land, labor, and commodities and capitalist forms of production organization.[15] His answer shows that a spatial division of labor with potentially sharp disparities in income would arise around the town. This mimics what happened in reaction to rising demand among the cities in Europe's maritime economy.

Von Thünen argued that agricultural activity would distribute itself in regular, concentric rings around the town, with each ring devoted to a particu-

lar type of product, and more important, using *different production systems.*
This spatial distribution of activity occurred because transportation costs to
market increased the farther a farm was located from town. Because distance
from market and thus transportation costs decreased the closer one got to
town, landowners closer to town were capable of charging a higher rent for
that land. Why?

Consider the situation when grain is the only crop grown outside the
town. Grain will cost the same to produce everywhere, since we assume
uniform fertility and knowledge. The price of grain in the town is equal to the
cost of production and transportation for grain coming in from the outermost
farm, because grain is a necessity. As rising demand pushes grain production
farther and farther out, causing rising transportation costs, town grain prices
rise. Grain produced at a distance will cost more than grain produced next to
the town, because in addition to the direct costs of production (P), this grain
also has to bear the cost of inward transportation (T). The implication is that
grain producers located next to the town will be able to capture extra profits
equivalent to the cost of transporting grain from the outermost farm, whereas
farms at intermediate locations will capture a similar but smaller extra profit
whose size depends on their own transportation costs to town. The shaded
area *R* in Figure 2.1 represents that extra profit, which in strict economic terms
is actually a *rent*. For analytic clarity, von Thünen presumed that landowners
and farmers were different actors. Landowners actually captured this extra
profit as rent. Landowners closer to town would charge higher rents than
those farther away; landowners located the same distance from town would
charge the same rent.

If we now free ourselves from the assumption that only grain is produced,
we can see that zones producing different commodities will emerge. Because
rents are higher closer to town, farmers bidding for access to that land would
opt to produce either products with a high value/yield per acre and/or
perishable products like fresh vegetables, milk, and flowers whose value depended on proximity to town. In contrast, high rents would force farmers
producing goods with a low value added per acre farther out. Producing
low-value-added goods close to town would be irrational, because rent costs
would overwhelm any profit the farmer might make from those goods.

With this theoretical device, von Thünen deduced that agriculture would
distribute itself in regular rings. Each ring produced a different mix of crops.
What was even more important, the kind of *production system* changed. This
change in the system of production allows us to construct a foundation for
and to amend the WST division of the world in core(s), semiperiphery(ies), and
periphery(ies). Going from ring one to ring six takes one from high value added
per acre to low value added per acre. The decline in value added per acre going
outward from the town reflects not only the kind of crop being grown, but
also the way it is grown. Put simply, when one is going from ring one to ring
six, the volume of labor inputs per acre decreases, but the proportion of labor
costs in total costs rises. Thus, from the economist's viewpoint, labor intensity
of production rises going farther out, whereas capital intensity rises coming in
toward town. In addition, the intensity with which land is used also rises

Figure 2.1 Relationship between Transportation Costs and Rent

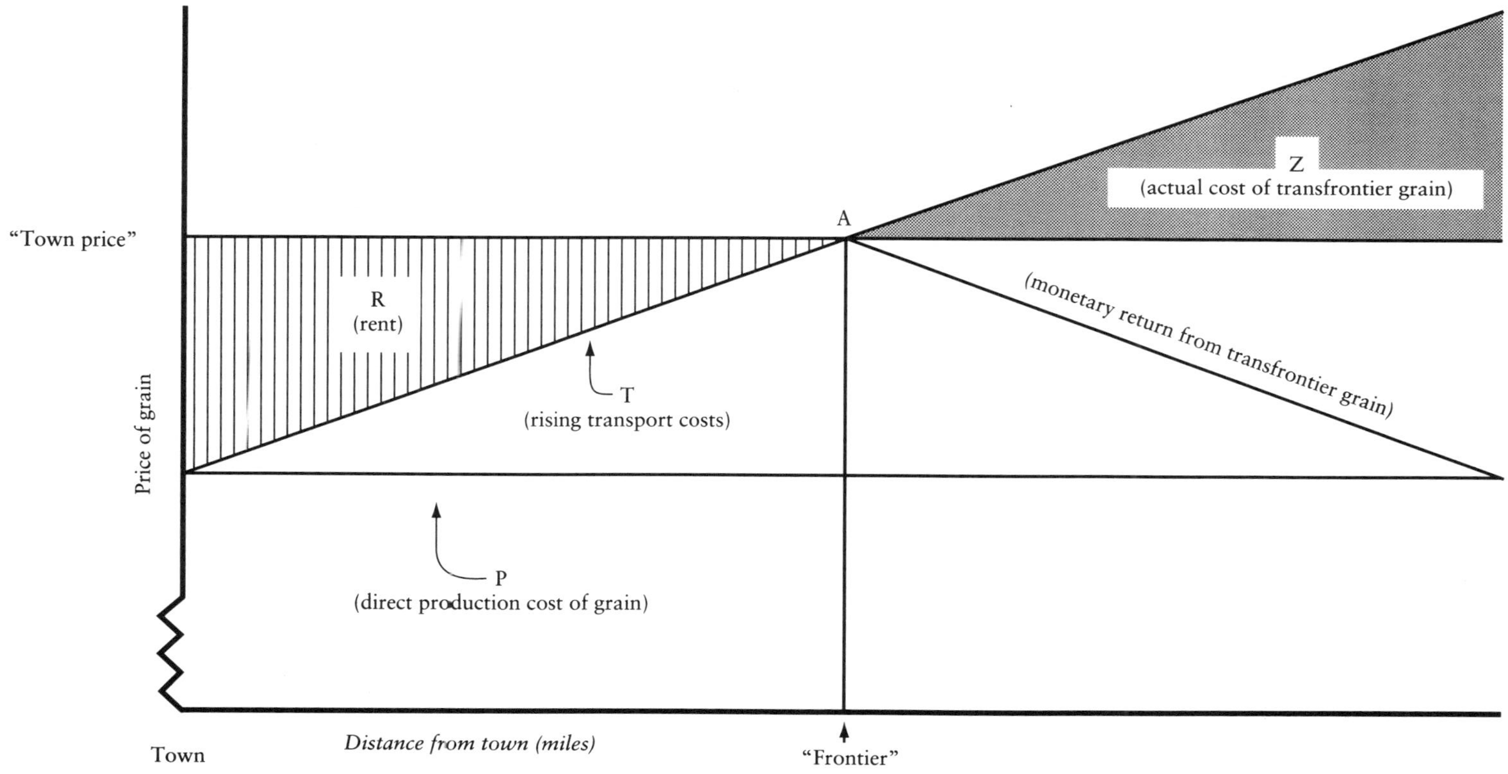

Z
(actual cost of transfrontier grain)

(monetary return from transfrontier grain)

A

T
(rising transport costs)

R
(rent)

P
(direct production cost of grain)

"Town price"

Price of grain

"Frontier"

Town

Distance from town (miles)

coming back toward town. Higher productivity per acre and per worker closer in to town means higher incomes there; low value added per acre and lower capital intensity farther out from town means low incomes there.

Von Thünen's first ring produced fresh milk, vegetables, and other high-value crops. This ring used very large amounts of labor, and neither left land fallow nor rotated crops. (Fallowed land is left unused to regain its former fertility, but because it is unused it generates no revenue.) Instead, manure from dairy cattle housed and fed in stalls, and manure trucked out from the city are used to restore fertility. Because this manure is easy to get, the market alone, not a crop rotation system designed to restore fertility, dictates what crops will be grown at any given time. Housing all those animals implies a big capital investment; feeding, milking, and caring for them, and preparing and harvesting crops constantly, means high year-round labor demands.

The second and third rings would produce a mix of root vegetables, such as potatoes, and a small volume of grains. Both of these rings would use a five- to seven-crop rotation. (I.e., in a five- or seven-year period, five or seven different crops would be planted.) This is the convertible husbandry referred to above. The crop rotation system wasted no land in fallow, feeding some root crops to stalled animals and using manure from those animals to restore fertility. As in the first ring, the enormous amount of work involved in feeding stalled animals and in preparing soil creates a huge demand for labor inputs and also uses lots of capital.

The fourth ring would produce an even mix of root crops and grains, using the three-crop (or improved) rotation. In this rotation, one field is used to grow grain, another is used for pasturing animals (whose manure partly restores fertility), and yet another is left fallow (to completely restore fertility). Animals raised in the outermost ring would be fattened here before final sale in the town.

The fifth ring would produce almost exclusively grain, using a three-field system. In the three-field system one field is left permanently as pasture, and the rest is divided between two grain fields and one fallow. Since this is almost a monocultural system, very little labor is needed, except at harvest time.

The sixth ring would be given over to stock-raising, because grazing uses such enormous amounts of land that it can be profitable only where land is cheap, that is, carrying a low-rent cost. Stock-raising uses very little labor and even less in the way of capital per acre. Butter and cheese might also be produced here.

This analysis has two important implications. First, von Thünen's location theory confirms the WST's assertions about zonal differentiation and inequality in the world market. Second, using NCE techniques, we can explain why some of the peripheralizing and exploitative consequences that WST predicts can occur. At the same time, it also shows why Brenner is more correct about why underdevelopment occurs. Underdevelopment is a possible but not a *necessary* outcome. Let's begin by discussing zonal differentiation.

Although von Thünen was no Marxist, his description of the spatial distribution of agricultural activity bears close resemblance to the spatial distribution of production noticed by WST, once we abandon the overly rigid division into three types of economy. (Von Thünen's graduated vision of space is preferable to WST's tripartite scheme anyway.) The most important coincidence is that production systems, labor demand, and the value of the goods produced change with increasing distance from the town/core. Von Thünen does not consider the consequences of this differentiation. For the sake of analytic simplicity, he assumed away issues of labor supply and wages, although he did consider the effects of the frontier on wages, as we will see in Chapter 5. Nonetheless, a number of powerful conclusions can be drawn from his analysis. Von Thünen's analysis also suggests that the NCE view that inequality — zonal differentiation — is not inherent in the system is wrong. Like NCE, von Thünen's analysis is based on marginalist principles, yet it shows that inequality can emerge for reasons that have nothing to do with the uneven diffusion of technology or "nonrational" behaviors.

What about peripheralization? The declining demand for labor, and particularly high-quality labor, produced by the shift to simpler forms of crop production farther away from the town potentially implies declining living standards. The total social product available for distribution among landowners, tenants, and laborers in the outermost rings will be small. First, while the price of grain in the town is set by grain brought in from the outermost ring, this does not imply high grain prices in the outer ring. Quite the opposite is true: the actual production cost of grain sets grain prices in the outer ring. The town price of grain reflects both production costs *and* the cost of transport. In the outer ring the grain is available without transportation costs, and thus its price simply reflects its production cost, including the normal rate of profit. Lower grain prices imply lower nominal wages, but not necessarily a lower standard of living. In the sixteenth century, grain prices in Danzig (modern Gdansk) were about half those in Amsterdam; similarly, the price of oxen loaded at Danzig was one-quarter of their landed price in Antwerp.[16]

Second, the higher percentage of land left fallow means that the average volume of good/NFA produced per acre is smaller than that closer to town. Therefore, a larger land area is necessary to maintain the same level of value produced per worker, and less income is available to distribute in that society.

Finally, the simpler production systems von Thünen observed imply lower Smithian specialization and thus lower productivity per worker, which in turn implies lower incomes. So, as in the WST scenario, the outermost rings (that is, the periphery) most likely will have lower incomes than the core, and precisely because they are engaged in commerce with the core. The market pressures emanating from the town/core will probably force production into a particular low-value-added mold.

These three conditions will not, as WST asserts, *necessarily* produce lower living standards or underdevelopment in this outermost ring, providing two interactive conditions hold. If the number of workers is small relative to the production area (i.e., if the ratio of available labor to land is low), then the total value produced per worker may be high enough to sustain high living standards. Small numbers of workers and large areas of land can imply high productivity, particularly if rational producers substitute capital for scarce labor. This high productivity will again result in high incomes per producer, despite low prices for what they produce. In both cases the increased volume produced per worker overcomes low prices and profit margins. The very areas WST finds most nettlesome for its tripartite scheme — for example, Australasia — are precisely those areas where highly capitalized, highly productive forms of agriculture offset the lower value produced per acre characteristic of the outermost rings.

Where either of these conditions did not hold, the low living standards of WST's periphery certainly result from participation. When labor is scarce relative to land but there is no incentive to increase productivity via investment, the value added per worker remains low. Consider Brenner's France. Widespread peasant proprietorship caused fragmented holdings and blocked investment by either lords or peasants. The absence of investment meant slowly falling living standards as land was split up and peasants were forced onto more marginal land. Alternately, when landlords use coercion to fix peasants to the land and squeeze additional labor out of them, the result will also be low productivity and low incomes. Landlords using coercion will invest in more coercion, not capital goods, to increase production. This is part of the reason for underdevelopment in Brenner's Poland; the other part derived from real exploitation.

Consider what happens in a von Thünen system when a landowner lies over the "frontier" set by transportation costs and the prevailing price of grain in the town (point A in Figure 2.1). This landowner earns negative rents if he engages in trade. That is, he would have to subsidize additional transport costs (the shaded area Z) in order to deliver grain to the town at the prevailing price. However, if that landowner could shift the cost of subsidy onto his labor force, then he could still ship grain to the town and make a profit. This is what happened in the Vistula River grain trade. Certainly, landowners proximate to the river could trade profitably with Holland, but those farther inland also wanted to trade. Their desire for income and the consumption that income bought moved them to exploit their peasants by squeezing additional labor time out of them — time that those peasants needed for their own subsistence production. It also motivated landlords to edge out as many middlemen as possible — destroying Polish towns — because the narrowness of the surplus generated by this system meant that few could share it. In Poland this coerced labor came at the expense of peasants' ability to feed themselves, and thus led to falling incomes and demographic collapse.

## The Von Thünenization of the European World Economy

Von Thünen's system may look good in theory, but what about reality? The world economy that grew up around Holland and, to a lesser extent, London provides the best example of the emergence of von Thünen rings during the period of state-building in Europe. (We will look at the same phenomenon in relation to British industrialization in Chapters 5 and 6.) Shipbuilding, fishing, commerce, and wool textile production were the economic core of Holland's huge urban economy. By 1622 Amsterdam had a population of over 100,000,

Leiden and Haarlem over 30,000, and seven other Dutch cities over 10,000. Initially, Holland's location in the Rhine and Scheldt river deltas and on the North Sea favored urbanization. Overseas grain then enabled Holland to become one of the most intensely urbanized areas of the world, with between 50 and 70 percent of its population living in cities during the 1500s and 1600s. About 15 percent of its grain consumption came from the Baltic. London, which also had riparian and littoral access, had a population of over 400,000 in 1660, making it the largest city in Europe. The specialization found in these cities made them centers of efficient manufacturing.

Rising urban (or, for WST, core) demand for food and raw materials created market pressures that in turn forced profound changes in both their own agrarian hinterlands and their overseas suppliers. The scale of demand in these urban centers pushed grain and animal production out into areas of Europe that were distant in geographic terms but still fairly close by in terms of transport cost. Holland fed on Polish grain and Danish grain and meat. Although geographically Denmark was closer, cattle walked to market, thus, Danish oxen were farther away than Polish waterborne grain. What happened? First Poland and peripheralization, or underdevelopment, then Denmark and development.

Precisely because they lay within Amsterdam's enlarged agricultural zone, the Polish nobility found that exporting grain there was profitable. (Some of this grain was then reexported, but it went to other urban centers such as Lisbon and Seville.) As WST asserts, the ability of the Polish landlords to export was limited by the relative lack of labor in Eastern Europe. Porous borders meant peasants could migrate to relatively empty lands to the east. Through law and force, the Polish authorities prevented their peasants from moving and then obliged them to work on nobles' estates, producing grain for export.

Much as WST argues, increasing Polish involvement in trade was paralleled by increased compulsory labor for peasants. From 1460 to 1560, Polish grain exports via Danzig increased from 12,500 bushels, a negligible quantity, to 300,000 bushels, and then doubled again over the next century to 600,000 bushels, an amount capable of feeding about 750,000 people per year. Beginning in 1493, a series of laws increasingly restricted peasant freedoms while introducing compulsory labor on nobles' land. (Poland's elected king remained a pawn of the nobility.) In 1500 Polish peasants were free from compulsory labor; a law in 1520 fixed compulsory labor at one day per week; by 1550, compulsory labor had reached three days per week; and by 1600, six days per week. The same process can be seen in other long-distance agricultural suppliers in Eastern Europe. In Hungary, a supplier for Vienna and Italy, compulsory labor was fixed at one day per week in 1514 after a peasant rebellion was crushed. It reached three days by 1550, and by the end of the sixteenth century landlords could fix compulsory labor at any level they liked.

This increase in compulsory labor, of course, left peasants little time to work on their own plots. The natural result was economic stagnation and the risk of demographic collapse from chronic malnourishment. Thus, the very system nobles elaborated to provide them with exportable grain blocked any efforts to increase productivity. If serfdom shackled a potentially mobile peasantry, it also tied nobles to primitive methods of cultivation by increasingly debilitated producers. The only way to increase exports was to increase the number of days peasants were forced to work the nobles' land, and this cut deeper into peasants' ability to feed themselves. Both Brenner and WST can find data to support their argument concerning this moment in economic history. Brenner maintains that Polish grain exports were too small relative to total Polish production — only 6 percent of total net grain production in the 1500s but 20 percent of marketed production — to have caused underdevelopment. If much of this grain was extracted at a loss to the local economy, its impact is greater than the numbers suggest, since some grain would have been used as fuel for the animals transporting the rest.

On the other hand, the importance of the factors Brenner cites, namely, the relative power of different social classes, can easily be seen by casting one's eyes around the rest of the Baltic coast. Denmark provides a salutary contrast to Poland. Like Poland, Denmark supplied cattle and grain for Holland, but unlike Poland it did not regress economically. In Denmark, unlike Poland, the king allied with merchants and protected the peasantry in order to dominate the nobility. The king fixed peasants to the land but did so by making peasants the property of the king, not the nobles. The king also prevented further expropriations of peasant land by nobles. To counterbalance the nobility politically, the king supported direct export production by the peasantry as well as the subsequent creation of a large middle peasant sector. Direct production for market made peasants responsive to market pressure to improve productivity, and they did make such improvements, just as Brenner's English tenant farmers did.

# International Trade: Two Responsive Strategies

Whereas NCE does not expect the world market to produce any kind of pattern of rich and poor areas, WST asserts that the world market determines both the kinds of goods and the kinds of production systems that emerge in specific geographical locales. A von Thünen analysis shows us that neither is quite right. Urban cores do exert market pressures that distribute economic activity in a definite pattern around them, but these pressures do not necessarily determine development, its absence, or its opposite. Peripheral areas may be fated to produce low-value-added goods by virtue of their location in terms of transportation cost, but von Thünen's model suggests that, even so, development and rising incomes are possible. Once a town emerges in the periphery, agriculture will redistribute itself in a new pattern around that town.

This analysis in turn confirms the importance of Gerschenkron's and Brenner's insights about the role of local classes and states in ultimately determining a given economic zone's relative position in the world economy. The market *does* distribute areas (which are not, however, always contiguous with states!) into different zones with different productive potentials. But distance is not destiny, and local actors can modify the consequences of market forces by changing the way production occurs. Raising productivity can raise incomes. Therefore, two different strategies for development are available to states, representing the extremes of a continuum of responses to world market pressures. As we will see, most real-world responses mix elements of both.

## Ricardian Strategies

The first strategy relies on comparative or factor advantages along the lines presented earlier in the section on NCE. I will call this a *Ricardian strategy* because David Ricardo (1772–1823) presented the first reasonably coherent model of trade based on comparative advantage.[17] Ricardian strategies typically use agricultural or other primary product exports to drive economic development. These strategies try to maximize the economic gains from the efficient allocation of the various factors of production present in the society in question, and so are necessarily export oriented. Ricardian strategies are subject to constant or to decreasing returns. At best, an increase in the factors of production (land, labor, and capital) yields a proportional increase in output. At worst, an increase in those factors may yield a lower output than it used to — as, for example, production is pushed onto more marginal land, or less able workers are taken on. Furthermore, to the extent that Ricardian strategies generate industry producing inputs for agriculture or processing outputs, the positive effects of rising exports are linked to the rate of growth of export volumes. As these exports taper off, so do industrial growth and increases in industrial productivity. In the short term, states can pursue a Ricardian strategy by providing the social overhead capital (e.g., transportation networks) needed to get exports to market, as well as a clearinghouse for the information generated and needed by the many small production units typical in farming. The agricultural extension service is the classic example of this kind of clearinghouse.

The long-term success of Ricardian strategies rests on their ability (1) to find new agricultural (or mineral) exports when the old one runs out or suffers from declining returns, or (2) to link other industries to the export sector and use export growth to create growth in those other industries. In the real world, all economies have industries that produce nontraded goods, as well as industries that either process agricultural outputs or provide inputs to agriculture. Accordingly, Ricardian exports can also generate a degree of industrial growth. For example, modern Saudi Arabia has tried to create downstream petrochemical industries using its cheap oil, gas, and petroleum by-products; in the nineteenth century U.S. flour milling was a major and sophisticated industry. Consequently, long-term Ricardian growth depends on the ability of the state both to organize the flow of exports outward and to connect the rest of the local economy to this external engine of growth. It also rests on the propensity of those local groups who are actually doing export production to invest. As noted earlier, however, reliance on a single exported commodity indicates that eventually the spinoff effects for related industries will end.

## Kaldorian Strategies

The second strategy relies on a set of interrelated phenomena like increasing returns to scale, learning by doing, imperfect competition, and economies of speed for growth. I will call it a *Kaldorian strategy,* after Nicholas Kaldor (1908–86), the economist who first presented a relatively coherent model of industrial growth. Kaldorian strategies attempt to take advantage of so-called verdoorn effects, namely, that the greater the rate of increase of output inside a firm, the greater the increase in productivity. The more a firm produces of any one good, the more experience it gets and the more efficient it becomes at producing not only that good but other, similar goods.

Kaldorian strategies are thus investment driven and partly ignore any existing factor disadvantages or advantages. Even though a country may not be competitive in the production of, say, microwave ovens at time A, by investing in additional capacity, selling at a loss, and increasing production volumes, it may learn enough about the production process to become more efficient and thus competitive at time B. (This is what in recent years South Korean firms did with microwave oven production.) By increasing skills, experience, and the division of labor, investment and production themselves change the nature of the factors available in the production mix, and so can override any initial factor disadvantages. Investment in an initially loss-producing activity is rational because many activities have increasing returns. That is, a given investment calls forth a disproportionate increase in output. Greater levels of output create greater specialization in the provision and processing of inputs and also induce process innovations as firms try to cope with increased throughput (economies of speed).

Kaldorian growth is thus much more likely with manufacturing, although as noted earlier, agricultural exports can also have some Kaldorian aspects. Because investment yields disproportionate increases, Kaldorian strategies are also necessarily export oriented. As the local economy grows, income is diverted into imports. The size of the local economy, and thus of effective demand for manufactured goods, is ultimately constrained by its ability to pay for its imports with exports. The best possible Kaldorian strategy exports goods that are themselves the fastest growing part of the economy, maximizing verdoorn effects and increasing return effects.

Kaldorian strategies carry a different kind of risk than Ricardian strategies. When Ricardian strategies are exposed to the risk that demand will eventually taper off for a given raw material, Kaldorian strategies are exposed to the risk that verdoorn effects and learning by doing may not occur. After all, ultimately, firms and not states produce and export goods. States pursuing a Ricardian strategy can invest in social overhead capital, knowing that local firms (or farms) already have a comparative advantage. However, the verdoorn effects and learning by doing in Kaldorian strategies are social processes; both emerge from the interaction of managers and workers on the factory floor. Management may be incompetent and fail to recognize ways to increase throughput or cut costs, and workers may be powerful enough to resist reorganization of work processes. In that case, a firm producing at a loss in order to increase production volumes may just take a bigger loss and go bankrupt; a state subsidizing exports may just run up a big debt, while subsidized firms fail to learn.

Kaldorian growth strategies attempt to construct a new town somewhere in the agricultural supply zones surrounding a larger town. These strategies try to reorient agriculture around this new town and eventually generate sufficient demand to contain or displace the pressures emanating from that larger town. Ricardian strategies accept a region's position in the international division of labor created by some other urban center, and try to maximize the gains from accepting that position. The next chapter looks at the processes we have described here from a dynamic point of view, in order to structure the discussion of Ricardian and Kaldorian strategies in Chapters 4 through 7.

# Notes

1. Paul Bairoch, "Europe's Gross National Product, 1800–1975," *Journal of European Economic History* 5, no. 2 (1976): 273–340; Paul Bairoch, " Economic Inequalities between 1800 and 1913," in Jean Batou, ed., *Between Development and Underdevelopment, 1800–1870* (Geneva: Librairie Droz, 1991), p. 25. For a somewhat contrary view, see Angus Maddison, "A Comparison of Levels of GDP per Capita in Developed and Developing Countries, 1700–1980," *Journal of Economic History* 43, no. 1 (March 1983):27–41.

2. World Bank, *World Development Report, 1992* (New York: Oxford University Press, 1992), pp. 218–220.

3. See Douglass North and Robert Thomas, *Rise of the Western World* (New York: Cambridge University Press, 1973) for an analysis based on property rights. Typical examples of NCE analysis applied to Europe are Sidney Pollard, *Peaceful Conquest: The Industrialization of Europe 1760–1970* (New York: Oxford University Press, 1981); C. Trebilcock, *The Industrialisation of the Continental Powers* (London: Longman, 1981); and David Landes, *The Unbound Prometheus: Technological Change and Industrial Development in Europe from 1750 to the Present* (Cambridge: Cambridge University Press, 1969). For an application to Third World development, see Lloyd Reynolds, *Economic Growth in the Third World* (New Haven, Conn.: Yale University Press, 1985).

4. Here I will conflate analysts using Immanuel Wallerstein's world-systems framework and those in the *dependencia* school. See Immanuel Wallerstein, *Modern World System*, 4 vols. (New York: Academic Publishers, 1974–89) and especially "Rise and Future Demise of the Capitalist World Economy," *Comparative Studies in Society and History*, no. 16, September 1974. Ronald Chilcote, *Theories of Development and Underdevelopment* (Boulder, Colo.: Westview Press, 1984), provides a concise overview of the *dependencistas*.

5. Arghiri Emmanuel, *Unequal Exchange: A Study of the Imperialism of Trade* (New York: Monthly Review Books, 1972).

6. Alexander Gerschenkron, *Economic Backwardness in Historical Perspective* (Cambridge, Mass.: Harvard University Press, 1966). Robert Brenner's original article, "Agrarian Class Structure and Economic Development in Pre-Industrial Europe," a collection of critiques, and his response can be found in T. H. Aston and C. Philpin, eds., *The Brenner Debate: Agrarian Class Structure and Economic Development in Pre-Industrial Europe* (Cambridge: Cambridge University Press, 1985). Brenner's attack

on WST can be found in "The Origins of Capitalist Development: A Critique of Neo-Smithian Marxism," *New Left Review* no. 104 (July 1977): 25–93.

7. Several of the critics in Aston and Philpin, *The Brenner Debate,* contest this notion; see, in particular, Heide Wunde, "Peasant Organization and Class Conflict in Eastern and Western Germany," pp. 91–100. See also Perry Anderson, *Lineages of the Absolutist State* (London: New Left Books, 1974).

8. In the 1980s in high-income areas, "better" has come to mean fresher foods, particularly more fruits and vegetables, in and out of season, and less meat and fat. But during the period 1400–1900 proteins were the prize for those with rising incomes. On the conversion of grain into animal calories, see Wilhelm Abel, *Agricultural Fluctuations in Europe from the Thirteenth to the Twentieth Centuries* (London: Methuen, 1980), p. 269.

9. Fernand Braudel, *Civilization and Capitalism, Fifteenth–Eighteenth Century,* vol. 1 (New York: Harper and Row, 1981). p. 482.

10. Fernand Braudel, *Civilization and Capitalism,* vol. 1, p. 511.

11. B. H. Slicher van Bath, *Agrarian History of Western Europe 500–1850* (New York: St. Martin's Press, 1963).

12. Braudel, *Civilization and Capitalism,* vol. 1, p. 170. On the potato, see Redcliffe Salaman, *The History and Social Influence of the Potato* (Cambridge: Cambridge University Press, 1949).

13. Kristof Glamann, "European Trade 1500–1700," in C. Cipolla, ed., *Fontana Economic History of Europe: The Sixteenth and Seventeenth Centuries* (Glasgow: William Collins, 1974), pp. 454–467.

14. Johann Heinrich von Thünen, *The Isolated State,* Peter Hall, ed., and Carla M. Wartenberg trans. (New York: Pergamon Press, 1966).

15. Von Thünen made a number of simplifying assumptions here: all land is of equal fertility, all farmers and landlords have access to the same information, all have equal access to transportation. None of these assumptions, if relaxed, substantially changes the point that agricultural activity will distribute itself in a regular fashion.

16. Peter Kreidte, *Peasants, Landlords, and Merchant Capitalists: Europe and the World Economy, 1500–1800* (Warwickshire: Berg, 1983), pp. 26–27.

17. Ricardian strategies are similar to staples-led growth—see among others Harold Innes, *The Fur Trade in Canada* (Toronto: University of Toronto Press, 1956) and Mel Watkins, " A Staple Theory of Economic Growth," *Canadian Journal of Economics and Political Science* no. 29 (May 1963). Since the staples theory has historically been used to explain development patterns in newly colonized areas in general and regions of primarily European settlement in particular, I wish to avoid this terminology. By Ricardian strategy, I hope to convey a more generic response than staples-led strategy does.

# CHAPTER 3

# Economic and Hegemonic Cycles

> The problem that is usually being [investigated by economists] is how capitalism administers existing structures, whereas the relevant problem is how it creates and destroys them. As long as this is not recognized, the investigator does a meaningless job.
>
> *Joseph Schumpeter*

Chapters 1 and 2 presented relatively static pictures of the interaction of states and markets. States transformed themselves from mafias into modern bureaucratic states by deploying increasingly more organized forms of violence internationally and internally. Much of the funding for this organized violence initially came from the international market, but over time regularized forms of internal extraction proved more secure. At the same time, the growth of industrial activity inside some nations (and more often than not in specific regions within those emerging nations) created opportunities for other nations/regions to specialize in the production of agricultural goods. Ultimately, each state's ability to project itself and its merchants/producers into the world economy and to protect itself from other states rested on its economic strength and its ability to transform that strength via taxes into organized violence.

While warfare and economic activity occurred continually, they did not occur continuously. Both warfare and its concomitant extensions of political power, as well as global economic activity, waxed and waned in what a large number of analysts argue are fairly regular cycles whose periodicity runs some multiple of 50 years.[1] These economic cycles reflect alternating periods of relatively rapid growth followed by periods of relative stagnation or slow growth. We will call these economic cycles Kondratieff cycles, after Nikolai Kondratieff (1892–1935?), the Soviet economist most credited for original insight into cycling,[2] although we do not necessarily agree with everything he asserted. The political cycles reflect the establishment of a hegemonic position by one state and its eventual disintegration in the face of challenges by other states. For the time being, we can define hegemony as a situation in which one country dominates the world economy intellectually, economically, and militarily. Again, without necessarily agreeing with everything, we will call these Modelski cycles, after George Modelski, the American political scientist who has tried to document these most systematically.[3]

William R. Thompson succinctly summarizes the argument about the interaction of these cycles:

> The governance of global politics, focusing primarily on the management of long distance trade, is intermittent and dependent on the concentration of capabilities of global reach. One state, designated the world power, emerges from periods of global war in a position of preeminence and with a commanding lead in these global reach capabilities. The ability to pay for these capabilities is predicated in large part on leadership in a prewar wave of economic innovation. Winning the global war and controlling a high proportion of the most valuable capabilities then enables the world power to develop policies for the management of the world's political economy.[4]

Let's take politics first. George Modelski sees five periods of hegemony punctuated by convulsive wars involving all major powers. (While Modelski provides precise dates, they should be taken as approximations, as should the dating of economic cycles.) According to Modelski, the Portuguese were dominant from 1494 to 1580, but their position disintegrated during the wars of 1572–1609, which pitted the Portuguese, as part of the Hapsburg empire, against the Dutch, the French, the English, and the Ottoman empire. Holland replaced Portugal as the hegemonic power from 1580 to 1688. England and France repeatedly attacked Holland, until the hostilities culminated in the wars of Louis XIV during 1684–1713. As a result, Holland was transformed into a junior partner of a coalition against France. During 1688–1792, Britain emerged from these conflicts as hegemon.

The French Revolution and the subsequent Napoleonic wars of 1789 to 1814 again pitted all of Europe against France, and again Britain emerged as hegemon from 1815 to 1914. The United States replaced Britain as hegemon after 1914; Modelski dates the decline of U.S. hegemony to circa 1973 but declines to provide a date for its passing. In contrast, Immanuel Wallerstein argues for longer cycles, and thus fewer hegemons, with the Dutch dominant from 1618 to 1815, the British from 1815 to 1945, and the United States after that. Thus, Wallerstein also argues that only the Thirty Years' War, the French Revolutionary and Napoleonic wars, and the two modern world wars were really hegemonic struggles.

No convincing data are available to project Kondratieff cycles back before the French Revolution. The historical data suggest, at best, Frank Spooner's or Fernand Braudel's logistical price cycles in Europe lasting 150 years, not the faster 50-year-long Kondratieffs. During the nineteenth century, sufficient statistical evidence becomes available to match economic cycles against these changes. Kondratieff and others have suggested that 1789, 1849, 1896, and 1940 all marked the end of downswings in economic activity, whereas 1815, 1873, 1920, and 1973 signified the end of upswings. These peaks and troughs correlate only roughly with major systemic wars and internal crises. The possibility of a fit raises several questions, however.

# Economic Cycles

First, what if anything, explains economic cycles? Second, why don't changes in overall economic growth rates affect both hegemons and challengers evenly? Why are the diffusion and adoption of technological advances related to changes in economic growth rates uneven? How did challengers turn relatively small technological advances into major advantages in world political and economic markets? Answering these questions requires examining the literature on long economic waves and hegemony in turn, but some foreshadowing is possible.

The predominant answer to these questions claims that the presence of one dominant power allows that power to assert hegemony or leadership in the world economy. By doing so, it creates the stability necessary for global economic expansion. This is a comforting claim, conjuring the image of a benevolent paterfamilias, but a different metaphor is perhaps more accurate. Hegemonic leaders are more like leaders in an endless race over uncertain terrain. For the moment they are ahead and can determine to an extent the path taken, benefiting from choosing terrain that suits them. Followers can take advantage of the hegemon's leadership to slipstream behind it, running on a beaten path, meanwhile looking for shortcuts.

## Kondratieff Waves

How plausible is the existence of long waves, and what explains them?[5] Kondratieff first proposed the existence of a long economic cycle in *prices* lasting 50 to 60 years. Using five-year moving averages, Kondratieff charted periods of rising and declining prices for a variety of commodities, including labor, over the period starting with the French Revolution and reaching to the Great Depression. Kondratieff's cycles were divided between a period of stagnation (downswings) in which bad economic years outweighed good economic years and a period of expansion (upswings) in which the reverse was true.

Kondratieff made only weak arguments on the origins of these price cycles, but subsequently, different economic schools have picked up and elaborated on each of his arguments. Each of these schools tries to move beyond Kondratieff with a causal explanation linking price movements to the underlying real economy. In each case, we will use the *locus classicus* of these arguments, adding more modern commentary when this is useful.

Kondratieff noted a correlation between agricultural depressions and periods of stagnation. Economists W. Arthur Lewis and W. W. Rostow used this idea to argue that only agricultural and raw materials output is characterized by long cycles. Kondratieff also observed that inventions intended to cluster toward the end of a downswing. Joseph Schumpeter used this notion to argue that entrepreneurial promotion of hard innovations — scientific innovations — caused long waves. (While innovations in the narrow sense — discovery — do not necessarily cluster, their uptake into products and production does.) Finally, Kondratieff proposed that cusp points — the turning points between downswings and upswings and vice versa — were characterized by wars, social upheaval, and the reorganization of economic life. A Marxist, Ernest Mandel, used this argument to maintain that workers' resistance to exploitation forced capitalists to reorganize production processes in fundamental ways that established the pattern for a new period of exploitation and later resistance. We will call these managerial innovations soft innovations in contrast to hard, scientific innovations. Each argument contributes important points, which later analysts have tried to synthesize.

## Raw Materials Cycles

Lewis makes the most limited set of claims but because his argument concerns agriculture it is very important for our analysis of the agriculturally centered period before the twentieth century.[6] Lewis argued that price cycles emerged from inverse relationships between agricultural and industrial prices. Agricultural production (and raw materials production in general) was inherently inelastic, because of a fairly tight connection between human life cycles and the formation of agricultural production units. Lewis noted that the creation of new family farms contributed most of the new agricultural production in the nineteenth century. While global grain acreage quadrupled in uneven spurts from 1870 to 1914, most of the expansion came outside Europe in areas like Australia, Argentina, and the United States characterized by family-based farming.

Families tended to start farms in response to periods of high agricultural prices created by booming industrial demand. Rising industrial profits, and thus investment, tended to lead to rising industrial demand for raw materials and industrial workers' demand for food. Rising demand for foods and non-food agriculturals in turn led to rising agricultural prices. It took time, however, for output to rise in response to these high prices, since family farms could not start instantaneously. Most new family farms began in the United States when grain prices were high in the 1860s and 1870s, and then in Canada, the U.S. Midwest, Argentina, and Australasia in the 1890s and 1900s when prices rose again. As farms did come "on line," agricultural production expanded and caught up with industrial demand for agricultural goods. Agricultural prices then fell. Although family farms were closely linked to the market, they did not exit markets in periods of overproduction and low prices. Thus, low prices continued.

Price cycles emerged from the interaction of farm formation and industrial demand. The two waves of agricultural investment noted above drove down agricultural prices, increasing real wages and reducing raw materials costs for industrial economies. This trend in turn decreased the rate of growth of agricultural output. With rising urban real wages, fewer people emigrated to new lands to start farms. Lower raw materials costs meant higher profits in industrial activity, so less capital was lent to new agricultural lands while industrial investment increased. This development pushed the rate of growth of industrial output, and thus industrial demand for agricultural raw materials, up above the rate of growth of agricultural goods, causing agricultural prices to rise again. The rate of growth of industrial demand outstripped the rate of growth of agricultural supply.

Rising agricultural prices then reversed these relationships: real wages fell, encouraging emigration, and industrial profits fell, encouraging investment in overseas agricultural areas. As new farms came on-line, agricultural prices fell once more, starting the cycle all over again. We have seen this argument before, albeit without the direct connection to family farms. As von Thünen's town (Lewis's industry) grows, it boosts demand for agricultural goods, pushing agrizones farther out into space. Lewis's argument could be strengthened by noting that the infrastructural costs of opening up new land for agricultural production also created discontinuous entry into the market and discouraged easy exit. Thus, the Lewis cycles reflect the spasmodic expansion of von Thünen rings in response to growing urban demand for agricultural goods.

Lewis's argument also dovetails with the arguments advanced by economists Simon Kuznets and Thomas Brinley to describe 20-to-25-year cycles in the United States and British economies in the late nineteenth century.[9] They argued that waves of immigration to the United States caused reciprocal waves of city-building in both economies, because both economies relied on the same pool of capital. Immigration to the United States led to building booms there; when those waves subsided, city-building boomed in Great Britain.

Lewis did not believe that these cycles in the general economy reflected anything inherent in industrial production. Rather, because agriculture tended to dominate economic life before 1914, agricultural price cycles propagated through the general economy much more strongly than they do today. Lewis thus argues that Kondratieff cycles exist only in the long nineteenth century. After 1920, industrial production dominated economic life, and while industrial production exhibited cycles, they were much shorter 3-year and 10-year cycles. Thus, Lewis also implicitly argues that international institutions or hegemony are irrelevant in any explanation of economic cycles, and vice versa.

More recent formulations of Lewis's argument encompass all raw materials. Rostow's analysis notes that each period of growth rests on specific sources of energy and characteristic raw materials,[8] whose production is inelastic. Like family farms, they generally require large, infungible, and illiquid investments. Because they are natural products, the cost of extracting raw materials rises as better and more easily extracted sources are exhausted. Rising extraction costs deter more investment and in turn create the kind of price cycles Lewis described. Because the driving force in all these analyses is urban demand, they all complement and provide a bridge to the leading-sector perspective of Joseph Schumpeter. This perspective looks at industrial investment as the driving force in economic cycles and argues that cycles reflect not only price movements but also underlying changes in the rate of growth of production volumes.

## Schumpeterian Leading Sectors

In contrast to Lewis and other analyses based on raw materials, Schumpeter sees long waves in industrial production.[9] Schumpeter is interested primarily in the relationship between entrepreneurship and innovation. The emergence, expansion, and saturation of markets for new leading sectors produce economic waves because innovations occur in clusters over time. These innovations force changes in the process of production and the objects produced across all industries. The dynamism of new leading sectors drags the rest of the economy forward.

For Schumpeter a leading sector is a cluster of innovations that create new products with high demand and new and cheaper forms of energy and transportation. Examples of leading sectors are the cluster of cotton textiles, iron, and water power (canals and mills) from the 1780s to the 1820s; steel, steam engines, and railroads from the 1840s to the 1870s; industrial chemicals, electricity, and intraurban trams from the 1890s to the 1920s; and the internal combustion engine, petroleum, and motor vehicles from the 1940s to the 1970s. Schumpeter saw these innovations as "gales of creative destruction" that swept away old production systems.

Schumpeter argued that the emergence of new leading sectors caused Kondratieff upswings. He viewed most economic activity as routine, providing daily necessities. This activity yielded a steady-state economy; if it grew, it did so because growing population forced an expansion of total GDP without materially changing per capita GDP. Investment merely covered depreciation or created capital to service a growing population without changing production systems or capital-to-labor ratios. Growth was basically extensive. Conservative administrators, not energetic innovators, ran enterprises. For Schumpeter, growth came only when entrepreneurs innovated new leading sectors and reenergized capitalism by raising the rate of profit. Schumpeter focused mostly on innovations in what here we will call hard technologies, that is, technology in its narrow, scientific sense, as opposed to soft technologies that are concerned mostly with the organization of production processes. Because he examined the organization of entrepreneurship, Schumpeter did look at soft innovation, but for analytic purposes we will leave production processes until later.

Bringing new leading sectors on-line both required and forced massive new investments. New leading sectors force new investment because they immediately threaten existing ways of doing business. Railroads undercut the vitality of canals, and long-haul trucking undercut railroads. Older firms had to adapt to these new technologies or go out of business. Leading sectors also require new investment to establish themselves because part of the new leading sector cluster involves innovations in transport and energy sources. The infrastructure for transportation systems and energy distribution has to be created from scratch. So, too, do new production systems using the new energy source and producing the new good. From our perspective as well, the change in transportation and energy sources significantly expands the potential division of labor by increasing the area open to profitable transportation of bulk commodities, thus enlarging the market.

Leading sectors therefore energize the economy through new, highly profitable investments. Their massive investment spurts cause rising economic growth, pulling existing firms along as they get reorganized and demand for their product increases. Once these new infrastructures and factories are built, investment slows, and economic growth grinds to a halt until a new cluster of leading sectors reenergizes it.

The growth rates of leading sectors display a clear s-type logistic curve of innovation, explosive growth, maturity, and stagnation or decline. (See Figure 11.1 on p. 246.) In the first phase, uncertainty about the extent of the market, the profitability and utility of existing production processes, and the reliability of new technologies keeps output low and prices high. As producers gain more experience, falling prices help the market expand. Increasing certainty and experience combine with falling prices to create rapid growth; producers settle on an accepted production technique. At the level of individual products, more consumers can now afford to buy the new good. At the level of the economy, more and more producers find they must adapt production processes to the new technologies, relocate to be closer to new transportation nodes, and reconfigure products to be compatible with new sources of energy. All this activity creates a surge in investment. However, as new transport and energy networks are completed, as new production complexes relocate near them, and as consumers' closets, houses, or driveways become clogged with the new product, growth rates level off. Instead of producing for new consumers, producers find they are merely replacing the existing stock of goods as they wear out. Producers depreciate their investments rather than investing for more output.

Consider the automobile. For about 30 years it was a toy for the rich. Cars were built by hand, with few interchangeable parts, and in limited numbers — about 4,000 in 1900. As a result, they were expensive. Then Ford combined the assembly line with interchangeable parts. Prices fell, gas stations and roads were built, and the number of standardized cars produced rocketed from 200,000 in 1910 to almost 4.5 million in 1929. By 1970 nearly everyone who needed a car had one, and sales leveled off at about 8 to 10 million cars per year. But this discussion has already signaled the degree to which managerial innovations (for example, the assembly line) are as important as scientific or technological ones (for example, the internal combustion engine).

## The Organization of the Firm and Work

Ernest Mandel's analysis closely parallels Schumpeter's, but as befits a Marxist, Mandel places more emphasis on the way work is organized rather than on the role of entrepreneurs in engendering new leading sectors.[10] While each of Mandel's phases rests on a particular set of hard technologies, he focuses more on the soft organizational technologies that constitute the actual process of production: how is work organized, who works, and on what? Mandel argues that the labor process has undergone four major shifts, breaking the postindustrial revolution world into five periods. The first period, from roughly 1789 to 1848, was characterized by craftworkers operating water- and steam-powered machinery in small factories. This machinery was fabricated on-site by craftworkers as "one-offs," unique machinery tailored to the idiosyncratic needs of whoever erected the factory. The archetypical machines of this period were spinning and weaving machines made of wood but using iron fittings, and driven mostly by water. The archetypical worker is the British textile worker, seeking to ameliorate working conditions through economic movements like Owenite unionism and political movements like Chartism.

These movements lead into the second period: the European upheavals and rebellions of 1848, the beginning of a new phase that lasted until the 1890s. The industrial production of machines by specialist firms and the emergence of specialist machine operators mark this period. The archetypical machines of this period were steam engines used in locomotives or steamships, or for forging rails or cutting pieces for increasingly standardized kinds of machines. The archetypical worker was the engineer, that is, a master craftsman with a practical knowledge of how engines or machines work, not the degreed engineer's theoretical training. This skilled worker controlled the flow of production and often acted as a subcontractor, hiring labor to work some capitalist's machinery. These workers attempted to form skill-based unions. This period comes to an end with a series of violent mass strikes in the 1890s.

The third period lasted from the 1890s to the 1930s and was characterized by the emergence of taylorist methods of production. These new methods shifted control of the production process from master craftsmen to professional, degreed engineers and allowed the emergence of limited kinds of continuous-flow production. Engineers organized the production of goods developed from systematic research, while workers merely followed orders. Foremen replaced skilled workers as the immediate overseers of the lowest workers. The 1930s saw a revival of mass unionism, the flowering of left-wing political movements in electorally successful parties, and the introduction of the assembly line.

The fourth period, the post-Depression era, was characterized by the grouping of electrically powered product-specific machines into assembly lines run by semiskilled workers. The archetypical machines of this period are assembly lines for the production of cars and other consumer durables. The archetypical worker is the assembly-line worker doing one repetitive task, organized into state-sanctioned mass unions. Mandel claims that this period came to an end in the great strike wave of the 1960s. A new form of labor organization, based on continuous-flow production systems organized by microelectronics and run by self-supervising, multiskilled workers appears to be emerging. This fifth period would correspond to a cluster of energy-saving technologies, microprocessors, and telecommunications (as "transport").

Mandel and Schumpeter overlap in their analysis of how work organization and the entrepreneur meet in the firm, which is an institutional arrangement for organizing investment in innovative labor processes making innovative goods. Firms successfully producing new leading-sector products usually do so in a new and characteristic institutional form: mills owned by individual capitalists; factories owned by small groups of capitalists; corporately owned multiplant firms; vertically and horizontally integrated firms producing everything they need for their assembly lines; and (probably) networked alliances of specialist firms, or Japanese-style *keiretsu*. Like the hard technologies in leading-sector clusters, innovative institutional forms also threaten old-style firms with "gales of creative destruction."[11] Old-style firms must adopt these new forms or die.

Not surprisingly, these new institutionalized forms, just like leading sectors, also emerged first in extant or potential hegemons. The British created the first mills and mill towns, and showed a strong and lingering preference for familial firms. U.S. and German entrepreneurs proliferated joint stock companies controlling multiple plants. U.S. firms created the assembly line and conglomerate. And everyone is rushing to emulate the *keiretsu*.

The fact that Schumpeter's leading-sector clusters and Mandel's new organizational forms overlap chronologically may be an indication that both are needed to spark a new upturn in the economy. The coincidence should not surprise us. The sheer scale of investment needed to utilize new technologies mandated both new organizational forms and new work practices. Neither kind of innovation could stand alone: new work practices and management systems made little sense unless changes in machinery and power systems accompanied them; new machinery could not be used to its fullest potential without changes in work practices and the management of production. Following business language, we will call the combination of new leading-sector technology and new institutional forms "best practice manufacturing."

Schumpeter and Mandel diverge from Lewis in two other ways. Lewis saw a regular, if temporary, cycling in the world economy, which died out around World War I. In contrast, neither Schumpeter nor Mandel believes that cycling in the economy is inevitable because the initiation of a new cycle rests in human agency. The advantages of new institutional forms and the infrastructure investment boom associated with a new cluster always exhaust themselves, leading to stagnation. Without entrepreneurs, however, or in the face of entrenched worker resistance, a new cycle might not start again. Each, however, saw enormous incentives for actors to innovate and thus start the cycle again. Schumpeter believed that inevitably entrepreneurs would search for and create new innovations during a search for higher profits in periods of stagnation. Mandel believed that worker resistance to exploitation drove down profits, forcing capitalists to search for new organizational forms to break down that resistance. Each saw an end to cycling only in a socialism that had not yet happened: Schumpeter because it would extinguish entrepreneurship and Mandel because it would end exploitation. In anticipation of the next chapter, we can introduce a third factor forcing new cycles, competition. Under competitive pressures from abroad that threatened to crowd them out of the market, states and their industrialists reacted by generating new organization forms and adopting new technologies more rapidly than they might otherwise have done. These late developers aggressively pursued best practice manufacturing, and by adapting it to local circumstance, they created new organizational forms and spurred locally appropriate technological advances.

## Economic and Hegemonic Cycles: Links

Leading-sector clusters are discontinuous over space as well as time. Leading sectors usually emerge inside one country and then spread to others. This observation allows us to begin to link economic and hegemonic cycles: in all cases new leading-sector clusters first emerged either in an existing hegemon or in the country that became hegemonic soon after. While all technologies do inevitably diffuse (though not everywhere and not evenly), the new hegemon has a period of unquestioned technological and thus economic superiority. This suggests that the emergence of new leading sectors creates the economic basis for hegemony. As our explorations of successive phases of domination in the Indian Ocean have shown, however, hard technology is an insufficient explanation for superiority. Much of the advantage of the Portuguese, Dutch, and British had come from soft technologies, innovations in the art of building and managing organizations. As Modelski shows, these institutional innovations also demonstrate cycling.

Study of the creation and diffusion of best practice manufacturing thus suggests both origins for and limitations to hegemony. Best practice manufacturing is both a blessing and a curse. The geographically uneven emergence of new best practice manufacturing provides a would-be hegemon with a highly competitive economic base. Until those best practices diffuse—which is itself an uneven process—the hegemon will enjoy productivity advantages over its rivals. These productivity advantages allow the hegemon to enjoy both guns and butter, for an expanding economy can support both investment in the new economy and the revenue to support the projection of military force abroad. The ultimate saturation of a leading sector's markets and the diffusion of its best practice technologies imply that the hegemon must either accept the reality that it is riding a slowing horse racing competitors who are gaining, or hope that its economy will generate a new technological and institutional cluster so that it can ride ahead once more. Unfortunately, as we will see in Chapter 8, the very success entrepreneurs in the hegemon enjoy tends to make them conservative, while the extreme competitive threat they pose to other entrepreneurs tends to spur these other entrepreneurs to seek the technologies and organizational forms that can help them overcome their backwardness.

## Hegemonic Cycles

What about political cycles? Modelski, Wallerstein, and others have argued that in a succession of periods a single, dominant, economic and political power orchestrates the global economy, and in other periods this domination unravels in the face of challenges. Convention labels these powers hegemons. Although different analysts mean different things by the term *hegemon,* all seem to agree that hegemon is dominant in both military and economic matters, without necessarily being predominant. In turn, these imply a degree of technological and cultural superiority insofar as others emulate the hegemon in order to uncover the sources of its success. The major differences center on these issues: whether hegemons are benign or malign dominant powers; and whether analysts approach the issue of hegemony from a static or dynamic perspective.[12] The first opposition is somewhat false because it presumes that states have unified interests and that international order is a kind of public good. Second, given the emphasis above on leading sectors, a dynamic approach is preferable to a static one. To the extent that technologies diffuse from the hegemon to other areas, hegemony cannot be viewed statically; each difference in turn.

## Benign versus Malignant Hegemons?

The dichotomy between benign and malign hegemons is somewhat false for two reasons, yet it lies at the heart of debates about so-called hegemonic stability theory (HST). The dichotomy arises mostly because of the similarities between HST and the realist school of thought in security studies. First, like the realist school, HST conceives of states as unitary actors possessing predefined interests.[13] Because these quasirealists conceive of states as unitary actors, they can also assume that the costs of maintaining hegemony and the benefits that flow from it accrue to states, and not to specific internal interest groups. Second, HST focuses on the question of order in the international economy. Like the international security system, the international economy is naturally unstable and prone to closure, to conflicts in which wars over trade and protection occur. Because HST sees order and openness as public goods, it questions whether any state would willingly take on the burden of providing these public goods. These assumptions lead naturally into game theoretical discussions of whether or not it is rational for a state to accept the burdens of hegemony — of providing order — and equally so whether it is rational for other states to support the hegemonic state or to "free ride" on its efforts.

HST argues that an open international economy — one characterized by free trade — can emerge only when the hegemon or leading economy provides certain collective or public goods. Public goods have peculiar properties: they are indivisible goods whose consumption by one person (state) does not reduce the amount that someone else can consume, and they cannot be provided on a discriminatory basis.[14] Classic collective goods are defense, roads, clean air, public transport, and reticulation networks for water, gas, and so on. The absence of possibilities for private appropriation means that it is difficult to charge for the use of public goods. HST thus makes an implicit analogy with the role of the state within societies. Hegemons provide international goods similar to those goods that states provide domestically, including stability (discussed above), and these make openness possible. The simple fact that hegemons might have the capacity to provide those goods neither implies that they will nor that others will cooperate with them. HST arguments thus rest on three legs: hegemons must have the capacity to be hegemons; they must have the motivation to pursue policies; and they must gain cooperation, grudging or willing, from other countries for these policies.

The empirical support for HST arguments is plausible but weak. A rough correlation has been established between hegemonic powers' periods of greatest military and economic power and international free trade. In their period of maritime cum mercantile supremacy, the Dutch promoted Hugo Grotius's doctrine of *mare librum* — the seas are free to whoever wishes to use them for commerce. The Dutch dominated international finance, with most credit originating from and most bills of exchange (a kind of check) clearing in Amsterdam. British domination of the international economy ultimately led them to adopt free trade in the mid-1800s. After 1815 the British navy dominated the oceans, suppressing pirates and intimidating the natives everywhere. The pound sterling, together with a network of banks and insurance companies, provided coin and credit, backed up by the Bank of England.

U.S. domination of the post – World War II period has the same features. The United States organized a relatively orderly process of decolonization and reconstruction of the old imperial economies. (Vietnam was exceptional for the scale, duration, and violence of U.S. intervention, not for the intervention itself.) U.S. dollars, particularly in the form of Eurodollars, provided a currency for international transactions, backed up by the Federal Reserve Bank's promise to redeem dollars for gold. And the United States pursued multilateral approaches to a more open international economy as early as 1933 and aggressively after 1944.

This story has both an empirical and a theoretical weakness. The theoretical weakness, which we have already touched on, is that it assumes that all political actors in a would-be hegemon will sign on to a free trade policy; states are seen as unitary actors. We will turn to that subject later. Meanwhile, some of the most severe empirical critics of HST have attacked the notion that hegemons actually pursue free trade policies. They note that British tariffs were consistently higher than either French or German (first Zollverein, then early Imperial) tariffs during the nineteenth century and that the chronology of mutual tariff reductions in Europe does not follow the pattern predicted by HST.[15]

These attacks show the importance of looking at intentions and at the weaknesses of the HST's belief that hegemony rests on the provision of public goods. HST can be rescued from this criticism only if it drops the notion of public goods. Not all the goods a hegemon provides are true public goods, and hegemons need not be uniformly in favor of free trade. The hegemon can provide collective goods discriminatorily, precisely in order to create transnational coalitions with converging interests. The British, for example, were oriented toward free trade in areas where it really counted from their point of view, namely, in the import of foods and other agricultural raw materials. Aside from wine, which was heavily taxed for revenue purposes, food and nonfood agricultural raw materials entered Britain tariff free. Britain's (limited) free trade policy created an empire that was (mostly) bound by trade ties, not by colonization and force.

This behavior is entirely consistent if we look at the process of interest formation from a von Thünen perspective and ask about the consequences of the hegemon's large import market. All states naturally pursue their own interests, but with the significant exception of physical security, the constitution of those interests is a politically contested activity. Groups/classes in society fight to define the national interest, and inevitably some groups lose. As Robert Cox has argued, international hegemony therefore has Gramscian aspects.[16] It rests on a convergence of interests among those groups that have managed to define a state's nonstrategic interests and groups in other states with similar interests. States controlled by groups with interests in common with those controlling the hegemon will see hegemony as benign, while those with diverging interests may very well see it as malign.

Before the twentieth century, hegemony rested on the complementarity of hegemonic von Thünen towns and their agricultural supply zones. The emergence of industrial activity in a von Thünen town created potential wealth elsewhere if producers were willing to orient agricultural activity toward that town. Once they did so, they constituted a powerful interest bloc favoring accommodation with the hegemon. In the twentieth century, a somewhat similar process has occurred, except that access to industrial markets looms large. In both cases, a hegemon's capacity comes mostly from the large import market that its rapidly growing economy creates, for this in turn creates market pressures elsewhere to reorient production toward that market.

The size of hegemonic countries, combined with their high levels of productivity and income, means that they usually constitute a sizable portion of world import markets. Britain's share of world imports, for example, fluctuated between the 33 percent of 1850 and the 25 percent of 1870. The U.S. share in 1950 was about 18 percent, falling to about 15.4 percent by 1990. (Japan's share in 1990 was 6.9 percent.)[17] Therefore, nonhegemonic countries will probably try to get access to the hegemon's domestic market in order to expand the potential market for their own producers, particularly since their own internal markets, largely composed of microeconomies before 1914, were difficult to sell into and had relatively low levels of purchasing power. From an economic point of view, capability and interests go hand in hand. The more a hegemon is capable of importing, the bigger will be the groups elsewhere who make a living by exporting to it, and the more states will tend to align around the hegemon.

Hegemonic capacity has a military side as well as an economic one. In order to function, businesses need security and stability—the assurance that goods shipped will arrive, that contracts will be enforced, and that the world in general is predictable. As we saw in Chapter 1, states replaced the internal anarchy and multiple sovereignties of the nobility with one law, Hobbes's leviathan, in exchange for taxes. Internationally, anarchy, in the sense of a Hobbesian state of nature in which contract is difficult or impossible, prevailed until 1815, if only because warfare was almost constant from 1500 to 1815. Because most commerce was made up of maritime commerce until after World War II, the relevant index of a hegemon's military power thus has to be overwhelming naval power.

Modelski and his colleague W. R. Thompson have shown that the powers that everyone agrees were hegemonic—Holland, Britain, and the United States—as well as Portugal, all apparently controlled roughly half the warships available during their period of domination.[18] The connection between control of the maritime economy and military security is relatively clear. Hegemons have always been firmly based in the maritime economy and have so far managed to beat off all challenges by continental powers whose predominant strength was land based precisely because they could call on extra-European resources present in the world economy.[19]

Is the provision of security a public good in HST's sense? Security and stability presume a continuance of the status quo, and as the dominant power and probably producer, hegemons naturally benefit from the status quo. Insofar as prestige and fear deter challenges to the status quo, especially to the interests and shipping of the hegemon, benefits accrue disproportionately to the hegemon. When the Dutch and British controlled most oceanic shipping, both also relied heavily on overseas sources of food. Security and economic interests commingled, and each would have had to have borne the costs of maintaining order anyway.

## A Dynamic View

We can now consider hegemony dynamically. Would-be hegemons need an economic base that is sufficiently strong to afford the cost of policing and sufficiently large to be able to serve as a market of last resort. So would-be hegemons have to have economies that are relatively large compared to the global economy. Some of the arguments rejecting a hegemonic position for Portugal, Holland, and the early period of English hegemony misunderstand this point. Looking only at the small absolute size of these economies, they call into doubt their ability to serve as hegemons. However, the global economy was a thin coastal crust surrounding a vast number of microeconomies that were not effectively integrated into the world market. Relative to this thin crust, the Dutch and English economies may well have been sufficiently large, although the Spanish and Portuguese certainly were not.

Would-be hegemons also had to have relatively efficient and dynamic economies, and in our terms had to be the site of emergence for a set of leading sectors. The productivity advantages conferred by this position were essential for two reasons. First, a rapidly expanding leading sector would create the kind of large import market that in turn would cause at least some external economies to reorient themselves around the hegemon's economy.

Second, the productivity advantages inhering to a leading sector also made a hegemon the center of international credit and money markets. Bills of exchange (a kind of check used to finance trade) only worked as an efficient medium for international trade if some cheap central pool of credit existed. Amsterdam, London, and New York (and Tokyo?) in turn have provided that pool of credit. Each of these cities drew this credit from the enormous pool of savings available from their economies. High domestic productivity rooted in best practice manufacturing generated too much capital for local reinvestment, particularly because part of the competitive potential of new leading sectors comes from the introduction of capital-saving technologies that reduced the cost of fixed and circulating capital. This pool of savings drove down local interest rates, giving the hegemon's banks enough of a cost advantage to dominate world lending. They can offer the cheapest credit to their own sellers, to buyers of their goods, while also financing foreign sellers.

Precisely this ability to take advantage of the difference between low interest rates at home and higher ones abroad allowed the Dutch, for example, to dominate Baltic trade.[20] The Dutch bought up the crops of Baltic grain exporters in advance of the harvest at large discounts. Grain sellers were willing to sell at a steep discount because the interest rate in the Baltic was quite high, and the present value of money they received was thus very high whether they were net creditors or debtors. Dutch traders in turn were financing grain purchases with money borrowed at low interest rates in Amsterdam. From their point of view, they obtained a deeper discount for the grain than they would have if Baltic sellers had access to equally cheap credit. British traders and American firms did similar things during their period of global dominance.

Hegemony also rests on political foundations that are not identical to those created by von Thünen effects. By means of analogy to best practice manufacturing, Modelski suggests that political power also rests on creating new forms of best practice statecraft. These can be seen in the discussion of the successive waves of European incursions into the Indian Ocean. Some of this best practice statecraft concerns military and diplomatic organization. It should not be surprising that during the 17th century the British pioneered both professional intelligence organizations and the building of dual-purpose ships capable of being used as both merchant and warships. Nor should it be surprising that during the mid- and late 1800s, the Prussians/Germans excelled at the use of railroads for mobilization and strategic maneuver and were virtually the only country with a general staff system for running its army. Or that the United States developed mass production armies and navies deployed on a global scale.

## Free Trade

What about the proliferation of free trade? As we have seen above, it should not be surprising that a hegemon might pursue free trade, as long as it had an obvious competitive advantage in world markets. Until the diffusion of best practice manufacturing associated with the new leading sector, a hegemon's productive and financial advantages should incline them to pursue free trade. After all, in most competitive battles their firms are likely to prevail. Open markets benefit the strong (i.e., competitive) and punish the weak. By drawing on a much wider source of agricultural and other primary inputs, hegemons could then expand their internal division of labor. Logically, strong coalitions favoring at least a limited free trade would be expected to emerge in a hegemon as its dominance of the new leading sector became clear. In practice, however, creating such a coalition might be difficult.

If hegemons have the capacity and the desire, why should other countries cooperate with them?[21] Steve Krasner notes that, while economic theory points to the virtues of an open economy, virtually all states have opted against free trade at some point. Krasner states that either something must be wrong with static theories of comparative advantage or that policymakers are stupid. He rejects the latter possibility. Looking at the dynamic aspects of the cycling of leading sectors suggests why countries might opt to cooperate for a time with the hegemon, and then defect by protecting their home market.

From the point of view of nonhegemonic countries, the existence of open markets in the hegemon means that they might be able to export to that enormous market. But what to export? Their ability to export into the hegemon's market implies production either of goods that are impossible to produce in the hegemon or of goods from sectors that are competitive. Since the hegemon by definition likely possesses a competitive advantage in the leading sectors, this means that exporters are selling raw materials, intermediate goods, or finished goods from other, nonleading sectors to the hegemon. In the classic free trade cases HST points to, the *pax britannica* of 1850–80 and the *pax americana* of 1950–70, both patterns existed. Countries often cooperated with Britain and the United States because they had complementary economic structures and were pursuing Ricardian development strategies. In that case, hegemony did exist in the sense that a true convergence of the elite interests existed.

Countries pursuing Kaldorian strategies also opted for free trade for a time because they were using exports into the hegemonic market to finance imports of capital goods that were needed to adopt/adapt the current leading sector. Here hegemony did bring about free trade, but because countries were looking for ways to undermine that hegemony, interests converged at the level of means, not ends. Thus, France's and Britain's coordinated reduction of tariffs in the Cobden-Chevalier Treaty occurred when France needed to import iron rails and railroad equipment for its first phase of industrialization.[22] Prussia also freely imported British rails and locomotives in the early stages of its industrialization. Both France and Prussia exported primary products (wine and grain, respectively) or fine products with stagnant local markets (woolens and linens, respectively) into Britain. Once these countries were capable of building their rail networks with local resources, they turned to protectionist policies. By opening up their internal markets to international competition, those same railroads boosted local political support for protection from uncompetitive sectors, especially agriculture.

The flip side to this picture is that the hegemon's efforts to open up markets have short-term benefits but in the long run these efforts undermine hegemony and free trade.[23] An open international economy facilitates the diffusion of the very leading-sector cluster and managerial technologies that constitute the hegemon's advantage. As its advantage erodes, the costs of maintaining collective goods that support an open economy begin to outweigh the benefits. The hegemon's commitment to free trade decays in train. But closure, though politically easy, does not resolve these problems. As noted earlier, hegemons must revive old leading sectors or generate new clusters. At the same time, countries playing catch-up have an incentive to play the hegemon's game for a while, and then move to close their markets in order to protect new infant industries in the leading sector.

The next three chapters detail the diffusion of the industrial revolution from Britain to the European continent and Britain's construction, in cooperation with local elites, of new zones of specialized, export-oriented agricultural production. European efforts to cope with Britain's economic preeminence created a variety of new institutional forms for organizing industrial activity. Just as the British benefited from apparent disadvantages in the Indian Ocean, the advantages of adversity allowed some European states to catch up with and surpass Britain by the end of the nineteenth century. In this process, they opted first for free trade and then for protection. British promotion of free trade primarily concerned its new agricultural suppliers. The flood of exports these countries released created a challenge paralleling that of Britain's industrial revolution, and as with manufacturing pushed a number of states to opt for protection. The evolution of British hegemony revolved around both of these developments.

## Notes

1. Joshua Goldstein, *Long Cycles: War and Prosperity in the Modern Age* (New Haven, Conn: Yale University Press, 1988).
2. Nikolai Kondratieff, "Long Waves in Economic Life," *Review of Economic Statistics* 17 (1935), translated by E. Stolper.
3. George Modelski, *Long Waves in World Politics* (London: Macmillan, 1987); George Modelski and William R. Thompson, *Seapower in Global Politics 1494–1993* (Seattle: University of Washington Press, 1990); William R. Thompson, *On Global War: Historical-Structural Approaches to World Politics* (Columbia, S.C.: University of South Carolina Press, 1988); William R. Thompson, "Long Waves, Technological Innovation and Relative Decline," *International Organization* 44, no. 2 (Spring 1990): 201–234; and William R. Thompson and Lawrence Vescera, "Growth Waves, Systemic Openness, and Protectionism," *International Organization* 46, no. 2 (Spring 1992): 493–532.
4. William R. Thompson, "Dehio, Long Cycles and the Geohistorical Context of Structural Transition," *World Politics* (January 1993): 143–144.
5. The most serious objection to all long wave arguments derives from work by E. Slutsky, which showed that moving averages of random data produced sinusoidal waves. However, reconstruction of Krondratieff's time series using discontinuous averages produces cycles that match Kondratieff's original cycles. While this does not *confirm* Kondratieff's argument, it suggests that it at least is not an artifact; see Brian Berry, *Long Wave Rhythms in Economic Development and Political Behavior* (Baltimore: Johns Hopkins University Press, 1991).
6. W. Arthur Lewis, *Growth and Fluctuations 1870–1913* (Boston: Allen and Unwin, 1978).
7. Thomas Brinley, *Migration and Economic Growth* (Cambridge: Cambridge University Press, 1973); Simon Kuznets, *Secular Movements in Production and Prices* (New York: Augustus Kelly, 1967).
8. Walt Whitman Rostow, *The World Economy* (Austin: University of Texas, 1978); Craig Volland, "A Comprehensive Theory of Long Wave Cycles," *Technological Forecasting and Social Change* 32 (1987): 120–145; Lorna M. Waddell and Walter C. Labrys, *Transmaterialization: Technology and Materials Demand Cycles* (Morgantown, W.Va.: West Virginia University, 1987).
9. Joseph Schumpeter, *Business Cycles: A Theoretical, Historical and Statistical Analysis of the Capitalist Process* (Cambridge, Mass.: Harvard University Press, 1939); Joseph Schumpeter, *Capitalism, Socialism, Democracy* (New York: Harper and Row, 1942).
10. Ernest Mandel, *Late Capitalism* (London: New Left Books, 1975), and *Long Waves of Capitalist Development: The Marxist Interpretation* (Cambridge: Cambridge University Press, 1980).
11. The literature on firms is growing and interesting. For an intensive historical discussion of the role of administrative and managerial forms, see the work of Alfred Chandler in *Strategy and Structure* (Cambridge, Mass.: MIT Press, 1962); *Visible Hand* (Cambridge, Mass.: Harvard University Press, 1977); and *Scale and Scope* (Cambridge, Mass.: Harvard University Press, 1990). See Oliver Williamson, *The Economics of Institutions* (New York: Free Press, 1985) and William Lazonick, *Business Organiza-*

*tion and the Myth of the Market Economy* (Cambridge, Mass.: Harvard University Press, 1991) for two completely opposing views on the significance of Chandler's findings.

12. See Richard Rosecrance and Jennifer Taw, "Japan and the Theory of International Leadership," *World Politics* 42, no. 2 (January 1990): 184–209 for an overview of this voluminous literature. See also Charles Kindleberger, *The World In Depression* (Berkeley: University of California Press, 1973); Stephen Krasner, "State Power and the Structure of International Trade," *World Politics* 28 (1976): 317–347; Robert Gilpin, *U.S. Power and the Multinational Corporation* (New York: Basic Books, 1975); Robert Keohane, *After Hegemony: Cooperation and Discord in World Political Economy* (Princeton, N.J.: Princeton University Press, 1984); Duncan Snidal, "The Limits of Hegemonic Stability Theory," *International Organization* 39 (Autumn 1985): 579–614; John Conybeare, *Trade Wars* (New York: Columbia University Press, 1988); and Joseph Greico, *Cooperation among Nations* (Ithaca, N.Y.: Cornell University Press, 1990).

13. See Stephen Krasner, *Defending the National Interest* (Princeton, N.J.: Princeton University Press, 1978) for the clearest defense of this approach, and Krasner, "State Power and the Structure of International Trade," for the clearest example of its application. Most of the game theoretic approaches to hegemony follow this line of thinking. For a game theoretic exception to this approach, see Robert Putnam, *Hanging Together: Cooperation and Conflict in the Seven Power Summits* (Cambridge, Mass.: Harvard University Press, 1987). The "epistemic community" literature takes a completely opposite approach. See Peter M. Haas, ed., *Knowledge, Power and International Policy Coordination, International Organization* 46, no. 1 (Winter 1992) (special issue).

14. Alternately, we can regard these as things for which property rights have not been specified in Ronald Coase's sense or cannot be specified in Oliver Williamson's sense. The former is explicitly and the latter implicitly the basis for Keohane's analysis in *After Hegemony*.

15. John Vincent Nye, "Revisionist Tariff History and the Theory of Hegemonic Stability," *Politics and Society* 19, no. 2 (1991): 209–232; Timothy McKeown, "Hegemonic Stability and Nineteenth-Century Tariff Levels," *International Organization* 37, no. 1 (Winter 1983): 73–91. Albert Hirschman, *National Power and the Structure of Foreign Trade* (Berkeley: University of California Press, 1945) remains the classic study of asymmetric trade relations.

16. Robert Cox *Power, Production and World Order* (New York: Columbia University Press, 1988); see also Peter Gourevitch, "The Second Image Reversed: International Sources of Domestic Politics," *International Organization* 32 (Autumn 1978): 881–912.

17. World Bank, *World Development Report 1992* (New York: Oxford University Press, 1992), p. 245.

18. Modelski and Thompson, *Seapower in Global Politics*.

19. For some interesting observations on this point, see Thompson, "Dehio, Long Cycles, and the Geohistorical Context of Structural Transition," pp. 127–152.

20. See Jonathan Israel, *Dutch Primacy in World Trade 1585–1740* (Oxford: Oxford University Press, 1989); Fernand Braudel, *Capitalism and Civilization*, vol. III (New York: Harper and Row, 1984).

21. Krasner, " State Power and the Structure of International Trade."

22. Charles Kindleberger, "The Rise of Free Trade in Western Europe 1820–1875," *Journal of Economic History* 35, no. 1 (March 1975): 38–40.

23. Gilpin, *U.S. Power and the Multinational Corporation*, has a fine analysis of this process.

# CHAPTER 4

# The Industrial Revolution and Late Development

The statesman who should attempt to direct private people in what manner they ought to employ their capital would not only load himself with a most unnecessary attention, but assume an authority which could safely be trusted, not only to no single person, but to no council or senate whatever, and which would nowhere be so dangerous as in the hands of a man who had folly and presumption enough to fancy himself fit to exercise it.

*Adam Smith*

The loss occasioned by protective duties consists, after all, only in values [i.e., money]; whilst the country thus acquires a power, by which it is enabled to produce a great mass of values. This loss in values must be considered as the price of the "industrial training" of the country.

*Friedrich List*

The industrial revolution in Britain did not change the inner workings of the world economy so much as it accelerated processes that were already under way. The industrial revolution, a clustering of innovations in cotton textile production, the systematic application of water and — to a much lesser extent —steam power to manufacturing, and the gathering of previously dispersed manufacturing operations under one factory roof had three major consequences. First, Britain's exploding demand for raw materials and rising industrial population pushed agricultural production outward from Europe, generating a global set of von Thünen rings with their attendant potential for spatial inequality and potential for opportunities for some agricultural producers to pursue Ricardian strategies.

Second, the industrial revolution in Britain threatened to blow away industry in other regions and countries with a Schumpeterian gale of creative destruction. If non-British manufacturers could not find ways to assimilate the hard and soft technologies of the industrial revolution, they faced declining competitiveness and perhaps extinction. Therefore, the industrial revolution generated effects similar to those already experienced in northwest Europe and the Atlantic economy, but on a much broader scale and at a faster pace.

Finally, the economic growth generated by the industrial revolution underpinned Britain's rise to global dominance after 1814. Britain's dominance in coal, metallurgy, and steam gave its navy the material basis for control of the seas, and thus control of a world economy that still largely moved goods over water. In general, most states reacted to this rising British dominance by continuing the mercantilist policies followed during the period before the Napoleonic wars. They tried to extend central state power into their microeconomies, homogenizing and routinizing the administration of law and taxation.

The industrial revolution presented a dilemma for states trying to continue these policies. States now intervened in their economies to promote industrial development because they feared the strategic consequences of industrial backwardness. These consequences were quite clear by the 1840s, when most European states began emulating Britain. At this point, Britain had already passed into the second stage of the industrial revolution, with an economy based on iron, steam engines, and the railroad. States' efforts to drag their economies forward therefore involved using the railroad industry as a leading sector. This transportation innovation tended to link microeconomies together, creating unified internal markets for the first time and advancing efforts at internal security.

Paradoxically, however, the more successful states were at industrialization through railroadization, the more they exposed themselves to shocks emanating from the international market and to British competition. Since most economies could not compete with Britain in basic manufactured goods, states risked the displacement of entire industrial sectors when they opened their economies to the world market.[1] If their firms succeeded in catching up with British firms, then better transport meant a bigger market. If their firms did not catch up, better transport meant easier pickings for foreign competition. Late industrialization thus was a difficult gamble: success reinforced success; failure, failure.

At the same time, the devices used to create industrial success typically created international trade friction. As we will see, successful late industrialization relied on Kaldorian growth strategies — rapidly increasing output to stimulate rapid increases in productivity. However, this rapid increase in output had to be sold somewhere, and so parts of it had to be exported. The sudden streams of exports generated by successful late industrializers tended to overflow the canals of international commerce, threatening to inundate other, less successful late industrializers and eroding the market share of existing industrial powers. Both of these resorted to protection to dam the flow of goods from a successful late industrializer.

This chapter looks at successful and unsuccessful European efforts to industrialize in response to the industrial revolution, and then contrasts it to Asian responses. This contrast is one of nuance. The threat was the same for all late industrializers; differences emerged from the different defenses European and Asian industrializers could muster against that threat. In general, most countries, including many in Europe, did *not* industrialize successfully. Among successful European industrializers, the first response was often increased specialization in agricultural production, not industrialization. The states and firms that responded successfully to British competition were successful because they created new institutions that allowed the state to aid industry and permitted firms to assimilate British technologies creatively. This chapter also sets up arguments that will be used in Chapters 8, 11, 12, and 14, because the problem of late industrialization recurred every time a new leading sector emerged. Chapter 12 studies late industrialization in Latin America and some additional Asian countries. Chapter 8 takes the story begun in this chapter about Germany and the United States forward to the point where these late industrializers were capable of challenging Britain. Chapters 11 and 14 retell the story in Chapter 8, looking at U.S. hegemony and the Japanese challenge.

Before that, however, come two chapters (5 and 6) that examine responses to the industrial revolution in agricultural supply areas. Putting Chapter 4 first seems to give priority to industrialization as a causal factor, but this priority should not be overstated. Industrialization in Europe and the global spread of European agriculture were mutually reinforcing sides of a growing division of labor. Industrialization required cheaper and more raw materials; agricultural suppliers provided a market for industrial goods. Just as was the case with late industrialization, however, export agriculture did not automatically come into being. Simply having the right climate did not guarantee an ability to export; areas with the right climates also had to have states that were able to organize (and often impose) Ricardian growth strategies. Like late industrialization, export agriculture–led growth needed and generated a range of new institutions.

Since our focus is international, we will not explore in any great depth the internal causes of the industrial revolution; instead, the discussion begins with two questions about external aspects of the revolution. Did empire and the industrial revolution interact, and if so, how? What role did international competitive pressures play in the development of the British textile industry? Then the chapter turns to influences on successful and unsuccessful late industrialization. The chapter ends with a discussion of the less obvious international consequences of late industrialization.

## International Origins of the Industrial Revolution

The interaction between empire and industry revolves around two questions.[2] Marxist historiography has repeatedly argued, first, that imperial depredations provided the capital for the investment that underlay the industrial revolution, and second, that imperial markets were places to dump exports. Liberal historians have repeatedly denied this contention, maintaining that colonial revenues at best constituted a very small part of capital investment and that domestic markets were more important. The truth seems to lie somewhere in the middle. While imperial profits could not have funded the industrial revolution, they did contribute to widespread wealth in British society, and this in turn created fertile ground for the investments that constituted the industrial revolution. Colonial markets augmented local markets, but to a disproportionately small degree. During the nineteenth century, Third World markets took at most about 10 to 15 percent of all developed country manufactured exports.[3] At best, Third World markets were important only for particular industries. Britain's cotton textile industry relied heavily on Third World markets by the end of the century. Also, captive colonial markets arguably allowed some producers with high fixed capital costs to expand production runs, thus lowering the average cost per unit produced and creating additional profits. This argument presupposes that producers could take for granted markets in the areas absorbing the bulk of their production, however. Colonial markets actually had a more important supply-side contribution. Their exports expanded the food and non-food agricultural (NFA) supplies available for European industrializers, thus overcoming the limits imposed by microeconomies on Europe's division of labor.

What about the reverse, namely, the consequences of competitive pressures on the British textile industry? For a while before the industrial revolution, it appeared that this British industry would be displaced. Colonial wealth and local agricultural advances created an increased demand for manufactured goods in Britain that actually threatened British cotton textile producers with extinction. They were unable to compete with low-wage Indian producers. The British government actually embargoed the import of Indian cottons in the early 1700s in order to protect local producers. Given the porous borders of the time, this effort was doomed to fail, forcing British producers to devise some other response. Even at subsistence levels, British wages were about 50 percent higher than those in India; unlike inland continental producers, British producers could not rely on high transportation costs to provide some kind of protection. Even counting transport costs, as late as 1780, Indian producers of calico and muslin fabrics had a 60 percent cost advantage over British producers.[4] Thus, British producers could not compete by lowering wages further or trying to close the market. Instead, they had to innovate, applying mechanical power to textiles production in order to reduce their production costs. This increased productivity by 300 to 400 percent. So parts of the industrial revolution's causes and consequences were the same: international competitive pressures causing innovation.

Roughly the same process occurred in iron production. Traditionally, iron was smelted using charcoal. British iron-smelters could not compete with Sweden. Low-wage Sweden had huge reserves of the timber used to make charcoal, while Britain was already deforested. During the 1700s British smelters began experimenting with coal-derived coke to smelt, refine, and forge iron. Production processes using coal and coke turned out to be more efficient. Meanwhile, rising demand for coal stimulated the use of steam engines in mining; later, these engines found application in metals production. With better and cheaper metals British producers had better and cheaper water mills to run metal looms and spinning jennies, and cheaper steam engines to use in metals and coal production, creating several virtuous cycles.

The existence of a world market both facilitated and forced British innovation. The enormous depth of the British market was matched only in

Holland, but the Dutch lacked cheap coal and iron ore, and perversely did not benefit in this case from their domination of Baltic trade. This domination made timber cheap relative to coal. Britain's successful reaction to the challenge of cheap Swedish iron and Indian cottons in turn created a challenge for other countries.

## Late Development as a Response to the Threat of Displacement

Just as they disagree about the origins of spatial inequality (see Chapter 2), NCE, WST, and agnostics disagree about the nature of the challenge Britain's industrial revolution posed for other countries. NCE argues that the natural and gradual diffusion of British technology allowed former agricultural exporters to become industrialized, usually along the lines of the British model.[5] Economies elsewhere responded to British demand for raw materials by specializing along the line of comparative advantage. In contrast, WST maintains that specialization in raw materials production is an economic dead end. This kind of specialization creates and perpetuates the inequality described in Chapter 2.

The record is rather mixed: many regions responded to rising British demand by increasing their agricultural exports or having such an increase forced on them by a colonial government, and if some of these regions did industrialize at a later time, by no means did all such exporters. Neither WST nor NCE accounts fully capture what happened. Instead, institutions mattered, because, within rather broad limits, actions by the state and social groups did affect a country's placement in the international division of labor. Understanding why some regions and states responded successfully to the flood of hypercompetitive British goods and the siren call of British demand for foods and NFAs, while others did not, means understanding how the British challenge differed from prior competitive threats, what kinds of institutional responses were available, and how states built those institutions with help or despite opposition from local social groups. However, if the requisite institutions are viewed abstractly, the whole thing can be put rather simply: if countries could use agricultural exports to stimulate growing demand and thus verdoorn effects for local industrial goods, they generally succeeded. If not, they failed.

The industrial revolution created a more serious rupture with prior economic patterns than did previous technological advances. In Britain the industrial revolution created productivity gains of 3.4 percent per annum in cotton textiles, the fastest growing sector. Although there has been a recent tendency to relabel the industrial revolution the industrial evolution and to downplay the role of cotton textiles, this growth rate was absolutely unprecedented in the context of what was and continued to be an agrarian society. The best contrast is with the so-called agricultural revolution that laid the foundation for industrialization in northwest Europe. Starting in the fifteenth century, productivity grew about 0.25 percent per year. Using a variety of new crops, new crop rotations, new and more fertilizer, and new implements, English and Dutch farmers needed 150 years (roughly 1450–1600) to raise the ratio of seed to yield from 1:3 to 1:6; it took another 100 years to get to a 1:10 ratio.

These innovations spread slowly. The major innovation, the three-field rotation, spread eastward into Europe at a rate of about 3 to 4 miles per year, reaching Poland and Hungary by 1825. This slow rate of diffusion makes sense given the inherent risk-averseness of peasants and their limited exposure to market pressures. The much higher rates of manufacturing productivity growth in the industrial revolution, and the fact that it largely affected producers who were already in the world market, meant that those producers could not afford this kind of passivity.

## British First Mover Advantages

As a result of the explosive growth of British production during the industrial revolution, even after satisfying domestic demand Britain could shower those parts of Europe accessible by water transport with goods. British cotton textile production doubled every 10 years from 40 million yards of fabric equivalent in 1785 to over 2 billion yards in 1850.[6] British iron production doubled every 13 years, rising from 68,000 tons in 1788 to 250,000 tons in 1806 and 678,000 tons in 1830.[7] Production of pottery, glassware, alcohols, kitchen goods, soap, and other household goods followed similar growth curves. This increased production flowed into British exports. In 1800 these exports had constituted about 18 percent of British gross domestic product (GDP), but by 1830 they were 35 percent of a much larger GDP, with textiles the largest single export. This shower of goods imposed enormous competitive pressure on producers in Europe and elsewhere, particularly because the British were not selling new commodities with untested demand but old commodities that they produced ever more efficiently.

This threat can be seen in Britain's rising share of world manufacturing output. In 1750 Britain had a little more than 1 percent of world population and produced less than 2 percent of manufacturing output. By 1860 it had approximately 2 percent of the world's population but produced about 20 percent of world manufacturing output. British per capita industrial production was about twice that of its nearest competitor, Belgium, and four to six times that in Central Europe.[8] Table 4.1 provides additional comparisons, but the reader should be aware that these are at best estimates.

European consumption of raw cotton indicates the size of its cotton textile industries relative to that of the British. It is thus a good proxy measurement of the displacement effects of the flood of British goods. As late as the 1770s, the raw cotton consumption of European firms exceeded British consumption, reflecting relatively equal productivity levels and Europe's much larger population. After the industrial revolution, however, total European consumption lagged the British until the 1880s, indicating the displacement of potential European production by British imports. Until 1860, the British cotton textile industry usually consumed more than twice as much raw cotton

TABLE 4.1

### British Industrial Dominance, 1800, 1860, and 1913
(per capita level of industrialization; Britain in 1900 = 100)

| 1800 | | 1860 | | 1913 | |
|---|---|---|---|---|---|
| Britain | 16 | Britain | 64 | United States | 126 |
| Belgium | 10 | Belgium | 28 | Britain | 115 |
| Switzerland | 10 | Switzerland | 26 | Belgium | 88 |
| France | 9 | United States | 21 | Switzerland | 87 |
| Netherlands | 9 | France | 20 | Germany | 85 |
| Norway | 9 | Germany | 15 | Sweden | 67 |
| United States | 9 | Sweden | 15 | France | 59 |
| Germany | 8 | Norway | 11 | Canada | 46 |
| Sweden | 8 | Netherlands | 11 | Denmark | 33 |
| Denmark | 8 | Austria-Hungary | 11 | Austria-Hungary | 32 |
| Austria-Hungary | 7 | Denmark | 10 | Norway | 31 |
| Japan | (7) | Japan | (7) | Japan | 20 |

Numbers in parentheses are best-guess estimates.

SOURCE: Paul Bairoch, "International Industrialization Levels from 1750–1980," *Journal of European Economic History* 11, no. 2 (Fall 1982), pp. 281, 286, 330.

as *all* of its European rivals. By the 1880s, the aggregate consumption of European textile producers caught up.[9]

Outside Europe, European efforts at colonization aggravated the difficulties of industrializing. The share of world manufacturing in colonized and soon to be colonized areas fell steadily in both relative and absolute terms. In 1750, at the beginning of the industrial revolution, productivity was relatively equal around the world, and about three-fourths of world manufacturing took place outside northwest Europe and North America.[10] By 1830, largely because of British industrialization, this share had fallen to about three-fifths; by 1880, with the United States and northwest Europe substantially industrialized, it was down to one-tenth. Third World manufacturing output seems to have fallen in absolute terms until 1900, producing an inverse verdoorn effect in which declining production led to declining productivity per unit labor.

The British enjoyed what we would today call first mover advantages and verdoorn effects. As the first to enter the market with industrially produced goods, the British acquired the expertise that comes from "learning by doing." They developed a workforce with the skills needed to run the machines they were using and a large pool of practical engineering talent to build those machines. In addition, fairly specialized firms emerged for particular fabrics, giving each firm some economies of scale. All the advantages listed above involve market imperfections that impede the diffusion of technology. While the technologies associated with the British industrial revolution did diffuse to the continent, they did so a generation behind their introduction in Britain, and quite unevenly.

Michael Porter's analytic model for industrial success can be used to explicate some of the difficulties confronting would-be late industrializers.

Porter argues that competitiveness arises from a "diamond" of competencies encompassing factor markets, supporting industries, firms' strategies and structures, and demand conditions.[11] Late developers lag in each of these, making it difficult for them to compete with established producers. Late developers lack skilled labor and experienced managers, have limited access to capital, do not possess established suppliers, finishers, and marketers of their goods, and by definition use backward technologies. Identifying these disadvantages also allows us to see some of the ways in which states might intervene to promote local industry. Alexander Gerschenkron has argued that institutional innovations that overcome each of these problems are the source of success in late developers.[12] The next two sections present Porter's and Gerschenkron's models.

## Porter's Model Applied to Late Developers

Porter basically argues that industrial structures and competitive success are interdependent. Firms are shaped by the kinds of labor and capital markets to which they have access — their factor markets. Their relationship to supporting industries providing services, final sales, components and other manufactured inputs, design, and research partly determines the technological dynamism of the industry and its overall competitiveness.

*Factor Markets*
Labor markets in preindustrial or agrarian societies are very weak for two reasons. First, workers lack skills that we take for granted, as well as more obvious technologically based skills. In agrarian economies around 1800, most workers lacked "skills" such as showing up for work regularly. Most males worked in agriculture, and the nature and intensity of their labor varied enormously depending on the season. It took several generations of urban life to get them to come to factory work every day and to work at a constant rhythm throughout the year. Even in the United States, as late as the 1920s and 1930s, automobile workers often deserted the factory during harvest season; in agrarian economies this problem was more acute. Unsurprisingly, most industrial workers in the 1800s were women and children, who could be spared from the field and who were accustomed to the more constant rhythms of domestic work.

Second, late developers also have problems creating labor discipline, including getting workers to abandon subsistence agriculture for paid work.[13] One of the late developers' few competitive advantages is relatively low wages, expressed in money terms. However, relatively low wages are an advantage only when productivity is as high as that of one's competitors. Late developers try to increase productivity by using the most modern technology available, but the lack of skilled labor makes this difficult, and even when skilled labor is available they often lack specific experience with this technology. Equally important, models of worker resistance, including unionization, travel just as fast as technological imports. High levels of worker mobility made communication reasonably instantaneous even in nineteenth-century Europe. Thus, while it took almost two generations for British workers to develop durable unions, similar unions emerged simultaneously with industrialization in Scandinavia and Germany. These unions could impede efforts to raise productivity to the point where low wages were actually a competitive advantage.

Late developers usually have no trained pool of managers to draw on. Most European and Asian firms were family firms. The absence of professional managers and engineers hindered the successful management of large-scale enterprise.[14] The only experience with large-scale organizations resided in the state, which had been running armies and bureaucracies for many years, and in its related colonial administrations and enterprises. In late developing countries, the military consequently played an important role in creating professional management cadres.

Creating new industry also requires capital. Here two problems hindered, and continue to hinder, late developers: they absolutely lack capital, and they lack an efficient means to link savers and investors institutionally. The earliest stage of industrialization can be accomplished on a shoestring: textile production is within the resources of an extended family. But canals, not to speak of railroads, steel mills, and production of bulk chemicals, require capital on a larger order of magnitude. This capital has to be gathered from many individual investors and concentrated in one institution, be it a firm drawing on equity markets, or a bank, or the state, to be invested in these "lumpy" projects.

Shortages of capital in turn usually reflected inefficient agricultural production. In the nineteenth century, "savings" in one year ultimately equaled grain left over from the preceding year's consumption, either as grain itself, as livestock fed with that grain, or as cash earned by exporting/selling that grain somewhere else. "Fixed capital" or "investment" equaled the structures or machines built by the workers fed with that extra grain. *A region's agricultural efficiency or ability to import foods thus set the upper limit on potential investment.* The amount of grain that landlords (and later the state) could squeeze out of peasants represented the practical limit on investment. This was true even where money capital existed: if peasants would or could not surrender extra food, and food could not be imported, then investment could not occur. Agriculture also set limits on the local labor supply. The more efficient agriculture was, the more labor that could be freed from agriculture for industrial employment.

Agricultural efficiency also set a second limit on industrialization. Late industrializers usually financed their initial imports of modern physical capital goods (i.e., machinery or rails) by exporting the surplus of some local agricultural good. However, agricultural modernization also required investment, that is, access to surplus agricultural production. A balance had to be drawn (usually by the state in later industrializers) between how much agricultural surplus was siphoned off for industrial investment and how much was left in agriculture. Taking too much might permanently cripple agriculture, making it useless as a source of investment funds and depriving the economy of labor supplies.

*Firm Strategy and Structure*
Even if an agricultural surplus and thus capital existed, it often was dispersed. Surplus food or the money representing surplus food had to be concentrated and made available to those who wanted to build canals and railroads. This problem of intermediation between savers and investors did not exist, for example, for family-owned textile mills; they were both saver and investor. The only practical way to capitalize and manage large firms was through joint stock companies, which institutionalized the raising and investment of capital. The absence of banks oriented toward long-term investment, or of stock and bond markets to facilitate the floating of company shares (stock), could inhibit the creation of joint stock companies. Firms also faced internal organizational difficulties. Reliable legal systems for regulating corporate enterprise had to be developed.

*Supporting Industries*
Leading sectors are actually made up of many individual industries and firms that contribute to a final product. British success in cotton textiles rested not just on the application of power to the spinning of fibers and weaving of cloth. It also reflected expertise in dyeing and the production of natural dyes, in the production of textile machinery, in marketing into a staggering variety of global markets, and in access to, control over, and transportation of colonial sources of raw cotton. Technological innovation in supporting industries can also spur innovation in related industries, because innovation in one particular industry will force innovation on its users or suppliers. The development of faster, water-powered spinning made it necessary to speed up the carding of cotton and wool.

*Demand Conditions*
The nature of end-users can also either promote or hinder technological development. Britain's large and wide domestic market and its control over most colonial markets provided its producers with a market big enough to support further extension of the division of labor, and thus big enough to support high-productivity manufacturing. In contrast, continental producers were limited to their own and adjacent microeconomies, had small domestic markets that were often oriented toward luxury goods, and were shut out of British colonial markets until the repeal of the Navigation Acts in 1841. A relatively sophisticated end market will force constant innovation on producers, as consumers demand more and better products.

---

# European Models
# of Late Industrialization

## Gerschenkron's Models

Alexander Gerschenkron provides a stylized model of late development that implicitly rests on Michael Porter's analysis. Gerschenkron's argument was quite simple: the later any given country's industrialization started after Britain's, the greater the degree of state intervention needed to make industrialization successful. Late industrializers could not replicate Britain's experience and institutions. Instead, they had to follow many different institutional paths to industrialization because new institutional forms were needed to overcome the barriers markets threw up to late industrialization. Countries that did not innovate new institutions usually failed to industrialize. From an institutional point of view, British industrialization rested on a mixture of individual entrepreneurs using their own savings and retained earnings to capitalize small-scale industry, while a large stock market helped to capitalize big industry. Britain largely pursued a laissez-faire policy, guaranteeing property rights, permitting the early and easy formation of joint stock companies, and avoiding interference in the allocation of investment funds. In this model, most banks concentrated on short-term commercial finance, while investment banks concentrated on overseas lending and the floating of new shares on the stock market. Only Holland's and Switzerland's states imitated Britain's. Everywhere else in Europe states intervened to support local industry, sometimes successfully, sometimes not.

Gerschenkron argued that four syndromes co-varied with the lateness of industrialization.[15] The later successful industrialization occurred,

~   the faster the rate of growth of output — usually faster than that in the current dominant economy — would be once industrialization started. Gerschenkron called this the industrial spurt.

~   the greater the degree of state intervention to support industry through special institutions to create, concentrate, and lend capital, and to control labor unrest.

~   the more concentrated the pattern of industrial ownership and the larger the institutional form of ownership would be.

~   the more likely that agriculture would remain undeveloped relative to local industry, hindering expansion of the market.

Each of these syndromes reflected the consequences of efforts to overcome competitive disadvantages relative to earlier industrializers.

Gerschenkron constructed two stylized models of institutional deviations from the British based on these features, arguing that bank-led development characterized countries industrializing one to two generations (20 to 40 years) later than Britain, and that state-led development characterized countries industrializing three to four generations (40 to 80 years) later. Germany was prototypical of the first. The novel institutional form here as compared with Britain was long-term investment banks using their control over capital to direct industrial investment. In Germany, banks concentrated capital for industrial investment and tended to control industrial firms. Most capital came from long-term loans rather than sale of stock shares (equity). Most capital was raised locally. The state used tariffs and purchasing policy to induce local production of industrial goods it wanted, but usually avoided direct ownership of production. The state preempted and repressed unions.

Russia was prototypical of state-led development. The novel institutional form here was state ownership of financial and industrial companies across a range of industrial sectors. The Russian state concentrated capital for investment in a mix of privately and publicly owned enterprises. The state raised capital by taxing agriculture and borrowing abroad. Indeed, Russia was absolutely Europe's largest foreign borrower. Because of an absence of local entrepreneurs, the state used state-owned firms to ensure production of goods, occasionally privatizing these—and thus creating a weak sort of entrepreneur—when they were on their feet. As with bank-led development, the state used tariffs and purchasing policy to secure the local market for domestic producers. Even so, the shortage of entrepreneurs and skilled labor meant that foreign investors and entrepreneurs assumed a major role in industrialization. (Foreign investors owned 41 percent of Russian joint stock companies in industry in 1914.)[16] The state repressed labor unions.

In both situations, late industrializers' difficulty in becoming competitive with the British forced them to adopt novel institutional forms. Like the British in the Indian Ocean, latecomers Germany and Russia had to make the best of a bad situation, and in doing so they stumbled into institutional arrangements that proved beneficial in the long term. An explanation of why these institutional forms matter is in order before examining Germany and Russia, among others, in greater depth later.

Each of Gerschenkron's syndromes reflects the fact that successful late industrialization required a shift to a Kaldorian growth strategy. In other words, they involved conscious efforts to create verdoorn effects in order to bring local industry's productivity up to a level that would enable them to compete with earlier industrializers. As noted earlier, verdoorn's law argues that the faster the rate of growth of output, the faster the rate of productivity growth. Most of the gain in verdoorn effects comes from learning by doing, as workers and management gain experience producing a particular good and overcoming temporary bottlenecks in production. The faster production grows—that is, the bigger the Gerschenkronian spurt—the more workers and management are forced to think up creative ways to expand production, and the greater the economies of speed as they reduce the amount of time it takes to actually produce something. Meanwhile, established competitors facing stagnant demand will be tempted to routinize production and in doing so are less likely to innovate more efficient production methods.

The rising level of state intervention thus partly reflects efforts to create the largest possible market—and thus the maximum possible verdoorn effects—for local producers. State efforts to maximize local producers' control of the market dovetailed with their strategic concerns. As stated earlier, in the nineteenth century nonindustrial states seemed likely to lose wars. Therefore, states typically tried first to build up a railroad network along with its supporting industries. Railroads helped unify the microeconomies over which the state ruled. Much of the local market actually was quite distant from local industry because of the absence of cheap transportation. Railroads helped overcome high transport costs. At the same time, important industries linked to the railroads, such as engineering, metals production, and mining, enjoyed rising sales and output. States used tariffs, contracts to buy output, and sometimes state ownership to ensure that local firms emerged or made a successful transition to modern production methods. From the firm's point of view, investing in high-productivity, high-volume production often was rational only if it could be sure of having at least the domestic market to fall back on. Otherwise, firms would not be able to gain economies of scale and scope by running their factories at full capacity.

Concentration of ownership and the use of the most modern production methods also reflected the positive effects of concentrating output and thus verdoorn effects into a handful of firms. Putting scarce resources such as skilled labor, management, and capital in one place concentrated profits and learning effects. Geographic concentration also fostered faster learning by doing, because it permitted interaction among different producers in the same area.

Because of the need to maximize verdoorn effects, the later industrialization occurred the more likely it was that agriculture would lag industry. Generally, the later industrialization took place, the greater the need for capital relative to the local supply and the greater the level of state involvement, making it probable that taxes and other coercive mechanisms would be used to squeeze as much as possible from agriculture in the shortest amount of time. States appropriated this surplus food in kind or as money taxes and used it to fund initial investment in heavy industry. When Stalin starved the Ukrainian peasantry to industrialize the Soviet Union in the 1930s, he merely continued, albeit in an extremely violent and telescoped way, nineteenth-century processes in Western Europe.[17]

This kind of rushed extraction could also divert investment funds from agriculture, leaving agricultural production unmodernized and thus less useful in the long run as a source of investment funds. Slower rural income growth would also hamper the expansion of the market for locally produced industrial goods and the expansion of agriculture as a source of exports. Late industrializers thus walked a fine line between too little extraction to fund industry on a competitive scale and so much extraction that investment in agriculture collapsed. A weak or decaying agriculture often forced reliance on foreign borrowing. Earlier industrializers could exploit agriculture more slowly, until industry became self-financing.

## "Early" Late Industrializers: The United States and Belgium

A quick survey of European industrialization demonstrates these points. Even in the first two countries to industrialize after Britain, Belgium and the northeastern United States, banks and state intervention played a much greater role than in Britain. In Belgium the state planned two strategic railroads, one going north-south from Antwerp to France and the other east-west from the Channel to Germany, in order to capture transit trade from the Atlantic economy to the European interior. The Société Générale and the Banque de Belgique, both long-term, joint stock investment banks, financed this system with state help. The system was completed by 1844, shortly after Britain began building railroads in earnest. Rail construction acted as a leading sector in Belgium, spurring a 100 percent increase in coal production. Belgian firms used railroad demand to become more productive and then sought the economies of scale they needed to compete with the British by exporting to backward neighbors like Holland, France, and the many German states; cast iron exports rose 800 percent from 1835 to 1845. By 1853, the Belgian railroads were profitable, and from 1850 to 1870, about 1,300 miles of privately funded railroads were constructed. Some capital for these lines came from Britain, as did most of the technology for modern iron production.

In the United States, contrary to received wisdom, the states and banks played a major role in the initial stages of industrialization.[18] Alexander Hamilton's views on the importance of a protective tariff for infant industry are well known. But the various states also created and financed, often with foreign capital, most of the early canals and railroads. In the southern states, the state usually helped planters capitalize cotton plantations and other export-oriented agriculture by backing their efforts to secure mortgages with state bonds. In the emerging Midwest, federal land policies supported another export-oriented agricultural complex centered on grain and pork. These policies culminated in the four great policies that built the Midwest: land grant railroads; homesteading; the land grant college; and the extension service of the U.S. Department of Agriculture. In the North, states provided about 40 percent of all railroad capital in the 1830s.[19] By 1850, the United States already had 50 percent more miles of railroad than Britain; more important, the extensive use of steamships on internal rivers and canals helped create and expand sophisticated machine tool and engineering industries. (Chapter 6 provides more information on the agricultural side of this story.)

## Second-Generation Late Industrializers: France

Because of France's overall economic backwardness relative to Britain, its leap into the railroad and industrial era took greater state and bank involvement than did Britain's. France's economic slowness can be seen at all levels: transportation, urbanization, technology, metals production, and sources of industrial power. Canal-building did not boom until a generation after the British canal boom. France built roughly the same number of miles of canals as the smaller Britain during the 1800s. The weakness of the transportation system and the lack of a unified national market can be seen in regional differences in grain prices. In 1800 wheat prices varied by as much as 400 percent in different regions; in 1817 by 200 percent; and as late as 1847 by 70 percent.[20] Without cheap transport to bring food to cities, urbanization also lagged behind Britain's. In 1806 only 7 percent of the population lived in towns over 2,000; and by 1846 only 25 percent. In Britain over half the population lived in towns by 1851.

Smaller cities meant less demand for infrastructure. Therefore, growth in French iron output also lagged a generation behind Britain (Table 4.2). France's metals output was so deficient that it had to import British rails

TABLE 4.2

## Relative Industrial Backwardness in Nineteenth-Century Europe, Selected Years

| | *Britain* | *France* | *German States* | *Russia* |
|---|---|---|---|---|
| | Iron Production (thousands of tons) | | | |
| 1818 | 330 | 113 | 85[a] | 127 |
| 1828 | 714 | 221 | 105 | 178 |
| 1847 | 2,000 | 592 | 230 | 195 |
| 1860 | 3,888 | 898 | 529 | 298 |
| | Mechanical Energy (thousand horsepower)[b] | | | |
| Steam engines | 1,641 | 243 | 100 | } 5 |
| Water mills | 674 | 462 | — | |
| | Railroad Mileage (kilometers) | | | |
| 1830 | 157 | 31 | 0 | 0 |
| 1840 | 2,390 | 410 | 469 | 27[c] |
| 1850 | 9,797 | 2,915 | 5,856 | 501 |
| 1860 | 14,603 | 9,167 | 11,089 | 1,626 |

[a]1823 for German states.
[b]Data for Britain are for 1839, France 1842, Germany 1860, and Russia 1860.
[c]1837 for Russia.
SOURCE: B. R. Mitchell, *European Historical Statistics* (New York: Columbia University Press, 1978), pp. 215–216, 315–316.

during its great railroad boom. In Britain most machines were already all metal by the 1830s and 1840s, while in France metal fittings on wooden frames remained common until the 1840s and 1850s. France also lagged in the application of water and steam power (Table 4.2). France's greater reliance on energy from water reflected its poorer supplies of coal and also hindered its industrialization. Industry had to move to water rather than bringing coal to itself. Industry therefore lost the economies that come from concentrating in urban areas, with their abundant labor, good transportation, and service sectors.

France thus faced considerable obstacles to the development of a modern rail system and metals industry. Its workforce was unruly and violently defended traditional work norms. While much capital existed in France in the form of metallic money, most was hidden under the mattress, so to speak, and unavailable for investment. Financial intermediaries, particularly banks, were highly fragmented, weak, and oriented toward short-term lending. Few firms were willing to undertake the very expensive task of building long-haul railroads.

In the 1840s the state intervened, legislating the basic outline for a national rail network in 1842. This network was to be a six-pointed star radiating from Paris to Marseilles, Toulouse (and Spain), Bordeaux (and Spain), Brest, Le

Havre, and Lille (and Belgium). The state provided the railroads with a significant subsidy by building the bed for the rails (the built-up ground on which the wooden cross-tie "sleepers" lie) and then leasing the beds to companies with a monopoly on each route. Building began immediately with help from British capital, engineers, and management. However, the financial crisis of 1847 and the revolution of 1848 caused English capital to flee.

The coup d'état of Louis Napoleon (1851–70) removed these obstacles and set off an explosion of building. Louis Napoleon outlawed unions and required workers to carry around the *livret*, which recorded whether or not they had been good workers. He also sponsored the Crédit Mobilier, France's first long-term finance bank. The Crédit Mobilier collected deposits on a short-term basis while lending on a long-term basis to railroads and other industrial ventures. The Crédit Mobilier fostered a fivefold expansion in the annual average railroad investment between 1850 and 1860.

This spurt of rail building had immediate economic consequences. By 1861 two-thirds of the grain harvest was being transported by rail, and the agricultural supply basin for Paris had expanded to 155 miles from the 30 miles of 1830. Regional specialties—eponymous products like Gruyère and Rocquefort—which had previously been produced in limited quantities saw their market expand rapidly once they could be transported cheaply. Grain prices in Paris began to dominate rural prices. Stock-raising also changed in response to integration of the national market. Despite rising demand for wool, the number of sheep fell 25 percent between 1840 and 1882, while the number of cattle increased 30 percent.[21] Fresh beef and dairy production displaced low-value-added wool production.

France reduced but never closed the gap with Britain during the nineteenth century. Per capita industrial production rose from about one-third the British level in 1860 to about half by 1913, so that despite a larger population, France's total output in 1913 lagged Britain's.[22] Yet France was a relatively successful case of late industrialization.[23]

## Second-Generation Late Industrializers: Germany

The states that Prussia cobbled into Germany were even more successful. As one of his classic cases, German development illustrates all of Gerschenkron's syndromes. Banks coordinated development, which occurred in two big waves. One centered on railroads and created basic iron and engineering capacity. The other centered on the new leading-sector cluster of electricity and chemistry, but ran in tandem with a further expansion of steel making on the basis of new smelting and casting technologies and new ways of organizing the flow of production. Ownership was highly concentrated in a small number of banks. The three largest firms in Germany during the late 1800s were also the three largest banks.

Initially, Germany was even more backward than France, experiencing virtually no urban growth from 1815 to 1848. Ninety percent of the labor force in textile mills in the early 1800s came from peasant households supplementing subsistence farming with part-time work. Sixty percent of those mills were worked by hand, compared to 20 percent by water power and 20 percent by steam. Even in highly industrialized areas like Saxony, steam power seems to have been a rarity in the first half of the 1800s.[24] The famous Zollverein toll was more of a revenue tariff than any protection, so in the 1830s and 1840s cheap imported British textiles drove many peasants out of textile production. Iron production was equally backward.

After a series of private efforts failed, the state intervened to promote railroadization. Railroad construction then acted as a leading sector, pulling the German engineering industry and the economy forward into modernity in Germany's first big industrial spurt. As in France the state laid down the basic rail network, with a star of six rail lines radiating from Berlin. The state subsidized construction with cheap loans, guaranteed the profits of rail firms, and, when necessary, purchased shares in rail companies to assure their flotation. The state also renovated an old state corporation, the Seehandlung, to create new exports and, equally important, to demonstrate new technologies to local entrepreneurs. The Seehandlung established a number of model factories in textiles, chemicals, mining, and luxury goods production, often in collaboration with expatriate British engineer/entrepreneurs and skilled workers. Nonetheless, in the first phase of industrialization, Germany, and particularly Prussia, relied on grain exports to Britain to finance capital goods imports.

German rail construction benefited from German backwardness and distance from the British town. Despite their later start, by the middle of the 1800s the Germans managed to build roughly twice as many miles of rail as France, essentially completing their "star" by 1853. Cheaper land, lower wages, and planning that took roads around difficult terrain rather than through it made German rail construction costs per mile roughly one-third those in Britain (on average £11,000 per mile versus £30,000 to £40,000 in Britain).

The entire economy accelerated through rail investment. From 1855 to 1870, railroad investment averaged over 20 percent of total investment in Germany, dwarfing any other single sector. The demand for locomotives also helped promote local engineering. Until 1842, all locomotives came from Britain. Tariffs and state contracts induced local production, and by 1854 all locomotives came from Central European sources. Germany imported British and Belgian skilled workers to speed this process. Rising output led to rising productivity, and by the 1860s Germany became a net exporter of rails and locomotives.

The second wave of industrialization centered on steel and chemicals, with banks playing an even more active role than before. Industrial production grew an average 3.7 percent per year during 1870–1914.[25] Reflecting a relative scarcity of capital, the big banks promoted high levels of concentration in Germany. The banks fostered cartels and vertical and horizontal integration in order to reduce competition and thus the risk of overinvestment, to exercise more control over raw materials prices, and to coordinate export efforts. By the 1870s the German iron and steel industry was already more concentrated than its British rivals. This pattern obtained in other growth sectors as well. By 1896 banks had founded thirty-nine firms in electrical goods. The banks then rationalized the industry into two great firms—an enlarged AEG and Siemens. The banks also rationalized the market for these firms, lending money to cities for electrical works on condition that they buy standardized products from AEG/Siemens. In 1904 the same thing happened in the chemicals industry with the creation of Farben-Cassella and Bayer-Agfa-BASF; in 1916 these merged into IG Farben.

The state, particularly under Bismarck, actively preempted unionization and outlawed the Socialist party. Bismarck developed a state system of health insurance and old-age pensions to break the working class into a series of strata defined by occupation and income. Even so, Germany had one of the most radical working classes west of St. Petersburg during the last quarter of the nineteenth century.

German late industrialization was highly successful. Per capita industrial production went from about one-quarter of British levels in 1860 to about three-quarters in 1913, and because of Germany's larger population, it actually outproduced Britain in gross terms that year.[26] Austria and Italy, industrializing about one generation behind Germany, replicated the institutional features of the German model, albeit less successfully. Countries industrializing after this period had much greater state involvement, particularly direct involvement in financing and running industrial enterprises.

## Japanese and Other Asian Models of Late Industrialization

### Russia—Three Generations Late?

Gerschenkron's classic case of state-led industrialization is Russia, but as a case Russia actually mixes elements of the Western European pattern and the Asian pattern. Because of this circumstance and Russia's relative failure to industrialize in the nineteenth century, Russia is discussed only briefly before we move on to Japan and Asia. The key difference between Russian industrialization and that farther west is that, where the state largely aided private entrepreneurs in Western Europe, in Russia and the east the state tended to replace private entrepreneurs. Thus, in Russia the Ministry of Finance played a key role in raising and allocating capital. The Russian state established a series of state banks, subordinated to the Ministry of Finance, to lend to industry, matching each bank to one particular industrial sector. These banks steered borrowed foreign capital into the sectors they were trying to promote. The state built most of the early railroads and also built a factory to produce rolling stock for them and an iron mill for rails. Consistent with Central European patterns, the Russian state also promoted private railroads by guaranteeing loans and paying dividends to investors. Despite these efforts, by 1914 European Russia had less than 20 percent of the railroad trackage of the comparably sized United States.

Russia's efforts ultimately failed because of the grim choices imposed by its backwardness. Its backward agriculture (Siberia aside) yielded a very small surplus, and the relative absence of rivers, canals, and railroads meant that most agriculture took place in microeconomies, making extraction of that surplus difficult. This situation forced the state to look abroad for capital, but this created a conflict between debt service and agricultural modernization. Russia relied on grain exports to finance its foreign debt payments. As international grain prices fell, peasants came under more and more pressure to deliver more grain without having any way to increase productivity. Rising rents led to peasant unrest, the abortive 1905 revolt, and finally the great uprising of 1917.

## Japan—Better Late Than Never

While the Russian pattern is typical of foreign debt–financed, state-led industrialization in Asia, Latin America, and elsewhere, Russian industrialization had only limited long-run success. This makes Japan a more interesting case of state-led industrialization, particularly as it demonstrates the first example of a fairly consistent Asian pattern of industrialization distinct from the European model. Japanese and other Asian industrialization mimics the Russian state-led model.

Two characteristics, however, distinguish the Asian model from the generic European model, with Russia viewed as a transitional case. In Europe, the state largely allowed private landlords to extract and invest agricultural surplus. In Asia and in Japan in particular, the *state* controlled the extraction and investment of the agricultural surplus. In Europe, late industrializers typically jumped into the middle of the market with modern technologies. In Asia and Japan, manufacturers initially targeted markets for low-quality, low-price goods ignored by European producers, and then they inched their way up into markets for higher-quality goods through continuous innovation and improvement. Asians industrialized from the bottom up. Both characteristics reflect efforts to cope with adverse circumstances created by European commercial and military dominance of the world. Asian industrialization differs from European not because the difficulty of industrialization intrinsically differed, but because the external political environment for Asian industrialization was much harsher than for European industrialization.

Japan avoided being hobbled by the agricultural problems that tripped up Russia by carefully cultivating the agricultural sector as a source of surplus for investment. As a result, Japan was able to industrialize without substantial foreign debt. Japanese agricultural reforms in the early Meiji period (1867–90) established capitalist relations of production in the countryside, removing nominal samurai landlords.[27] The state systematically helped peasants increase their yields in order to increase its ability to tax peasants. As in Russia, peasants frequently revolted, but, in the absence of any external shocks, the Japanese state easily quelled these revolts. Because the Meiji state taxed land values, not the harvest, peasants had an incentive to increase productivity; the more they could squeeze out of the land, the more they could keep. The tax structure pushed marginal farmers off the land and replaced them with more productive farmers. Because the land tax had to be paid in money, it forced peasants into the market and commercialized the entire countryside. The land tax extracted about 30 to 40 percent of the value of agricultural production for the state, providing between 60 and 70 percent of state revenue.[28] The state then invested this money in railroads, in generic heavy industries critical for military security, and in its military per se. These investments secured Japan from the colonization typical of the rest of Asia.

The Japanese state also channeled capital extracted from agriculture to the large family-owned merchant companies that had emerged during Japan's long self-imposed isolation under the Tokugawa shogunate. In this sense, the state was building capitalism from the top down, as in Russia. These merchants transformed themselves into banks, which, as in Russia and Germany, controlled much industrial investment and fostered considerable centralization. Japan also adopted joint stock company institutions right from the start of its industrialization. The combination of bank control and joint stock organization led to an early form of conglomerate that the Japanese called *zaibatsu*, or financial clique, in which banks controlled and coordinated a group of firms. Many of these industrial firms had been started by the state and then sold off to the *zaibatsu* banks.

Meanwhile, Japan also industrialized from the bottom up in response to European colonization of Asia. After 1842 the British and other Europeans opened Asia to Western trade via colonization and unequal treaties. The Europeans integrated Asia into their world economy as exporters of primary products to Europe and importers of manufactures from Europe just as they did colonial areas in Latin America and Africa. (See Tables 4.3 and 4.4.)

The Asian economies differed in two respects from Africa and Latin America. First, strong local state structures survived the European incursions, particularly in Japan, but also in Siam and China. Even in India and what became Malaysia much rule was indirect. Second, as noted in Chapter 1, Asia possessed a deep and vibrant economy based on intra-Asian trade. This intra-Asian trade provided the market that supported Asian industrialization from the bottom up. European demand for raw materials added a dynamic motor to this existing trade, driving an extremely rapid increase in local trade. Total exports by Asian countries rose from about £82 million in 1883 to £214 million in 1913. However, the intra-Asian component of this trade rose from

TABLE 4.3

### Composition of Asian Trade with Europe, c. 1912

| | Exports (%) | | Imports (%) | |
|---------|---------|--------------|---------|--------------|
| Country | Primary | Manufactures | Primary | Manufactures |
| Japan | 69 | 31 | 34 | 66 |
| India | 92 | 8 | 8 | 92 |

SOURCE: Kaoru Sugihara, "Patterns of Asia's Integration into the World Economy 1880–1913," in Wolfram Fischer et al., eds., *The Emergence of a World Economy 1500–1914*, vol. II (Wiesbaden: F. Steiner, 1986), pp. 711–713.

TABLE 4.4

Distribution of Asian Trade, c. 1913[a]

| Country | Exports (%) | | Imports (%) | |
|---|---|---|---|---|
| | Asia | "The West" | Asia | "The West" |
| China | 48 | 50 | 16 | 83 |
| Japan | 47 | 50 | 44 | 53 |
| India | 27 | 63 | 22 | 75 |

[a]Rows do not add up to 100 because of exports to/imports from other regions.
SOURCE: Kaoru Sugihara, "Patterns of Asia's Integration into the World Economy 1880–1913," in Wolfram Fischer et al., eds., *The Emergence of a World Economy 1500–1914*, vol. II (Wiesbaden: F. Steiner, 1986), pp. 711–713.

£31 million to £149 million during the same period, a rate of growth of 5.4 percent per annum compared to the 3.2 percent growth for exports to Europe.[29] Much of the increase in intra-Asian exports came from industrial goods aimed at Asian consumers, who were spending money derived from exports to Europe.

The same leading sectors that produced the expansion of the European economies also drove expansion of Asian industry via European demand for Asian raw materials. European demand rose in two waves. The first was linked to the diffusion of the initial industrial revolution cotton textiles leading-sector cluster to continental Europe and the simultaneous railroad cluster in Britain. The second, much larger wave was linked to the chemistry and electricity cluster, and centered on demand for rubber (for insulation and bicycle tires), tin and palm oils (for canned and processed foods for an enlarged urban working class), and petroleum (for the emerging motor industry). Most Asian exports to Europe came from plants introduced to or transplanted within Asia. Rubber in Malaya, tea in northeast India (Assam) and Sri Lanka (Ceylon), and systematically cultivated palm and coconuts almost always occurred in new monocultural production zones. New mining ventures, such as tin in Malaya, also boomed. Labor for these new production zones came from displaced peasants turned into indentured or migrant labor. (See Chapter 5.) These ex-peasants now worked full-time for money incomes and turned to the market to buy food and manufactures they previously had made for themselves or in isolated microeconomies. In turn, this additional demand for food called forth new rice production zones in Siam, Vietnam, and Bengal, adding to demand for manufactures by enlarging incomes there.

Parts of this expanding Asian market remained the preserve of European firms: rail and oceanic transport, electrification, colonialists' consumption. Nonetheless, a huge market segment remained untouched by European producers. This segment catered to local consumption and involved goods that European firms could not profitably produce in Europe for Asian markets. Local Asian producers, particularly the Japanese, jumped into this market segment. One Japanese scholar precisely marks the divide between the European and Asian textile markets as cotton textiles with thread counts above about 25 and those below.[30] Thread count is a measure of fineness and quality, with higher thread counts denoting finer fabrics. European, especially British textile producers in search of higher profits, systematically moved up-market into higher thread counts at the end of the nineteenth century. They abandoned the lower ranges of the market to Asian producers in textiles and other household goods.

With their low wage rates, Asian producers could compete in these low-priced goods. Japanese manufacturers particularly introduced a wide range of knockoffs of European goods into local Asian markets. Verdoorn's law held in Asia as in Europe, and rising output for the Asian part of their market helped the Japanese increase their productivity to the point where they could begin to compete with European producers at the bottom of the market for higher-quality goods. Japan's successful creation of a textile industry allowed it to become a kind of Britain within Asia, exporting finished textiles to India and China while importing raw cotton from India and rice from Taiwan, which it colonized after 1895. Its large agricultural surplus, its successful exports, and its colonies allowed Japan to industrialize without the need for significant amounts of borrowed capital.

Finally, the Japanese state also interfered in factor markets. Unlike Central Europe, which could rely on a voluntary migration of skilled workers from West European countries to help start up modern industry, Japan actively had to seek out skills. It sent students overseas to acquire technical knowledge and imported Western academics and professionals to teach local students. As in Germany, the military was a key training ground for management personnel. The state ruthlessly suppressed labor movements. Local firms also innovated lifetime employment in a bid to retain skilled labor. Japanese per capita industrial production rose from about one-tenth the British level in 1860 to one-fifth that level in 1913, reflecting a growth rate about 50 percent higher than Britain's.[31] Later Asian industrializers like Taiwan and South Korea would imitate the Japanese model, squeezing agriculture to fund their initial round of industrial investment and using low-grade consumer nondurable exports to drive industrialization in the entire economy. Textiles continued to play a crucial role in this process. (See Table 4.5.)

Late development succeeded only in economies where the state intervened to protect local producers, provide investment capital by squeezing agriculture, and control labor. Among European countries with failed or stunted industrialization, the Iberian states failed to protect local industry, the Italian state did not come into being until the late nineteenth century, and the Balkans lacked stability and sometimes independence. Eastern Europe's generally impoverished agriculture proved a weak base for investment in manufacturing and later marketing. Even the most successful late industrializer, Germany, had a stunted consumer goods sector because of the need to divert long-term capital to the capital goods industry. The segmentation of the Asian market between high-cost, high-quality and low-cost, low-quality goods allowed certain Asian countries to industrialize, even though Asian industrializers and Asia overall remained exporters of raw materials to Europe. Colonized nonindustrializers, failed industrializers, and deindustrializers in the

TABLE 4.5

## Share of Raw Materials and Textiles in Asian Exports, Selected Years[a]

|  | Raw materials as % of total exports | Textiles as % of total exports | Textiles as % of manufactured exports |
|---|---|---|---|
| Japan |  |  |  |
| 1874/83 | 82 | 4 | 25 |
| 1892/01 | 54 | 23 | 52 |
| 1912/21 | 34 | 34 | 51 |
| 1930/39 | 20 | 35 | 44 |
| South Korea |  |  |  |
| 1954/56 | 94 | — | — |
| 1964/66 | 41 | 27 | 46 |
| 1971/73 | 16 | 39 | 46 |
| 1976/78 | 12 | 33 | 38 |
| Taiwan |  |  |  |
| 1954/56 | 90 | — | — |
| 1964/66 | 55 | 14 | 32 |
| 1971/73 | 18 | 30 | 36 |
| 1976/78 | 14 | 25 | 29 |

[a]Dashes indicate that no data are available.

SOURCE: Kim Anderson, "China and the MultiFibre Arrangement," in Carl Hamilton, ed., *Textiles Trade and the Developing Countries* (Washington, D.C.: World Bank, 1990), p. 143.

nineteenth century had two other options: Ricardian strategies using agricultural or other raw materials exports as a prerequisite to industrialization, or even more extreme state involvement to create successful Kaldorian growth in industry. The next two chapters deal with the agricultural option. Chapter 12 picks up the second option for late industrializers in Latin America and East Asia.

## International Consequences of Late Development

What were the international consequences of late industrialization? Late industrialization created pressures for increased protection. The late industrializers' drive for wider markets usually led to trade frictions, particularly with the dominant economy, which after all was usually the world's largest market.

Because late industrialization rested on Kaldorian growth—rapid increases in output to stimulate rapid increases in productivity—it inevitably stimulated conflicts among countries for domestic and foreign market share. Late industrializers generated two kinds of export streams. The first usually consisted of some kind of raw material or a traditional manufactured good that, because of its fineness or quality, had so far resisted mechanization and retained its niche in the market for quality goods. Late industrializers exported these in order to finance their initial imports of the capital goods needed for industry. These exports often threatened agricultural producers in the dominant economy, who often had higher implicit rental costs than producers in late industrializers. The second export stream consisted of new industrial goods.

Consequently, the opportunities for reciprocity between the existing dominant economy and late industrializers—mutual tariff reductions—usually shrank. As noted earlier, late industrializers needed to maximize local firms' share of the domestic market in order to run their plants at full capacity and to maximize overall output. Late industrializers had a strong temptation to free ride on the dominant economy's openness to international trade.[32]

In one sense, then, late industrialization occurred at the sufferance of the dominant economy. Almost always the largest market in the world, the dominant economy was a logical target for late industrializers trying to expand output. If the dominant economy chose to protect its market from the export streams of late industrializers, those late industrializers would have a more difficult time starting and sustaining a virtuous circle of rising output–rising productivity–rising competitiveness–rising sales. On the other hand, if late industrializers produced products that firms in the dominant economy were abandoning, then the dominant economy could benefit from cheaper low-value-added industrial goods. In effect, the dominant economy could shed industries along the lines of comparative advantage, allowing low-value-added agriculture and low-value-added, labor-intensive industry to shift location, while hoping that higher real incomes at home would stimulate more output in local high-value-added industries. This is why protectionism in the nineteenth and twentieth centuries seems to be very closely related to the business cycle.[33] During upswings, as new leading sectors emerged in the dominant economy, older sectors could be abandoned at relatively low political and economic cost. Capital and labor could redeploy into new sectors with higher returns via profits or wages. In periods of relatively slow growth, however, the political and economic costs would be higher.

In another sense, successful late industrialization also occurred at the expense of other would-be late industrializers. To the extent that one late industrializer's export stream spilled over into third-party markets—neither the dominant economy's market nor the late industrializer's home market—then firms in that and other third-party markets lost the ability to generate a virtuous Kaldorian circle. Nineteenth-century German success in heavy industry implied slower growth in French, Austrian, and Russian heavy industry, and blocked the emergence of heavy industry in the Balkans, the Ottoman empire, and other agricultural peripheries to Europe's industry.

Paradoxically, then, the dominant economy's efforts to take advantage of its economic superiority by opening up markets creates pressures to close markets. The dominant economy's structural power comes from the pressures its enormous market generates, inducing producers everywhere to reorient their production toward that market. The only way to resist that pressure is to close off the local market and force local producers to look inward, until the demand generated by the local von Thünen town is large enough to draw in those producers on its own.

# Notes

1. Dieter Senghaas, *The European Experience: A Historical Critique of Development Theory* (Dover, N.H.: Berg, 1985) makes the clearest statement of this while providing a typology of states' strategic responses.

2. See Eric Hobsbawm, *Industry and Empire* (London: Weidenfield, 1969) for a lovely and more detailed survey of these questions.

3. Paul Bairoch, "International Industrialization Levels from 1750–1980," *Journal of European Economic History* 11, no. 2 (Fall 1982): 279. Bairoch's estimates should be used as yardsticks.

4. Heita Kawakasu, "International Competition in Cotton Goods in the Late Nineteenth Century: Britain versus India and East Asia," in Wolfram Fischer et al., eds., *The Emergence of a World Economy 1500–1914*, vol. II (Wiesbaden: Franz Steiner, 1986), p. 636.

5. Sidney Pollard, *Peaceful Conquest: The Industrialization of Europe 1760–1970* (Oxford: Oxford University Press, 1981), p. v, says succinctly, "The industrialization of Europe took place on the British model." See also David Landes, *Unbound Prometheus: Technological Change and Industrial Development in Western Europe from 1750 to the Present* (Cambridge: Cambridge University Press, 1969) and W. A. Lewis, *Growth and Fluctuations, 1879–1913* (Boston: Allen and Unwin, 1978).

6. Unless noted, all statistics on production and consumption levels and population come from B. R. Mitchell, *European Historical Statistics, 1750–1970* (New York: Columbia University Press, 1975).

7. All tons used here are metric tons, or 2,200 pounds.

8. Bairoch, "International Industrialization Levels," pp. 275, 281.

9. William Lazonick, *Competitive Advantage on the Shop Floor* (Cambridge, Mass.: Harvard University Press, 1990); P. T. Ellworth, *The International Economy: Structure and Operation* (New York: Macmillan, 1950), pp. 421–422.

10. Bairoch, "International Industrialization Levels," p. 275.

11. Michael Porter, *Competitive Advantage of Nations* (New York: Free Press, 1990). Each corner of Porter's diamond incorporates a well-mined area of research. See, for example, John Zysman, *Governments, Markets, Growth* (Ithaca, N.Y.: Cornell University Press, 1982) on capital markets; Alfred Chandler, *Scale and Scope* (Cambridge, Mass.: Harvard University Press, 1990) on strategy and structure; and Giovanni Dosi, ed., *Economic Theory and Technical Change* (London: Basil Blackwell, 1988) on innovation.

12. Alexander Gerschenkron, *Economic Backwardness in Historical Perspective* (Cambridge, Mass.: Harvard University Press, 1962) p. 44; see also ch. 1 and pp. 353–364.

13. E. P. Thompson, *The Making of the English Working Class* (New York: Vintage, 1966); William Lazonick, *Business Organization and the Myth of the Market Economy* (Cambridge: Cambridge University Press, 1991), and Lazonick, *Competitive Advantage on the Shop Floor* provide an overview of studies of everyday forms of resistance in the textile industry. See Charles Sabel, *Work and Politics* (Cambridge: Cambridge University Press, 1982) for an effort to synthesize and systematize Marxist and Weberian theories of worker (non-)militancy.

14. Jurgen Kocka, "Entrepreneurs and Managers in German Industrialization," in Peter Mathias, ed., *Cambridge Economic History of Europe*, Vol. 7, Part I (Cambridge: Cambridge University Press, 1978), p. 553, puts this point bluntly regarding German industrialization: "It was difficult for German factory owners around 1850 to find

qualified and reliable officials and office staff to perform those tasks which the entrepreneur could not closely control himself."

15. Gerschenkron, *Economic Backwardness in Historical Perspective*, pp. 353–354; Gerschenkron actually lists six syndromes, which I have collapsed into four.

16. M. E. Falkus, *The Industrialization of Russia 1700–1914* (London: Macmillan, 1972), pp. 63–71.

17. See Michael Ellman, "Did the Agricultural Surplus Provide the Resources for the Increase in Investment during the First Five Year Plan?" *Economic Journal* 85 (December 1975): 844–864 for a broad discussion of the sources of investment capital in the 1930s. A subtle discussion of the significance of agricultural surpluses in development and Soviet thought can be found in Chih-Ming Ka and Mark Selden, "Original Accumulation, Equity and Late Industrialization: The Cases of Socialist China and Capitalist Taiwan," *World Development* 14, no. 10 (1986): 1293–1310.

18. See G. Callendar, "The Early Transportation and Banking Enterprises of the States in Relation to the Growth of Corporations," *Quarterly Journal of Economics* 17, no. 1 (November 1902): 111–162; Colleen Dunlavy, "Mirror Images: Political Structures and Early Railroad Policy in the United States and Prussia," *Studies in American Political Development* 5, no. 1 (Spring 1991): 1–35.

19. Dunlavy, "Mirror Images," p. 12.

20. Roger Price, *An Economic History of Modern France* (London: Macmillan, 1981), pp. 72–73.

21. Price, *Economic History of Modern France*, pp. 78–79. A similar pattern can be seen in "Germany." After railroad building began in 1860 in the German states, the number of sheep fell rapidly from about 28 million head to less than 4 million head in 1900. In contrast, the number of pigs (a sign of both rising dairy production, as pigs are raised partly on skim milk, and rising urban meat consumption) rose from about 5 million to nearly 20 million over the same period. Wilhelm Abel, *Agricultural Fluctuations in Europe: From the Thirteenth to the Twentieth Centuries* (London: Methuen, 1980), trans. Olive Ordisk, p. 275.

22. Bairoch, "International Industrialization Levels," pp. 292, 294.

23. Some would even argue that on its own terms France was very successful and that the absence of bigness in French enterprise helps explain its success in niche markets for fine linens, woollens, glassware, and fashion products. See Michael Piore and Charles Sabel, *Second Industrial Divide* (New York: Basic Books, 1984); and Patrick O'Brien and Caglar Keyder, *Economic Growth in France and Britain 1780–1914* (Boston: Allen and Unwin, 1978).

24. Knut Borchardt, "The Industrial Revolution in Germany 1700–1914," in Carl Cipolla, ed., *Fontana Economic History of Europe*, vol. 4 (London: Collins/Fontana 1972–1977), p. 104.

25. Kocka, "Entrepreneurs and Managers in German Industrialization," p. 555.

26. Bairoch, "International Industrialization Levels," pp. 292, 294.

27. See Perry Anderson, *Lineages of the Absolutist State* (London: Verso, 1974), for a comparison of the consequences for capitalist development of different forms of feudalism in Japan and Eastern Europe; see E. H. Norman, *Origins of the Modern Japanese State*, John Dower, ed. (New York: Pantheon, 1975), on the Meiji Restoration and subsequent land reforms.

28. Norman, *Origins of the Modern Japanese State*, pp. 250–258.

29. Kaoru Sugihara, "Patterns of Asia's Integration into the World Economy 1880–1913," in Fischer et al., eds., *The Emergence of a World Economy*, vol. II, pp. 712–713.

30. Heita Kawakasu, "International Competition in Cotton Goods in the Late Nineteenth Century: Britain Versus India and East Asia," in Fischer et al., eds., *The Emergence of a World Economy*, vol. II, pp. 626–631.

31. Bairoch, "International Industrialization Levels," pp. 292, 294.

32. David Lake, *Power, Protection and Free Trade* (Ithaca, N.Y.: Cornell University Press, 1988).

33. Timothy McKeown, "Hegemonic Stability Theory and Nineteenth Century Tariff Levels in Europe," *International Organization* 37, no. 1 (1983): 73–91; Susan Strange and Roger Tooze, *Politics of Surplus Capacity: Competition for Market Shares in the World Recession* (Boston: Allen and Unwin, 1981).

# CHAPTER 5

# Agricultural Exporters
# and the Search for Labor

It is not the land that we want, but the use of it. The use of land may be
got . . . by means of exchange.

*Edward Gibbon Wakefield*

## The Opportunity for Ricardian
## Development and the Problem of
## Labor Supplies

The industrial revolution's voracious appetite for agricultural goods caused a
system of von Thünen agricultural production rings to emerge around a rapidly
industrializing northwest European "town." In Britain and then most of continental Europe the population exploded, and on a per capita basis consumed
more. Northwestern Europe's market for agricultural goods grew both absolutely and relatively, forcing von Thünen rings farther out into the world. The
expansion of those rings triggered successive waves of international migration.
It also created successive windows of opportunity for some peripheral areas to
develop and perhaps industrialize on the basis of agricultural exports back to
the European town.

These Ricardian development strategies relied on the availability of land
with the proper climatic characteristics to produce the foods and nonfood
agriculturals (NFAs) consumed first by British and then by European industry.
The right kind of land often created not just comparative advantage but also
absolute advantage in world markets. However, even when land was available,
labor often was not. The biggest limit on the expansion of von Thünen rings
around Europe was a pervasive shortage of labor. Would-be producers used
various forms of coerced labor to compensate for this shortage.

Successful Ricardian development strategies created their own problems.
Food and NFA supplies expanded faster than demand, as W. A. Lewis notes,
driving down prices toward the end of the nineteenth century. At this point
some economies simply failed, while a few shifted to Kaldorian strategies.

**110**

Most Ricardian developers did not respond to falling prices by discarding their Ricardian strategy in favor of a Kaldorian strategy. Instead, they shifted out of the production of the agricultural good experiencing falling prices and began producing a different agricultural good with stable or rising prices. This second effort at Ricardian development was also vulnerable to falling prices, creating a second crisis in the 1930s. This crisis forced countries to shift from Ricardian to Kaldorian development strategies. Again some countries missed the boat (or, in the case of colonies, were denied a boarding pass). Chapter 6 examines the institutional prerequisites for and paradoxes of successful Ricardian strategies, the problems that states encountered using them, and initial efforts to use Ricardian strategies to finance a shift to Kaldorian strategies, comparing the Australian, Argentine, and U.S. experiences. Chapter 12 picks up the shift from Ricardian to Kaldorian strategies in the rest of the periphery. Both chapters, in other words, look at the process of Ricardian development from the vantage point of Ricardian developers.

This chapter, however, examines the process from the outside. It looks first at the general expansion of von Thünen rings outward from Europe. Rising European demand for food and NFAs in effect turned industrial Britain and then the industrial triangle in northwestern Europe (defined by Hamburg-Paris-Frankfurt) into a gigantic von Thünen town; this town drew commodities from a global agricultural supply zone. As the urban population in this town grew, the very opportunities it created for Ricardian development in more distant zones like the U.S. Midwest, the Southern Hemisphere's temperate zones, and parts of Eastern Europe also created competitors for West European agricultural producers. Expanding urban demand caused a 50 percent expansion in world crop production from 1840 to 1880, of which half was in North America and Australia. World wheat acreage experienced even greater expansion: from 1885 to 1929 it grew 78 percent, with virtually all of this growth occurring outside Western Europe.[1] Paradoxically, the more successful European industrialization was, the greater the competitive pressures on European agriculture. It had either to adapt or to die.

The next section of this chapter deals with Irish agriculture, to show how adaptation occurred and how it generated the migrations that provided labor for the emerging agricultural periphery, and to demonstrate the successive expansion of von Thünen agrizones through a fixed geographic space. The Irish case is useful because, unlike most new agricultural supply areas elsewhere, Ireland already had a labor supply. In addition, Ireland's colonial status meant that the local state could not resort to protection as a way of slowing the passage of von Thünen rings through the geographic space Ireland occupied. Typically, agricultures threatened with death sought protection from their states. These more typical problems and responses are discussed in Chapter 8. Meanwhile, Ireland provides us with a sort of natural experiment in which market pressures to create von Thünen agricultural zones operated unimpeded. The discussion of Irish agriculture provides a control against which to judge what happened in other old and new supply areas.

The last part of this chapter concentrates on the creation of labor supplies in the agricultural periphery and on the shift from slavery to non-slave forms of labor, focusing mostly on Caribbean sugar and Southern Hemisphere wool production. Unsurprisingly, as their numbers and wealth increased, Western Europeans tended to eat or wear more of what they had historically eaten or worn, as well as some new foods that grew in temperate climates. Outside Europe the areas best suited to an expansion of temperate agriculture turned out to be in those relatively unpopulated lands lacking complex local state or political structures, namely, the Southern Hemisphere's temperate zones and temperate North America. This presented both a major opportunity and a problem. The absence of settled populations and states meant a relatively easy conquest and no prospect of the kind of continual guerrilla warfare present in Ireland. While this land was easy to take, the absence of labor meant that, once acquired, the land had little or no productive value until a labor force (or the combine harvester) could be created. Most colonists chose not to wait one to three centuries for the marriage of McCormack's reaper and the gasoline engine. Nor could they wait for the market to provide labor. Market mechanisms alone could not generate a flow of labor to these empty places. So at first the rise of wage labor and industrial capitalism in Britain and Europe created slavery virtually everywhere in the agricultural periphery.

## The Rise of Global Von Thünen Zones

Most industrial activity up to World War I involved the transformation of agricultural raw materials into some finished or intermediate good, so the industrial revolution's explosive increases in output implied proportionately increasing demand for inputs. Increased demand rapidly outpaced local production capacity. By 1871 over 90 percent of Britain's imports by value were foods and NFAs. While the share of foods and NFAs declined to about 80 percent by 1913, the absolute value grew from £234 million to £436.[2]

Specific commodities linked to leading sectors experienced exponential growth in demand, rising more rapidly than population. In 1759 Britain consumed about 1,000 tons of raw cotton per year, enough to make one shirt for every person there.[3] By 1787 Britain consumed roughly 10,000 tons, by 1829 100,000 tons, and by 1913 nearly 1 million tons. Demand doubled every twelve years in the early 1800s. Demand for wool, after mechanization of production in the 1830s, also doubled about every thirteen years, from 4,400 tons in 1820 to 196,000 tons in 1910. By 1900 Britain imported 80 percent of its wool consumption. Demand for wood (to produce machinery), for leather (to bind machinery and connect it to rotary power sources), and for tallow (to grease machines) rose similarly. In the 1890s expansion of the electrical industries and of bicycling caused a similar explosion in rubber imports.

Like its machines, the industrial revolution's growing urban proletariat also had to be fed. Despite massive emigration, Britain's population exploded during the nineteenth century, doubling from 10.2 million people in 1801 to 20.8 million in 1851 and almost doubling again to 37 million in 1901. Despite increased productivity and good inland transport, local food production increasingly lagged demand, forcing Britain to import vast quantities of food. By 1900 Britain imported 84 percent of its wheat, 37 percent of its beef and 47 percent of its mutton, and 53 percent of its dairy and poultry. About 17 percent of Britain's caloric needs came from sugar, virtually all of which was imported, and roughly 60 percent of its total calories were imported. As northwest Europe industrialized, it increasingly resembled Britain. Continental Europe's population (excluding Russia) also doubled in the 1800s, creating rings south and eastward from Europe. By 1914 Germany imported about one-fifth of its calories, concentrated mostly in meats and fats.[4]

Increased demand for agricultural raw materials and food created von Thünen–style agrizones on a global scale, with industrial Britain/Europe becoming a gigantic von Thünen town surrounded by a plethora of roughly concentric production zones. At the beginning of the 1800s, Britain imported only about 10 percent of its consumption of temperate agricultural products. Britain's supply zones essentially ended in Ireland (for grain). Nontemperate products had to come longer distances, from the U.S. South (cotton) and the West Indies (sugar), but with water transport these areas were "closer" than their distance in miles might indicate. The European economies were largely self-sufficient, excepting sugar and cotton. As Britain's population grew, it drew first on Holland, Denmark, and Prussia for grain. But industrialization in northwest Europe increased demand, causing Britain to import grain from the Ukraine, the United States, and eventually Argentina. By 1900 the growing population and diminishing local supply capacity of the British and European economies pushed their von Thünen agrizones outward as far as Australasia. (See Figure 6.1.) By 1900 dairy and extensive grain production emerged there alongside the grazing of sheep for wool and cattle for frozen beef. In the 1830s, Britain imported negligible quantities of fruit, vegetables, and live animals — all products of the innermost rings. By 1900 these imports traveled an average distance of 1,880 miles to London. Similarly, wool and hides, products of the outermost ring, traveled an average distance of 2,330 miles in 1830 but 10,900 by 1910 (Table 5.1).[5]

This global playing out of the von Thünen model caused enormous ecological changes around the globe, for only a few of the foods and raw materials grown for Britain and, later, Europe naturally occurred in the areas Europeans came to control. Even where they occurred naturally, their geographic range was fairly limited. We tend to perceive places like Australia, Malaya, Brazil, or Iowa as having a natural comparative advantage, but the ecology in virtually all of today's agricultural areas with obvious comparative advantages was in fact conquered and transformed by transplanted animals, weeds, pests, predators, and pathogens. Part of this process involved a great swap of plants and animals by the new and old worlds. In exchange for the potato and maize (corn), Europeans brought sugar from the eastern Mediterranean to the West Indies; released cattle, sheep, and horses in the Pampas, Australasia, and temperate North America; sowed wheat everywhere; and deforested enormous swaths of the Americas and Australasia.[6] It also involved the deliberate transplantation of species in order to create new supply areas, particularly in the tropics and Southern Hemisphere. For example, Brazil, the

TABLE 5.1

Expansion of Von Thünen Rings around Britain,
1831–1909, Selected Years[a]

|  | 1831–35 | 1856–60 | 1871–75 | 1891–95 | 1909 |
|---|---|---|---|---|---|
| Ring 1 |  |  |  |  |  |
| Fruit and vegetables | 0 | 324 | 535 | 1,150 | 1,880 |
| Ring 2 |  |  |  |  |  |
| Butter, cheese, eggs | 262 | 530 | 1,340 | 1,610 | 3,120 |
| Live animals | 0 | 630 | 870 | 3,530 | 4,500 |
| Ring 3 |  |  |  |  |  |
| Feed grains | 860 | 2,030 | 2,430 | 3,240 | 4,830 |
| Flax, linseed | 1,520 | 3,250 | 2,770 | 4,080 | 3,900 |
| Ring 4 |  |  |  |  |  |
| Wheat and flour | 2,430 | 2,170 | 4,200 | 5,250 | 5,950 |
| Ring 5 |  |  |  |  |  |
| Meat and tallow | 2,000 | 2,900 | 3,740 | 5,050 | 6,250 |
| Wool and hides | 2,330 | 8,830 | 10,000 | 11,010 | 10,900 |
| *Weighted average* | 1,820 | 3,650 | 4,300 | 5,050 | 5,880 |

[a]Average distance traveled by agricultural imports in miles.

SOURCE: J. Richard Peet, "The Spatial Expansion of Commercial Agriculture," *Economic Geography* 45, no. 4 (October 1969), p. 295.

source of rubber, became a coffee producer, while the British made Malaya into a rubber plantation.

The constant changes in the production profile of these areas also reveal the artificiality of the notion of natural comparative advantage. Comparative advantage changed as population growth in the European town turned former outlying zones into inner zones, making it profitable, rational, and necessary to produce higher-value-added goods. These shifts involved enormous changes in established production practices and thus the demand for labor. Changes in Irish agriculture clearly show this process. Ireland's proximity to industrial Britain meant that every von Thünen zone passed through its geographic space as Britain's population grew between 1600 and 1900. Ireland differs from most of the other areas we will discuss because it already had a labor supply and a state. It thus shows the expansion of rings without bringing in the problem of labor supply and state-building, which will be discussed later. Precisely because Ireland is an easy case, it allows us to isolate purely economic processes so that we can later introduce the effects of more political processes.

## Zonal Shifts in Irish Agriculture

Ireland started out mostly outside the frontier of the stock-raising ring and ended up in an inner zone of Britain's economy. As transportation links improved and as Britain's population grew, pushing agrizones offshore, Irish agricultural production processes, population, and exports changed. Each improvement in transportation brought Ireland one ring closer in to the

English town (which actually was growing out to Ireland), changing what Ireland produced. These transformations superficially support the notion that technologies diffused outward from Britain, for each change increased the value added per acre in Ireland. But markets drove this diffusion. As falling transportation costs brought Ireland's competitors in agricultural markets closer to England, Ireland had to invent new comparative advantages for itself. The Irish story thus reflects a complex interplay between market opportunities and local action. This story should be examined in depth because of what it reveals about the creation of new agricultural zones elsewhere and about the creation of labor for those new zones.

Before English colonization, the Irish herded cattle and grew oats. English colonization did not begin in earnest until the 1600s. Until then, Ireland had supplied very small amounts of money rent, wood, and iron for England. At that time, Ireland was over the frontier from the point of view of the English economy. It could only supply goods with either extremely low transportation costs (e.g., money) or quasi-luxuries. Because England was deforested, both wood and iron (a disguised export of wood via the consumption of charcoal) could be profitably exported. Because Ireland exported wood products to England, the interaction of the Irish and English economies left unchanged the peasantry's basic diet, which consisted largely of oats, milk, and beef (providing peasants had managed to keep the British from stealing their cattle).

During the seventeenth century, all this changed as London's population grew. Ireland became part of the outermost grazing ring, supplying range-fed cattle to England. Cattle exports, averaging 60,000 head in the mid-1600s, accounted for 75 percent of Irish exports.[7] Meat began to disappear from the peasantry's diet at this point, and the specter of a year-round Lent ignited a rural Catholic rebellion. Oliver Cromwell restored English rule, driving the population down to 900,000 by slaughtering thousands of Irish and exporting others as slaves to British sugar and tobacco plantations in the Caribbean. With order restored, Anglo-Irish landlords expanded their production of low-quality beef to the point where they posed a competitive challenge for English producers. Consequently, in a response later imitated in Europe, the English closed their market to nonmainland producers, including their Anglo-Irish kin, in 1666. This action diverted Irish beef exports, as salt beef, to the Royal Navy and to the West Indian colonies.

From 1700 on, the number of cattle increased rapidly as these markets grew. The Irish peasantry found its diet shifting from oats to potatoes as "cattle ate men" in the Irish version of the enclosures. Landlords pushed peasants off oat-producing land and onto wastelands so that the landlords could graze their cattle on former oat fields. Peasants unsuccessfully resisted this displacement, and those arrested were again shipped off to the West Indies to eat salt beef and make sugar and tobacco. The rest converted former wastelands to potato fields, creating a large number of smallholdings.

As in urban-centered microeconomies, the introduction of the potato promoted this compression of the population. The potato's higher caloric yield per acre allowed the peasantry to subsist on a smaller area while freeing up land for other uses. The population increased slowly, reaching 1.7 million by 1739. At that point, potatoes constituted half of local food consumption, and virtually all meat was exported, which removed it from the peasantry's diet.

The British population doubled during the 1700s. Consequently, Britain became a consistent net grain importer by the early stages of the industrial revolution, as demand outstripped mainland grain production. Politics and location made Ireland the major supplier of these grain imports, and grain soon displaced beef as Ireland's major export. Foster's Corn Law in 1784 subsidized Irish exports to Britain until the Union of Britain and Ireland opened the British market to Irish grain. The British Corn Law also favored Irish grain over somewhat cheaper competitors in the Baltic. Under these influences, the area tilled for grain increased sixfold from 1784 to 1805 and peaked at 272,000 hectares in 1846. In the 1780s Ireland had been a marginal net exporter of grain; by the 1800s it exported ten times more grain than it imported and provided half of British grain imports. Where low-quality cattle had displaced peasants in the 1700s, grain now displaced both in the early 1800s.

Rising grain exports presented Anglo-Irish landlords with a dilemma. In order to grow more grain, they had to push cattle and peasants off the land, but to harvest that grain they needed more labor. Landlords resolved the dilemma by compressing the peasantry's smallholdings, forcing them into an increasing, almost exclusive reliance on the potato. These displacements provoked a century-long guerrilla war against landlords. (With postrevolution America useless as a prison and African slavery institutionalized in West Indian sugar production, Irish prisoners were now sent to Australia.) About 1 million Protestant cottagers began migrating to the North American colonies. Despite rising emigration, the population rose from 5.4 million in 1805 to nearly 8 million by the 1840s.[8] So Irish grain and potato production rose steadily in tandem.

The interaction between rising grain production and rising potato consumption on a shrinking area reached its natural limits in the 1840s during the Famine. Although the potato blight (1845–49) triggered the Famine, the population was already debilitated and any further increase in grain production would have created a demographic catastrophe. Roughly 1 million peasants starved while grain exports to England increased. (The same process can be seen today; Ethiopia continuously exported livestock foods like rapeseed, linseed, and cottonseed meal during its catastrophic 1984 famine.) Another 4.3 million people emigrated between 1851 and 1918. Why were landlords unconcerned about this sudden shrinkage in their labor force?

The doubling of the British population had pushed its agricultural supply zones outward once again, creating both a threat and an opportunity for Anglo-Irish landlords. The repeal of the Corn Law in 1846 confronted Irish producers with world market competition from Prussia, Denmark, and Russia, which had more extensive acreage and cheaper, more docile labor. However, Ireland *was* positioned to export higher-quality live cattle for fresh slaughter and fresh cream, so landlords switched from wheat production to these goods. This shift caused the landlords' harvest labor requirements to drop so precipitously that emigration slightly outpaced the rate of natural increase. Meanwhile, grain acreage fell from its 1846 peak of 272,000 hectares to 18,000 hectares in 1887.[9]

This outcome had been foreshadowed in 1824 with the first regular steamship connection to Britain. This induced Protestant colonists in Northern Ireland and some farmers around Dublin to export eggs and butter. The landlords' continuous conversion of production from wheat to cattle grazing during 1848–1914 eliminated thousands of Irish smallholders, provoking Ireland's last, longest, and greatest rebellion against the English. Smallholders and the village and urban middle classes united under Charles Parnell's Home Rule party to press for self-governance. Meanwhile, peasants and landless laborers united behind the violent Irish National Land League. This dual struggle matured into the two-wing Sinn Fein–IRA struggle and eventually won independence in 1922 for the 26 southern counties, which formed the Republic of Ireland. Irish agriculture still sits in the innermost ring, supplying fresh meat and dairy goods for Britain, but with a family farmer–based agriculture that reflects the diminishing power of Anglo-Irish landlords.

## Slavery as a Last-Resort Labor Supply

European industrialization re-created Ireland's experience around the world, as von Thünen production rings rippled outward, but with one key difference: the best places for production of temperate agricultural goods lacked an existing population to serve as a labor force, and the second-best places lacked a tractable labor force. If not for this key limiting factor, the transformation of available agricultural land into supply zones for Europe would have been even faster. Although the industrial revolution triggered enormous population movements, prior to 1800 few people moved voluntarily. Of an estimated 9 to 15 million transatlantic migrants before 1800, fewer than 10 percent were free; most of the unfree were slaves from Africa. After 1800 coerced labor played a declining but still significant role, particularly for non-Europeans. Most of the roughly 50 million European migrants during the nineteenth century went voluntarily, that is, not as indentured servants. In contrast, most of the 50 million Asian migrants went as indentured labor and an additional 3 million Africans as slaves. Because labor represented the great limiting factor to agricultural transformation, most production in the New World and Asia relied on some form of involuntary labor: slaves, indentured servants, convicts, or peasant production compelled by imperial authority. What explains the labor shortage, and why did coercion give way to nominally free labor later in the 1800s?

### Explaining Slavery: Frontiers, Workers, and Coercion

Von Thünen and economist W. A. Lewis provide two opposite models that explain the initial resort to coercion and its eventual replacement by market forces. They come to the same general conclusion, however, albeit from different directions reflecting their different premises: wages at the frontier had to be high enough to draw people out of subsistence production. They part company in their definition of what was "high enough." For von Thünen high enough was quite high, and for Lewis, quite low. Actually, von Thünen is talking about peripheries with high land-to-labor ratios, and Lewis about peripheries with low land-to-labor ratios.

Von Thünen starts with his isolated state model, assuming an active, commercialized economy centered on an urban area. This economy has a frontier past which, owing to the high cost of transportation inward to the town, production for the urban market is uneconomical. Only subsistence production takes place in the transfrontier area. Von Thünen assumes that the availability of free land just outside the outermost ring allows workers simply to migrate over the frontier and to establish a self-sufficient existence. To pull workers back into the system of agrizones, a farmer must offer these transfrontier workers a wage greater than the implied value of production possible on their own subsistence farm. The availability of land makes von Thünen's frontier wage very high.

Like von Thünen, Lewis assumes a capitalist zone, corresponding to von Thünen's urban-centered zone, and a subsistence zone, corresponding to the transfrontier area.[10] Unlike von Thünen, Lewis assumes no open land over the frontier. Instead, he assumes that absolute overpopulation characterizes the subsistence sector. By this he means that the marginal productivity of labor in the subsistence sector is so low that any subtraction from the labor supply does not decrease production in the subsistence sector. Lewis agrees with von Thünen that the wage necessary to induce someone out of subsistence production into the capitalist economy equals the implied value of subsistence production, as well as an increment for the economic and social costs of dislocation. However, the labor surplus keeps that wage very low.

Both models assume that the actors they describe are pure economic beings for whom a positive wage differential suffices to impel greater effort. In the language of economics, they assume forward-leaning labor curves. Suppose, however, that those actors have backward-leaning labor curves. Then higher wages lead to fewer hours of work. Actors simply maintain their desired level of consumption by working fewer but better-paid hours. On the basis of studies in India, Colin Clark calculated that the inducement wage — the wage necessary to draw people over the frontier — had to be about twice the subsistence wage. Presumably, this doubling would apply in both the Lewis and the von Thünen frontier situation. In von Thünen's case, with available land, only extremely high wages would induce transfrontier labor to participate in labor markets inside the frontier. And in Lewis's case, even moderately high wages might not induce labor market participation. Peasants might be happy producing just enough to feed themselves and buy goods they cannot produce locally. Why work harder?

Von Thünen and Lewis explain the origins of coercion and its transformation. Would-be agricultural capitalists faced a dilemma. Empty places — places without a rooted peasantry, landlords, and a state — were the best places for production. As it happened, most of the empty places were in temperate climatic zones suited for the bulk of the foods and NFAs that

Europeans devoured. In empty places would-be capitalists did not have to pay the political, social, and police costs of controlling an extant peasant population and stealing land; in Ireland these costs had proven quite high. In empty lands like the temperate zones of the Americas, Australasia, and southern Africa, von Thünen frontiers meant owners had to use bound labor to prevent their workforce from walking over the frontier onto available land. (Actually, these places were not absolutely empty, for many people did live there already. As we will see, however, they either died out or were killed off.)

In full places, with their high population density, would-be capitalists had access to labor but often could not use it. In those areas, owners' ability to find a steady workforce depended on their ability to squeeze peasants out of the subsistence economy. Accomplishing this objective was fairly difficult. First, even outside the temperate zones, in most cases the great agricultural supply zones came into being in empty areas. The great tea plantations of Assam and Ceylon, the rubber plantations of Malaya, the coffee plantations of Africa, and the palm and coconut oil plantations everywhere were started in empty highlands with imported workers.

Second, most of the areas with settled populations that did engage in extensive commerce had been doing so for hundreds of years. Peasants were already responsive to market or landlord pressures to boost production. Equally important, landlords were unwilling to simply move out of the way just because Europeans wanted them to do so. The pepper coasts of India best exemplify this situation.

Third, few areas really approximated Lewis's unlimited supply of labor model. In most places, peasants did not have to rely on the market for their survival. Simply making them increase production was problematic, without also trying to get them to work outside the subsistence zone. Wage work generally was discretionary.

Wherever would-be agricultural capitalists faced von Thünen frontiers they resorted to coercion to remedy their lack of labor. As these von Thünen transfrontier areas filled in and began to resemble Lewis's transfrontier subsistence zone, coercion relaxed. In most places, however, Lewis-type subsistence zones came into existence only through the application of state or political power. The colonized temperate zones of the Americas and the Southern Hemisphere started out closely resembling von Thünen's frontier situation. Tropical Asia began somewhere in between von Thünen and Lewis, but pressure from the colonial authorities' tax and land tenure policies transformed it into a Lewis-type frontier.

We will consider each of these transitions by looking at a specific case. The West Indies began as a von Thünen–type frontier, but after manumission from slavery it moved closer to a Lewis-type situation with low wages. Australia and Argentina began as a von Thünen frontier, but state action closed the frontier prematurely, creating an open but high-wage labor market. British colonial policy in India created a Lewis-type frontier in which parts of India served as subsistence zones in relation to commercial production located inside and outside India.

In the temperate zones of the Americas (Argentina, Chile, Uruguay, the

Rio Grande do Sol region of Brazil, the United States, and Canada) and some of its tropics (the Caribbean littoral and most of Brazil), in Australasia, and in southern Africa, European incursions quickly eliminated fairly large local populations, thus eliminating local sources of labor. The combination of disease, deliberate extermination, and ecological change caused by significant European incursions into these areas destroyed local populations, including areas with population densities rivaling Europe's.[11] European predators, like dogs, and domesticated animals, like pigs, horses, and cattle, thrived and often became feral in the empty places in the Americas, driving local species out of their ecological niches. Ecological change and demographic collapse wiped out the initial labor supply in these areas. Why didn't the Europeans simply replace them, filling in the empty places?

Eventually the Europeans did just that. After all, Europeans ought to have been and were able to thrive in those areas, and today "European emigrants and their descendants are all over the place."[12] However, from 1500 to roughly 1824 the number of voluntary European migrants was extremely low. Most Europeans still lived in microeconomies, where their direct access to land gave them a secure existence. Getting to the Americas, and later Australasia, required an enormous amount of money and also had huge social and emotional costs. Therefore, where people could still feed themselves, push factors as outlined by Lewis were weak, as were the pull factors described by von Thünen. America was a raw, unknown, and dangerous place that yielded an uncertain improvement in living standards. Even counting involuntary immigrants, before 1824, only about 1 to 2 million Europeans migrated to the Americas — less than 10 percent of the entire transatlantic flow.

Even that minimal number did not create much of a labor force in the Americas. Once there, many migrants died; among indentured servants only about 20 percent lived to see the end of their term of bound labor.[13] Others dropped out of the labor market voluntarily; they crossed the frontier and went native, intermarrying with indigenous peoples and melting into the countryside. They and their descendants served as intermediaries between surviving indigenous peoples and the markets for some of the goods those people hunted and gathered. Métis in Québec/Canada, gauchos in the Argentine/Uruguayan Pampas, llaneros in Colombia, vaqueros in northern Mexico, griqua in southern Africa, cossacks in the eastern Ukraine, and, a rare naval example, buccaneers in the Caribbean — all facilitated a trade in beaver, hides, jerked meat, and the like. Yet these people did not constitute a stable, disciplined workforce capable of producing the consistent, continuous, and sizable flow of raw materials England's industry demanded. Moreover, because weapons were an essential part of their means of production, these intermediary populations also undercut any local state's monopoly of violence and thus its stability.

Since markets alone could neither restore original native populations nor pull in European replacements, would-be exporters resorted to slavery and coercion everywhere in the outermost von Thünen rings supplying Britain and northwest Europe. We tend to think of slavery in the United States as the great exception to the rule that settler colonies were born free, while the Caribbean and tropics were born slave colonies. Appearances are deceiving. Slavery occurred in all but one of the temperate zone colonies as well as the more obvious plantation economies in the tropics and subtropics. Temperate zone slavery started out in the disguised forms of convict labor and indentured servitude. Meanwhile, slavery in the tropics and subtropics mutated into a form approaching that of Eastern European serfdom, particularly after it was paired with indentured labor. If the United States is exceptional, it diverges for two reasons. Because of the dynamic demand for cotton and the relatively open frontier, it took longer for slavery in the United States to change to a peasantlike situation than it did elsewhere. On the northeastern coast one could find virtually the only sizable collection of pre-1800 voluntary migrants anywhere. These, like most voluntary migrants, were religious fanatics, suggesting that the only difference between the English and Iberian colonies is happenstance: England's religious fanatics reproduced, whereas Iberia's entered the priesthood and convent.

All in all slavery was a last-resort kind of labor. Despite its high purchase and supervision costs it was used mainly because of the utter insufficiency of any other kind of labor, including wage labor.

## Open Slavery in Response to Von Thünen Frontiers: Caribbean Sugar

Slavery emerged as a last-resort effort to overcome extreme labor shortages in the von Thünen–type frontiers in the Atlantic and West Indian (Caribbean) islands. Slaves were used almost exclusively to produce high-profit agricultural commodities, because slavery was very expensive. Only highly productive agricultures growing very valuable crops could afford it for long periods of time. In the Americas, slavery is associated with sugar, a mildly addictive food; tobacco, a highly addictive drug; and cotton, the raw material for the industrial revolution's leading sector. Sugar is the most interesting of these crops, because slavery and sugar have been linked from the eastern Mediterranean in the 1200s to Cuban manumission in 1886.

Sugar is valuable as a crop because of its high productivity in terms of calories created per acre. One acre of subtropical land under sugar yields about 8 million calories; to produce the same amount with potatoes requires 4 acres, with wheat 9 to 12 acres, and with beef about 135 acres.[14] Sugar by-products can be burned for steam or used as animal feed. Its high productivity made it profitable to pay for the kidnapping of humans and their shipment, with extraordinary wastage, to distant areas. High demand in Europe for this mildly addictive food assured high prices.

The Portuguese started production of sugar with African slaves off the coast of Africa. There was nothing unusual about the use of slavery in sugar production. The Venetians had been using Slavs (captured and sold by Christians and then Turks in Constantinople) as slaves to make sugar on Mediterranean islands ever since the Crusades. Portugal itself already had a large slave population acquired during the reconquest of Iberia from the Muslims. For the Portuguese, Africa was a convenient source of bodies. It already had an established, though small, slave trade. The introduction of American crops like the potato and corn (maize) facilitated the expansion of African slavery by helping to double the West and Central African populations (despite slaving) from 1500 to 1800.[15] Hence, the peculiar aspect of slavery was not its existence, but its scale.

The Portuguese landed in Madeira in 1402, in the Azores in 1430, and in São Tomé (off present-day Cameroon) in 1470. Disease, slaughter, and Portuguese efforts to use them as slaves killed off the indigenous population in each area. Emigration from Portugal itself was very low, totaling perhaps 40,000 people in the 1500s and 1600s combined, and thus unable to provide more than a minimal administrative and military presence for a Portuguese empire stretching from Brazil to Malacca. Thus it was that the Portuguese resorted to slavery to man (almost literally) their sugar plantations. The Portuguese experience with slaves on islands near Africa naturally led them to repeat this scenario in Brazil after 1520. From 1450 to 1600, Portuguese sugar planters in Brazil and Dutch, French, and English imitators in the West Indies bought about 275,000 African slaves. As the imitators caught up with and surpassed the Portuguese, the flow of slaves from Africa increased rapidly. From 1600 to 1700 about 1.3 million slaves were sent to the greater West Indies, with Brazil absorbing about 40 percent, and the English, French, and Spanish colonies each about 20 percent. During the 1700s demand for sugar and then tobacco boomed. British North America and the British and French sugar islands split another 6 million or so slaves. Finally, despite British efforts to stamp out the slave trade after 1807, Cuban and Brazilian sugar and coffee production absorbed another 2 million slaves until 1870.[16]

The Dutch, French, and British established sugar production with slaves in a two-stage process. First, each set up the slave-sugar system on a small island, respectively, Curaçao, Martinique, and Barbados. These relatively small islands served as incubators for plantation systems that were later deployed on a larger scale after 1750. When improved transportation made it possible to exploit part of the interior of the larger Caribbean islands, they shifted production, respectively, to Surinam, Haiti (then known as St. Domingue), and Jamaica, as well as to a myriad of other nearby islets. On each island, slavery evolved away from a pure slavery into a situation resembling that of Eastern European serfdom, and eventually, after manumission, indentured labor replaced slaves.

Dale Tomich's fine-grained study of Martinique details this transition nicely.[17] Labor demand in sugar production varied considerably over the course of a year. Harvesting and processing had to be done quickly and required massive amounts of labor. Sowing and routine maintenance required much less labor. Plantation owners permitted their slaves to work their own gardens, thus freeing them from feeding their slaves during off-peak periods. Over time and with considerable struggle, the slaves' rights to both free time and land increased. By the 1800s masters had to pay slaves when they wanted to absorb slaves' plots into cane production, and slaves could inherit plots. So slaves essentially had property rights in their plots. Increased property rights and built-in free time meant that masters could in effect extract a labor rent of only 5 to 5.5 days per week for their land, much like the Polish landlords in the 1500s. Hence, slaves had become serfs.

Manumission (or, in Haiti's case, revolution) simply changed this de facto status to a de jure status, reinforcing this situation of quasi-serfdom. Despite legal freedom, most ex-slaves continued to work on plantations as part-time, part-year workers, who now truly had to fend for themselves in the off-season. Owners initially opposed manumission but found they could live with it. Manumission freed owners from the necessity of feeding slaves during slack periods of the year. Manumission threw all ex-slaves into the nascent subsistence economy on the periphery of the plantation. While plantation owners still needed labor, they could buy labor in discrete amounts that corresponded to their need for labor.

From the point of view of ex-masters, this situation worked best on the smaller islands. The smaller islands had no frontier between cultivated and wild land; the ocean stopped slave-serfs from running away. On the larger islands and continental coastal areas like Surinam, however, the availability of unused but arable land in the interior made it possible for some ex-slaves simply to walk across the frontier and create a subsistence life, often joining existing communities of runaway slaves. In Jamaica, for example, ex-slaves walked up the mountainside, grew dreadlocks, and glared red-eyed at labor recruiters coming up from the coastal plantations. They were useless as a labor force for the plantations, but their presence made it possible for plantation owners to import *nonslave* labor for the first time. Manumission made it physically possible to use indentured labor, because it closed the frontier on the larger West Indian islands and the Caribbean littoral.

With ex-slaves covering all the land available for subsistence, incoming indentured workers had no option but to continue working for wages once they arrived. Since successive waves of voluntary and involuntary migrants to the area could not escape over the frontier, slavery yielded to a cheaper and more elastic form of workforce.

## "Covert" Slavery? Wakefieldism in the Temperate Colonies

European transformation of the tropics generally gets more attention than its transformation of temperate zones. However, the temperate zones were more important than the tropics in terms of global investment flows and the supply of agricultural raw materials. Europe's industry and people could have lived without tropical jute and vegetable oil, but not without temperate wool and wheat. Subtropical cotton is the only real exception to this generalization. Like those in the tropics, European settlements in temperate areas also began as von Thünen frontiers, and production started with various forms of involuntary labor: indentured servants and convicts in North America, convicts in Australia, slaves and forced labor in Latin America's southern cone. As in the West Indies, these coerced labor regimes gave way to open labor markets. What explains the transition? Australia and Argentina are the most interesting examples.

As in America, few voluntarily came to Australia at first. When the American Revolution closed off their usual dumping ground, the British started shipping convicts to Botany Bay. Like tropical slavery, the convict labor regime passed through a period in which production was clubbed out of the labor force. Like the tropics, this passed into a less malign regime in which owners conceded considerable autonomy to their convict workforce in order to increase production. With the rise of sheep grazing for wool, the prison administration (i.e., the state) began to rent convicts to graziers for use as shepherds. The difference between this and West Indian slavery was at best a matter of two degrees: ownership rested in the state, not in individuals, and in principle convicts were freed once they had served their term. Otherwise, workers were essentially chattels.

Australia's twin in the Southern Hemisphere, Argentina, also relied on slave and coerced labor in the early 1800s. The various areas that became Argentina utilized overt African slavery well into the middle of the 1800s, with Africans constituting up to one-third of the population by some estimates. After independence, the state (such as it was — Argentina's great misfortune was perhaps not to have been run from London) in Buenos Aires imposed a system of coerced labor. Workers without papers showing current employment could be automatically impressed into the army; thus enlarged, the army set about to hunt down other potential workers.

The mechanization of wool textile manufacturing in the 1830s created intense demands for wool which rapidly outran Europe's own supply capacity. Western Europe's internal raw wool production peaked in the mid-1800s at around 200,000 tons. By 1895, however, British production alone consumed almost that amount, and German and Belgian production together an additional 340 tons per year. From 1840 to 1860 demand doubled. Rising prices spurred Australian and Argentine producers to increase output, but they found that convict and impressed workers did not make good shepherds. Argentine landowners began importing Irish shepherds displaced by British cattle; Australian graziers began political agitation to end shipments of convicts.[18] However, both were still living in a von Thünen frontier. How could they be sure that immigrants and freed labor would not cross the frontier?

Edward Wakefield, the English advocate of systematic colonization and a contemporary of von Thünen, solved their problem. Wakefield understood practically what both von Thünen and Lewis appreciated theoretically. Ironically, Wakefield worked out the answer while he was in debtors' prison, thinking about how it would be possible to re-create English society in new lands like Australia. English society rested on landownership by the gentry and hard work by the landless laborers they hired. The only way to assure that the right sort of people ended up possessing the land and that their social inferiors ended up working for them was for the state to set the price of land so high as to preclude landownership by the many. So Wakefield suggested a high minimum price at land auctions in the Australian colonies.

Although this sounds simple enough, it took time to institutionalize as policy, because de jure state ownership of land did not necessarily convey de facto control. Both would-be escapees from the labor market and would-be sheep graziers challenged state ownership. The effort to institute state owner-ship over land sparked conflicts in all the Southern Hemisphere societies: figures like Ned Kelly in Australia, Hone Heke in New Zealand, and Martin Fiero in Argentina all symbolize the conflict between state and property owners on the one hand, and free-ranging intermediary groups and indigenous peoples on the other.

In the Australian colonies and New Zealand, the state proved strong enough to institute and maintain wakefieldism, suppressing outlaws and more or less enforcing the principle of crown ownership of land by forcing squatters to pay rent. In Argentina the state was weak, almost nonexistent at periods, and so had a harder and more violent time instituting wakefieldism. Where the Australian colonies could suppress Jesse Jamesian bushrangers like Ned Kelly with police actions, the Argentine/Buenos Aires government had to mount sustained military campaigns against organized revolts like those of the gaucho montoneros in the 1850s. Owing to the weakness of its state, Argentina ended up with a private kind of wakefieldism where ranchers asserted control over all available land and backed their claim with private armies. Uruguay ended up with the reverse of wakefieldism: gauchos defeated the state's armies, and labor control crumbled in the resulting anarchy. Wakefieldism, public or private, succeeded in preventing an overly large leakage of labor across the frontier in the Southern Hemisphere dominions. Buenos Aires abolished slav-ery and the slave trade in 1853; beginning in 1851, the Australian colonies began to legislate against further transportation of convicts to Australia.

The shift from coerced to free labor in all the new temperate producers helped boost output of foods and NFAs. In turn, this increased output generated a steady stream of migrants from Europe. Competition from the new temperate producers forced many European peasants off the land. Crowding into nearby cities, they depressed wages, and both they and existing urban workers then took off for higher wages and more opportunity in the Southern Hemisphere and the United States. As in Ireland, the largest flows occurred when former wheat production zones encountered increased compe-tition from wheat producers farther out, particularly in the Americas. The peaks of migration from the United Kingdom, for example, occurred in the 1840s, 1880s, and 1910s, coinciding with the arrival of grain from the old U.S. Northwest, from the U.S. Midwest, and from Argentina and Canada. Migra-tion from the greater British isles averaged 6 people per 1,000; 19 million people migrated during the 1800s. This migration also included many skilled workers attracted to the industrial activity that occurred in conjunction with agricultural production.

Overall, 40 percent of the natural increase in Europe's population in the nineteenth century migrated, with about 60 percent of these going to the United States. Put another way, two out of every five surviving babies left Europe permanently. The significant immigrant influence in the United States is obvious and constant, but the immigrant influence on non-U.S. areas was even greater, since they started out with smaller populations. (It still is; immi-grants account for a higher proportion of Australia's population than the United States population.) Argentina absorbed 5.4 million immigrants, Canada

4.5 million, Australia 1 million, New Zealand 0.5 million, and South Africa 370,000. With their arrival, local land prices rose to the point where wakefieldism became unnecessary. People had to work for wages. In recognition of that fact, workers in all of these societies agitated for bans on non-European immigration, hoping to slow population growth and thus keep wages high. Why, aside from racism, were they afraid of being swamped by non-Europeans?

## Asian Migration: Creating Lewis Frontiers

Asians were also on the move, and, although in proportion to total population fewer migrated than in Europe, absolutely the numbers are almost the same. India and China supplied nearly 50 million migrants to new and old production zones during the nineteenth century, most of whom traveled as indentured labor.[19] With industrialization occurring, only 1 million Japanese migrated in a mixture of free and indentured labor. As noted earlier, indentured Indians replaced or supplemented Africans in sugar production in the West Indies and Africa's coastal islands, and supplied labor for emerging tea, rubber, palm oil, and sugar plantations in Asia and the Pacific. Chinese became miners in Malaya, cut sugarcane in Cuba, quarried guano in Peru, and in more limited numbers mined, built railroads, cooked, and did all manner of things in Australia and the Pacific coast of North America. Japanese tended coffee and pineapples in Brazil and Hawaii and gardened in California. Unlike Africans, indentured Asians did not travel as slaves, at least de jure, although their de facto work conditions and lack of personal freedom at times closely resembled chattel slavery. What explains the de jure difference and the motivation for seeking indenture?

Europeans in Asia encountered relatively durable states and societies that were able to resist outright colonization. They also found that they, not the locals, got sick. Most of Europe's diseases originally came from Asia, so the local population had one up on the Europeans, who had no experience with tropical diseases. Aside from a few exceptions, like Hong Kong, Asia remained Asian. European firms and colonial governments found it difficult to get enough European labor to do anything more than man the top layers of their administrative and military networks. As a result, in Asia European enterprises had to rely on Asian labor; and European armies had to depend on Asian soldiers.

Asia obviously did not have the kind of von Thünen frontier that disease created in the Caribbean basin, but, when the Europeans arrived, neither did it have a classic, overcrowded Lewis frontier. European colonial governments had to use various forms of coercion to get Asians to labor for them. Colonial policy in Asia and, later, Africa sought to create a Lewis-type frontier.[20] Africa was even further from being a von Thünen frontier than was Asia. Thus, even more coercion was applied to motivate wage work.

Precolonial Asia, despite occasional famines, was not overcrowded in Lewis's sense. Contrary to Lewis's model, the emergence of a commercial and export-oriented economy did not attract labor in search of higher wages from neighboring subsistence economies. The reverse happened. Imperial tax policies and laws that encouraged an expansion of commercial production in settled areas crowded peasants into smaller and smaller subsistence areas, just as in Ireland. In other words, rather than commercial agriculture drawing in labor from subsistence areas, the emergence of commercial agriculture often crowded workers off the land into subsistence areas. These displaced workers then flooded into newly opened export production zones elsewhere in search of any possible livelihood.

In India, for example, British tax and land policies caused a massive emigration of Tamils from southern India to a variety of new export agricultural areas. The British assigned landownership to individual farmers, or *ryots*, and introduced a fixed land tax. As in Japan, the tax forced peasants to reorient production toward the monetized, commercial economy. As in Japan, weak peasants lost their land as production for export began. Stronger peasants absorbed this land. Unlike Japan, the state did not use these revenues to industrialize the country. Instead, British colonial policy promoted increased market share for imported textile and household goods. So where landless peasants in Japan became a new urban labor force, in India they either crowded onto the land left over from commercial production or opted to emigrate.

Thousands of newly landless Tamils thus indentured themselves to work in the new rubber plantations in Malaya, in new tea plantations in the relatively empty highlands of Ceylon and Assam (in northeastern India), in new rice plantations in Burma, and in mines in Natal in southern Africa. Once there, they provided an expanded market for Indian rice exports, speeding the reorientation of rice production toward export markets and the process of emigration in an echo of the temperate zone – European agricultural interaction. About 1 million Tamilese, mostly from the lower castes, migrated during the 1800s, followed by a flood of exported rice. The rest of India saw similar processes.

Meanwhile, local populations avoided working on plantations, reinforcing planters' reliance on indentured labor. In Ceylon, the local Sinhalese population had an easy subsistence existence in the lowlands, just as native Malays had in Malaya. Why should a peasant family perform year-round backbreaking work on a tea or rubber plantation, especially when it could supplement its income by planting a few coffee trees?

The extraordinary lengths to which the British and French imperial authorities went to generate labor supplies in Africa also show this pattern of commercial expansion generating a surplus labor supply. Africa resembled a Lewis-type frontier even less than did Asia, for it had a lower labor-to-land ratio, capable of absorbing a rough doubling of population before 1900. Imperial authorities had to employ hut and head taxes paid in coin and mandatory production of cash crops to force the local peasantry into the market. Getting wage labor was even more difficult, as the British found in their southern African colony of Rhodesia.[21] African peasants in the Rhodesia area assimilated European plants and cultivation techniques. Their ability to assimilate European agricultural technologies enabled them to compete with

European farmers as a source of food for mining operations in South Africa proper. It also enabled those peasants who desired to maintain a transfrontier existence with limited contact with world markets to do so at relatively high levels of consumption for relatively little effort.

In either case, would-be British agricultural employers found themselves at a disadvantage: they could neither engage Africans as workers nor compete with African peasant producers. Settlers used their state to impose taxes, first in kind and then in cash, on African peasants, hoping that this would drive them into the labor market in search of cash wages. Instead, peasants stepped up their production for the market, earning cash by selling more food in the South African markets. Settlers then turned to a policy of land expropriation, forcing peasants into a serflike situation in which they offered their new settler landlords labor rents. Land expropriation also diminished the area available for subsistence production, forcing transfrontier peasants to shift from direct production and marketing to sale of their labor.

The Rhodesian case shows even more clearly than southern India the degree to which labor surpluses in Lewis-style transfrontier subsistence zones were as much a creation of politically deployed violence as of market forces. In Africa, European settlers deployed political power to generate a labor force for internal use; in India, the colonial state imposed taxes and intermediaries whose actions then generated a pool of labor willing to migrate; in the Southern Hemisphere, artificially high land prices kept workers inside the frontier. Aside from the postrevolutionary United States, simple market mechanisms rarely motivated migration for participation in a wage labor market.

The shifting legal status applied to laborers arose mostly from differing population levels at the time those laborers came to the places where they worked. Sugar and tobacco, which were most closely associated with slavery, took root at a point in time when population in the Americas was at its nadir. Extant slave systems in turn were extended to cotton production once the Native Americans were cleared out of the southeastern United States. Slavery everywhere mutated into a kind of serfdom, with rents paid in labor or in kind (via, e.g., sharecropping in post–Civil War America). Indenture flourished at a later date. The demand for products that could be produced in tropical Asian climates exploded at a time when Europeans could find (or make) few empty zones. Empty places in Asia tended to be surrounded by full places, so they lacked a frontier over which labor could escape. Plantation owners could therefore use indentured labor from foreign areas for tea, rubber, and vegetable oil production. These workers could not cross the frontier in the same way that manumitted slaves had on the larger Caribbean islands.

The industrial revolution thus created agricultural peripheries with noncapitalist labor forms. The expansion of industrial demand for agricultural goods also created new production zones in temperate areas. Like tropical America and Asia, these areas also started life with coerced labor, which was sometimes indistinguishable from slavery. In spite of their common origin in coerced labor and in spite of the ready availability of root stock for products demanded in industrial Europe, not all areas prospered equally. What explains the variation in the economic success of the agricultural periphery? Why did some areas develop much more than others using Ricardian strategies?

# Notes

1. Eric Hobsbawm, *Age of Capital, 1848-1875* (New York: Scribner, 1975), p. 179; Harriet Friedmann, "World Market, State and Family Farm," *Comparative Studies in Society and History* 20, no. 3 (1978): 546.

2. Brian Mitchell and Phyllis Deane, *Abstract of British Historical Statistics* (Cambridge: Cambridge University Press, 1962), pp. 298-301.

3. As in the previous chapter, all tons here are metric tons; 1 metric ton = 2,200 pounds.

4. J. Richard Peet, "The Spatial Expansion of Commercial Agriculture in the Nineteenth Century: A Von Thünen Interpretation," *Economic Geography* 45, no. 4 (October 1969): 297; Sidney Mintz, *Sweetness and Power: The Place of Sugar in Modern History* (London: Penguin, 1985), p. 113; Dale Tomich, *Slavery in the Circuit of Sugar* (Baltimore, Md.: Johns Hopkins University Press, 1990), p. 18; Avner Offer, *The First World War: An Agrarian Interpretation* (Oxford: Clarendon Press, 1989), pp. 25 and 81.

5. Peet, "The Spatial Expansion of Commercial Agriculture," pp. 295, 297.

6. Alfred Crosby, *Ecological Imperialism: The Biological Expansion of Europe 900-1900* (Cambridge: Cambridge University Press, 1986).

7. Richard Peet, "The British Market and European Agriculture, c. 1700-1860," *Transactions of the Institute of British Geographers* 56 (July 1972): 5.

8. Lest this seem unusually rapid, it should be noted that many poor countries today have even faster growth rates.

9. Peet, "The British Market and European Agriculture," p. 6.

10. W. A. Lewis, "Economic Development with Unlimited Supplies of Labour," *The Manchester School Journal*, 22, no. 2 (May 1954).

11. Crosby, *Ecological Imperialism*, remains the best general guide to this process.

12. Ibid., p. 2.

13. Eric Wolf, *Europe and the People without History* (Berkeley: University of California Press, 1986), p. 202.

14. Mintz, *Sweetness and Power*, pp. 190-191.

15. Wolf, *Europe and the People Without History*, p. 204.

16. Ari Zolberg, "Wanted but Not Welcome," in William Alonso, *Population in an Interacting World* (Cambridge, Mass.: Harvard University Press, 1987), pp. 36-73; Wolf, *Europe and the People Without History*, pp. 200-201.

17. Tomich, *Slavery in the Circuit of Sugar*, especially pp. 271-278. Similar processes appear to have been at work in the tobacco plantations of Virginia and North Carolina, until the demand for slaves in the expanding cotton South created an export trade from those two states to the states on the Gulf of Mexico. See Eugene Genovese, *Roll, Jordon, Roll: The World the Slaves Made* (New York: Pantheon, 1972).

18. See Philip McMichael, *Settlers and the Agrarian Question* (Cambridge: Cambridge University Press, 1984), on Australia, and James Lynch, *Argentine Dictator: Juan Manuel de Rosas* (Oxford: Oxford University Press, 1981).

19. Internal migration was also high: about 20 million Chinese migrated to Manchuria between 1900 and 1930.

20. Joseph Furnivall, *Colonial Policy and Practice: Burma and the Netherlands East Indies* (New York: New York University Press, 1956).

21. This section draws on Giovanni Arrighi, "Labor Supplies in Historical Perspective: Proletarianisation of the Rhodesian African Peasantry," *Journal of Development Studies* no. 3 (April 1970), pp. 180-234.

# CHAPTER 6

# Agriculture-Led Growth and Crisis in the Periphery: Ricardian Success, Ricardian Failure

It is quite as important to the happiness of mankind that our enjoyment should be increased by the better distribution of labour, by each country producing those commodities for which by its situation, its climate, and its other natural or artificial advantages, it is adapted, and by thus exchanging them for the commodities of other countries, as that they should be augmented by a rise in the rate of profits.

*David Ricardo*

The industrial revolution in Britain and Kaldorian late industrialization in much of Europe and in the U.S. Northeast created a space for Ricardian development elsewhere. Relatively steady growth in industrial country economies engendered equal or faster growth in peripheral agricultural production. The rise of these new production zones in turn induced massive waves of involuntary and voluntary migration out to those production zones, as distant agricultures displaced and transformed more proximate ones.

As we saw in Chapter 2, the opportunity to produce agricultural goods for Europe's von Thünen town did not guarantee development. Quite the contrary, out in the periphery created by Europe's town, the value produced per acre was necessarily low. How did some peripheral areas use Ricardian strategies to develop? In late industrializing Europe, industrialization rested on the concentration of verdoorn effects in local industry through timely and appropriate state interventions to deflect market pressures that would have displaced local industry.

Successful Ricardian development depended on state intervention to position an exporter advantageously in world markets and to reduce the peripheralizing effects of market pressures. The state in Ricardian developers did everything late industrializers' states did, and to an even greater extent. The state constructed both society and economy in all of the European settlements in the Southern Hemisphere and, to an unrecognized extent, in North America as well. The state organized inward flows of labor and capital and, confronted with a common period of crisis in the 1890s, in most cases helped to reorient the economy around a new Ricardian strategy using different agricultural exports.

Even more so than in most late industrializers in Europe, the state in the agricultural periphery controlled a fairly high proportion of investment. At any given time, these states controlled between one-quarter and half of all investment in their economies during the nineteenth century. This investment, primarily in rail systems and other social overhead capital, made it possible for private producers to undertake the massive export of agricultural and other primary products. Therefore, as with late industrializers, economic success among these agricultural exporters was relative and depended on the art of the state as much as on the art of the entrepreneur. Unlike late industrializers, Ricardian developers first had to construct states, and many were hampered by the presence of an externally imposed colonial state.

Putting aside the question of relative state competence, all Ricardian developers faced an extra, significant limitation that was not present in Kaldorian strategies. Ricardian strategies for development could be successful — contrary to many arguments that raw materials exporters face insurmountable obstacles. Raw materials exports could create a dynamic growing economy.[1] However, both food and to a certain extent NFA exports were vulnerable to the phenomenon expressed by Engel's law: as income rises, the proportion of income spent directly on food declines.[2] The same is true of fibers. This phenomenon led to boom and bust cycles in Ricardian developers. Booming demand for a particular export led many countries (and individual producers) to initiate production; production volumes soared; the market saturated; and prices fell. Paradoxically, falling prices did not stimulate increased consumption in industrial areas; instead, consumers diverted this extra income into higher quality foodstuffs.

Meanwhile, most Ricardian developers with colonial states faced an additional barrier to successful development. Usually, colonial governments are blamed — correctly — for deliberately hindering industrialization during their tenure. However, much of the industrialization that would have taken place in the periphery in colonized Asia and Africa did occur, because, as we saw in Chapter 4, market segmentation prevented European firms from penetrating local markets. Colonial governments hindered future development in a more significant way when they deliberately created Lewis frontiers in order to create a supply of labor for European enterprises. The oversupply of labor there depressed wages and thus inhibited investment across the economy. Why substitute expensive capital for cheap labor?

Successful long-term development for Ricardian developers thus rested on their ability to shift from one commodity to another, higher-value-added commodity when the first commodity experienced price declines. Alternatively, they had to be able to use the local demand for industrial inputs created by agricultural exports to create local industry. Most Ricardian developers managed the first, but only the United States, Australia, and Canada (and perhaps Holland) managed both of these in the nineteenth century. Most lived through a series of boom and bust cycles until the Depression of the 1930s, when a second set of Ricardian developers shifted to Kaldorian industrialization strategies.[3]

This chapter will look at Ricardian development in temperate agriculture, comparing Australia, Argentina, and the U.S. Midwest to show how a Ricardian strategy could lead to industrialization. It will stint tropical agriculture for two reasons. First, temperate agriculture was far more important for the world economy during the long nineteenth century. Second, it was difficult to industrialize using a Ricardian strategy, even in the relatively favorable terrain of the temperate zones, where states were at least nominally independent, demand for exports rose rapidly, and wages were high. If very few states actually succeeded under favorable conditions, it should not be surprising that areas with unfavorable conditions failed. As with late industrialization, failure was the norm and success unusual. This chapter will give less attention to some topics that usually receive treatment out of proportion to their economic importance, like the imperial scramble for Africa after 1880. From all perspectives, including most politico-military ones, Africa was marginal to the world economy centered in Europe.

## Temperate Agriculture and Ricardian Development

The temperate agricultural periphery included the U.S. Midwest, Siberia, and a group of countries we can call dominions for the sake of brevity. The dominions encompass a large and diverse set of societies in the Southern Hemisphere temperate zone. Four of them became self-governing British dominions: six Australian colonies (federated in 1901), New Zealand, four southern African colonies (federated as the Union of South Africa in 1910), and the two Canadas (federated in 1869 and eventually incorporating all of British North America). The dominions also include the areas of the Latin American southern cone which, after considerable conflict over borders, eventually turned into Uruguay and Argentina; arguably, Chile and Brazil's Rio Grande do Sul province should also be included in this zone. These were called informal dominions because their economic and social ties to Britain were as close as those of the formal colonies but without, of course, the political tie.[4]

These areas had five things in common:

~ Europeans displaced or eliminated the indigenous populations.

~ The economy grew using high-productivity (often mechanized), export-oriented agriculture as its leading sector.

~ All of the areas grew on the basis of extensive state intervention in the economy and borrowing overseas, and, in the case of the U.S. Midwest, from eastern bankers too.

~ All faced significant debt crises in the late 1880s and 1890s. Their states responded to these crises by creating new social classes to revitalize production and stabilize society.

~  Obviously, given what they made and sold, all actively acquiesced in British hegemony.

The dominions' economic significance in the nineteenth and, to a lesser extent, twentieth centuries is generally overlooked, although that of the United States is not. Quantitatively, in 1913 Australia's 4 million people alone exported £75 million of goods compared to a total trade in tropical agricultural goods of £438 million and total British agricultural imports of £464 million. The population of the tropics, while clouded by measurement problems, surely was more than six times Australia's population whether we take gross population or merely use those living in monocultural export zones. To Australia should be added exports from Argentina (£80 million), New Zealand (£23 million), Canada (£100 million), Uruguay, southern Africa, and, arguably, the U.S. Midwest and Siberia. The dominions received 40 percent of British overseas capital investment (60 percent if the United States is included); Australia alone received as much British capital as India. The six Southern Hemisphere dominions imported 125,000 miles of British-produced rails, and the United States another 125,000. Together, this amounted to roughly Europe's total trackage by 1914.

The qualitative impact on the division of labor is even more important. By making food cheap, U.S. and dominion exports enabled a rapid expansion of the British domestic market and its internal division of labor without a corresponding rise in nominal wages. In 1800 the average British worker family spent 75 percent of its budget on food, half of which went for bread. By 1900 only 33 percent of the budget went for food, and the average diet included considerable quantities of dairy and frozen meat from the dominions. Real wages in Britain rose about 60 percent from 1860 to 1900 because of falling prices for imported foods. (Figure 6.1 compares Britain's wheat imports from various supply regions.) The United States and dominions also provisioned slave plantations with jerked meats, provided the woollen industry with its raw material, and supplied much of the leather used in industrial production and for clothing. I will briefly touch on the most outstanding case of a successful Ricardian strategy, the United States, and then turn to the more typical cases in the dominions. The United States will get short shrift since its story is more familiar.

## Ricardian Growth in the United States

The United States emerged as the most successful Ricardian developer for five reasons.[5] First, simply, it was first! The United States began exporting staple bulk foods to, for example, the sugar islands as early as the 1600s. In the 1800s, the United States emerged as the first major overseas exporter of foods to Britain and then Europe. Because of its high productivity and location, it easily competed with and displaced exports from peasant-based agricultures in Eastern Europe by the 1860s. When the dominions finally developed into competitive food exporters at the end of the nineteenth century, this was partly because growing U.S. internal demand was absorbing a much larger share of total U.S. production and so pushing up the price of U.S. exports.

Second, as a consequence of the Revolution and even more so of the Civil

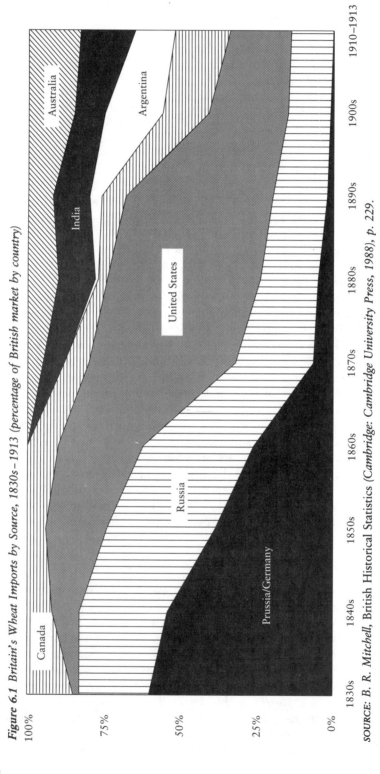

**Figure 6.1** *Britain's Wheat Imports by Source, 1830s–1913 (percentage of British market by country)*

SOURCE: B. R. Mitchell, *British Historical Statistics* (*Cambridge: Cambridge University Press, 1988*), *p. 229.*

134

War-inspired 1862 Land Grant Act, land was freely available, making the United States a much more attractive destination for migrants from Europe than the other agricultural societies. Overall, about three out of five migrant Europeans ended up in the United States, as did thousands of Chinese and Japanese. More migrants meant more farmers, even if many migrants stayed in cities or peopled midwestern towns. From 1870 to 1900 the number of farms and farm acreage doubled. The Revolution, the refounding of the United States as a stronger federal state in 1789, and the Civil War also constructed a powerful and durable state apparatus in the United States.[6]

Third, state intervention provided many of the collective and private goods needed for export agriculture. The individual states all intervened in the provision of rail and canal transport, as Chapter 4 notes. After the Civil War, the land grant system helped capitalize transcontinental railways, linking the agricultural heartland to export markets. Land grants were a particularly efficacious form of subsidy, because the value of the land the railroads received in part depended on their ability to promote agricultural production in adjacent areas.

In the pre-Civil War cotton South, the individual states also organized a flow of capital to private planters. The states set up quasi-public banks by giving them state bonds. Potential and existing planters could get capital by mortgaging their land to these banks; in return, the banks then gave the planters those bonds. Planters would sell those bonds in the global capital market, receiving British pounds, which they could then use to set up production. When those planters sold cotton overseas, they received pounds and dollars that they could use to pay the bank; the banks used those dollars to repay the state; and the state used those dollars to repay the original British lender. At least, in principle; many planters and a few states defaulted! Default or no, cotton production exploded in the 1800s, rising from 3,000 bales in 1790 to 180,000 bales in 1810, to 732,000 bales in 1830, and, finally, to 4.5 million bales in 1860. Despite the Civil War, cotton production continued to grow, doubling to over 10.1 million bales by 1900.

Fourth, the federal state, through the U.S. Department of Agriculture (U.S.D.A.) Extension Service, also provided agriculture with grading services (to improve the image of U.S. exports in world markets), with a vast amount of technical and scientific information and their accompanying new seed varieties, and with marketing information. The 1862 legislation that created the homestead system also created a system of land grant colleges that initially specialized in agricultural R&D, generating the information disseminated by the U.S. Department of Agriculture. When the growth of cotton output began to level off, corn (maize) and wheat output and exports picked up because of this extensive state support. Corn output doubled from 1870 to 1900; wheat output doubled from 1870 to 1880 and then rose another 20 percent by 1900.

Finally, the distance of the U.S. market from Europe provided a degree of covert protection, which Congress supplemented with overt tariffs. This huge market, the need to provide inputs for agricultural production, and the need to process agricultural outputs before export created a wide range of industries. The U.S. steam engine industry, for example, grew by providing small simple engines for the thousands of steamboats plying the 30,000 miles of navigable rivers and canals in the United States. Because this engineering industry provided marine engines, rather than the railroad and industrial engines Europeans produced, it obtained a degree of natural protection. This process can be seen in a wide range of industries attached to agriculture.

From 1850 to 1880, for example, flour milling was the single largest industry by value of product in the United States, the fourth largest by value added, and generally the highest or second highest in terms of capital intensity, with productivity per unit labor twice that of the U.S. manufacturing average. Whether or not railroads served as a leading sector in the U.S. economy, clearly advances in transportation per se were driven by the potential volume of agricultural produce that could be exported or shipped to the East Coast.[7] By the 1870s agricultural machinery accounted for 25 percent of U.S. machinery output. Equally important, much generic manufactured output, particularly of metal goods, was consumer nondurables for farm families, including items like kettles, pots, plows, stoves, axes, nails, guns, and saws. Despite their small scale, these many diverse industries accounted for roughly one-third of U.S. manufacturing output by 1890.[8]

## The First Ricardian Boom in the Dominions

After a variety of mini-booms based on different commodities, the dominions boomed together on the basis of wool exports, while the U.S. Midwest was booming on cotton and then wheat. As the previous chapter noted, European settlements in the dominions (New Zealand aside) began as von Thünen frontiers, and thus production started with involuntary labor. As in the tropics, the original use of coerced labor represented a last-resort choice. The dominions started out as relatively uneconomic imperial outposts. Buenos Aires was a minor "backdoor" port for Peru, exporting hides; New Zealand an "R&R" stop for whalers, exporting wheat to the Australian prisons; the Cape Colony in southern Africa a way station to the Indian Ocean, exporting fruit; Australia a dumping ground for Britain's perceived human refuse, exporting seals and whales; and Canada's maritime colonies provisioning grounds for the more important fish and fur trades. Consequently, they remained relatively underpopulated. As late as 1825 the nonindigenous population of Australia was around 70,000; of Buenos Aires about 50,000; and of New Zealand as few as 1,000. In contrast, even as small an island as Barbados had a European population of 10,000 as early as 1700; tens of thousands of slaves would augment this total in the 1700s.

Just as labor was in short supply, potential wool producers lacked capital in two senses. On the one hand, they personally lacked the capital necessary to expand production by buying more sheep, setting up homesteads, and shearing sheds, and to carry them through the growing season until they could harvest their wool and get paid for it. On the other, their raw colonial societies lacked even the most rudimentary infrastructure, including the infrastructural sine qua non, transportation. Just as European planters in Asia found themselves confronted by an enormous but unusable pool of labor, would-be graziers in the dominions confronted an enormous but unusable landscape.

During the first third of the 1800s, shortages of labor and capital in the dominions were irrelevant, for the European periphery could have supplied enough wool to meet industrial demand. Two developments changed this. First, the reorientation of Europe's peripheral agriculture to the British town forced its own peripheral wool growers to shift to finer, higher value wools. This change opened a space for the dominions to supply coarser wool. Second, wool textile production was mechanized in the 1830s. With rising demand, producers and potential producers found themselves unable to expand production as much as they would have liked. Because price signals alone could not induce capital and labor to migrate to the dominions, dominion states began creating systems for providing capital and labor to expand the production of wool and hides.

The ideal response took the following form. States abolished coerced labor but closed the frontier so as to assure that migrants stayed in the labor market. States used their own credit to borrow overseas capital for infrastructure investment. This infrastructure investment, primarily in rail systems, opened new land for productive exploitation and also provided employment for new migrants. Sale of this new land allowed states to amortize their debts and to sponsor more immigrants to work on newly opened land. Ideally, this created a self-sustaining cycle in which foreign investment funded railroads, which opened new land, which attracted new migrants, whose imports of consumer and capital goods provided the state with customs revenue to service its debts, thus sustaining the state's creditworthiness and allowing it to borrow more money for more railroads. First, however, there had to be states.

In each country the political struggles of the 1850s and 1860s revolved around efforts to create new states or expand existing state structures and activities. The core structures of these states mirrored those in Europe. In the 1850s and 1860s agricultural exporters tried to establish consistent and centralized fiscal apparatuses and to assure internal order by monopolizing the means of violence. British hegemony and the maritime frontier largely guaranteed external security, though somewhat less so for Uruguay than the others. In Australia, Britain's passage of the Australian Colonies Government Act in 1850 created a space for the emergence of local constitutions, legislative arrangements, and institutions. Although these varied across the six colonies, all took control over customs and land sale revenue. All began systematically to stamp out bushrangers (small-scale sheep-rustlers living off the land). And all forced sheep graziers to acknowledge crown ownership of land through payment of land rents.

In Argentina, creation of a central fiscal and military apparatus took more time, because Argentina's longer history of settlement had created several competing and autonomous centers of power, and after the overthrow of Spanish rule these could not reconcile their differences. After export-oriented graziers overthrew the dictator of Buenos Aires province in 1851, a decade-long civil war erupted between inland provinces and Buenos Aires. The steady convergence of the economic interests of Buenos Aires and the other provinces with access to water transport provided a basis for compromise, because the other provinces also wanted to enter the wool trade. Despite its control over customs revenue, Buenos Aires was never able fully to centralize control over other revenues or fully to establish control over the provincial militias. (This makes the significance of being first for the United States clear; it was busy exporting and growing while others were trying to birth states.) All of these states were instrumental states. In these extremely small societies, public and private elites almost completely overlapped, either in one person or through extended families. Thus, the behavior of dominion states is understandable. They strove to maximize the private good of the graziers who controlled them.

In the 1850s both Argentine and Australian graziers sought more reliable supplies. The prior chapter discussed the shift to wakefieldism. Once this process was complete, both Australia and Argentina advertised extensively in Britain and Europe, and then subsidized transport costs for migrants. Each country averaged over 20,000 immigrants per annum in the 1860s; by the 1880s nearly 100,000 people per annum migrated permanently to Argentina and nearly 40,000 to Australia. One in seven Britons migrated to Australasia; Argentina absorbed 10 percent of European migrants to the Americas. Even so, graziers still had to pay extremely high wages to attract European migrants, most of whom preferred to go to the United States. These high wages forced graziers and other employers in these societies to search for high-productivity production methods. Paradoxically, this helped attract capital rather than driving it away: high productivity meant higher profits. Nonetheless, the dominion states had to organize a flow of capital just as they organized a flow of labor.

As with labor, the dominions initially faced an absolute shortage of capital. Unlike late-industrializing Europe, where the creation of new forms of intermediation sufficed to pull existing capital out from under mattresses and into investment in railroads and steel mills, the dominions needed both new forms of intermediation and the capital itself. They imported capital by floating public bonds and private corporate enterprises in Britain; they also created legal structures that facilitated private borrowing. An inherent contradiction between the way they raised public debt and facilitated the expansion of private debt brought most dominions into a debt crisis by the 1890s.

Each state established a legal context for railroad development and began borrowing abroad for capital to develop railroads. In Australia each individual colony borrowed directly on the London bond market, and built and operated its own rail system. From 1861 to 1890 these rail systems expanded 2.5 times as fast as GDP in general.[9] By 1890 southeastern Australia had 10,500 miles of railroads. Even more so than in industrializing Europe, railroads proved too costly and too large for individual investors to attempt without public help; the organization of these enterprises also required the state to run them.

Argentina opted for a mixed public and private system. Local investors began the first rail line in 1854, but Buenos Aires province took over the line after only 25 miles were built. As part of the deal cementing an end to the civil war of 1851–62, Buenos Aires agreed to the use of customs revenue and central government borrowing to subsidize the construction of important private railroads, guaranteeing their profit rates and buying some of their stock shares. The Central Railroad, connecting inland but sheep-grazing Cordoba with the river port Rosario, was the most important of these. The central state also built rail lines in the less economically active interior provinces. By 1900 Argentina had about 10,350 miles of railroad. In both countries the extension of railroads inland opened up millions of acres of land for export-oriented production. Unlike grain, wool could be profitably transported overland about 80 miles. Even so, the extensive nature of sheep grazing demanded more land than could be accessed by riverine transport. Railroads made that land accessible.

Each state also established a legal regime for private individuals to mortgage land, creating a basis for private credit. In both Australia and Argentina graziers contracted about half of each country's foreign debt. Until the 1850s mortgages on land were not legal in Australasia; the shift to dominion status enabled local states to make mortgaging possible. Argentina did not really get a mortgage system until the Banco Hypotecario de Buenos Aires was established in 1872. In contrast, mortgage finance was not readily available in Uruguay until about 1896, considerably slowing investment in rural production and productivity increases.

States loaned their creditworthiness to the private sector to enhance its ability to borrow overseas. For example, Argentina used a system similar to that in the U.S. South. The state "loaned" its bonds to local banks. These banks then sold state bonds to overseas investors in order to raise specie that they could use to back their loans to agriculturalists. Planters or graziers borrowed from those banks by mortgaging their land, assuming that their increased production and exports would generate enough specie to pay the bank. The bank could then use the specie to repay the state for its bonds, and the state could use the specie to buy back its bonds from overseas investors.

States went beyond simply creating a legal framework to help capitalize private enterprises in ways that ultimately conflicted with their ability to repay public borrowing. The extension of railroads created enormous opportunities to speculate, because railroad building created a fictitious capital in land. Generally, land has economic value only to the extent that production occurs on it. Access to railroads increased the value of land by increasing the potential value of the production that would be carried out on it.

Dominion states tried to capture the increase in land values brought about by the extension of transportation networks. By so doing, they could earn enough money to pay back the debt they contracted building or subsidizing railroads in the first place. Generally, however, private firms captured these speculative profits through the contemporary version of insider trading. Either by advance knowledge (typical of Australasia) or simply by appropriation of the land in advance of the state's assertion of ownership (typical of Argentina), private speculators generally captured the increase in land prices. These insiders then sold land to outsiders, typically new migrants. These outsiders paid what they perceived to be a fair market price, based on the stream of income they expected from wool produced on the land they were buying. The states' failure to capture increased land values created a potential fiscal crisis that could and did undermine the entire process of state-led development.

Despite this situation, states' success in organizing inflows of capital and labor created a classic Gerschenkronian spurt for the wool economy. Sheep flocks and wool exports in each country grew exponentially. In 1813, Australia had 50,000 sheep; by 1850, 16 million; by 1880, 60 million; and by 1895, almost 110 million. Argentina lagged slightly, with 250,000 sheep in 1815; 5 million by 1850; and 61 million by 1880.

As with leading sectors in late-industrializing Europe, in the dominions leading-sector agrobusinesses were highly capitalized and highly concentrated enterprises. The dominions saw the first widespread application of the joint stock company to the production of agricultural goods. In both Argentina and Australasia, large landholders and large corporate bodies predominantly owned sheep stations. More interesting, a few large commercial banks and financial agencies dominated lending to the pastoral sector. These firms were bi- and sometimes multinational in orientation, usually being chartered and capitalized in Britain but lending in Australia and/or Argentina. In effect, these commercial firms replicated and anticipated the role played by banks in continental Europe, aggregating the savings of millions of Britons for use in large-scale overseas enterprises.

Curiously, considering that the dominions began with coerced labor, these enterprises immediately took on a modern, fully capitalist form. They relied on a fully proletarianized but itinerant workforce to shear sheep. This fully proletarianized workforce presented a considerable political problem for the state. In Argentina graziers relied on their private armies, vote rigging, and careful admixtures of shearers from different areas to block any opposition. In Australia, workers could vote and by 1890 were capable of mounting a general strike. These fully capitalist enterprises retreated after the common debt crises in the dominions during the 1890s, giving way to less fully capitalist family farming. In family farming, land and especially labor are not fully commoditized; they take on a fixed aspect, as families cannot easily dispose of family members who are unwanted labor. What caused these common crises, and why did they create family farming in all the dominions except Uruguay and Chile?

## The Failure of Ricardian Strategies: The Crisis of the 1890s

The crisis of the 1890s was a debt crisis with simultaneously international and domestic causes and ramifications. Here we look mostly at the domestic side of the debt crisis in order to explain the shift from highly modern capitalist production forms to family farms, and the shift both within Ricardian strategies and from Ricardian to Kaldorian strategies. The international aspects wait until Chapter 7.

Successful development of agricultural production flooded the world market with agricultural commodities, causing prices to fall. Falling prices in turn made it difficult for indebted (corporate) individuals and states to carry the fixed burden of the debts they had contracted to finance development. The obvious solution to a fixed-debt burden was to increase productivity and production, shifting to higher-value-added crops. Then a new round of Ricardian development could start. But getting from *A* to *B* involved domestic political struggles and often new injections of foreign capital that debt-burdened states could not get.

Speculators' appropriation of most of the rise in land values deprived dominion states of the revenues they needed to pay back their overseas debt. Generally, the dominions' debt-financed railways charged freight rates that allowed them to recoup their operating costs but not to amortize their debt.[10] Without this revenue, dominion states found themselves unable to continue borrowing abroad and thus to continue building railways and other infrastructure. Aware of the dominions' impending inability to generate enough revenue to service their debts, London bankers began to demand higher interest rates on dominion bonds and to shut some borrowers out of the market. Between 1880–85 and 1890–95, Australian borrowing fell by almost half; by the second period, debt service exceeded new borrowing. Capital flows to Argentina ceased from 1890 to 1895 after Buenos Aires defaulted.

Rising interest rates and the reversal of net capital inflows broke the virtuous cycle of dominion growth. Less lending meant fewer new railroads, fewer new railroads meant lower land sales, lower land sales fewer immigrants, fewer immigrants slower customs revenue growth, and slower or lower customs revenue made debt service more problematic. New South Wales provides an instructive example: from 1880 to 1890 its total per capita revenues fell, led by a fall in land sale revenue from 42 to 24 percent of total revenue.

The debt crisis had a private side too. First, speculators had rushed to invest in land over the frontier, expecting continued expansion of the rail net. The states' fiscal crises prevented rail building, trapping millions of pounds of speculative investment in overvalued land. Second, declining wool prices meant that new migrants who had bought productive land when wool prices were high now found themselves unable to meet mortgage burdens that had been hypothecated on the basis of high rising wool prices. As they began to default on their mortgages, their banks found themselves possessing millions of acres of land. Given falling wool prices, selling this land would not help the banks recoup their initial investment via the mortgage loan.

This double debt crisis also triggered efforts by workers to organize economically and politically. Graziers' efforts to squeeze out the maximum return from their properties to service increasingly burdensome mortgages made them confrontational with their workers. The year 1890 saw a general strike followed by several smaller but violent strikes in Australasia, and Argentina experienced civil disorder in the early 1890s and a series of violent general strikes in the 1900s. Workers' parties emerged in both countries in this period.

How could states, speculators, and banks escape their economic dilemma? How could states control the new unions and workers' parties? Partly by design, partly by accident, states tried to create a class of small landholders to resolve these difficulties. If wool could not yield enough revenue per acre to support both mortgage payments and the grazier, then perhaps more intensively produced commodities like grains, meat, and dairy would. The very success of prior Ricardian development in flooding Europe with basic grains had pushed urban incomes up to the point where workers there could now afford these foods. However, precisely because these commodities were intensively produced, they were less suited for large corporate enterprises. Family farms were more appropriate for reasons of both scale and resilience.

Family farms operated on the right scale to produce meat and dairy products. With the application of machinery, family farms could also handle grain production. Family farms were also more resilient than fully capitalist enterprises, which had to pay both wages to workers and profits to their owners.[11] In contrast, family farms did not accumulate profit or pay wages to family members in the strict sense. They merely survived, at a level they found tolerable, after paying their fixed obligations to creditors and suppliers of inputs. Thus, family farms could ride out periods of economic turbulence and declining prices more easily than corporately organized farms. (This is still true today.)

Different paths carried the dominions to family farming. In Argentina, graziers defaulted on their loans or devalued them through inflation. With the money they saved from not paying their debts, they upgraded their cattle and sheep populations, breeding for meat, not hides and wool. They hired immigrant Italian families to produce grain on their land, integrating meat and grains in a complex and highly productive rotation. The economic change wrought by the shift to family farming is visible in the changing ratio of fatter crossbred animals, which could be used for frozen and chilled beef, to scrawny native cattle, suitable only for jerked and salted meat. In 1895, just after the crisis, the ratio was 1:1, but by 1908 it had risen to 10:1. The importance of wool diminished, and grains replaced it as the major export. Wool composed 58.1 percent of exports in 1880–84, but by 1900–1904 was down to 26.5 percent; grains were only 5.2 percent of exports in 1880–84, but by 1900–1904, 48.3 percent.

Australia saw similar changes, but more slowly than in Argentina, because of Australia's inability to default. There, banks foreclosed on graziers and then sold land to family farmers. The state subsidized these sales by advancing low-interest mortgages to would-be farmers. New Zealand's transition also lagged Argentina's. In New Zealand graziers subdivided land among their children, breaking estates up into more manageable units. The state also subsidized the creation of new family farms. Because these new family farms generated greater revenue per acre than wool grazing had, banks could sell off former wool estates at prices high enough to recoup their initial investment. Exports increased 250 percent from 1896 to 1913, with wool falling from 47 percent of the total to only 35 percent, and dairy and meat products rising from 17 to 36 percent.

For all the dominions wheat, meat, and dairy products provided a second successful Ricardian boom. Global wheat exports, for example, sextupled from 1873 to 1929 to nearly three-quarters of a billion bushels. All the dominion states supported this shift with a new round of infrastructural investments, borrowing anew to build a second, denser network of railroads and to establish agricultural research centers; the United States had already done this forty years before.

The increased exports these new farms generated saved the state from its own debt crisis. Increased exports meant increased imports, and thus increased customs duties. This allowed the state to renew borrowing and railroad building, bailing out speculators. Family farming also constituted a circuit breaker between the state and the restive working class in the dominions. These new small property owners evidenced a potential for upward mobility, and also created a solid mass of voters for conservative parties.

This second round of Ricardian success re-created the cycle experienced in the first round of Ricardian success. By the 1920s and 1930s, meat and dairy exports markets were glutted, and the dominions as well as the tropical Latin American agricultural exporters experienced a second severe debt crisis (see Chapter 8). The recurrent crises related to Ricardian strategies forced a shift to manufacturing-based economies. The foundation for this shift to manufacturing had already occurred as a natural result of Ricardian based growth.

## From Agriculture to Industry in Ricardian Development

The shift from extensive production of wool to relatively more intensive production of grains, dairy, and meat products also created an opportunity for the first stages of industrialization in the dominions. More farmers meant broader demand for daily necessities. Construction, food processing for local and export markets, and light industry emerged in all the dominions at this time. All of these industries benefited from a kind of natural protection because the cost of transportation from older, more established industrial centers was high enough to be prohibitive. This agricultural export-led industrialization in light and nontradable industries was a fairly common phenomenon extending across most agricultural exporters, with the dominions experiencing much greater success than either tropical or Eastern European agricultural regions, but much less than the U.S. Midwest.

Grain and dairy exports generated the greatest impulses for industrialization. First, these goods tended to be produced by family farmers, creating a relatively flat distribution of income that enlarged the local market for light consumer goods. Small local entrepreneurs could easily jump into the production of garments, and furniture and food processing, especially milling and beer making. All of these had relatively low capital requirements. Second, family farmers relied heavily on machinery. Wheat farmers needed it to compensate for the fixed nature of labor inside the family, and dairy producers needed cream separators and refrigeration equipment. The larger and more sophisticated the overall economy, the more likely that production of this machinery would start. Thus, outside of the United States, the most sophisticated and largest of the agricultural export economies, agricultural machinery production had strong Gerschenkronian aspects. Both Canada and, to a lesser degree, Australia became producers of harvesting and other grain production equipment by virtue of tariff protection for local producers. Australia used this in turn to promote a local steel industry. Argentina, lacking both iron ore and coal, and any deliberate industrial promotion policy, achieved industrialization only in nontradable light consumer goods.

The same pattern can be seen in dairying equipment. Sweden became the world's largest producer and exporter of dairy equipment, partly by accident and partly because its tight links to the vibrant Danish dairy export sector enabled existing machinery producers to capture demand for equipment. Other dairy producers had to compete with first mover Sweden, so a dairy equipment industry emerged in the United States only behind tariff barriers.

Outside the United States, whose early settlement and vast domestic market gave local manufacturers considerable advantages, industrialization in the Ricardian periphery depended crucially on local social pacts between manufacturers and labor that expanded the potential domestic market. Australia shows this most clearly, because Canadian industrialization was distorted by its proximity to the United States and by the U.S. firms' early multinationalization into Canada. In Australia during the early 1900s, local manufacturers and labor exchanged high regulated wages for tariffs and other forms of protection from outside competition. High wages expanded the market for locally produced products, in turn spurring increased investment and thus increased employment in a primitive kind of Keynesianism. The agricultural sector and foreign consumers bore the cost of this protection and higher wages via a disguised export tax on the agricultural and minerals sector.

This strategy was extremely fragile. It depended on timing; were world markets for agricultural products expanding? It depended on agriculture's ability to invest, increase productivity, and remain competitive despite the imposition of additional costs. And it depended on a low minimum scale for entry to key industries. When Juan Perón tried the same strategy in Argentina in the 1940s and 1950s, none of these things was true. Stagnant agricultural markets reduced the utility of agriculture as an engine for the rest of the economy; soaking agriculture led to a drought in agricultural investment and declining production; and the minimum scale for entering key manufacturing sectors probably exceeded Argentina's domestic capacity both to consume output and to generate investment funds at that time.

# Tropical Agriculture
# and Ricardian Development

Ricardian development in the tropics largely proceeded along lines similar to those in the dominions, with one key exception. Unlike the self-governing or independent dominions, tropical exporters were mostly de jure or de facto colonies. Central American states were fragile; Africa was easily colonized at the end of the 1800s. Only Brazil and Siam (modern Thailand) were sovereign. Colonial administrations imposed export crops in several cases (bringing, for example, rubber from Brazil to Malaya and tea from China to India and Ceylon). Colonial administrations also taxed local producers heavily, pulling much of the surplus into their treasuries and further limiting the pool of funds available for investment. Aside from this, the state played basically the same role it did in the dominions, establishing a legal regime for private property in land, borrowing overseas to build transportation infrastructure, and ensuring labor supplies. As in the dominions, the better they did these, the greater their competitive advantage relative to other suppliers in the same markets.

As Chapter 5 noted, in much of the tropics, labor had to be imported. Even though European diseases did not depopulate Asia as they had the Americas, the political costs of clearing thousands of settled peasants off the land meant that export production often took place in areas empty of labor. Areas with smaller populations and the right climate were more likely to emerge as supply regions than areas with more dense populations, because it was easier for would-be planters to assert their right to landownership. This easier access to land in turn meant that planters had to import labor.

Railroad construction also proceeded along lines similar to those in the dominions. Colonial or local states floated bonds overseas to finance state-owned networks or to subsidize foreign-owned firms, and these networks directly served new export production zones.

When local states got the proper mix of capital, labor, and crop, the tropics experienced the same kind of explosive growth in output as the dominions. Brazil's pre–World War I coffee exports, for example, which amounted to about 200,000 tons during 1821–30, doubled five times to peak at 7.8 million tons in 1900–10. Brazil's success stimulated market entry by other producers and states in Latin America and colonial Africa. The coffee market became glutted, and prices began dropping around 1900. Brazil encountered difficulty servicing its debt and defaulted in 1898–1900, and then made only partial payments in the next decade. Its major competitor, Colombia, also defaulted for part of that decade.

## Ricardian Strategies and British Hegemony

Britain's superiority in the manufacture of textiles and railroad-linked goods was the bedrock for its hegemony during the nineteenth century. These allowed it to dominate world export markets for manufactured goods and conversely to become a major market for other countries' exports. Put simply, a lot of money could be made from cooperating with the British. Because the dominions were empty places, the political and economic costs of cooperation were quite low. Britain's initial industrial supremacy was leveraged by its access to cheap foods and raw materials; the dominions came into being precisely because the British industrial behemoth and its import market existed.

Ricardian strategies, whether locally adopted or inherited from colonial administrations, provided the soil in which British hegemony flourished. The Formal Dominions, all British colonies, had considerable freedom to buy, borrow, and sell from and into third-party markets. However, 80 percent of their exports usually went to Britain anyway, and virtually all the overseas capital they borrowed came from Britain. The informal dominions, though not legally bound to Britain, show a similar pattern. Exports meant money, and capital inflows meant money for existing property owners. Only the United States followed a slightly different pattern, and that largely because industrialization in the Green Bay–St. Louis–Baltimore–Portland (ME) quadrangle ultimately created a market rivaling Britain's. By the end of the nineteenth century, most U.S. agricultural production went to domestic markets.

The close connection between Britain and the dominions is also evidenced by Germany's behavior. As it industrialized, it became increasingly like Britain in its raw material needs. Although it never went so far in relying on external sources of food, it began to colonize or infiltrate all the areas contiguous with the British dominions. Germans migrated in large numbers to southern Brazil's cattle country and to southwest and southeast Africa, and they invested heavily in South Africa, Argentina, and, to a lesser extent, Australia. Germany also penetrated Eastern Europe, a major food supply zone despite its low productivity.

Britain's hegemony created cooperation by giving local elites massive incentives to cooperate. If those elites took advantage of Britain's market, so much the better for both Britain and the local economy. Competition among would-be exporters for capital and for the profits accruing to those using best practice agriculture disciplined those elites, allowing Britain to exert its hegemony without the costs of intervention. Competition also gave Britain access to cheaper raw materials than its competitors. Finally, the reliance of the supply zones on British capital allowed Britain to obtain a considerable portion of its imports as loan repayments; Britain ran a consistent and growing trade deficit during the nineteenth century. All in all, these relationships were the core of British hegemony and more important than Britain's relationships with European economies.

## Notes

1. W. A. Lewis, *Growth and Fluctuations* (Boston: Allen and Unwin, 1978), makes the clearest statement of this. See also Douglas North, *Economic Growth of the United States 1790–1860* (Englewood Cliffs, N.J.: Prentice-Hall, 1961), for this argument applied to the United States; Harold Innis, *The Fur Trade: An Introduction to Canadian Economic History* (New Haven, Conn.: Yale University Press, 1930) and Mel Watkins, "A Staples Theory of Economic Growth," *Canadian Journal of Economics and Political Science,* no. 29 (May 1963) for more general interpretations of growth led by staple exports; and W. A. Lewis, ed., *Tropical Development 1880–1914* (Evanston, Ill.: Northwestern University Press, 1970) for applications to tropical agriculture.

2. This is Ernst Engel, the Prussian statistician, not the Friedrich Engels of the famous tag-team Marx and Engels.

3. These countries were Mexico, Brazil, Argentina, India, and perhaps Colombia. A handful of European economies also made the transition from Ricardian to Kaldorian strategies: Denmark, Holland, and Finland. See also Lloyd Reynolds, *Economic Growth in the Third World* (New Haven, Conn.: Yale University Press, 1985).

4. Donald Denoon, *Settler Capitalism* (Oxford: Oxford University Press, 1983) provides an eclectic but comprehensive study of the dominions in the nineteenth century. See also D. C. M. Platt and Guido Di Tella, *Argentina, Australia, and Canada: Studies in Comparative Development 1870–1965* (New York: St. Martin's Press, 1985).

5. Unless otherwise cited, statistics in this section come from the U.S. Department of Commerce, Census Bureau, *Historical Statistics of the United States, Colonial Times to 1970*, 2 vols. (Washington, D.C.: Government Printing Office, 1976).

6. See Richard Bensel, *Yankee Leviathan* (Cambridge: Cambridge University Press, 1990).

7. Albert Fishlow, *American Railroads and Transformation of the Ante-Bellum Economy* (Cambridge, Mass.: Harvard University Press, 1965); Robert Fogel, *Railroads and American Economic Growth* (Baltimore: Johns Hopkins University Press, 1964).

8. Brian Page and Richard Walker, "From Settlement to Fordism: The Agro-Industrial Revolution in the American Midwest," *Economic Geography* 67, no. 4 (October 1991): 294–295.

9. Noel Butlin, *Investment in Australian Economic Development, 1861–1890* (Canberra: Australian National University Press, 1972), p. 16.

10. The U.S. policy of railroad promotion through land grants neatly sidestepped this problem: railroads directly captured increased land values. Most U.S. railroads in fact made more money from land sales than from transportation in their formative years. From a historical point of view, grant railroads proved a superior policy choice compared to alternatives like direct state ownership or state subsidy of operating costs. In principle, though, had states been able to appropriate increased land values, direct state ownership would not necessarily have led to a debt crisis.

11. See Harriet Friedmann, "World Market, State and Family Farms," *Comparative Studies in Society and History* 20, no. 3 (1978): 545–586, for a complete analysis of this question.

# CHAPTER 7

## Foreign Debt, Hegemony, and the Gold Standard

The last chapter showed how Ricardian responses to Britain's industrial revolution relied on British capital. British hegemony rested on reciprocal and complementary flows of capital and agricultural exports. As it turns out, so did the international monetary system. In earlier periods of hegemony, metallic money and various forms of commercial credit (of which bills of exchange were the most important) constituted the basis for international exchange. But the limited supply of metallic money and bankers' risk aversion limited the degree to which the volume of international commerce could expand by limiting the supply of internationally acceptable money. (When the growth of the money supply lags behind the growth of real product, deflation occurs, which can slow growth. The money supply needs to grow in proportion to real output.)

During the late nineteenth century, British lending overseas helped create a new source of international liquidity. Metallic money and bills of exchange remained important, but the enormous pool of liquid securities — stocks and bonds — created by British overseas investment also provided a source of credit expansion. This expanded credit enabled a vast expansion in trade. It also enabled would-be export economies to run massive balance-of-payments deficits while they invested in infrastructural projects with long gestation periods. The strengths and weaknesses of this system can be seen in the events leading up to and resolving the 1890s debt crises. In Chapter 6 we examined the domestic side of those crises; now we will look at their international aspects and compare them to later, but similar, debt crises in the 1930s and 1980s.[1]

Each of these global debt crises has unfolded in roughly the same way, with the 1890s proving the easiest to resolve, the 1930s the most difficult, and the current one somewhere in between. Three factors explain the differences among these crises: different institutional structures linking debtors and creditors (that is, different intermediation structures); different strategies by creditor states for the political management of debtor–creditor economic relations; and the presence or absence of a concurrent debt crisis involving developed nations. We will concentrate on the comparison with the 1980s crisis but will bring in the 1930s crisis where relevant; the 1930s crisis receives an expanded treatment in Chapter 8. The discussion here will ask why there was a generalized debt crisis in the dominions in the 1890s and why it was more easily resolved than the proportionately smaller developing country debt crisis of the 1980s. Then the discussion will shift to the relationship between Britain's global lending and the functioning of the international monetary system.

# Three Debt Crises

## How Much Was Lent?

The dominions, understood loosely to include the United States, owed about £3.5 billion to European creditors by 1914. In current terms, this amounts to about $150 billion, but, since the entire world economy then was perhaps only one-tenth as big as today's, it is proportionately one and a half times more than all the developing countries owe today (about $1 trillion). Thus, all European foreign investment by 1913, about £7.5 billion, was about three to four times as large as developing country debt today. This investment flowed out relatively evenly, unlike the enormous leap in bank lending during the 1970s. British net overseas investment in real terms was roughly the same in the 1860s and 1870s, doubled in the 1880s, and even in the crisis decade of the 1890s never fell below the level of the 1870s.[2]

The 1920s duplicated the patterns of the nineteenth century, so that here we can speak of a long nineteenth century encompassing the period up to World War II. Most investment continued to occur as portfolio lending, that is, as bonds, and the same borrowers—Argentina, Australia, Brazil, Canada, New Zealand, and South Africa—bulked large. The exceptions are instructive, however. Direct foreign investment, mostly by U.S. corporations, was rising rapidly, but, compared with the stock of portfolio debt, it was still insignificant in terms of volume. The deviations from the pattern of developed countries lending to agricultural exporters were more important. World War I had created a set of developed country debtors and borrowers. Germany was the most important borrower, absorbing about one-fifth of U.S. capital exports during the 1920s. This laid a set of developed country–developed country debt relationships over the older core–periphery pattern of the nineteenth century. In the 1930s German and other Central European defaults complicated resolution of the parallel debt crisis in the agricultural periphery.

In contrast, borrowing in the contemporary period has shifted three distinct times, in terms of both volume and form. In the 1950s and 1960s multinational corporations conducted most overseas investment (as direct foreign investment—DFI) and, overall, invested only about $200 billion in 1990 dollars. In the 1970s, DFI shrank somewhat in response to a wave of expropriations by developing countries. During the 1980s, direct investment continued to flow into LDCs at a fairly steady but low rate of about $20 billion per year. In contrast, DFI flows into developed countries tripled to $120 billion during this decade as firms sought to position themselves in the world's three major markets.[3] In the 1960s, concessional lending by multilateral and other development agencies approached earlier DFI levels. This investment constituted a low-cost transfer of resources. Lending-as-aid generally had concessional interest rates and terms, making the debt-service burden light. This lending continued through the 1970s but became less important as bank lending boomed.

During the 1970s, portfolio lending by banks became the most important source of capital for developing countries, as development-minded states tried to bypass transnational corporations by borrowing directly. In constant 1990 dollars, in 1970, developing countries owed commercial banks about $200 billion, but by 1979 they owed about $450 billion and by 1988 $650 billion. At that point, overall developing country debt, including concessional lending, amounted to around $1.2 trillion. Unlike in the 1890s, increasing debt in the 1980s did not represent new net lending; most of the debt increase came from negotiations that capitalized interest payments then in arrears. That is, they simply added unpaid interest to the total debt, much as unpaid interest accumulates on an unpaid credit card bill (and with the same dire long-term consequences for the debtor).

## Why Lend?

Three characteristics of their economies drove nineteenth-century European, and particularly British, lending. All derived from the fact, as we have noted in previous chapters, that the division of labor could expand only as fast as the supply of food and raw materials for urban workers and manufacturing activity. Manufacturing output and its labor force expanded more rapidly than agricultural production through most of the 1800s, raising relative prices for agricultural goods. Rising agricultural prices meant rising agricultural profits, which attracted investment. Few lenders consciously attempted to keep agricultural production in sync with manufacturing growth. However, high agricultural prices made would-be agricultural exporters out in the dominions willing to pay relatively high interest rates to get capital, and lenders quite reasonably invested for the maximum return.

The first characteristic driving investment was the difference between the social structures of European agricultural production and dominion production. This difference made production in the dominions more profitable than European agriculture, even when transportation costs were taken into account. This greater profitability meant that dominion agriculturalists could afford to pay higher interest rates than inland European producers, attracting capital to the dominions. The social structure of European food and raw material production also inhibited investment.

Europe was cluttered with noble landlords and peasants, neither of whom necessarily had to accommodate market forces. Noble landlords inherited their land (or, as Hegel once said, the land inherited the man) and thus avoided mortgages. Without the whip of mortgage payments, the residual nobility could indulge in the luxury of ignoring market signals. Similarly, peasants could avoid market pressures by reverting to subsistence production or sending extra children off to the city. With few exceptions, both classes proved remarkably resistant to market pressures to improve and so continued to use archaic production methods on small plots. Thus, European agriculture continued to be a low-productivity agriculture supporting many rural mouths through rents and direct consumption (see Table 2.2).

In contrast, the empty or emptied lands in the dominions lacked landlords and peasants. Modern large-scale production methods could be used right from the start by modern large-scale corporations. Dominion producers also benefited from very fertile virgin land. These corporate and individual producers thus reaped high profits and also appropriated rents that would have gone to landlords. As a result, they could afford to pay high interest rates on borrowed money.

With regard to the second characteristic, transportation cost considerations reinforced incentives to lend overseas. Despite declining freight rates, transport costs still bulked large in final cost. By 1913, transport still accounted for 20 percent of the cost of wheat delivered to Liverpool. Despite railroads, sea transport continued to be the cheapest way to move bulky goods, giving producers in coastal and riverine areas a second distinct competitive advantage over inland European producers. The flip side of peasant and landlord indifference to market signals to produce more output was an inability to consume manufactured goods. Substantial internal markets did not exist in most European countries outside of England and the industrial corner of northwest Europe. Thus, in 1913 Australia imported more British goods than France did, although France had ten times Australia's population. Figure 7.1 presents a geographic breakdown of overseas investment.

The third consideration was one of momentum; new investment drew more investment later on. The economies of the nineteenth century were very

**Figure 7.1** *Distribution of Foreign Investment by Area, 1913 ($million)*

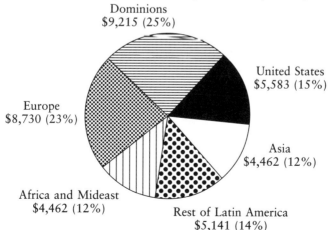

Dominions
$9,215 (25%)

United States
$5,583 (15%)

Europe
$8,730 (23%)

Asia
$4,462 (12%)

Africa and Mideast
$4,462 (12%)

Rest of Latin America
$5,141 (14%)

SOURCES: Cleona Lewis, *Debtor and Creditor Countries* (Washington, D.C.: Brookings Institution, 1945); Albert Fishlow, "Lessons from the Past," *International Organization* 39, no. 3 (1985): 394.

outward oriented. By "economies" here, we mean the world market–oriented producers who had access to decent transportation, and not the well-integrated national economies that emerged after World War I. European economies looked overseas to buy their raw materials and to sell their manufactured goods; the dominions and tropics looked overseas for places to sell raw materials and to buy manufactures. The interaction between these two complementary zones allowed each to grow, while both ignored their respective interiors. Unsurprisingly, the level of investment in each area converged. In 1860, for roughly every £7 Britain had invested in its domestic economy it had £1 invested overseas. By 1913 the ratio was 2:1; the British investors' stake in overseas economies equalled half their stake in their own economy.[4]

The major exceptions to this pattern were found in states that encouraged private investors to support development efforts in other countries for strategic reasons. Both France and Germany put about half their investments into other European countries, with France making about 25 percent of its investment in Russia (its counterweight to Germany) and Germany about 25 percent in Austria-Hungary, Romania, and the Ottoman empire (its corridor of states running southeast to the Mediterranean and supplying it with food and fuels).[5]

The interwar period continued the patterns set in the nineteenth century. Aside from loans to Germany, however, U.S. and British lending and investment followed the usual patterns. Although the British mostly lent via bonds to their traditional agricultural suppliers, British firms also used direct foreign investment to secure their major foreign markets in the United States, Canada, and Australia. U.S. firms set up subsidiaries in Europe and the richer dominions. Both the United States and Britain supported their oil companies' massive direct investments in the Mideast and Asia. Figure 7.2 shows the geographic distribution.

*Figure 7.2 Distribution of Foreign Investment by Area, 1938 ($million)*

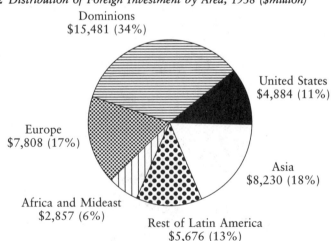

Dominions
$15,481 (34%)

United States
$4,884 (11%)

Europe
$7,808 (17%)

Asia
$8,230 (18%)

Africa and Mideast
$2,857 (6%)

Rest of Latin America
$5,676 (13%)

SOURCES: Cleona Lewis, *Debtor and Creditor Countries* (Washington, D.C.: Brookings Institution, 1945); Albert Fishlow, "Lessons from the Past," *International Organization* 39, no. 3 (1985): 394.

What about the 1970s and 1980s? Here a similar, though not identical, process occurred. In the long nineteenth century, the limiting factor on growth was the scarcity of land free of archaic social structures. In the post–World War II period, the limiting factor was the scarcity of labor willing to work the dirty, dangerous, and dull jobs typical of the assembly line. The emergence of assembly-line-based manufacturing created relatively standardized production processes that could be easily transferred to countries that had already started shifting from Ricardian to Kaldorian strategies in response to the Great Depression of the 1930s. (See Chapter 13 for a more extensive analysis; Figure 7-3 shows the geographic distribution.) Those countries had a pool of low-wage labor willing to work dirty, dangerous, and monotonous jobs. However, those would-be industrializers lacked capital. The oil shocks of 1973 and 1979 created a pool of capital from which those states could borrow. After quadrupling prices, the oil exporters socked their cash away in U.S. banks. Those banks had to lend the money to someone, but the post–oil shock recession deterred their traditional customers in developed countries from borrowing. Consequently, they lent to would-be industrializers.

## Investment in What?

A truly global economy tied together by underseas telegraph cables and steamships emerged from the mutual dependence of industrial and agricultural regions in the long nineteenth century—a global economy that until recently was much more integrated than today's global economy. Relative to gross world product, international investment flows in the 1800s dwarf post–World War II flows by a factor of about three or four. On average, between 1873 and 1914 the British invested about 5 percent of their GDP overseas, making it possible for Australia, Argentina, Canada, and other nations to finance between 30 and 50 percent of their gross capital formation from overseas sources. The French and Germans averaged outflows of 2 to 2.5 percent of GDP. During the 1920s the United States lent about 1 percent of GDP overseas annually. In contrast, during the peak years of U.S. direct investment overseas and during the 1970s recycling of petrodollars, outflows rarely breached 1 percent of U.S. GDP. Even in 1987, their peak year for overseas investment, the Japanese lent less than 1 percent of their GDP. The flip side of this situation is that today's late-industrializing debtor countries rely much less on foreign capital for investment funds. Few countries used foreign capital for more than 25 percent of capital formation, and then only in peak years.

Nineteenth-century investment went out in discrete waves to specific geographic areas, each of which, at the time of inflow, seemed the most promising location. Thus, investment swamped each area with capital, making possible the construction of bulky rail networks as a whole, rather than piecemeal. Argentina and the U.S. cotton South caught the first investment wave in the 1820s and 1830s. The United States and Canada caught the second wave, building their first intercontinental railroads in the 1860s and 1870s. Russia, the Ottoman empire, and Egypt also began borrowing heavily during this period. Then New Zealand, Australia, Argentina, and southern Africa

154

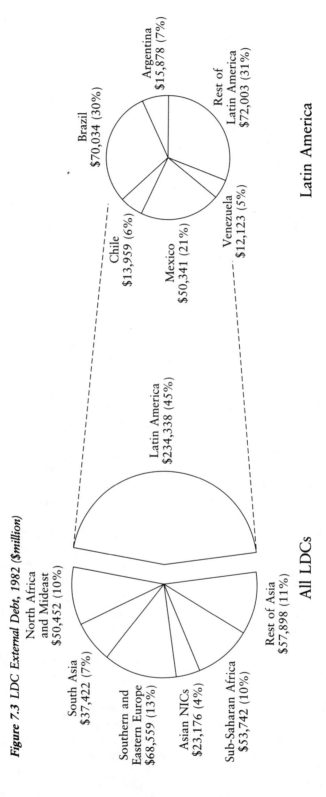

**Figure 7.3** *LDC External Debt, 1982 (*$million*)*

North Africa
and Mideast
$50,452 (10%)

South Asia
$37,422 (7%)

Southern and
Eastern Europe
$68,559 (13%)

Asian NICs
$23,176 (4%)

Sub-Saharan Africa
$53,742 (10%)

Rest of Asia
$57,898 (11%)

Latin America
$234,338 (45%)

**All LDCs**

Brazil
$70,034 (30%)

Argentina
$15,878 (7%)

Rest of
Latin America
$72,003 (31%)

Chile
$13,959 (6%)

Mexico
$50,341 (21%)

Venezuela
$12,123 (5%)

**Latin America**

*SOURCE:* IBRD, *World Debt Tables* (Baltimore: Johns Hopkins University Press, 1984).

caught successive waves in the mid-1870s, early 1880s, late 1880s, and 1890s
—all oriented toward infrastructure for the wool economy. In the immediate
prewar period, South Africa, Argentina, and especially Canada caught the last
big wave. Diamonds and gold drew investment to South Africa, and grain
production to Argentina and Canada. This pattern continued during the
1920s, although British investment shifted away from the United States and
back toward Britain's empire. The empire, particularly Australia, took more
than half of British investment in the 1930s. The bulk of U.S. investment went
to Canada and industrial Europe. The United States aside, the biggest borrowers of the nineteenth century—Australia, Argentina, and Canada—
remained the biggest borrowers of the 1920s.

About 40 percent of all nineteenth-century British investment went directly to railroads, and a further 30 percent went indirectly, through government borrowing, to railroads and other social overhead capital. The remaining
30 percent went to directly productive enterprises. Over 70 percent of this
lending was in the form of portfolio investment, in which lenders do not
control the enterprise. Instead, states, local entrepreneurs, and a bevy of
binational corporations controlled the actual deployment of capital. The
1920s continued this pattern, with about 60 percent of British lending going to
states. U.S. investment, however, was relatively evenly divided between direct
investment and portfolio lending, of which about 60 percent went to public
borrowers.

The emphasis on infrastructure *cum* portfolio investment reinforced the
degree to which local agents benefited from investment. Most investment
opened up new lands, making it possible for local entrepreneurs to produce
and export for the Anglo-European industrial town. Michael Edelstein's analysis of various investments shows that, while overseas investment yielded rates
of return well in excess of British domestic investment opportunities, it yielded
less than other investment opportunities in the dominions and the United
States.[6] Local investors were better positioned to capture those opportunities.
Local, or insider, advantages are explained by transportation and information
barriers facing investors, and in turn explain why nineteenth-century investors
overwhelmingly chose portfolio investment over direct investment and why
most investment banks acted as intermediaries and not as principals in invest
ment transactions. Both of these had important consequences for the later
emergence and resolution of the 1890s debt crisis.

## The Advantages of Portfolio Investment

Limits imposed by organizational techniques, political and prudential reasons
for arm's-length transactions, and the structure of banking all combined to
favor portfolio investment over direct investment. In direct investment, lenders
actually establish or buy a corporation overseas and run it. The modern
transnational corporation is the preeminent example of direct investment.
Successful direct investment requires high levels of supervision to generate
profits. In portfolio investment, lenders receive their payback as invariable
interest or as rental payments. Lenders either buy real estate or make loans to

firms or states. Portfolio investment leaves the detailed, day-to-day management of firms to the borrower. Most British firms did not have the level of organization necessary to supervise overseas ventures on a month-to-month basis, let alone day to day.

Britain's overt unwillingness to get militarily embroiled in the local politics of foreign countries after the 1850s also inhibited direct investment. Direct investments had no guarantee of security from violent or legal forms of expropriation. Portfolio investment was somewhat safer, insofar as creditors could sometimes take control of defaulters' fiscs. Even there, creditors could not often rely on their *states* for help. Out of 90 defaults by indebted states in the long nineteenth century, only two resulted in military action, seven in some kind of cession of sovereignty to foreign states, and seven others in a cession of sovereignty to foreign private investors themselves. Debtors ceded sovereignty by allowing foreign experts to take control of, for example, their customs houses, thus assuring creditors that tax revenue would be used to service debt first and foremost.[7] British investors thus tended to avoid direct investment except in areas of exceptional political stability, such as the United States, or places where British law prevailed, such as the self-governing and directly governed colonies. In contrast, portfolio investment allowed investors to diversify their holdings away from single countries and single markets, lowering their risk.

More subtly, however, the concentration of investment in government and infrastructure rarely made it necessary for the British to resort to overt or covert pressure on recipient governments. Colonies obviously were subject to imperial vetoes on default. But even in formally sovereign countries and in the partly sovereign, self-governing formal dominions, formal supervision was largely unnecessary. The largely instrumental states in the dominions wanted to retain their creditworthiness because the rancher class dominating those states needed overseas capital to make money. Land speculation yielded fantastic fortunes and routine production more moderate ones, but both would evaporate if the flow of inward investment dried up. Most defaulters were relatively weak states with relatively weak economies.

The banking structure also inhibited direct investment, particularly by British banks. British commercial banks specialized in short-term lending for trade purposes; they abhorred holding physical property or equities. British merchant (i.e., investment) banks preferred to act as intermediaries in transactions between savers and borrowers. They avoided being direct creditors. Neither commercial nor merchant banks, therefore, wanted direct investment, and when, through either accident or default, they found themselves in possession of real property they moved as quickly as possible to dispose of it.

Conversely, the legal infrastructure in many investment areas also deterred direct investment. Setting up limited liability corporations was difficult or impossible. Therefore, both local and overseas investors tended to incorporate firms in London and then to draw on the London share or bond markets for their capital. Even firms that were wholly owned and run in the dominions often used this approach. Many Argentine firms, for example, preferred to live under British company law rather than under the more chaotic and incomplete Argentine law.

Finally, physical infrastructure also selected for portfolio as opposed to direct investment. A transatlantic telegraph cable was laid in 1851, and by 1914 every continent was linked to London. Other cables linked North America to Australia and South America. The telegraph network sufficed to create a global market in money, linking primarily banks and stock exchanges and only secondarily firms. Firms had to rely on physically moving people and information via the mails and regularly scheduled shipping, which could take weeks to go from London to Australasia. This made it virtually impossible to manage firms from a distance.

This discussion should also make it obvious why the share of capital flows taking the form of direct investment increased after the long nineteenth century. Technology, law, stock markets, and organizational capacities all changed in directions that made investment easier to manage at a distance. Thus, the environment became increasingly favorable to direct investment. Chapter 11 presents a more detailed discussion of why firms took advantage of this opportunity.

## What Went Wrong?

Albert Fishlow divides borrowing into two types for analytic purposes.[8] In the first category (Figure 7.4), revenue borrowing, states/entrepreneurs borrow to sustain current expenditure. The borrowed money is not invested and does not generate a future stream of income. In the second (Figure 7.5), development borrowing, countries/entrepreneurs borrow for investment or, in our

*Figure 7.4 Revenue Borrowing*

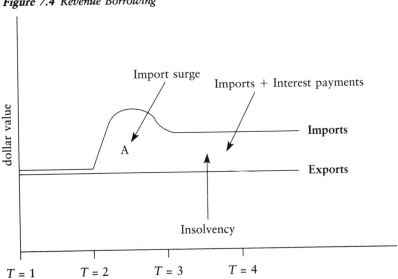

*Figure 7.5 Development Borrowing*

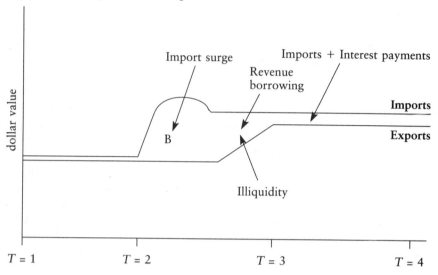

terms, for either a Kaldorian or a Ricardian development strategy. They hope that the additional stream of export income generated by this investment will allow them to service their foreign debt and retain some profits.

These two characteristic borrowing patterns may lead to two characteristic debt crises, insolvency and illiquidity. Revenue borrowing is obviously a quick road to a solvency crisis, while developmental borrowing may produce a liquidity crisis. Since lenders usually have to be repaid in foreign currency, increased exports are needed to make future payments. Because all revenue borrowers and some inept developmental borrowers will fail to create any productive, export-oriented firms/farms, their future stream of export income is zero (Figure 7.4). Exports are constant from time $T = 1$ through $T = 4$. Meanwhile, imports increase immediately (area A, from time $T = 2$ through $T = 3$) because of the surge of imports through which the capital transfer occurs. "Imported" capital takes the form of increased physical imports of some goods. Imports also increase over the long run (time $T = 3$ to $T = 4$) because debt service payments count as an "import" for balance-of-payments purposes. Thus, total imports equal the constant level of preborrowing imports as well as the additional imports constituted by debt service payments. As was already noted, the typical crisis associated with revenue borrowing is insolvency (i.e., bankruptcy). Unless exports accidentally grow as a result of revenue borrowing, a country will surely be unable to service its foreign debt unless it constricts imports in order to free up foreign exchange. Of course, it can also bring its payments back into balance by defaulting, which roughly 90 countries did in the long nineteenth century.

In contrast, liquidity crises involve a temporary inability by developmental borrowers to service debt. Because developmental borrowing involves investment in new productive facilities or infrastructure, it potentially creates exports and export revenues. Thus we see the surge of imports in area B. These exports earn foreign exchange that can be used to service foreign debt. Over the long run (i.e., from time $T = 3$ to $T = 4$), new export income will equal new outflows for debt service (imports). However, because it takes time for investment to produce a stream of exports — a gestational lag — there is almost always a period in which export income falls short of payments (Time $T = 2$ through $T = 3$ in Figure 7.5). During this period of illiquidity, the developmental borrower has to engage in revenue borrowing simply to cover its ongoing interest payments. The longer the gestational lag, the more likely it is that a developmental borrower will end up permanently indebted.

Fishlow's analysis has two flaws. First, it focuses on a single country's choice of investment/consumption patterns and a single country's choice of responses to rising debt payments. As argued above and in Chapter 6, individually rational investment decisions created collectively destructive outcomes, for example, when the creation of multiple new sources of wool production drove down wool prices. Investors in the dominions predicated their borrowing on continued rises or stability in wool prices. When prices declined, all debtors experienced illiquidity crises verging on solvency crises.

The second flaw in Fishlow's analysis is the sharp line drawn between borrowing for consumption and borrowing for investment. Few countries actually borrowed for consumption per se. Rather, most borrowing was for development purposes. What really distinguished healthy from unhealthy developmental borrowers was the competence of their state and local investors. At the level of intention and execution, for example, Egypt was a developmental borrower investing in infrastructure and agricultural development.[9] As with the Australian colonies, the Egyptian state's ability to pay back these debts depended on its ability to extract revenue. In Egypt, however, the state's ineffective fiscal administration made it difficult to collect any taxes, pushing the state over the edge into insolvency. Land taxes provided Egypt's major source of revenue. Village headmen were responsible for collecting land taxes, and they did so haphazardly. Part of the Egyptian state's problem was that it was trying to do in about 30 years what the European states had already done over a period of 200 to 250 years.

Finally, as noted above, even developmental borrowing had significant revenue aspects. Creating new agricultural areas involved considerable time. Rail lines did not appear overnight, and building up a large enough pool of livestock also took several animal generations, even when new graziers had access to supplies from older areas. However, payments on new debt began immediately, requiring either continued borrowing (and thus the implicit capitalization of interest) or a decrease in discretionary imports. In practice, most dominions resorted to continued borrowing, despite its quasi-revenue character. Decreasing discretionary imports would only have cut customs revenue and thus imposed limits on today's growth. Instead, the dominions opted to put crises off to the future, hoping that export production would catch up with debt service demands for foreign exchange.

Roughly the same phenomenon occurred in the 1970s, even though by then states were cultivating manufacturing, not agriculture and transport. Manufacturing competence — at least at a level sufficient for exports — took a long time to develop. Even in South Korea, about 12 years elapsed from the initiation of automobile manufacturing until the initiation of large-scale exports to developed countries. Consequently, individual debt crises would likely crop up in all the time periods under consideration here.

## Different Structures, Different Outcomes

The proximate cause for all three crises was default by one major debtor. This event triggered a sharp, indiscriminate reduction in new lending, which threw otherwise healthy debtors into illiquidity and sometimes insolvency. In 1889 Baring Brothers, one of the largest London investment banks, failed to sell a large issue of Argentine bonds. Shortly afterward, in 1890, the Argentine government defaulted on some of its bonds, driving the value of Barings's holdings to zero, and bankrupting Barings. From its 1890 peak of about £100 million per year, total British overseas lending collapsed to about £23 million in 1898. For countries that opted not to or could not default (e.g., Britain's formal colonies), net capital inflows shifted to net outflows during this decade, driving most countries into depression. Defaulters got a somewhat better deal in that they did not suffer net capital outflows.

In the 1930s, the collapse of world trade also drove most sovereign peripheral debtors, as well as Germany, into default. The United States and Britain, which had provided about two-thirds of lending, stopped lending. Shrinking possibilities for trade and an end to lending produced depressions and then various experiments with Keynesianism and industrialization in the periphery.

The year 1982 also resembles 1890. Mexico declared its inability to service its debt to the high priests of international finance in Washington — the International Monetary Fund, the U.S. Treasury, and the Federal Reserve. Banks immediately ceased lending to all debtors, driving some into de facto default and most into a decade-long depression. As in the 1890s, net inflows of capital shifted to net outflows, driving down debtors' domestic investment levels an average of 20 percent.

The underlying causes for debt crisis in both the 1890s and 1980s are the same and slightly paradoxical. In the 1890s, individual, successful, debt-financed Ricardian development strategies were *collectively* unsuccessful. As with all borrowing, these strategies rested on myriad individual and public gambles that the future income stream from investing borrowed money would cover debt service. When all the dominions began borrowing to start up wool production, demand for wool and thus wool prices were rising rapidly. With so many new wool producers coming on line in the 1880s, however, prices began to fall steadily. As was observed in the last chapter, falling prices drove many producers and states into or close to default. The gamble proved wrong for most borrowers (and thus also for lenders).

The crisis of the 1980s had the same underlying causes, although important proximate causes can also be found in policy decisions in creditor countries. Many states borrowed for debt-led, Kaldorian development. (Chapter 12 discusses these development strategies in more detail.) Like the dominions, they all gambled on a relatively narrow range of seemingly promising industrial sectors: textiles and garments, shoes, toys, basic steel production, and cheap automobiles. By the early 1980s their production was booming just as the Reagan-Volcker recession in the United States led to declining demand for those goods, and as protectionist policies in the United States and Europe set severe quantitative restrictions on the volume of sales. Stiff interdebtor competition and volume limits on exports made it quite difficult for debtors to generate enough foreign exchange to service their debt. From 1974 to 1986, terms of trade for most LDCs fell about 60 percent. This decreased their ability to service their debt just as the U.S. Federal Reserve raised real interest rates — and thus debtors' interest costs — to unprecedented levels to fight inflation.

In the 1930s, the proximate causes of the crisis were the U.S. stock market crash in 1929 and bank crashes in Central Europe in 1930. Yet peripheral borrowers would have eventually found themselves in difficulty anyway, as their situation before the crash strongly resembled that of the late 1880s: prices for their exports were falling, and Britain's willingness and ability to lend was shrinking. Britain actually had a net capital inflow during the 1920s and 1930s, slowing growth in the periphery by draining liquidity from their economies. Meanwhile, from 1928 to 1933, export revenues for the 41 largest primary product exporters fell 50 percent.[10]

These crises played out in different ways because of differences in the financial institutions linking savers and debtors, that is, intermediation structures. In the 1800s, investment banks generally facilitated a transfer of funds from savers to debtors but rarely directly held debt themselves. Because debt largely took the form of bonds, default threatened the bondholders and not the investment banks. Bankers (like junk-bond mogul Michael Milken or the fictional Sherman McCoy of Tom Wolfe's *The Bonfire of the Vanities*) made money by taking a cut out of every bond sale. Thus, debtor defaults rarely threatened banks with financial catastrophe, and banks were willing to arrange debt relief and reorganization, bridging loans and new bond flotations as long as debtors tried to get their house in order. It was the many small bondholders who lost from these defaults. They organized the Corporation of Foreign Bondholders (CFB) to protect their interests, but this protection proved much weaker than that which the International Monetary Fund provided for creditors in the 1980s.

The 1930s resembled the prewar period in that most developing area debt was held by individuals. U.S. bondholders created their own CFB in 1933, called the Foreign Bondholders Protective Council. But the United States did not recognize this group, and it had little impact. As in the 1890s, the multitude of small individual bondholders lost from default.

In contrast, in the 1970s banks acted as *direct* creditors, aggregating savings and lending directly to states and foreign firms. Debt took the form of loans, not bonds. Banks made their money by paying their depositors a lower rate of interest than they charged overseas borrowers. Thus, unlike in the 1890s and 1930s, default in the 1980s threatened the lending banks themselves with bankruptcy. These banks still owed their depositors the money they had lent out to but no longer could get back from indebted developers. Since the United States and other states guaranteed the safety of depositors' savings, the potential for multiple bank failures also threatened creditor states in ways that the defaults of the 1890s had not. This difference in the form of debt and the kind of intermediation explains why the 1980s crisis has been more difficult to resolve. Banks could be more forgiving and flexible in the 1890s than they could be in the 1980s.

The nature of economic relationships between debtor and creditor countries also tempered the 1890s crisis as compared to the 1980s crisis. This difference reflected different political realities as much as economic realities. In the 1890s debtor and creditor economies engaged in complementary activities. Debtors exported primary products almost exclusively, while importing manufactured goods. The crisis of the 1890s scared British investors away from foreign investment, reducing lending in the 1890s to three-fifths of its 1880s level. By redirecting their capital into domestic investment, they caused an expansion in the British economy. After creeping forward only 8 percent in the 1880s, British GDP roared ahead with 27 percent growth over the decade of the 1890s. This growth in turn meant much greater demand for debtors' exports, driving up primary product prices and restoring debtors' ability to service their debt. Although debtor exports did cause employment losses in British agriculture, displaced agricultural workers were politically and economically unimportant; they could not vote until 1919.

Relationships between developing debtor and developed creditor nations in the 1920s and 1930s were still complementary, but the degree of complementarity was declining. Many of the major debtors, like Canada and Australia, were already beginning to move beyond the industries thrown up by their old Ricardian strategies. Thus, they tended to restrict manufactured imports from developed countries, which in turn limited those countries' ability to import from debtors. At the same time, many developed European countries had artificially stimulated their agricultural sectors during the war, limiting debtors' ability to export. The sudden emergence of developed debtor–developed creditor ties created uncomplementary relations. It was the developed country problems that precipitated the 1930s debt crisis.

In contrast, debtor–creditor economic relations are neither as complementary today as they were in the 1890s nor as free of political impediments to trade. Both debtors and creditors export manufactured goods. Although these exports can be complementary, they have not been. Debtor exports of low-quality manufactures have created unemployment in creditor countries, lowering demand for debtor exports. For example, during the 1970s job losses in textiles and garment production in the United States and Europe amounted to between 20 and 50 percent of the increase in persistent unemployment during the 1980s, depending on which country is considered. Similarly, debtor exports of small cars put car workers out of jobs. Unlike European agricultural workers displaced by imports in the 1880s, those textile and car workers and their employers constitute important political actors. They pushed their states into establishing quantitative restrictions on debtor exports. Thus, debtor terms of trade fell, and creditor growth could not pull debtors out of their slump because creditor growth did not lead to a reduction in the quantitative restrictions on debtors' exports. In this regard, the 1980s are more like the 1930s than like the 1890s.

Finally, creditor states were more vulnerable to both the economic and political costs of default in the 1980s than in the 1930s or 1890s. Thousands of dispersed individuals were direct creditors in the 1890s and 1930s. They had a much harder time organizing themselves to pressure their respective states than did the relatively small number of banks that had participated in loan consortia and the even smaller number of lead banks. Furthermore, these banks and the state had a mutual interest in preventing the collapse of banks.

The 1890s debt crisis could have been more profoundly disturbing to the larger world economy than the current crisis. Not only were the sums involved proportionately larger, but also international debt and equity (stock) instruments played a much greater role in providing liquidity—a money supply— for the late 1800s than is generally realized. The so-called gold standard could not have functioned in the absence of a large, well-articulated pool of debt instruments in both London and colonial/dominion financial centers. In any event, the 1980s crisis has been the more destructive of the two.

Why was the 1890s crisis resolved relatively painlessly? Because in the 1890s banks were only intermediaries and not direct lenders, they had a stake in providing bridge financing for *illiquid* borrowers. Even in the case of Argentina, which had defaulted outright in 1890, London bankers were willing to put together two debt-restructuring packages in 1893 and 1895. These packages tided Argentina over until rising prices for and rising volumes of exports created an enormous trade surplus. Banks controlled access to lending, but banks, aside from the unfortunate Baring Brothers, were not directly hurt by default. Default hurt the thousands of small savers. If banks could find new savers willing to buy foreign bonds, lending could resume.

Savers had little institutional recourse and little institutional memory with which to block such lending in the hope of recovering part of their lost interest or principal. Generally, the only opponents to new bond issues for old defaulters were ad hoc groups of the specific creditors affected by default. The CFB tried to pressure investment banks to prevent the listing of new securities from countries in default, but with limited success. The CFB's lack of formal ties to the investment banks, the state, and alternative foreign lenders weakened its position. Consequently, it tended to take a soft line with defaulters, offering bridge financing and debt writedowns.

For its part the British state had preferred since 1849 to let private investors deal with debt problems. It countenanced Bank of England efforts to revive Barings but not to the extent of a British involvement in Argentine domestic affairs. The exceptions to this rule are revealing: Britain formally intervened to take control of the finances of the Egyptian and Ottoman (Imperial Turkey) states when they defaulted, and joined France and Germany in blockading a defaulting Venezuela in 1902. Strategic considerations dominated the first two decisions. Control of the Suez Canal meant control of the shortest route to India, but even so the British collaborated with the French in restoring fiscal order to Egypt. Britain had gone to war in 1856 to protect the

Ottoman empire from Russia; even so, it waited for the Congress of Berlin to create a multilateral agency to oversee the Ottoman treasury. Similarly, the Venezuelan intervention was a multilateral European exercise.

In the absence of institutional memory and strong discipline on the part of savers, investment banks soon revived the flotation of foreign bonds. The hiatus in lending lasted only about five years. The consequences of this intermediation structure can be seen most clearly in the somewhat paradoxical treatments afforded Australia and Argentina. Argentina, which had openly defaulted in 1890 and had obtained debt writedowns in 1893 and 1895, was rewarded after 1898 with one of the single largest spurts in British investment before World War I. Australia, which had neither formally defaulted nor written down debt, suffered net disinvestment by the British owing to the rising power of the Australian Federal Labor party. Banks promoted lending on the basis of future expectations, not past behavior.

In the 1930s the Great Depression and World War II precluded any quick resolution of the various debt crises. Britain organized austerity budgets for its dominions and colonies, enabling them to maintain their debt service. The United States tried but failed in similar efforts in Latin America. Eventually, wartime inflation erased the real burden of most debt, leaving only the administrative details to sort out.

In the 1980s the structure of intermediation blocked a quick resolution of the crisis, but because developed country debt is not as large, it was settled sooner than in the 1930s. Unlike the situation of the 1890s, banks are direct creditors of today's debtors, and creditor state guarantees for banks and the banking system mean those states cannot be indifferent to the fate of banks. In 1982 the collective exposure of New York City's money center banks to LDC debt roughly equaled their capital. Consequently, when Mexico threatened default in 1982, banks rushed to stop lending lest they increase their own risk of collapse. These individually rational actions by banks created a collective disaster, for they meant the cessation of lending to solvent but potentially illiquid debtors like Brazil, and even to solvent and liquid debtors like South Korea. In this respect, the situation resembled that of 1890. Unlike in 1890, when banks had an interest in reviving lending, 1980s banks refused to continue to lend. Instead, the state had to step in and organize new lending.

Unlike the 1890s crisis, the 1980s crisis directly affected creditor states. Virtually all these states explicitly or implicitly guaranteed the depositor base of their banking system through schemes like the United States' FDIC (Federal Deposit Insurance Corporation). The collapse of major banks would have forced these states to raise taxes or to print enormous sums of money in the high-inflation environment of 1982. Rather than risk bank collapses, the fiscal core of the U.S. government, the Treasury and the Federal Reserve, used the IMF to force banks to commit new loans to debtors. Because the Federal Reserve and the Treasury regulate banks, they could pressure banks to cooperate. The banks balked at this commitment, and they in turn received assurances that they would not have to write down the value of their loans to LDCs.

De facto, some writedown did occur during the 1980s, for many banks dumped a portion of their loan portfolio into the secondary market at a loss.

However, the banks retained the bulk of the debt at face value. They then demanded full interest payments on the nominal value of that debt. When debtors could not make payments, the IMF arranged for a rescheduling of loans. This usually added the interest in arrears onto the existing debt, helping it to roughly double over the 1980s. *In effect, the banks forced debtors to do more revenue borrowing, creating a bigger long-term problem.* Because debtors cut investment back by an average of 20 percent in order to service their debt, they reduced their ability to grow out of debt.

This picture contrasts sharply with the 1890s, when debt was implicitly or explicitly written down quickly, when debtors refused to make interest payments, and when creditors lost out. (It contrasts even more sharply with the 1930s, when less than a third of interest in arrears was ever paid back; but the 1930s are not a good model for policy!)[11] In the 1980s, creditors largely retained the nominal value of their loans until the 1989 Brady plan broke with the previous seven years of policy by encouraging banks to write down debt. In the meantime, banks' persistent refusal to write down debt also disrupted the complementarity of economic flows between debtor and creditor countries. In order to make their debt service payments, and pressured by the IMF to maximize their noninterest current account surplus, debtors depressed their imports through massive devaluations and the proliferation of import controls. Debtor import cuts decreased economic activity in creditor countries, in turn decreasing demand for debtor exports. In the 1980s, the United States, for example, lost about $25 billion annually in exports to Latin America owing to Latin American debtors' efforts to maximize their noninterest current account surpluses. Creditors' exports to Latin America did not return to the absolute level of 1981, in *current* dollars, until 1988. In real terms, they still have not returned to 1981 levels. The banks' fear of extending new credits has also slowed the transition to new export commodities, which, as we have seen, was the key to resolving the 1890s debt crises. Most indebted LDCs are still trying to export the same old commodities into the same glutted and protected markets.

The 1890s crisis by definition marked a sharp departure from the regular patterns and consequences of investment in the 1800s. What about its more quotidian workings and consequences? Investment had important consequences for the normal functioning of the global economy in the 1800s: investment flows constituted the political and monetary foundations of the global economy. (Chapters 8 and 15 will deal with the international monetary consequences of the 1930s and 1980s debt crises.)

## Investment and the Gold Standard

The international monetary system is usually considered in abstract terms, but this treatment has the effect of disconnecting the monetary tail from the investment dog. The monetary system is not just a means for making exchange easier. Today, as in the late 1800s, the monetary system reflects two variables: domestic political arrangements and the scale of international investment.

International money exists to make nonbilateral, nonbarter transactions possible, particularly those that are discontinuous in time and thus impossible without some form of credit. Like the domestic monetary supply, in order to function efficiently international money should provide a source of liquidity that is noninflationary. Equally important, the supply of money should grow in tandem with the growth of transactions and the economy in general. If it does not, then deflation can occur, which is just as destabilizing as inflation. The key attraction of monetary systems based on gold (and precious metal) is also their key problem: the global supply of money cannot be increased through policy decisions. This makes metallic money, as well as systems of paper money tightly connected to a metallic base, immune to inflation. But, because the supply of gold and silver is partly determined by the accidental discovery of ore deposits, the money supply cannot be increased during periods of deflation.

From 1870 to 1914, the fact that the gold standard worked owed more to a large and growing supply of credit instruments, including stocks and bonds, than to any expansion in the supply of metallic money. Increased credit money accounted for 90 percent of the expansion of the global supply of bank reserves from 1816 to 1914.[12] The classic description of how the gold standard actually functioned is a better explanation of how international money function before 1850, and descriptions of the early post-World War II gold-dollar standard provide better explanations for the period 1850-1914 than do the original descriptions of that period.

## The Gold Standard: Theory

The classic description of the gold standard system usually runs as follows. Precious metals served as the basis for both international and domestic money. Banks, including the primitive central or official banks of the time, bought and sold gold or silver at fixed rates, exchanging bank notes for metallic money. Any ongoing purchase of foreign goods that exceeded exports would thus cause a net outflow of specie in one of two ways. First, domestic purchasers could remit specie directly to sellers to pay for imports (as happened overall with European imports from the Indian Ocean in the early years). Second, as foreigners redeemed bills of exchange and bank notes taken as payment for their exports, banks would have to remit gold to foreigners. This drain of specie money would cause bank reserves to fall, making banks call in loans and their bank notes (paper money). In turn, this situation would cause deflation —a fall in the price of goods in local currency terms—making imports more expensive and exports cheaper to foreigners. The flow of specie would then reverse itself as the change in relative prices made imports decline and exports grow. The converse was also true: successful exporters would experience rising prices as their metallic money supply grew, which in turn would price their exports out of other countries' markets but make imports cheaper, causing an outward flow of specie.

This system seemingly eliminates all the perplexing and political problems of international trade. As long as national currencies are not debased, their exchange relationship to gold gives them fixed exchange rates versus other gold-backed currencies. Similarly, the fungibility of domestic and international money means that balance-of-payments disequilibria automatically equilibrate through flows of gold. As long as all banks play by the rules and do not prevent gold flows, replace gold currency with paper money, or debase the currency, everything should work automatically (aside from time lags).

This system is actually a better description of the period before 1850, which is to say before the Bank of England was given a monopoly of paper currency issue in 1844, before the laying of transatlantic telegraph cables (from New York to London in 1851), and before the explosion of British overseas lending after 1860 created unified asset markets on both sides of the Atlantic. Before this period, a mixture of bullion and metallic money served as international money. Bills of exchange also functioned as money, but typically within merchant communities, not across them.

## The Gold Standard: Reality

The reality of the late 1800s was verbal acknowledgment of the rules and constant disobedience of them.[13] The Bank of France and the Bank of Prussia seem to have intervened freely to prevent gold outflows. Instead of flows of gold between countries, what made the system work was exchanges of sterling balances and bills of exchange *within* Britain, among British and non-British banks. These intra-British exchanges eliminated the need for physical flows of gold. Instead, banks settled their claims with one another, leaving a residue of unsettled claims. This residue was not settled by gold shipments. Instead, if favorable to Britain, claims would usually be settled by new borrowing in Britain on behalf of those who still owed money to British entities. If the claims were unfavorable to Britain, changes in the Bank of England discount rate (the "bank rate") would usually suffice to draw in an offsetting flow of short-term capital, thus obviating the need to export gold from Britain. *The monetary system mirrored the complementary flow of investment and goods in the real economy.*

This system worked for two reasons. First, world trade, though not identical to trade with Britain, closely approximated it. Sterling and sterling-denominated bills of exchange drawn on London banks could thus be used as a substitute for gold in international transactions. Outstanding international bills of exchange on London banks roughly approximated British trade at any given time. The institutional structure of banking also reduced the need for gold and gold flows. Many colonial and quasi-colonial banking systems were anchored in London. The London branches of these banks held sterling balances that effectively functioned as a country's "gold reserves." Exporters to those countries would draw funds from these London branches for payment, and the drawdown of those reserves would then cause the bank's other *home* country branches to restrict lending. In 1892 foreign and colonial banks based in London had funds amounting to about £370 million; these rose to £952 million by 1908 — or roughly one-third of total bank funds in Britain.[14]

A whole group of London banks specialized in the buying and selling of bills of exchange at varying rates of discount. These banks helped the market for bills clear. They bridged the time gap between otherwise offsetting flows of bills for export and import payments from any given area. Bills also avoided the problem of the gold supply not growing in tandem with trade. Trade grew at an annual average rate of 3.3 percent from 1870 to 1913, but the supply of physical gold grew only 1.4 percent per year from 1873 to 1892, and then only 3.7 percent per year up to World War I.[15] Even in the depressed years after 1873, gold lagged trade. Therefore, the expansion of trade relied heavily on the creation of credit forms of money.

The second reason why the sterling-based gold standard worked was the enormous volume of paper assets created by British investment overseas. The bills of exchange system worked more efficiently because of the pool of securities British investment created. Investment flows meant that balance-of-payment deficits could be financed for extremely long periods of time without requiring any adjustment — any shipment of gold or constriction of the money supply — on the part of the deficit country. Theoretically, this was not possible under the gold standard. Practically, however, the United States consistently ran trade deficits from the 1860s until 1900, as did many other agricultural exporters.

This system worked because the stocks and bonds created by British investment themselves were used to settle outstanding claims.[16] Securities (stocks and bonds) were used as a form of money. So-called finance bills were created when holders of the same security simultaneously sold and bought that security on both sides of the Atlantic. For example, a Canadian importer of British machinery would need pounds sterling to settle his debt to the British machinery producer, but, of course, his customers paid him in Canadian dollars. Using Canadian dollars, this Canadian might buy Canadian railroad bonds or stocks in the amount he owed, and transfer ownership to his bank. The bank would then sell the bonds/stocks in London, receiving sterling to pay off the machinery producer. By 1913 three-fifths of settlements via bills of exchange were done with such transactions. Unlike simple bills of exchange, whose value roughly corresponded to the value of British trade, the asset base on which the value of finance bills rested was a *multiple* of British trade. Thus, this asset base could be tapped whenever the rate of growth of the physical money supply or of bills of exchange fell short of the growth of trade. This asset base also grew procyclically: rising trade was closely associated with rising economic activity. This activity usually entailed higher profits for firms, which meant rising capital values for their shares and higher interest rates on bonds as the demand for credit grew. In turn, this caused the potential money supply to expand.

The so-called gold standard system of the late 1800s was thus actually a sterling–credit money standard. Gold remained the ultimate backing for money, but a backing that was rarely if ever relied on. The relatively small gold reserve maintained by the Bank of England shows how unnecessary gold actually was in a highly commercialized economy. Instead, the stability and value of the stocks and bonds making up Britain's foreign investments determined the stability of the monetary system. A series of defaults by Britain's supply zones constituted one of the few real threats to the monetary system.

Furthermore, the gold standard was not economically neutral, although in a peculiar way, despite its reinforcement of British hegemony, it was *politically* neutral. The concentration of bank balances and countries' reserve holdings both in sterling and often physically in Britain reflected and reinforced British domination of international financial flows. This domination rested in the first place on superior British manufacturing and productivity, which created an available pool of profits waiting for reinvestment. This pool depressed interest rates in Britain, making it possible for banks to engage in a discounting and rediscounting of bills of exchange for international transactions. This was the financial equivalent of the earlier Dutch practice of buying up Baltic harvests in advance, and at a discount. Like the Dutch, the British benefited from their hegemonic position; their suppliers conformed to British commercial practices, ideologies, and fashions.

As with earlier Dutch practices, this practice worked to the disadvantage of the economically weak. Smaller economies, economies with political authorities that were not committed to gold, and economies with weak tax capacity all had to pay higher interest rates on their public and private debts, reflecting greater uncertainty about repayment. This spread could be enormous: Uruguay, bereft of an effective state until the end of the century, highly indebted, and with a fiduciary internal currency, paid interest rates on its public debt almost two and a half times as high as those paid by the British state in 1889. In contrast, the premiums demanded for the Australasian colonies' public debt averaged only one-third over that for British public debt.[17] Thus, the gold (i.e., securities–bill of exchange) standard tended to reward the strong and further hamper the weak. To make investments based on borrowed overseas money profitable in the weak economies required nearly speculative rates of return and thus effectively discouraged it.

Curiously, the system was politically neutral in the sense that it could not be used as an instrument. Again, as with earlier Dutch practices, the expansion of credit money based on financial assets meant that political authorities had at best blunt instruments for influencing the money supply. The Bank of England could raise and lower its discount rate, and thus affect the underlying flow of short-term bills of exchange, but it could not control the long-term evolution of the money supply. The money supply ultimately rested on the supply of securities created by the capitalization of economic growth on a world scale. The Bank of England could not use monetary policy to punish British enemies. While markets could be such an agent of punishment, they did not define enemies in a political sense, but only in the sense of "a good credit risk is a friend, a bad credit risk an enemy."

This political neutrality reinforced the structure of incentives that underpinned informal imperialism in the dominions. Countries could opt out of the gold system and pay only *economic* penalties expressed as higher interest rates. Except in the formal dominions, elites retained control over their money supply, as the Argentine case demonstrates. There, ranchers opted to go off gold in the late 1880s so as to devalue their debts in a time of falling world market prices for their exports. When world market prices began to rise, they opted to go back on gold in 1900. The absence of extraeconomic coercion reinforced the elites' perception that participation in the British system was discretionary and to their benefit.

## The Collapse of the Gold Standard: Prewar Problems

The gold standard rested on Britain's centrality in international exchange, on British ability to manufacture efficiently and thus control its merchandise trade deficit, and on London's centrality as a market for raising capital. Once these strengths began to fade, the pre-1914 gold standard began to unravel. The next chapter describes the erosion of British supremacy during the chemical/electricity leading-sector cluster. Here it suffices to make only a few observations. First, as the Americans and Germans began to outperform the British in these new industries, the British were less and less able to export and thus more and more forced to draw down their overseas assets to pay for their imports. Put simply, as countries believed less and less that the British could actually export, they believed less and less in the ability of the British to honor outstanding sterling balances. So the gold standard was already eroding in advance of World War I: financial crises after the mid-1890s were more severe than those before that date. The Boer War, globalization of the U.S. Panic of 1907, and the crisis started by war in the Balkans all forced the Bank of England to raise its bank rate to unusually high levels in order to prevent a liquidation of sterling balances in favor of gold. In 1914 the threat of war — not actual British participation — was enough to start banks liquidating their outstanding short-term loans.[18] Exchange controls, closure of the stock exchange, and a bank holiday stopped this process, but at the cost of adherence to all the rules of the gold standard. World War I pushed an ailing system into its grave.

## Notes

1. Barry Eichengreen and Richard Portes, "Debt and Default in the 1930s: Causes and Consequences," *European Economic Review* 30 (1986): 599–640; Albert Fishlow, "Lessons from the Past: Capital Markets during the Nineteenth Century and Interwar Period," *International Organization* 39, no. 3 (Summer 1985): 383–439; Barry Eichengreen and Peter Lindert, eds., *The International Debt Crisis in Historical Perspective* (Cambridge, Mass.: MIT Press, 1989); Christian Suter, *Debt Cycles in the World-Economy* (Boulder, Colo.: Westview, 1992); William Cline, *International Debt and the Stability of the World Economy* (Washington, D.C.: Institute for International Economics, 1983); Herbert Feis, *Europe: The World's Banker, 1870–1914* (New Haven, Conn.: Yale University Press, 1930).

2. Michael Edelstein, *Overseas Investment in the Age of High Imperialism* (New York: Columbia University Press, 1982), p. 22.

3. United Nations Centre on Transnational Corporations, *World Investment Report 1991* (New York: United Nations, 1992).

4. Edelstein, *Overseas Investment in the Age of High Imperialism*, p. 27.

5. Feis, *Europe: The World's Banker*, pp. 49–59, 73–80. Note that Feis's concentration on European borrowing leads him to overstate the politico-strategic factors influencing lending decisions.

6. Edelstein, *Overseas Investment in the Age of High Imperialism*.

7. Suter, *Debt Cycles in the World-Economy*, pp. 92–93. Britain participated in only one of the military interventions. See also Charles Lipson, *Standing Guard: Protecting Foreign Capital in the Nineteenth and Twentieth Centuries* (Berkeley: University of California Press, 1985).

8. Fishlow, "Lessons from the Past."

9. For a strong argument that Egypt consciously pursued a Kaldorian development strategy, see Jean Batou, "Muhammad-'Ali's Egypt, 1805–1848: A Command Economy in the Nineteenth Century?" pp. 181–218, in Jean Batou, ed., *Between Development and Underdevelopment* (Geneva: Librairie Droz, 1991); a more balanced consideration can be found in Roger Owen, *The Middle East in the World Economy 1800–1914* (New York: Methuen, 1981).

10. Eichengreen and Portes, "Debt and Default in the 1930s," pp. 605, 612.

11. Suter, *Debt Cycles in the World-Economy*, p. 94.

12. Robert Triffin, *The Evolution of the International Monetary System: Historical Reappraisal and Future Perspectives* (Princeton, N.J.: Princeton University Press, 1964), pp. 2–20.

13. Barry Eichengreen, ed., *Gold Standard in Theory and History* (New York: Methuen, 1985); see also Marcello de Cecco, *The International Gold Standard: Money and Empire* (New York: St. Martin's Press, 1984).

14. James Foreman-Peck and Ronald Michie, "Performance of the Nineteenth Century International Gold Standard," in W. Fischer et al., eds., *Emergence of a World Economy 1500–1913*, vol. II (Wiesbaden: F. Steiner, 1986), pp. 383–412.

15. Triffin, *Evolution of the International Monetary System*, pp. 2–20.

16. Foreman-Peck and Michie, "Performance of the Nineteenth Century International Gold Standard, *passim*.

17. Marcello de Cecco, "Choice of a Monetary Standard: National Dilemmas and National and Supranational Solutions 1890–1914," in Fischer et al., eds., *Emergence of a World Economy 1500–1913*, vol. II, p. 396.

18. Marcello de Cecco, *The International Gold Standard: Money and Empire* (New York: St. Martin's Press, 1984).

# CHAPTER 8

# The Collapse of the
# Nineteenth-Century Economy:
# The Erosion of Hegemony?

*The superiority of Prussian enterprise over British lies in good organization; this
outweighs many major advantages of the English.*

*Werner Siemens*

## British Decline?

By the end of the nineteenth century, all the institutions of British hegemony
were slowly decaying. The major European states had abandoned free trade
during the 1870s and 1880s; Britain itself after 1890 began a slow retreat into
its colonial markets. Britain used its surpluses with imperial markets to offset
rising deficits with third parties like Germany and the United States. The slow
shift away from Ricardian to Kaldorian strategies in the dominions presaged
rising protectionism, to Britain's ultimate loss, in agricultural production zones
as well. The international monetary system proved increasingly vulnerable to
crisis with the decentering of trade from Britain. Industrialization on the
continent, particularly by Germany, and in the United States created zones in
which the mark and dollar, not the pound sterling, were used for exchange.
Britain's share of world import markets also declined relatively in the run-up to
1914, decreasing incentives to cooperate with Britain. Britain's share of world
trade fell from its midcentury peak of about 30 percent to 14.1 percent in
1913, while the U.S. share rose from 8.8 to 11.1 percent and Germany's from
9.7 to 12.2 percent. By 1929 the British share had slipped further, to 13.3
percent, despite World War I's detrimental consequences for Germany.[1]

The irony of this process is that Britain's initial success both led to the
successes of its competitors and undermined its hegemony. Under the pressure
of British competition, industrialists in Germany and the United States created
a range of institutional and technological innovations that propelled them
ahead of British producers. Starting from relatively low levels of output, both
experienced substantial increases in output and thus verdoorn effects, enabling
them to surpass British productivity levels. British rail exports also helped by

enlarging both the domestic and neighboring markets of late developers. European countries and the United States used trade protection to shelter these enlarged markets. Britain's success in creating highly competitive export-oriented agricultural producers overseas exacerbated political pressures for protection. As the extension of rail networks exposed more and more of Europe's microeconomies to world markets, it created a potential for protectionist alliances between European agriculturalists and industrialists.

Britain's declining hegemony can be seen at two levels. From below, despite continued absolute growth, Britain's productive base declined relative to those of the United States and Germany. This decline compromised Britain's ability to export. Both competitor countries captured increasing shares of third-party, nonimperial markets, forcing Britain back into its own empire. From above, Britain's ability to offer access to its own import markets declined, limiting the incentives it could offer for cooperation. Declining export share obviously led to declining import share, even though Britain could and did finance a considerable proportion of its trade imbalance out of its existing overseas investments. In the past, investment income had been plowed back into more overseas investment, enabling the British to extend their financial control over the major supply regions. Now it kept them from losing ground.

## The Erosion of British Hegemony from Below: Production

British hegemony eroded because its productive base eroded relative to that of its two main competitors, Germany and the United States. Four soft (managerial and organizational) innovations underpinned the rise of the U.S. and German economies: professionalization of management, cartelization of industry, electrification of production, and taylorization of production processes. These innovations allowed the United States and Germany to draw the maximum benefit from the hard electrical, chemical, and smelting technologies that became available at the end of the century. Britain's uneven and relatively slow adoption of these innovations caused it to lose ground during the chemical/electric upswing starting in the 1890s.

Britain's competitors took full advantage of the new innovations in steel, electrical goods, bicycle, and chemicals production. These innovations translated into higher rates and absolute levels of productivity growth and national income. U.S. productivity per unit labor grew by 2 percent per year from 1890 to 1907 compared to British growth of 0.1 percent; by 1909 U.S. productivity was over two and a half times as high as British productivity in 15 major industries.[2] From 1870 to 1913, U.S. GDP grew 4.9 percent annually and German GDP 3.9 percent, while Britain's grew only 2.6 percent.

Why did the British miss out on the chemical/electrical cluster? The new hard technologies of the 1890s created enormous opportunities for firms to profit from economies of both scale and scope, if they could successfully create managerial structures and workplace processes to take advantage of those opportunities. Economies of scale come from using the same highly specialized (and extensive) machinery to produce enormous quantities of the same standard product. Spreading the fixed cost of this investment over many units of output lowers the final cost per unit produced. Economies of scope come from using the same knowledge to produce similar, though not identical, products.

British firms responded differently to the new technologies than did German or U.S. firms not because the British failed to adopt some of the hard technologies or enter some of the new product markets. For the most part they did. The key difference is that British firms did so without fundamentally changing their managerial or production structures. Their failure to adopt the new organizational technologies decreased their ability to draw maximum benefit from the hard technology they did adopt.

## Hard Technologies and Firm Structures

The new process technologies emerging at the end of the nineteenth century made possible enormous profits from enormous economies of scale in activities such as food canning and processing, soap and chemical production, steel production, oil refining, and transportation.[3] These new processes also required equally enormous investment in product-specific production and transportation equipment, such as large tilting furnaces and mechanized feeder systems in metal smelting. These investments were profitable only if plants could run at high levels of capacity utilization and throughput, which allowed their large fixed costs to be amortized over many units of production. If they were run at low capacity utilization or throughput, then per-unit costs were high because each unit had to bear a proportionally greater share of the cost of amortizing a big investment in fixed capital. High capacity utilization implied relatively continuous usage of the machinery, and thus created pressures for stable sources of inputs and stable ways to market output.

Simultaneously, systematic research and development created possibilities for economies of scope. Firms with dedicated research and development (R&D) facilities could apply the knowledge they produced to a wide range of goods using similar production processes, like organic chemicals. The first university–industry complexes, forerunners of areas like Silicon Valley, started in Germany's chemical industry and in U.S. agriculture. The German chemical industry combined university brain power with waste products from coal mining to develop a wide range of organic dyes for the textile industry and an even wider range of organic pharmaceuticals, soaps, and fertilizers. By spreading research costs and production knowledge over many products, the Germans drove down costs. By 1913 a typical large chemical firm like Bayer spread its research knowledge over 2,000 different marketed dyes. By the end of the nineteenth century, the U.S. Department of Agriculture's Extension Service was systematically channeling knowledge generated in agricultural colleges to farmers.

## The Professionalism of Management

Only a new kind of firm — the multidivisional firm — could adequately capture these economies of scale and scope. These new U.S. and German multidivisional firms were bigger than most competing British firms. Qualitative differences in the way the new firms handled management, marketing, and manufacturing also distinguished these firms from the family-run firms typically found in Britain. Only larger firms could afford to make the investment in dedicated production and research facilities needed to capture the new scale and scope economies. In turn, these firms also needed more professionally trained management in order to use these investments efficiently. They needed marketing professionals to develop consumer loyalty in order to ensure that production systems could run at the highest possible capacity. These firms also needed to reorganize manufacturing processes to prevent workers from interfering with the flow of production and the introduction of new production technologies. Professional managers not only replaced the bevy of cousins with imprecise responsibilities found in British firms but also substituted CEOs for paterfamiliases.

These new firms first emerged in the United States because of the difficulties railroads were having in managing continental-scale operations. These railroads created complex pyramidal structures in which tasks like finance, personnel, purchasing, R&D, operations, and legal matters were centralized into specialized internal divisions, while daily supervision was decentralized to regional offices. Eventually, this format diffused to the entire manufacturing sector in the United States, spreading from boxcar and steel manufacturing to a variety of machinery producers and food processors. Banks enforced a similar process in Germany, albeit with initially smaller firms.

## The Cartelization of Competition

The amalgamation of many small firms into a few larger firms may have allowed for larger investments in these new technologies, but it also increased the risk of overinvestment and what the Japanese are fond of calling "excessive competition" by too many ambitious firms. As these new firms relied on high levels of capacity utilization to remain profitable, they greatly desired stable demand. This risk spurred implicit or explicit efforts to create cartels, or trusts, which the smaller number of firms made it easier to do. Through cartels (or trusts), firms coordinated their investments, selling prices, and production volumes in order to prevent overcapacity and dangerous levels of competition.

Cartelization occurred in both the United States and Germany but in different forms. The major differences between the two cartels were legal and financial. In the United States the passage of the Sherman Anti-Trust Act (1890) made cartels and cartel agreements illegal. In Germany, however, not only were cartels legal, but cartel agreements were enforceable as contracts. Thus, German firms often retained their separate identities inside the cartel structure, while U.S. firms had to merge their organizations into one company in order to avoid prosecution. In the long run, this approach enhanced the U.S. competitive position in world markets in the new industries of the late 1800s, because it forced a more thoroughgoing reorganization of production.

This legal difference dovetailed with a financial difference. U.S. multidivisional firms that developed out of smaller firms financed themselves through the stock market. They had to form new, unitary firms in order to get around the basic provisions of the Sherman Anti-Trust Act. Consequently, they incorporated themselves as new firms and floated new issues of stock shares to capitalize themselves and make payouts to the owners of the old firms. Most banks were too small to finance these new enormous firms. As a result, banks had less power over these corporations than in Germany. In Germany banks typically were larger than firms and used their control over access to capital to persuade recalcitrant owners to participate in cartels. Although later these cartels often gave way to a formal amalgamation of firms, no legal or financial necessity impelled this change.

These cartels took advantage of state policies that protected industry through high tariffs and helped them to maximize scale economies through military purchasing. High tariffs enabled cartels to capture their local market and then use that as a platform for expanding into foreign markets. Cartels dumped production into overseas markets at low prices, accepting short-term losses in order to maximize output and thus spread their fixed costs over the longest possible production run. By maximizing their production volumes and thus market share, they hoped to outcompete British producers in the long run. At the same time, state purchases of armaments helped absorb considerable amounts of steel and engineering goods.[4]

By World War I, most of the 200 largest firms in Germany and the United States were multidivisional firms. For example, in the United States the amalgamation in 1901 of firms representing 65 percent of steel production capacity created U.S. Steel. Similarly, in Germany the amalgamation of the electrical machinery industry under AEG and Siemens created firms that, in effect, combined the German equivalents of Western Electric, Westinghouse, General Electric, and the larger public utilities under one corporate roof. In contrast, before World War I, fewer than 10 percent of the 200 largest British firms were of the new multidivisional type.

The British organizational response to the competitive pressures of the late 1800s was federations of firms, or cooperatives, but they arose largely in the textile and consumer goods sector and not in producer goods or heavy industry. Cooperatives did block purchasing of raw materials and intermediate goods, raised capital jointly through cooperatively owned banks, and sometimes marketed jointly. Yet production decisions remained under the control of individual families/firms who made no effort to coordinate production or to change the scale of production. In textiles, this represented a reasonably successful adaptation to competition from abroad, and the British textile industry retained its global dominance, particularly in Third World markets.[5] In producer goods industries like basic metals, in chemicals, and in machinery, however, this cooperative solution was inadequate. Globally, Britain's two-thirds share (in 1880–84) of machinery exports from the four leading economies fell to only one-third by 1909–13. More telling, by 1912 General Electric, Westinghouse, and Siemens—U.S. and German firms—controlled two-thirds of the electrical equipment production *inside* Britain.[6]

British slowness to adopt new organizational forms led to glaring differences in the production of one of the key goods of the era, steel.[7] From 1850 to 1880 the British dominated world iron and steel production, accounting for about half of production and almost three-fourths of world exports. By the 1880s, however, the British had already begun to lose ground to the United States, where the average Bessemer furnace (used mostly for rail production) produced three times as much as the average British furnace. A bigger change came with the shift from Bessemers to open hearth furnaces. Although the British actually adopted the new hard technology somewhat earlier and more thoroughly than did U.S. or German producers, they did so in the context of a relatively stagnant domestic market. Consequently, the British tended to build relatively smaller furnaces than either competitor, attaching them to existing steel mills without changing the organization of work. Total British steel output rose only 3.4 percent per annum from 1890 to 1913, compared with 9 percent growth in U.S. output.[8]

In the United States and Germany, rail building continued at high volumes. Between 1880 and 1914 the United States added over 150,000 miles of track (three times the total British and German trackage combined) to its system, and Germany about 16,000. These extensions drove investment in Bessemer and then open hearth technologies for steel production, and permitted firms, particularly U.S. firms, to build furnaces that were much larger than those in Britain. U.S. and German metals producers thus benefited much more from verdoorn effects than did the British. Growing demand also permitted the construction of completely new mills, whose layout incorporated new strategies for organizing work processes and new auxiliary technologies for steel making. After a late start, by 1913 the average U.S. or German open hearth furnace was twice the size of the average British open hearth furnace. By then, U.S. and German firms had captured around 15 percent of the British domestic market for steel.[9]

## The Electrification of Production

German and U.S. metal smelting firms installed these larger-scale production facilities only because they could introduce electrically driven machinery for loading ore into the furnace and unloading molten metal. Adopting electrical machinery also spurred growth in the electrical machinery industry, passing verdoorn effects on to that industry while British competitors had to sell to a slow-growing metals industry whose scale of production did not require such machinery. Electrification of production overcame many of the limitations inherent in steam-powered machinery, as well as being much more productive than hand methods for loading and unloading furnaces.

Steam engines were bulky and immobile and had to be placed in close proximity to production sites. Motive power from steam engines was delivered by looping multiple leather belts around a large rotating shaft in the ceiling of the factory. This made it difficult to deliver precise amounts of power to individual machines. It also made it difficult to rearrange machinery on the shop floor in order to change the flow of materials or introduce new production methods.

Electrically driven machinery overcame these problems. Fractional amounts of metered power could be applied to specific machines, making it possible to machine metals more cheaply and to finer tolerances, which was critical for products made of interchangeable parts. Machines and factories could be located at some distance from power generation sites. Electrically powered cranes, tilting furnaces, and roller belts in the steel industry could replace human-powered charging and draining of the furnace, as well as the transport of hot raw steel. Bigger furnaces could be loaded and run continuously.

Because British firms tended to be family owned, they could not afford to shut down what often was their only furnace to reorganize production around the new technologies, while their larger U.S. and German competitors could selectively shut down works for reorganization. If their sales had been falling absolutely, British family firms might have risked shutting down to reorganize. Because the absolute level of sales continued to rise slowly, and continued to be fragmented over a large and diverse number of steel shapes, British firms had fewer incentives to make such costly and risky investments.

## The Taylorization of Work Processes

Electrification only boosted productivity if work processes could also be changed to take maximum advantage of electrical machinery. Work processes had to be "taylorized": workers' ability to control the flow of materials and the pace of work had to be removed in order to make electrification profitable. Existing work processes in the steel and related industries gave workers considerable control over output levels. Workers in mining and steel production were paid piece rates based on the volume of output and world market prices per ton. Skilled workers in the steel industry and shift bosses in mining acted as subcontractors, promising to produce a certain volume of output for the mine/mill owner, and then hiring enough unskilled workers to turn out the contracted amount. Until the advent of open hearth furnaces and electrification, mill and mine owners were content with this system because it minimized their risks; workers absorbed part of the loss should prices fall because their wage was linked to world market prices. They also shared part of the profit should prices rise. This system blocked full utilization of electrical machinery and newer, larger furnaces. Skilled workers – cum – master contractors had no desire to increase their workload, and owners could not really use wages to induce more work since wages were linked to world market prices. Skilled workers' control over the loading and emptying of furnaces and their insistence on using human labor for those tasks introduced bottlenecks in what was potentially a high-volume production system.

Just as their fragmented and relatively stagnant market dissuaded British metal firms from introducing electrical machinery, it also made them unwilling to attack the existing system of labor relations. The structure of ownership and management reinforced the disincentives for British owners to attack their unions. As individual owners, British mill owners could not compensate for lost output at their mill by increasing production at someone else's mill. At the same time, long institutionalized arbitration boards prevented individual owners from provoking strikes in order to reorganize production. These arbitration boards kept the labor peace, but they also perpetuated the system of tonnage-based wages.

The reverse was true for U.S. and German mill owners. They faced a rapidly growing and absolutely large market and so had huge incentives to try to destroy the union impediment to the use of electrical machinery. Cartelization in the United States and Germany facilitated coordinated lockouts of workers. Owners also found allies in unskilled workers, whose wages and job security were limited by the subcontracting system. Thus, U.S. and German owners attacked unions with abandon. Krupp led the way in Germany, combining an extensive welfare system (later imitated on a national level by Bismarck) with equally extensive police surveillance to preempt unionization. In 1892 Andrew Carnegie locked out the skilled steelworkers' union at his Homestead steel mill. Within two years, the skilled steelworkers' union was destroyed, and mill owners began introducing electrically driven trolleys, casters, cranes, and mixers, creating a form of continuous casting. The price of American steel dropped by two-thirds over the decade, and the elimination of many jobs made possible a 50 percent rise in wages as productivity rose by 300 percent. The unskilled benefited most from this hike in wages.

Although British mill owners adopted parts of the new technologies, they did not adopt the managerial and work practice changes associated with it. What occurred (or did not occur) in steel more or less occurred everywhere else in the British economy. The British did not quite miss the boat on the new cluster of leading sectors, but they sailed dinghies while the competition used cigarette boats.

## Conclusion: Decline from Below

British reluctance to adopt innovations readily available to them both reflected and reinforced the market situation they faced. Experiencing and expecting slow growth, they resisted investment in new, high-productivity machinery, new ways of organizing work processes, and new approaches to organizing their firms. In contrast, U.S. and German firms made self-fulfilling investments in the new technologies. U.S. iron production doubled every 10 years from 1870 to 1900, and then again by 1914; steel production experienced even faster growth, doubling every 10 years in the 1880s and 1890s, and then doubling every five years in the 1900s as electric machinery and taylorism swept the industry. By that point, total U.S. iron and steel production was four times British output. German iron output doubled roughly every 15 years from 1870 to 1914, and steel output every seven years. Rapid increases in output led to rapid increases in productivity, first in pig iron and then in steel. Rising productivity meant lower prices; lower prices meant increasing demand; and increasing demand meant higher output. Developments in metals were mirrored in the rest of the economy. Britain's gross capital formation locally and overseas averaged only 13.3 percent of its GDP from 1895 to 1913, while domestic capital formation alone in the United States and Germany averaged over 22 percent from 1890 to 1913.

U.S. and German firms were able to squeeze the British out of their respective domestic markets. Once those U.S. and German firms controlled their domestic markets, they used profits from sales there to subsidize exports into the large and lucrative British market as well as third-party markets. Britain bought U.S.-produced sewing machines, agricultural machinery, boot-making machines, light machine tools, and processed foods, and German-produced steel products, electrical goods, specialized machine tools, and quality chemicals. By producing for both domestic and export markets, U.S. and German firms were able to run at full capacity. Their size in turn dissuaded competitors from challenging their control of their market. Firms like Singer, for example, controlled about 80 percent of world sewing machine production and, along with a host of other U.S. firms, were able to transnationalize into the British market, squelching competitors (see Figures 8.1 and 8.2).

# The Erosion of British Hegemony from Above: International Trade

British hegemony ultimately rested on an import market big enough to induce cooperation and to cause its suppliers to reorganize their production processes in ways that favored Britain. As British preeminence in production decayed, so, too, did the basis for cooperation with Britain's particular ways of organizing world trade. Again paradoxically, the erosion of those arrangements was in part a function of British success in setting them up. This was particularly so with respect to the rise and decline of a general pattern of global free trade, as

*Figure 8.1 Share of World Pig Iron Production by Britain, Germany, and the United States, 1870–1914 (as percentage)*

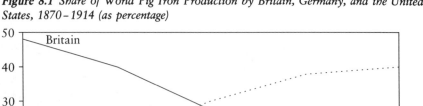

**Figure 8.2** *Share of World Steel Production by Britain, Germany, and the United States, 1870–1914 (as percentage)*

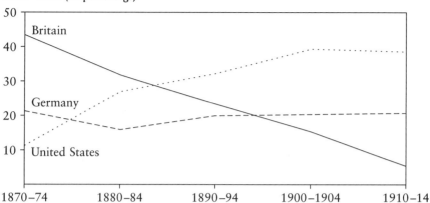

opposed to the smaller zone of free trade in the complementary British-dominion economy.

Hegemonic stability theory argues strongly that British decline led to a resort to protection on the continent and that this policy represented a major reversal of the pattern of British dominance. The present volume, in contrast, argues that the end of free trade in Europe signified the erosion of British hegemony at the margins, not at its core. The core of British hegemony in and over world markets lay in the complementary, market-based relationship between Britain and its raw materials–producing zones. It did not lie in Britain's trade with the European continent. Protection on the continent (and in the United States) by itself did not undermine British hegemony or reflect a declining hegemony. It was successful late development subsequent to protection that undermined British hegemony, by creating alternative von Thünen towns whose market pressures created their own agricultural peripheries. These competing towns threatened, but never displaced, Britain's dominance over its agricultural periphery. The best indicator of Britain's decline is its increasing resort to *political*, not market, mechanisms to maintain that dominance. These efforts began with informal preferential tariffs in some colonies and culminated in the Ottawa agreement of 1932, which set up a formal preferential tariff for all of Britain's empire.

Hegemonic stability theory usually attributes the brief flowering of European free trade in the mid-1800s to the rise and decline of British hegemony.[10] The first generation of arguments about hegemony maintained that structural factors at the international level caused the emergence of free trade. This focus on Europe and on free trade per se is somewhat misplaced, however. As argued above, hegemony arises from a coincidence of interests between the specific groups making state policy in the subordinated countries and those making policy in the hegemon. This convergence of interests arises from the market pressures emanating from the hegemon's industrial zone.

In the nineteenth century, interests converged around Britain's need and desire for cheaper raw materials and new markets, and the desire of potential suppliers of raw materials to cash in on this demand. This convergence established a durable free trade system in which the continued reliance on Ricardian strategies best signals Britain's hegemony. Free trade in this core area survived until most of Britain's suppliers opted for or were forced to choose Kaldorian strategies during and after the Great Depression.

The convergence of interests between Britain and European late developers and the United States was more tenuous. This convergence involved the late developers' desires to gain access to cheap capital goods imports and to finance those imports via exports to Britain and other areas. Britain gained access to markets this way, but never permanent access. Once these late developers could satisfy their need for capital goods locally, they closed off their markets and began preying on third-party markets in Britain's periphery.

## Free Trade among Complementary Economies

Free trade among complementary economies did not pose problems, at least until agricultural exporters began to develop manufacturing sectors through Kaldorian strategies. Agricultural imports allowed Britain to expand its internal division of labor and to become an almost exclusively manufacturing-based economy, at least relative to its European and North American competitors. By 1914 only 8 percent of the labor force remained in agriculture, and from the 1870s on the area of land under cultivation contracted by 30 percent. As in Ireland, the flood of imported grain after repeal of the Corn Laws in 1846 forced British agriculture to move into higher-value-added products. Agricultural exporters in turn used the British market to enrich themselves.

When agricultural exporters attempted industrialization, complementary trade began breaking down. When the British opened their market to agricultural imports, all of the great agricultural exporters reduced their tariffs. (They never eliminated them because tariffs were virtually their only source of state revenue.) The few agricultural exporters that attempted industrialization before the crisis of the 1930s (e.g., Canada in 1879 and Australia in 1904 and 1907) did so by cautiously imposing tariffs on manufactured goods. Only the United States stands out with an early protectionist tariff, reflecting the political dominance of the late-industrializing areas in the Northeast and parts of the Midwest over agricultural exporters first in the South and then in the Midwest. The earlier emergence and longer persistence of free trade in the complementary British-dominion economic system needs little explanation.

This complementary system eroded slightly under the pressure of U.S. and German export drives. Among the third-party markets, markets not under the direct colonial domination of one or another power, the most important was Latin America. There British exporters lost ground relative to German and U.S. exporters after 1880. Although British exports roughly doubled from 1890 to 1913, German exports tripled, and U.S. exports more than sextupled.[11] By 1913 the United States and Germany combined sold more to Latin America than did Britain. Meanwhile, in Europe, particularly Central Europe, the Germans carved out their own sphere of influence. Most of the overall increase in German exports went to European destinations. Consequently, Britain became less and less important as a market for the agricultural exporters on the global periphery.

As third parties shifted away from Britain as an import source, they still remained disproportionately reliant on Britain for finance. Thus, British lending, instead of helping British domestic industry, helped industry in the United States and Germany to expand by lowering its raw material costs and expanding its export markets. This undermined British competitiveness more than did the British investment banks' traditional indifference to long-term lending to British industry. (In any case, as we have seen, those industrial firms might not have taken up the investment anyway.) From the point of view of third-party countries, there was still no reason to abandon free trade. To the contrary, they could have their British financial cake and eat their higher-quality U.S. and German imports too. And since British exports continued to rise in absolute terms, no successful outcry for protection arose there. In the long run, however, Britain's declining share of exports and imports reduced the incentives for elites in the periphery to cooperate with Britain, while undermining British industrial supremacy.

## Free Trade among Competitive Economies

The more difficult question concerns free trade among competitive economies—for example, Britain and late industrializers in Europe and the United States. Here the progression of bilateral treaties that reduced tariffs and then the reimposition of high tariffs suggests that the sequencing of late industrialization efforts determined receptivity to British efforts to promote free trade. The classic example of bilateral tariff reduction is the 1860 Cobden-Chevalier Treaty between Britain and France, but Louis Napoleon III's unilateral reduction in tariffs on imported iron rails in 1853 anticipated this treaty. As Chapter 4 noted, Louis Napoleon's policies helped initiate railroad construction and late industrialization in the French economy. In the initial stages of this process, France could not produce enough iron to supply demand for rails. Maintaining a tariff would have slowed the expansion of the rail net. Cobden-Chevalier extended this earlier tariff reduction. Cobden-Chevalier also gave French exporters access to the much larger British market. Exports of wine and high-quality wool textiles funded French imports of capital goods. Prussia similarly reduced tariffs on imported rails during its first great railroad spree, but then raised both these tariffs and those on textiles and other manufactures during the 1870s. Once domestic output caught up with domestic demand, the need for imported commodities evaporated. Both France and Germany raised tariffs after the 1870s and 1880s.

The depression of the 1870s—so called because it was marked by falling prices and profits despite rising output—exacerbated this pressure for protection for two reasons. This depression and the shift to protection in some sense represented a perverse outcome of British drives to export rails and create new agricultural protection zones. Railroad building overseas opened up micro-economies to competition from the new agricultural producers, and the application of the steam engine to transatlantic shipping cut oceanic freight costs by two-thirds from 1880 to 1900. As the new exporters flooded the world market with cheap food, competing producers in Western Europe pressured their states for relief. The easiest way for states to grant relief was to raise tariffs. French grain tariffs equaled 40 percent of world market prices by the 1880s, and German tariffs 30 percent.

Successful late industrialization also created pressures for protection by creating overcapacity in the area of basic producer goods such as iron and steel. During the 1870s, steel production generally used the Bessemer process. However, its follow-on technologies — the open hearth furnace using electrically powered loading equipment — were most profitable on a larger scale of production than the Bessemer process, so that producers sought to assure themselves the greatest possible share of the domestic market. In the 1880s and 1890s, industrialists were able to find allies in agriculture for protectionist policies, for by then the gradual extension of railroads had exposed most of Western European agriculture to world market competition.[12]

## The Declining British Trade Presence

Britain's ability to function effectively as a hegemonic power rested ultimately on its competitive position in world markets. Declining British hegemony, understood at its simplest level as a declining dominance of world import markets, shows up clearly in the statistics on trade and manufacturing among the three big economies (see Table 8.1). From the beginning of the 1880s to just before World War I, world manufacturing output rose about 310 percent and world exports about 239 percent, but British manufacturing production and exports rose by much less — only 162 percent and 175 percent, respectively. These aggregate statistics conceal two important trends.

First, both the United States and Germany captured large shares of the British domestic market for the new leading-sector goods and of each other's market to the detriment of British exporters. The German and U.S. economies combined two features that were not found elsewhere: both were big economies experiencing rapid rates of growth. For the British, missing out on these import markets meant losing the rapid growth in output critical for verdoorn effects in new industries. Together the United States and German economies roughly doubled their share of world manufacturing to nearly half between

TABLE 8.1

### Share of World Trade and Manufacturing by Britain, Germany, and the United States, 1880, 1900, and 1913

|  | Share of World Trade (%) | | | Share of World Manufacturing (%) | | |
|---|---|---|---|---|---|---|
|  | 1880 | 1900 | 1913 | 1880 | 1900 | 1913 |
| Britain | 23 | 20 | 17 | 22.9 | 18.5 | 13.6 |
| Germany | 10 | 13 | 13 | 8.5 | 13.2 | 14.8 |
| United States | 10 | 11 | 11 | 14.7 | 23.6 | 32.0 |

1880 and 1913. Where the British economy more than doubled between 1870 and 1913, the German economy tripled, and, fueled by massive immigration, the U.S. economy sextupled.

Britain provided 26 percent of U.S. imports in 1899, compared to Germany's 19 percent. Although the British share rose slightly to 27 percent in 1913, Germany leaped ahead of Britain to supply 31 percent of U.S. imports. Similarly, the U.S. share of Germany's imports jumped from 12 to 21 percent in the same period, while the British share declined from 15 to 8.1 percent. Meanwhile, the United States and Germany were Britain's two largest sources for imports, particularly for machinery, chemicals, processed foods, and some kinds of metals. The multinationalization of U.S. producers into the British market in the 1890s and 1900s also undermined British hegemony. Britain's ability to export goods from the new leading sectors waned as the United States and Germany muscled out its domestic producers. In turn, this reinforced Britain's dependence on relatively unsophisticated colonial markets to balance its trade accounts. Selling to unsophisticated customers does not force producers to upgrade production, and apparently this strategy helped erode British industry's competitive position.[13]

As part of the second important trend, the United States and Germany began to force Britain out of third-party noncolonial markets and construct counterhegemonies in Latin America and Central Europe. Both used credit and investment to pry open markets and create zones in which the dollar and the reichsmark rivaled sterling. By 1914, the mark was used more widely in Europe as a reserve currency than sterling. The British increasingly relied on their enormous and politically created trade surpluses with India and a few other colonies to offset their trade deficits with Germany and the United States; both of those countries ran deficits with India. In 1910, for example, Britain's £60 million surplus with India offset a £50 million deficit with the United States.

Having failed to launch its boat with the tide of new hard and soft innovations associated with the chemicals/electricity cluster, Britain lost ground in global export markets. More and more, Britain had to use its investment income to cover its trade deficits; more and more, investment went overseas because of a relative lack of industrial activity at home. In the long run, this situation diminished Britain's ability to consume other people's exports. British productive weaknesses eroded the foundations for cooperation.

This erosion of British hegemony was just that, however—an erosion. Although the United States and Germany had surpassed the British in specific sectors, neither as yet had the kind of overwhelming productive advantage needed to displace Britain. The German economy still had lower overall productivity than Britain, reflecting the protection of an obsolete agricultural sector. Only Germany's larger population gave it a larger market overall. Although the United States had both higher overall productivity *and* a larger population, it was still a net debtor in the pre–World War I period. In the absence of some catastrophe, British dominance probably would have continued for some time. As it was, a catastrophe came along. World War I and the Great Depression finished off an otherwise slow process.

# World War I and the Collapse of British Hegemony

World War I destroyed the fundamental prerequisites for a stable international economy: stable exchange rates and easy access to credit. As we saw earlier, the gold standard rested on massive investment flows and the assets these investment flows created. It also rested on a presumption that gold would be freely exchangeable for paper money at fixed parities. European economies' underlying ability to support the gold standard through investment flows disappeared after 1914. Wartime inflation destroyed the presumption of convertibility. This discussion will look first at monetary and trade issues, and then at the link between trade and investment. Monetary problems alone could not have destroyed the institutions of the nineteenth-century economy, but investment and trade problems could and did. Chapter 15 will compare the collapse of British hegemony with the situation today.

## Exchange Rates

World War I killed the existing gold standard by aggravating all of its underlying weaknesses. During the war every European country abandoned free conversion of paper money into gold and issued paper currency on a scale unseen since the last continental war. Differential rates of inflation destroyed the old prewar exchange parities among different currencies and gold. If we set 1913 price levels at 100 for all countries, by 1920 price levels in the United States were 221; in Japan, 259; in Britain, 307; in France, 488; and in Germany, 1,000. Inflation disrupted the countries' ability to import and export at levels that reflected their underlying competitiveness in world markets and that would thus produce a balance of payments. The sharp deflation in 1920–21 also occurred unevenly across the major industrial countries. Two forces blocked immediate postwar efforts to set parities among currencies that reflected real underlying levels of productivity. The relationship between parity levels and prestige created political incentives to set some national currencies too high; the relationship between parities and overall economic activity created an enormous incentive to set some exchange rates low, in order to maximize exports.

Britain (1925) and Italy (1922) set their exchange rates too high for political reasons. Britain had an additional economic reason for choosing a high par value, for an overvalued pound would make imports cheaper, and Britain depended heavily on imports to make its economy work. This short-term good effect had an enormous long-term bad effect, because it priced British exports out of world markets. The French set their exchange rate relatively low (1926) in order to maximize exports. For its part, the United States tended to sterilize its current account surpluses by hoarding gold, thus taking demand out of the world economy.

In the crisis of 1929–32, unresolved exchange rate problems erupted into competitive devaluations. The British tried to counter a series of bank failures in Austria and Germany by extending sterling credits to those countries. The smaller European countries feared this would weaken sterling, and they also needed to offset their losses on holdings locked up in Central European banks. They began to convert their holdings of sterling into gold to boost their reserves, producing a run on the pound and forcing Britain off the gold standard. At that point, many countries devalued their currency either to maintain parity with the falling pound or to maximize their export surplus. This action in turn set off successive rounds of devaluation.

In varying degrees, virtually every country resorted to currency controls in order to manipulate the value of its currency and to control the level of imports. Currency controls forced exporters to turn foreign exchange earnings over to the central bank or some other authority, which then allocated foreign exchange to importers chosen for political or economic development reasons. Obviously, this meant that the freely exchangeable currencies of the gold standard had disappeared.

## Trade

World War I also disrupted the prewar trade system. Although most of the prewar period was characterized by protectionist tariffs, trade otherwise was largely unregulated. During the war, however, states imposed direct trade controls to assure adequate wartime supplies of raw and finished goods. The postwar disruption of foreign exchange rates created pressure to continue regulating the growth and volume of trade. For example, during the war the British state bought as much wool and butter as Australia and New Zealand could produce, at guaranteed prices, through joint organizations like the British Australian Wool Realization Authority. After the war, these organizations stayed in place as voluntary producers' organizations, financed by taxes on producers. These organizations attempted to regulate trade in primary commodities and built up enormous buffer stocks as prices fell during the 1920s.

Again, the Depression intensified this break with prewar patterns. States began using explicit quotas to regulate the volume of imported goods. States worked out bilateral exchange agreements that replaced the old multilateral (often triangular) patterns of exchange. These bilateral deals segmented the world's markets into blocs. One bloc centered on Britain, including British colonies, dominions, and a few of Britain's more important trading partners like Argentina and Denmark; a second centered on Germany, including Eastern Europe; and a third centered on the United States, including Canada and parts of Latin America.

This segmentation into blocs hurt some countries more than others. Lacking a significant imperial market, and so competing on the basis of productivity rather than power, the United States suffered the greatest fall in exports. Countries unable to export were also unable to import, and so they began encouraging the production of commodities that in an open market would have been uncompetitive. During this period many European countries became self-sufficient in wheat production, for example; this was one reason why U.S. grain exports fell.[14] These specific trade and monetary problems were not sufficient to cause a complete collapse of the world economy. Rather, the interaction of trade stresses with the enormous shift in global investment patterns caused by the war set the stage for the 1930s collapse. A stylized model of trade and debt conditions will help show why.

# A Stylized Model of the Interwar Period

A stylized picture of the world economy in the 1920s (and perhaps today; see Chapter 15) clarifies the salient issues. Imagine an international economic system with three types of countries: a large developed country that is also a large net creditor; several other, and often smaller, developed countries that are only marginal net creditors or perhaps even marginal net debtors; and a large group of highly indebted developed and less developed countries (LDCs) that are mostly primary product exporters. To service their debts, the developed and LDC agricultural periphery must either run large trade (goods and services) surpluses with developed countries in general or attract new lending to cover cumulating deficits on the investment income side of their accounts.

All developed countries that are themselves net debtors must run trade surpluses with the creditor country in order to prevent their own net investment income deficit from cumulating into more debt. (These developed countries obviously cannot run surpluses as a group with developing countries as a group, because this would only expand the latter's deficit and thus debt.) Economic stability in this system depends on the large creditor country either running a current account deficit, and thus boosting exports from debtor countries, or directly financing debtors' ongoing current account deficits. When the large creditor either cannot or will not provide either type of finance, trade flows will tend to contract as countries try to maximize their merchandise surplus by restricting their own imports. This individually rational constriction is collectively and systemically pernicious, however. By reducing everyone's exports, constriction forces all countries to further close their markets and perhaps default on their debts. In this situation, the large creditor must act as a lender or market of last resort, in order to prevent a collapse of markets as individually rational decisions cumulate into collective disaster.

The proximate causes of crisis in this stylized system are easy to see. If for some reason the major creditor country no longer can provide credit directly, all other countries will immediately be forced to reduce their imports. The more abrupt the contraction of lending, the more abrupt the efforts to constrict imports will be. How did the interwar period resemble this stylized picture?

# The Structure of International Debt in the 1920s

## The Problem: Round One

World War I undid the relatively complementary debt structure created by British lending in the nineteenth century. The war created a massive overhang of European debt on top of the existing high levels of debt outside Europe, while eroding Britain's creditor position. Neither Europeans nor Britain could import as much from the agricultural periphery as they had before the war, although the British continued to try. At the same time, both the Europeans and Britain had to export more to cover their increased debt payments. This conflicted with the agricultural periphery's need to expand its exports.

As Chapter 7 observed, the agricultural periphery had contracted high levels of developmental debt before 1914. By 1914 the dominions had foreign debts amounting to their combined gross domestic product and debt-to-export and debt-to-GDP ratios rivaling those of today's Latin American debtors. But Britain actually ran enormous merchandise trade deficits with the agricultural periphery, in effect trading its interest earnings for food. Similarly, the industrial European countries imported foods and raw materials, although not on the British scale. They paid for this by exporting to Britain and the agricultural periphery. Britain's trade surplus with major colonial markets such as India paid for its imports from Europe. The war destroyed these complementary flows in two ways. First, by creating overcapacity in global agriculture, it caused serious price declines that made debt service more difficult for the periphery. Second, it reduced British and European ability to import from the periphery.

During the war the agricultural periphery massively expanded output of foodstuffs and raw materials to supply European combatants. Britain spurred this expansion by promising to buy at fixed prices as much wheat, wool, and other primary commodities as its traditional suppliers could produce. Wheat acreage, for example, expanded by 34 percent in non-European areas during the war.[15] After the war, the Europeans resumed local food production. The ensuing oversupply of agricultural products relative to demand drove primary product prices down an average of 30 percent from 1923 to 1929, well in advance of the Depression. Among the most important traded commodities from 1920 to 1931, wheat prices fell by 75 percent, coffee 75 percent, wool 70 percent, and cotton 66 percent. Falling prices made it harder for agricultural exporters to service their debts, because they now had to export a greater volume of merchandise in order to earn the same amount of currency for debt service. Worse, by exporting more, they drove prices down even further.

If the agricultural exporters had encountered open markets, falling prices might not have been as big a problem; after all, the agricultural periphery had survived falling prices in the 1880s. However, all of the European industrial countries began protecting their markets, again well before 1930. What was going on in the periphery's traditional European market? Rising European protectionism reflected efforts by indebted European countries to maximize their own export surpluses. The Europeans after all had their own debt problem. Continental Europe emerged from the war as net debtors, because of inter-Allied borrowing; Britain's net creditor position was severely eroded by war debts. Only the United States emerged from the war a major net creditor. This shift in the status of most European industrial nations, including Britain, upset the balance between flows of capital and goods achieved in the nineteenth century.

In continental Europe, this situation forced each country to try to maximize its dollar or pound sterling surplus in international trade in order to have foreign exchange to service its foreign debt. Ultimately, everyone needed dollars to pay off their debts to the United States. Meanwhile, German reparations (or the lack thereof—nominally they were set at 132 billion gold marks, but the Germans paid only a fraction) aggravated existing debt-related trade imbalances. If the Germans ran current account surpluses large enough to pay their reparations, this would unbalance the accounts of both traditional debtors and other non-European countries. German nonpayment, however, put additional burdens on the new European debtors, particularly France.

Before the war, the larger European countries had generated surpluses by running merchandise surpluses with Britain or by skimming off surpluses that their tightly controlled colonial economies made with the external world, including the United States. Thus, Britain offset trade deficits with the United States and Europe through trade surpluses with and investment income from its dominions; they in turn ran trade surpluses with the United States and Europe. The postwar terms of trade decline and debt overhangs in the periphery forced those areas to restrict imports. Colonial empires thus generated less foreign exchange for the imperial countries at a time when those countries needed to rely even more heavily on their colonies. Nor could European countries run surpluses with one another to pay the United States; one country's surplus implied a deficit (and crisis) for another.

Britain's own declining competitiveness and weakened position as a creditor hampered its responses to this problem. Its heavy wartime borrowing from the United States transformed it from the international system's major creditor into a marginal net creditor overall and a net debtor vis-à-vis the United States. As a net debtor to the United States, the United Kingdom had to run either a bilateral trade surplus with the United States or a huge surplus with other countries that themselves ran surpluses with the United States. For example, in 1923 British exports to the United States amounted to a bit over £61 million. But the British government alone needed to find about £33 million annually to pay off war debts to the United States. Britain ran an annual average merchandise trade deficit of roughly £400 million during 1923–1929. Overall, its current account surplus amounted to only about £100 million.[16]

British policy choices aggravated the situation by lowering Britain's ability to export. The British restored convertibility between the pound sterling and gold at prewar parities in 1925, which made British exports too expensive. Overvaluation increased imports and decreased the incentive to invest in the domestic economy. Capital formation as a percentage of British GDP during 1921–29 fell by about 25 percent compared with 1900–13 levels.

Its economy weakened, Britain had difficulty maintaining the prewar structure of debt and trade. Diminished exports ultimately meant diminished imports and lending. Unable to do both, Britain mostly bought and only grudgingly lent. In the 1920s Britain lent less than half as much overseas in real terms as it had lent in the prewar decade. Unable to lend as much to old debtors, Britain opted to buy more, thus helping its debtors generate the revenues they needed to pay back their debts. During the 1920s the United Kingdom's merchandise trade deficit increased by 43 percent in real terms compared to the prewar decade. Consequently, Britain ran down its overseas assets to pay for the increase in imports. As a result, Britain's invisible (interest) trade surplus fell by about 20 percent during the 1920s.[17]

Unable to hold up global lending and trade flows by themselves, the British tried to lead by example and to promote cooperative solutions to the problems of German reparations and overseas debt. U.S. lenders, however, hesitated to commit capital outside of traditional areas like Canada and Central America, or the politically secure (Germany excepted) European countries. Britain also helped sponsor four failed multilateral conferences on mutual tariff reduction.

With Britain's ability to import eroding, why couldn't debtors simply increase exports to the United States in order to earn dollars for debt service? European countries and periphery alike found it very difficult to run surpluses via direct exports to the United States.[18] Few European countries or agricultural exporters had goods marketable in the United States. The United States was self-sufficient in most natural resources and agricultural products; where it was not self-sufficient, mostly in the area of tropical products, it drew much of its supply from captive sources like Liberia (rubber) or Central America (fruit).

Exporting manufactured goods to the United States was also difficult. The United States had high tariffs. More important, World War I had consolidated the domination of highly productive, taylorized, assembly-line methods of production in the United States. (See the Introduction to Part II.) Added to the natural advantages of market proximity, extant distribution networks, and customer loyalty, this productivity advantage made it impossible for Europeans to export all but a handful of products to the United States. The European countries' share of finished manufactured exports to the United States plummeted after World War I, reflecting a more general decline in the share of manufactured goods in U.S. imports.[19] The advantages inherent in assembly-line production allowed U.S. firms to go transnational, consolidating or creating subsidiaries in Europe. (See Chapter 11.) These hypercompetitive transnationals increased the flow of U.S. exports to Europe, as indicated in the sharp increase in the share of manufactured goods in U.S. exports—from 35 to 45 percent—in the 1920s. The U.S. trade surplus with Europe not only actually increased during the 1920s but also offset U.S. deficits elsewhere.

## The Solution?

Absent more exports to the United States, only three things could make international transactions balance. First, Germany could be made to provide the reparations the European allies demanded. The failed French occupation of the Ruhr proved this would not happen. Second, creditors could write down the debt overhang from World War I, freeing debtors' cash for commodity trade. The United States did write down small parts of inter-Allied debt after 1924.[20]

Third, the United States could become a lender of last resort to the world, financing the debtors' dollar deficits. During the 1920s the United States lent about $10 billion overseas. By way of comparison, this $10 billion in real terms equaled about one-quarter of all nineteenth-century lending by all creditor countries; rivaled the post–World War II Marshall Plan (though over a longer time period); and represented in *cumulative* terms an export of about 12 percent of average U.S. GDP in the 1920s. The United States more than recycled its current account surpluses during the 1920s, much as Japan more than recycled its current account surplus in the 1980s. U.S. lending prevented a 1930s-style explosion in tariff levels during the 1920s.

U.S. lending began in earnest with the 1924 Dawes Plan and its associated reductions in inter-Allied debt.[21] The $100 million government-to-government Dawes loan to Germany sparked a flood of U.S. lending overseas. From 1924 to 1929, the U.S. financial community floated $6.4 billion in loans, roughly double the rate of the 1920–23 period, with about 75 percent of it going directly to foreign governments. Nearly half of American lending went to Europe, one-quarter to Latin America, one-sixth to Canada, and the remainder to Asia, primarily Japan. European and peripheral debtors recycled this U.S. lending as debt payments to and imports from Britain. This indirect U.S. help for Britain and British exports in turn helped Britain to resume its lending, albeit at lower levels than before the war.

U.S. lending solved the problem of how to balance primary flows among trading countries. Compared with simply having the U.S. import more, lending only put off the eventual day of reckoning. For if the flow of capital were shut off, the underlying problem not only would remain, but would also have been worsened by five years of additional debt accumulation. And this is precisely what happened. For example, debt service for the major British colonies and dominions increased from $725 million per annum in 1923 to $900 million by 1928, implying that a proportional increase in exports had to occur.[22]

The system could keep going only if the United States continued lending. However, economic events and policy in the United States brought an abrupt end to capital outflows. By the end of the 1920s, loose monetary and regulatory policies had encouraged speculative excesses, including a near doubling of the stock market from 1926 to 1929. Hundreds of firms rushed to issue equity to raise capital for assembly lines. The 1929 crash, in which the stock market slid to half its 1929 peak, precipitated a recession. This recession trapped the billions of dollars invested in additional capacity during the late 1920s, as well as wiping out speculative financial gains. Although the Federal Reserve initially moved to increase liquidity in 1929, the money supply contracted by about 20 percent from 1931 to 1932.

During the 1920s, U.S. transnational manufacturing and financial firms had made large, long-maturing investments in Europe and consequently forged tight and complex ties with European financial and industrial circles. By 1929, about one-fifth of U.S. portfolio investment was in foreign, albeit mostly short-term, bonds.[23] But domestic economic and political realities defeated this group's desires to bind the United States to Europe's fate during the 1930s. Most U.S. firms were still oriented to the domestic market, and U.S. holders of liquid capital were not as tied to Europe as transnational manufacturers. When the 1929 stock market crash was aggravated by bank failures and tight domestic monetary policy, little capital was left for investment overseas. Without a last-resort lender or buyer, most countries tried to generate trade surpluses by resorting to tariffs to shut out imports. International trade collapsed by two-thirds from 1929 to 1932. The structures and institutions defining the world economy of the long nineteenth century were dead.

## Consequences of British Decline

British decline (and American ascent) before and after World War I was reflected in and reinforced four fundamental changes in the international political economy. Each change germinated in the interwar period but did not develop fully until after World War II. First, direct foreign investment (DFI) began to replace portfolio investment as the mode for overseas investment. Related to this development was a shift from investment in agricultural production, although mostly in developed areas, to investment in manufacturing. Since major agricultural producing areas lay inside the United States, U.S. firms went abroad looking for markets for manufactured goods, not sources of foods and NFAs. Before World War I and even more so before World War II, the most successful and technologically advanced U.S. firms set up production in Britain: Ford, General Electric, National Cash Register, Otis Elevator, Dupont, Singer, and so on. German firms like Hoechst (chemicals) and Siemens (electrical equipment) also made DFI in Britain. Absolutely, this investment was small, supplementing more traditional investment flows into raw materials extraction — for example, U.S. copper mining in Chile or German iron mining in Morocco. But it was both a harbinger of things to come and an indicator of Britain's decline. While British firms also began to go multinational, they largely went to colonial markets. If British firms could not compete with foreigners producing in Britain, drawing on the same labor and raw materials pool as British firms, they could not compete with them elsewhere.

Second, the intrusion of U.S. and German firms into British home markets created a novel problem for Britain. Now it was Britain that had to adapt, adopt, or create new institutional innovations so as to be able to compete with best practice manufacturing elsewhere; Britain now faced the challenges of late development. Like its erstwhile competitors at the beginning of the 1800s, Britain faced deindustrialization through competitive processes. Britain's former industrial success and the huge market this had created might guard against an absolute decline in living standards, but it did not guarantee future increases or competitiveness.

Third, the old complementary trade patterns between Britain and geographically peripheral agricultural economies began to give way to trade among high-income, developed areas in differentiated and branded goods. The old trade patterns rested mostly on an exchange of commodities between Britain and the periphery: railroad systems in return for bulk foods such as wheat and frozen meats. In the new, emerging trade pattern, Fords were exchanged for Mercedeses.

Finally, by 1914, fully articulated rail and steamship networks connected all parts of the world. Substantial parts of Europe still remained only diffusely connected to the world economy, but the beginnings of overroad trucking would soon fill in the holes in the lacelike pattern of areas tied together by steam transport. As this happened, true domestic markets began coming into existence in countries besides the United States, Britain, and dominions. These domestic markets would begin to have greater importance than foreign markets. The rise of direct investment from one developed country to another also signaled this shift, as manufacturing firms moved to secure access to their most important markets.

All of these changes foreshadowed shifts that would bloom in the interwar period and then mature fully after World War II. In the meantime, World War I would sweep away British hegemony and make a German hegemony politically untenable in Europe. The world economy then experienced an extreme and probably unavoidable period of instability in the 1920s and 1930s before the United States invented a new set of institutions to replace Britain's decaying ones.

The breakdown of British hegemony disrupted the international economy completely. With virtually all countries resorting to exclusionary tariffs, using currency devaluations to position their exports favorably in the few remaining open markets, and either defaulting on their overseas debts or refusing to lend more money, the value of world trade dropped by over two-thirds from 1929 to 1932. Because this collapse of trade seemed both cause and effect of the horrendous economic costs of the Great Depression, it imbued policymakers with a profound distaste for all the measures they saw as responsible for that collapse: bilateral trade treaties, managed currencies, exclusionary tariffs, and default. Aversion to these policy responses would color every institution of the international system America re-created after World War II. Nonetheless, a newly hegemonic America could have constructed many possible international orders around these aversions. The substance of the international system the United States created grew out of the particular domestic compromises achieved in U.S. politics during the 1930s and 1940s. Part II in general and Chapter 9 in particular deal with these compromises and the essential elements of U.S. hegemony.

# Notes

1. David Lake, *Power, Protection and Free Trade* (Ithaca, N.Y.: Cornell University Press, 1988) p. 31.

2. Marcello de Cecco, *The International Gold Standard: Money and Empire* (New York: St. Martin's Press, 1984).

3. Alfred Chandler, *Scale and Scope: The Dynamics of Industrial Change* (Cambridge, Mass.: Belknap Press, 1990) is the best single source on this phenomenon, but see also Alfred Chandler, *The Visible Hand: The Managerial Revolution in American Business* (Cambridge, Mass.: Harvard University Press, 1977) and Alfred Chandler, *Strategy and Structure* (Cambridge, Mass.: MIT Press, 1962).

4. Rudolf Hilferding, *Finance Capital*, Tom Bottomore, trans. (London: Routledge and Kegan Paul, 1981), chs. 21 and 22. For a provocative analysis, see James Kurth, "Political Consequences of the Product Cycle," *International Organization* 33, no. 1 (Winter 1979): 1–32.

5. See William Lazonick, *Competitive Advantage on the Shop Floor* (Cambridge, Mass.: Harvard University Press, 1990), especially ch. 5.

6. Alfred Chandler, "The Emergence of Managerial Capitalism," *Business History Review* 58 (Winter 1984): 497; P. T. Ellsworth, *The International Economy: Structure and Operation* (New York: Macmillan, 1950), pp. 421–422.

7. In general, the discussion of steel is drawn from William Lazonick and Frank Williamson, "Industrial Relations and Uneven Development: A Comparative Study of the American and British Steel Industries," *Cambridge Journal of Economics* 3, no. 3 (September 1979): 275–303; Katherine Stone, "Origins of Job Structures in the Steel Industry," *Review of Radical Political Economy* 6 (1974):113–173.

8. Bernard Elbaum, "The Steel Industry before World War I," in Bernard Elbaum and William Lazonick, eds., *Decline of the British Economy* (Oxford: Oxford University Press, 1986), p. 58.

9. Chandler, *Scale and Scope*, p. 491.

10. Charles Kindleberger, "The Rise of Free Trade in Western Europe, 1820–1870," *Journal of Economic History* 35 (1975): 20–55.

11. D.C.M. Platt, *Latin America and British Trade* (New York: Barnes and Noble, 1973), pp. 99–100.

12. See Kurth, "Political Consequences of the Product Cycle," for an argument linking protection to industries' position in the product cycle, and Peter Gourevitch, *Politics in Hard Times* (Ithaca, N.Y.: Cornell University Press, 1985) for an argument about coalition building between agriculture and industry.

13. Lazonick, *Competitive Advantage on the Shop Floor*, ch. 5.

14. Paul de Hevesy, *World Wheat Planning and Economic Planning in General* (New York: Oxford University Press, 1940).

15. Wilfred Malenbaum, *The World Wheat Economy, 1885–1939* (Cambridge, Mass.: Harvard University Press, 1953), pp. 236–237.

16. William Pullen, *World War Debts and United States Foreign Policy 1919–1929* (New York: Columbia University Press, 1987), p. 143; B. R. Mitchell, *European Historical Statistics* (New York: Columbia University Press, 1978), p. 307; M. E. Falkus, "United States Economic Policy and the 'Dollar Gap' of the 1920s," *Economic History Review* 24 (1972): 599–623. See also Harold Moulton and Leo Pasvolsky, *War Debts and World Prosperity* (Washington, D.C.: Brookings Institution, 1932), and Cleona Lewis, *America's Stake in International Investments* (Washington, D.C.: Brookings Institution, 1938).

17. Anne Orde, *British Policy and European Reconstruction after the First World War* (Cambridge: Cambridge University Press, 1990), pp. 328–329; Brian Mitchell, *European Historical Statistics 1750–1970* (New York: Columbia University Press, 1975).

18. See Falkus, "U.S. Economic Policy and the 'Dollar Gap' in the 1920s," for a systematic analysis.

19. Ibid., p. 607.

20. Pullen, *World War Debts and United States Foreign Policy.*

21. Steven Schuker, *American "Reparations" to Germany* (Princeton, N.J.: Princeton Studies in International Finance No. 61, 1988); William McNeil, *American Money and the Weimar Republic* (New York: Columbia University Press, 1986).

22. Charles Kindleberger, *World in Depression* (Berkeley: University of California Press, 1973), p. 84.

23. Kees van der Pijl, *Making of an Atlantic Ruling Class* (London: Verso, 1984); Jeffry Frieden, "Sectoral Conflict and Foreign Economic Policy 1914–1940," *International Organization* 42, no. 1 (Winter 1988): 64.

# PART II

# Back to the Future: The Reemergence of a Global Economy

# Introduction

Cars changed America and, by doing so, changed the world and the global economy from the bottom up. Cars, in our terms, mean the cluster of leading-sector industries that emerged first in the United States in the early 1900s and expanded rapidly there in the 1920s. This cluster diffused to Europe in the 1920s and 1930s and then expanded rapidly there in the 1950s and 1960s. This Schumpeterian cluster encompassed petroleum as an energy source, motor vehicles as a new mode of transportation and as a consumption good, and consumer durables as an additional consumption good. At the level of production processes, the common factor here is the use of continuous-flow processes, in particular the assembly line. As with Britain's industrial revolution, the emergence of this new best practice manufacturing paradigm based on the assembly line posed a variety of different and extreme challenges for actors in the global economy. Most of the chapters in Part II deal with one of these challenges or a part of one.

One common challenge can be summarized thus: Britain's industrial revolution and late industrialization elsewhere caused rapid growth in global trade, investment, and immigration flows. Although World War I interrupted this rapid growth and the 1920s saw international economic instability, these flows did not shrink. There was every possibility that they might once again regain their former rates of growth. Similarly, while the 1920s were politically unstable, World War II was by no means preordained. America's inability to cope with the macroeconomic consequences of assembly-line production led in part to the Great Depression of the 1930s and in turn to World War II.

Both events caused a sharp reduction in global trade, investment, and population flows. And because the growth of road transport opened up all the remaining microeconomies in Europe to the world market, it created social pressure for protection similar to that caused by the extension of railroad transport in the late nineteenth century. The common challenge thus had two parts: could global economic flows be restored to their nineteenth-century levels? And if they did regain those levels, what would the political consequences be?

First, we will discuss cars, then the specific problems, and, finally, the common problem.

## Cars: or, The Disruptiveness of a New Leading Sector

American firms produced about 4,000 cars in 1900. Only 180 out of 1,100 car producers ever made more than two cars, considerably limiting verdoorn effects and economies of scale. By 1910, production had risen to just under 200,000 cars per year, or about the annual average output of a typical car factory in the United States today. By 1921, output was 1.5 million vehicles, and prewar production peaked in 1929 at 4.6 million. The sudden jumps reflect the transition in the industry from stationary assembly by a collection of low-volume producers to assembly-line production by consciously high-volume producers. Henry Ford was the first to make this transition. His first and most important step was to insist on extremely high levels of standardization and interchangeability for parts going into the Model T in 1908. Standardization permitted Ford to introduce the moving assembly line, with its tightly scheduled, machine-paced flow of parts and assemblies, in 1913–14. By 1929, only eight firms remained in the U.S. industry, with Ford accounting for about two-fifths of this industry's annual sales.

Ford combined in one place all the elements from the prior cluster of leading sectors—professional management, cartel control over competition, electrification of production, and taylorization of work processes—and put continuous-flow production at its heart. This combination yielded spectacular increases in productivity. Ford's first crude assembly line in 1913 produced components, cutting production time for magnetos in half. What could be done for component assembly could also be done for car assembly, and the first assembly line for cars cut production time by more than half. Application of this logic to the entire production process cut the time required to assemble a car from 13 to 1.5 hours in 1914. This gave Ford an unbeatable edge over his domestic and foreign competitors until they, too, adopted the assembly line. During the 1920s Ford produced about 20.5 cars per worker per year; partly reorganized U.S. firms produced 4.3 cars per worker; and Europeans still using stationary assembly produced 2 cars per worker.

This combination of continuous-flow assembly and the prior cluster did not really represent any scientific edge on the part of U.S. industry; none of Ford's hard technology was particularly novel at first. Ford's system was a managerial innovation. The United States actually lagged behind Europe, particularly Germany, in many technologies such as electrical engineering and chemicals. Yet the assembly line allowed the United States to use its resources more efficiently.

## Specific Problems Created by U.S. Industrialization

This institutional innovation created four problems, which first surfaced during the interwar period and blossomed after World War II. The first problem had two aspects emanating from the links among economies of scale, productivity, and continuous-flow production. Continuous-flow production required large investments in machinery that could only be used to produce one type of product.[1] In and of itself, this investment guaranteed a high level of productivity, in the sense of a high volume of goods produced per unit of labor applied. Unless this machinery were used continually, however, the rate of return on it would be very low, because the machinery's large fixed cost could only be spread over a small number of units. If that machinery could be used constantly, then high profit rates would encourage even more investment in labor-saving machinery. More investment created a virtuous circle in which investment raised productivity and rising productivity increased the profits available for investment. This virtuous circle was vulnerable to unstable and inadequate levels of demand, however. Unstable demand discouraged investment by raising fears of cyclically high unit costs and low profits; inadequate demand could trap investment by creating excess capacity. So problem one boiled down to two questions: how could demand for products produced on continuous-flow principles be stabilized? And how could the increased supply of goods be balanced with increased demand?

This problem mostly confronted the United States in the 1920s and 1930s, with Europe later adopting variations on the U.S. solution. The diffusion of the assembly line out from the car industry and into allied industries like refrigerators, washers, dryers, and radios meant that major portions of the economy became vulnerable to sudden changes in aggregate demand. In the short run, the absence of any solution to this problem was an important domestic cause for the Great Depression. In the long run, domestic politics in the United States created the institutional basis for postwar Keynesianism, which both matched supply and demand and stabilized demand; the war set those institutions in motion. Chapters 9 and 10 deal with the U.S. efforts to create domestic and international institutions to cope with this problem.

The second problem was as follows. U.S. innovation of the assembly line made the production systems of other countries uncompetitive, threatening them with the same kind of displacement Britain's mechanized textile production had wrought on premodern textile producers. How could the Europeans avoid this displacement? In the short run, Europeans again could not find any solution to this problem. During the interwar period, employers attempted to introduce the assembly line and other American managerial styles in the face of considerable labor resistance.[2] European firms were unable to introduce American-style production until after World War II destroyed both employers' fixed capital stock and, through systematic deportation of leftists to concentration camps, most European unions. After World War II, many American firms began multinationalizing into Europe, threatening to displace European firms from their own home market. Chapter 11 deals with European fears and responses to this problem, as well as considering the multinational firm in general. In the long run, the European firms assimilated U.S. production technologies, and unions were recast along more cooperative lines. Europe created its own stable domestic market through generous welfare states, agricultural subsidies, and centralized collective bargaining systems. The Japanese response, which took a different form, will be considered in Chapter 14.

The U.S. and European answers to these two problems created the third problem: what happens in the global agricultural periphery when dissolution of the last European microeconomies reoriented European economies inward? European adoption of motor vehicles opened up all their residual microeconomies, with two effects. First, memories of World War II and the politics of the Common Market dictated increased European reliance on domestic food sources. Second, increased industrialization and income levels in Europe caused the proportion of income spent on food to decline. As demand for peripheral agricultural goods began to fall as a proportion of total demand, peripheral economies found it hard to earn a living as a national economic unit totally oriented toward external trade. This occurred despite absolute increases in peripheral agricultural exports, for those exports and the income they generated increased much more slowly than local population.

So Ricardian development strategies became less useful. In the 1930s, most peripheries tried to respond to this challenge by joining one or another imperial bloc and continuing a Ricardian strategy. Those that could not join, starting with Brazil and Mexico, switched to Kaldorian growth strategies based on domestic market – oriented industrialization. These inward-looking import substitution industrialization strategies rested on social pacts that stabilized urban real wages and offered considerable protection to nascent manufacturers at the expense of the agricultural sector. In short, the Australian model diffused to Latin America. After World War II rapid expansion of global trade created an opportunity, which several Asian economies exploited, for more export-oriented Kaldorian strategies. These Asian and Latin American industrializers, generically known as newly industrialized countries (NICs), exhibit all the classic symptoms of late industrialization. Those economies that could neither join blocs nor switch strategies stagnated economically. Chapter 12 deals with the shift from Ricardian to Kaldorian strategies, as well as considering the operations of multinational firms in the periphery. It compares industrialization strategies in East Asia, Eastern Europe, and Latin America during the twentieth century.

The first two problems, and to a lesser extent the third, created the fourth problem: would a hegemonic power (re-)structure the world economy, and, if so, how? Britain collapsed as a hegemon during the 1930s. The United States was the only plausible replacement, but the absence of any solid domestic backing for such a U.S. role in the 1920s and 1930s left the international economy vulnerable to collapse. After World War II, political maneuvering in the United States created a domestic coalition willing to support a limited international role. As noted above, Chapter 9 deals with this matter. In turn, Chapters 10 and 13 examine different aspects of the problem of re-creating a stable hegemonic order. Both examine the international cooperative institutions the United States proliferated after the war in order to cure international disorder. Chapter 10 looks at the international monetary system, while Chapter 13 discusses trade.

Chapters 14 and 15 close the discussion of the post – World War II period by arguing that U.S. hegemony is beginning to erode in much the same way as Britain's did during the 1880s. Chapter 14 looks at the erosion of U.S. hegemony from below. Like the United States and Germany with steel, the Japanese have introduced a number of institutional innovations enabling them to surpass the United States in assembly-line production. Chapter 15 brings this part to a conclusion by examining the erosion of U.S. hegemony from above. The "Introduction to Part III" — there is no Part III — signals the major conclusion of these two chapters. Contrary to the arguments of many analysts that Japan is poised to wrest hegemony from the United States, the sources of U.S. strength and advantage continue to be numerous and diverse. However, the United States does find itself in Britain's position circa 1890: challengers have generated institutional innovations that the declining hegemon must adopt, adapt, or surpass in order to preserve its position.

## States and the Regulation of the International Economy

Although so far this discussion has been cast in terms of countries' specific responses to the specific problems, a more general problem and response can be discerned. A recap of some themes from Part I will help here. As Chapter 1 discussed, states needed stable and large sources of revenue to survive in a militarily competitive world. At first, they relied on external sources of revenue, but the security and stability of domestic sources encouraged them to try to open up their internal economies. The dismantling of internal tariffs and the concurrent construction of internal transportation systems eroded the barriers to trade between microeconomies, enlarging the domestic economy. The very success of these simultaneous efforts to build transport networks and states also exposed newly created domestic economies to world market competition. In the late nineteenth century, states responded by using tariffs to control the degree of world market pressures experienced by uncompetitive economic sectors, particularly agriculture. By the beginning of World War I, however, most of northwest Europe had been truly incorporated into the world economy, for the truck brought nearly all rural areas within reach of imported goods.

As Karl Polanyi has argued, the extreme policy responses of states to the falling prices characteristic of the 1930s can be seen as reactions to the dislocating effects of markets on producers newly exposed to world market pressures. Above the foundation of tariffs from the 1880s and 1890s, states erected formidable barriers to international trade out of the bricks of quantitative restrictions on imports, foreign exchange controls and allocation, control over capital movements, selective exchange rate devaluations, and bilateral trade deals. They also stepped in to regulate directly output and investment in industry and agriculture. Tariffs in the 1880s and 1890s merely slowed the rate of growth of trade, but the barriers of the 1930s caused trade and capital movements to fall absolutely.

Relative to GDP, the foreign trade of most industrial countries fell to about two-thirds of the level prevailing before 1914. This level was akin to that in the early nineteenth century, when trade and capital flows were negligible,

**TABLE II.1**

**Imports' Share of GNP for Industrial Countries, 1880–1987[a]**

| Years | Values as a % of Nominal GNP | Volumes as a % of Real GNP |
|---|---|---|
| 1880–1900 | 12.7 | 12.4 |
| 1901–13 | 13.4 | 13.3 |
| 1921–29 | 10.0 | 13.0 |
| 1930–38 | 7.8 | 12.8 |
| 1948–58 | 8.4 | 10.1 |
| 1959–72 | 8.8 | 15.4 |
| 1972–87 | 15.1 | 21.7 |

[a]Data are means; the industrial countries are (until 1960) Western Europe and the United States; (after 1960) the same plus Japan, Australia, and New Zealand.
SOURCE: Timothy McKeown, "A Liberal Trading Order? The Long Run Pattern of Imports to the Advanced Capitalist States," *International Studies Quarterly* 35 (1991): 157–158.

representing exchanges between the skins of nations whose interiors were largely composed of microeconomies. World War II further depressed trade and capital flows. *While the thrust of U.S. policy after World War II was to reopen European economies to world trade, trade and capital flows did not recover to pre–World War I levels until the 1970s and did not surpass them until the mid-1980s.*[3] The entire period from 1914 until the 1970s constitutes an enormous divergence from the trends unleashed by the industrial (and transportation) revolution of the nineteenth century. (See Table II.1.)

The international institutions that U.S. policy created reflected and sustained this abrupt divergence in two ways. First, they tended to create escape hatches to protect domestic economic activity at the expense of international trade. Second, those institutions were not capable of handling the kinds of goods and capital flows characteristic of the late nineteenth century, for their institutional missions reflected a politically determined willingness to contain trade and capital flows, which was uncharacteristic of the nineteenth century. These postwar international institutions became less and less capable of handling tensions arising from an international economy that more and more resembled the nineteenth-century economy. Because the international economy has gone back to the future, those institutions have either crumbled or seen their missions change substantially. It is the states' resistance to this past as future that has caused the greatest conflicts in international economic relations.

# Notes

1. See Michael Piore and Charles Sabel, *Second Industrial Divide* (New York: Basic Books, 1985), especially chs. 2–4.

2. Charles Maier, *Recasting Bourgeois Europe* (Princeton, N.J.: Princeton University Press, 1975).

3. Timothy McKeown, "A Liberal Trade Order? The Long Run Pattern of Imports to the Advanced Capitalist States," *International Studies Quarterly* 35 (1991): 151–172.

CHAPTER 9

# The Depression, U.S. Domestic Politics, and the Foundation of the Post–World War II System

American hegemony in the international economy after 1945 reflects an enormous paradox. After World War II, the United States possessed a level of economic, moral, and military superiority never seen before, and certainly in excess of Britain's position even in the years immediately after the Napoleonic wars. Nonetheless, in contrast to Britain's unilateral style of hegemonic leadership, the United States pursued a more cooperative style of leadership. In a limited way before World War II, and much more so after, the United States constructed a series of multilateral international organizations in which U.S. preeminence but not dominance was assured.[1] What explains this paradox?

Two intertwined political and economic factors militated against an effort at a unilateral U.S. hegemony. Politically, no domestic consensus for an international U.S. role existed. Economically, both the necessities of postwar reconstruction and a preference for macroeconomic policies oriented toward full employment and stability precluded the kind of externally oriented, complementary international economy over which the British presided. Within the United States, many political actors opposed any international role for the United States, and so internationally oriented actors had to settle for a multilateral role. Those actors needed and used European demands for an international U.S. role as leverage against their domestic opponents. Because internationally minded U.S. actors needed this European help, they could not put forward institutions that embodied unilateral U.S. dominance. Postwar structures and institutions had to reflect European as well as U.S. interests.

## From British to U.S. Hegemony

In economist Charles Kindleberger's famous formulation, the problem with global economic leadership in the 1920s was that, while the British wanted to continue playing hegemon, they could not afford to, while the United States, which could afford this role, did not want it. What capabilities made it possible for the United States to become a global hegemon, and what changed its intentions? The innovation and diffusion of the assembly line in the U.S.

economy gave the United States more than enough latent economic capacity to play hegemon. The innovations of the late 1800s allowed the United States to catch up with Britain, albeit in tandem with Germany, and the assembly line propelled the Americans ahead of both.

During the 1920s and 1930s, however, the U.S. state was both weak and uninterested in a global role. Institutionally, it lacked an effective central bank (and thus any way of coordinating domestic and international monetary policy), deployed an army approximately the size of Portugal's, and relied on informal and personal contacts to coordinate macroeconomic policy with other countries.

Furthermore, state power and interests ultimately reflect the power and interests of the social groups supporting it, and a powerful bloc of business interests was indifferent to international problems. This nationalist or isolationist group centered in the Midwest and in midwestern heavy industries successfully stalemated efforts to assert U.S. leadership by a second, more internationalist group, centered in the eastern seaboard, East Coast industries, and the eastern establishment, particularly the major New York banks.

The Depression and World War II changed both capability and intentions. The war enhanced the U.S. government's ability to control its domestic economy and the global economy, and to confront potential challengers with unchallengeable military might. The assembly line permitted the United States to build the world's largest navy and air force. U.S. experience in managing multidivisional firms translated into the capacity to handle the complex logistical task of supplying military forces deployed worldwide, for it was only the United States that actually fought a *global* war from 1941 to 1945. Managerial technologies for running assembly lines and multidivisional firms in continental-sized economies eventually diffused to Europe and Japan. Nevertheless, as the Persian Gulf War of 1991 showed, the United States remains the only power whose military has the institutional memory, experience, and capacity to manage global and distant wars.

The war also created a capacity for domestic economic management. The war transformed the Federal Reserve system into a true central bank, and the Office of Price Management bequeathed to the state and the Federal Reserve the personnel, experience, and machinery to control aggregate demand and prices. The war expanded the reach of income taxation to the bulk of the working class, giving the state an enormous and broad source of revenue. A self-consciously Keynesian and expanded Bureau of the Budget gave the executive branch ideas about how to spend that money in the pursuit of macroeconomic stability.[2]

The war also changed *intentions*, partly by changing perceptions of self-interest on the part of the nationalists and partly by creating a third group, security internationalists, who were centered in the emerging sun belt/gun belt aerospace industrial bloc, to break the deadlock between nationalists and internationalists.[3] The third group was also internationally minded, but in a different way than the second, economically internationalist group. This three-sided struggle over U.S. state policy produced an amalgam of international agencies to handle global economic problems rather than the unilateral policies typical of the British model. Despite internal differences, the United States did reconstruct the international economy, and the fact that postwar institutions mirror the terrain of U.S. domestic political conflicts simply shows the degree of power the United States possessed at the war's end. The first part of this chapter thus explains why U.S. hegemony took the peculiar multilateral form it did. The second part explains the content, or the missions, of those multilateral organizations. It shows how the content of those organizations emerged out of the first problem mentioned in the Introduction to Part II — how to balance supply and demand in a stable fashion in the age of the assembly line — and, of course, from a balancing of interests among the three groups in U.S. politics.

## The Political Problem: Coalition-Building in the United States

### Three Contenders in U.S. Politics

During the 1920s and 1930s U.S. passivity toward international economic problems reflected a political deadlock between two groups of firms and farmers. The first group, which, following convention, we can call *nationalists*, was made up of firms and farms oriented almost exclusively toward the domestic market. These were steel and iron firms, railroads, coal mines, machine tool manufacturers supplying those firms, the banks that financed them, and the thousands of midwestern food-producing farmers whose production by the 1920s was mostly consumed at home. These firms were largely oriented toward domestic markets, and, because they produced undifferentiated goods like basic steel or coal, they did not have the technological advantages needed to transnationalize into Europe. In fact, some were uncompetitive and supported higher tariffs during the 1920s and 1930s. They were suspicious of any initiatives by the U.S. state to channel loans to Europe, fearing that this would make capital more expensive in the United States. Farmers supported state efforts to subsidize exports. They had strong connections to the Commerce Department, which for many years had acted to support U.S. exports but not overseas investment. For obvious reasons, they also had strong ties to the Department of Agriculture, ties that became even stronger when the state began directly regulating agricultural output after 1933. The Republican party largely represented this group.

The second group — the *internationalists* — included auto firms, electrical equipment makers (including makers of consumer electronics), producers of much electrically powered machinery, and the oil firms. Although these firms also sold the majority of their production in domestic markets, their incorporation of continuous-flow production processes made them extremely competitive in world markets. Consequently, all of them sold a substantial portion of output overseas or had transnationalized into Europe, Latin America, or even the Pacific before World War II. Roughly 15 percent of automobile firms' investment and nearly a quarter of machinery firms' capital was in foreign countries, compared with an average level of 6.5 percent for all U.S. manufacturing.[4] This group also encompassed two other elements traditionally oriented toward world markets: the large New York banks that financed U.S. international investment and trade, and the cotton and tobacco South. In the 1920s roughly half of cotton production and one-third of tobacco production were exported. This group had strong connections to the State Department and to a lesser extent the Treasury. The Democratic party largely represented this group after 1932, adding the industrial group to its existing base in the southern states.

Put simply, the first group did not see how spending tax money and political capital on saving Europe or the international economy during the 1930s advanced their interests. The second did. The first group dominated the executive in the 1920s, and the second in the 1930s, but the balance between them was too fine during these periods to produce any decisive outcome. U.S. policy in the 1920s and 1930s thus made only hesitant and erratic moves toward a larger international role.

For example, in 1924 the U.S. Treasury helped stabilize the hyperinflating German economy and tried to settle the war reparations question by providing start-up capital for a new German central bank and a new (and hopefully stable) currency, the reichsmark. This had to be done through private lending institutions, such as J. P. Morgan and Company, which underwrote the $100 million Dawes Plan loan. Meanwhile, nationalists had successfully instituted a procedure that allowed the State Department to veto private flows of capital overseas. Nationalists and internationalists also fought over debts left over from World War I, with nationalists demanding full payment while internationalists favored a writedown of debts to the United States. Again, neither side fully got what it wanted, for while interest rates were reduced and payments schedules lengthened, thus lowering the immediate burden of debt service, the debts' principal was not reduced. Consequently, the United States attempted to mediate a second round of informal talks to settle German reparations and war debts.[5] Finally, the New York Federal Reserve Bank also maintained close ties and tried to coordinate policy with the Bank of England, but largely because of the close friendship between the banks' heads.

Franklin Roosevelt's election in 1932 shifted policy in a slightly more internationalist direction, but only after an initial effort at unilateralism. Partly in order to be able to inflate U.S. farm incomes, FDR delinked the dollar from gold just before the 1933 London World Economic Conference. At that conference, the British proposed an international fund to help stabilize currencies and to remove controls over capital movements, a forerunner of the International Monetary Fund created in 1944. The United States rejected this proposal; instead, in 1934, Roosevelt devalued the dollar. Fears of the consequences of further competitive devaluations and trade restrictions led Cordell Hull, then secretary of state but also a longtime representative of southern cotton interests, to press for a more multilateral approach in both money and trade policy. Roosevelt obtained legislation permitting an enlarged role for the executive in international trade. The 1934 Reciprocal Trade Agreements Act shifted negotiating power over tariff levels from Congress to the president, bypassing the vested interests that had passed the highly restrictive Smoot-Hawley Tariff in 1930. It did so only for limited periods of time, requiring Congress to renew this delegated power. The 1936 Tripartite Monetary Accord created a basis for cooperation among the central banks of France, Britain, and the United States to control exchange rate fluctuations in their currencies. It paved the way for a return to a mixed dollar–gold standard. Finally, in 1938 the United States and Britain agreed to a trade pact, partly to counter Germany's rising power.

## Breaking the Deadlock

These two domestic groups remained deadlocked until the war changed everyone's positions, partly by changing the nationalist group's calculation of interests, partly because, as mentioned earlier, a third group emerged to tip the balance between nationalists and internationalists. The nationalists' position changed in response to the domestic and international consequences of World War II.

The great state-sponsored expansion of aggregate demand during the war convinced the nationalist group that an interventionist state was not necessarily a bad thing. Steel mills that had run at one-third capacity during the 1930s suddenly found demand forcing them to expand capacity. The nationalists conceded the need for Keynesian policy, as long as it was oriented toward the domestic market, but they wanted Keynesianism via massive tax cuts, not via a continuation of the enlarged and intrusive wartime state. The most they desired in the way of state-sponsored economic development was provision of social overhead capital like the Tennessee Valley Authority. They also wanted to try to roll back the power of the new and militant labor unions, like the Congress of Industrial Organizations (CIO), which had emerged during the late 1930s. In terms of their foreign policy, the war permanently removed the temptation toward genuine isolationism. Through support for the Marshall Plan and, for example, the 1948 Vandenberg Resolution expressing U.S. willingness to intervene militarily in Europe, they signalled a grudging acquiescence in a larger international role for the United States. Militarily, however, they favored a small, cheap army based on selective service, which would limit the means available for meddling overseas.[6] Similarly, they saw the ultimate source of American prosperity in its domestic markets only.

In contrast, the internationalists continued to push for a strong U.S. presence overseas. Their domestic and international interests were intertwined. Because labor peace was essential for continuous use of assembly-line factories, they favored an accommodation with the new labor unions as long as management controlled investment decisions. They also favored Keynesianism, but they argued that full employment ultimately required the expansionary effects of further exports. In 1947, the peak year for immediate postwar exports, some 5 million jobs and 7 percent of GDP relied on exports. The internationalists also hoped to tempt midwestern farmers out of the nationalist bloc with subsidized overseas grain sales. More exports were impossible without help for European reconstruction and without efforts to open world markets. Thus, internationalists wanted the United States to take up Britain's old pre–World War I role and restore an open trading order, free capital movements, and convertible currencies. While they preferred an accommodation with the Soviet Union to hostility, they ultimately settled on George Kennan's initial vision of containment to provide a measure of security for Europe. This vision called for a continued U.S. presence in Germany and Japan and revitalizing those two economies. Thus, militarily they favored universal military training and a large conscript army in Europe to deter any Soviet attack, but not to threaten the Soviet Union with invasion. Overall, the internationalists favored a state that was much more intrusive internationally and domestically than that which the nationalists favored.

The war created a third, albeit small, group — *security internationalists*. During the war, military procurement industrialized previously agrarian regions of the United States like the Pacific Coast and the South as shipbuilding and aircraft production moved there. The security internationalists' interests merged with those of existing West Coast groups oriented toward Asian markets. The military component of this group faced massive cutbacks in spending as the United States demobilized. For example, War Department forecasts estimated that postwar civilian demand could not support more than one-twentieth of wartime aircraft production. The civilian component faced sagging export sales as decolonization destabilized Asian markets. This group was fervently anticommunist and wanted to roll back the Soviet Union, and even more so the People's Republic of China after 1949. Naturally, this effort involved an expansion of military spending. They therefore had some interests in common with each of the older two groups. Like internationalists, they favored an expansion of the state's role: domestically, they wanted more government spending and thus taxation; internationally, they wanted a strong U.S. presence overseas, especially in Asia. Like nationalists, they feared the power of labor unions, which they saw as communist dominated and with whom they had had numerous conflicts during the war.[7]

This emerging third group resolved the old prewar deadlock, for now two groups could line up along a common axis of interests against the remaining group. Logrolling produced a series of compromises after 1944 on international economic and security issues. While significant conflicts over the conduct and content of foreign policy continued, consistent policy could be made where interests converged. The internationalists and security internationalists combined to press for a major international role for the United States. As the nationalists wanted, this would not be an expensive, unilateral role. Instead, the United States would attempt to create multilateral institutions in which all countries would be expected not only to cooperate but also to contribute. While significant conflicts continued over the conduct and content of foreign policy, consistent policy could be made in areas where interests converged. Thus, the International Monetary Fund would act as a lender of last resort, but not by forcing the United States to accept any increase in imports that might cut into domestic firms' sales. Similarly, the internationalists had to settle for the General Agreement on Tariffs and Trade, which was a watered-down version of the International Trade Organization they had originally wanted, but which threatened Congress's prerogatives over trade policy.

Because nationalists and security internationalists had common ground at the level of anticommunism, U.S. efforts to restructure the world economy would be justified by an ideological crusade against communism at home and abroad, which at times would take priority over the internationalists' economic interests.[8] Economic interest might have inclined the United States to try to accommodate the new People's Republic of China in 1949 as France and Britain both did. U.S. security interests, defined by internationalists in terms of containment, tended to favor adding China to the collection of states containing the Soviet Union. However, security internationalists' ties to the old Kuomintang regime, now displaced to Taiwan, prevented recognition of the new People's Republic. Finally, the security internationalists demanded a greater level of hostility to the Soviet Union than the internationalists might have preferred. In contrast, nationalists and security internationalists could agree that priority should be given to air and naval forces, and thus implicitly to nuclear weapons as well, rather than to the universal military training that internationalists favored.

## The Rise of Multilateral Organizations

Domestic political compromises thus forced the United States to pursue a peculiar kind of hegemony. Unlike Britain, which was content to act unilaterally and rely on markets to enforce its interests, the United States created and acted via a host of multilateral international institutions. Each of these institutions dealt with one of the tasks a hegemon might normally undertake. After trying to absorb its functions into the International Monetary Fund, the United States acquiesced as the Bank for International Settlements, a hangover from the 1930s, expanded its role as a clearinghouse among European central banks. The International Monetary Fund (IMF) would act as a lender of last resort, supervising and supporting fixed exchange rates among currencies. The International Bank for Reconstruction and Development (IBRD or World Bank) and the Organization for European Economic Cooperation would help European economies recover from the war, shortening the period in which controls over trade and capital flows were necessary. GATT, the successor to the still-born International Trade Organization (ITO), would help maintain open markets by supervising an orderly reduction in tariff barriers.

What about the substantive missions of these multilateral organizations? The new international organizations contained an economic paradox that shaped their missions. While they were supposed to undo the consequences of the 1930s and promote an open international economy in the mold of the nineteenth century, virtually all states had made full employment and macroeconomic stability an overriding goal of domestic economic policy. Why did international and domestic economic policy come into conflict, and what consequences did this conflict have? The answer lies partly in perceptions about the 1930s and partly in the peculiar economic problems created by the assembly line. Both suggested that a closed economy was a prerequisite for full employment and stability, even though closure in the 1930s had precipitated the Depression.

## The Economic Problem

### Supply and Demand and the Mass Production Firms

The assembly line and other continuous-flow production processes yielded enormous economic gains from a combination of economies of scale and productivity increases. The economic rationality of mass production rested on its profitability, and this was hostage to three different problems created by mass production's very productivity.

First, mass production was not profitable if demand was unstable. By using large numbers of capital goods dedicated to the production of single commodities, mass production was highly efficient, but this enormous fixed investment in product-specific machinery was profitable only if its cost could be spread over the largest possible number of units produced. Mass production systems were profitable only if they ran at something approximating full-capacity utilization. Unstable demand created unpredictable periods of low utilization during which the fixed cost of investment in dedicated machinery dragged down the rate of return. Thus, while mass production might be more productive than other systems in terms of output per hour of labor, in economic terms its profitability rested on conditions that were largely outside the firms' control. Fear of surplus capacity related to the business cycle thus inhibits investment in mass production processes, despite their absolute productivity advantages over other types of production processes.

The economic rationality of mass production was therefore hostage to its supply rigidity. Because dedicated facilities had to be used continuously, supply could not be changed; instead, some way had to be found to both stabilize demand and raise it to a level adequate to absorb supply. The first efforts at monopolization and/or cartelization offset unstable demand by restricting output to a level well below average demand. These efforts allowed firms to match supply to the stable part of demand. As the proportion of mass production firms grew in the economy and as they became more dependent on one another, this unilateral solution could not work. If a few firms misjudged markets or acted out of narrow self-interest, all would suffer.[9]

Second, even when demand is stable, the absolute level of demand determines the extent to which mass production techniques can be used. Although mass production increased the productivity of the average worker, wage increases and thus the ability to consume lagged productivity. While many mass production firms raised wages in the United States during the 1910s and 1920s, they did so with an eye not toward balancing supply and demand but toward stabilizing their own workforces. Ford introduced its famous $5- a-day wage in order to lower labor turnover from a crippling 300 percent per year to more tolerable levels.

Finally, the assembly line was extremely vulnerable to strikes. Because of the high level of interdependence among all the different components and subassemblies flowing into or down the line, a strike by only a small fraction of workers could paralyze the entire line. It made no sense to produce automobiles without transmissions, or radios without power cords. During the 1930s, U.S. workers would make an institutional innovation of their own: the sit-down strike. This tactic allowed them to shut down assembly-line production without drawing a violent response by owners.

## Unionization and Macroeconomic Stabilization

In the United States the innovation of the sit-down strike helped resolve these problems. Franklin Roosevelt's victories in 1932 and 1936 created a climate favorable to unionization. When the economy began to climb out of depression in 1935, workers used sit-down strikes to pressure employers to recognize unions, give higher wages, and provide a measure of dignity at work. The automobile industry had experienced catastrophic levels of underutilized capacity after demand fell from over 4 million cars in 1929 to under 1.5 million in 1932. Firms, wanting to take advantage of rising demand in 1935–37, were reluctant to risk prolonged strikes. In 1935 the United Autoworkers Union (UAW) conducted its first sit-down strike, which then spread to the car assembly lines. In 1937, a total of 28 million person-days of labor were lost to strikes, the all-time high for the prewar period.

The Congress moved to help workers. In 1935 it passed the National Labor Relations (Wagner) Act, which the Supreme Court affirmed in 1937. This act confirmed the legality of unions and established conditions for collective bargaining. This law was reinforced in 1938 by the Fair Labor Standards Act, which set a minimum wage and created a uniform 40-hour workweek. The number of unionized workers rose from 4 million in 1934 to 15 million in 1945; by then, about 70 percent of industrial workers were unionized, and many employers offered nonunionized workers union-level wages to preempt unionization.

Workers and/or employers may or may not have understood the macroeconomic consequences of unionization. In hindsight, however, unionization resolved most of the problems of macroeconomic stabilization associated with the assembly line. High and rising wages meant that aggregate demand rose. Long-term contracts with generous health and unemployment benefits stabilized aggregate demand by removing the long-term risk of going into debt to buy cars and houses. The United States promoted its style of unionization in Europe after the war, diffusing this particular solution to macroeconomic stability.[10]

Unionization, mass production, and Keynesianism all conflicted with the norms of the old pre–World War I British-dominated international system. In that system, economic cycles were allowed to run their course, and production levels rose and fell in response to demand. If firms could not survive through a recession/depression, they went out of business. Internationally, the pulsation of people and capital from Europe and to the agricultural periphery mirrored domestic waves of expansion and stagnation. Over the long run, nations' trade surpluses and deficits matched because the international production structure was complementary. In the new system, however, everyone tried to damp down the business cycle. Firms produced through recessions, gambling that demand would eventually catch up with supply; unions demanded rising real wages; states accommodated both by expanding the money supply during recessions. States could not allow trade surpluses or deficits to disrupt their management of aggregate demand. Nor did they countenance much in the way of internationally imposed limits on their ability to manage their own macroeconomy in accordance with local political demands.

## The International Consequences

Each of the multilateral international organizations created by the United States and its European allies thus reflected their determination to have their domestic cake while dining in international markets. The mission of these organizations reflected contradictions between the domestic and international lessons of the Great Depression of the 1930s. Before World War I, states had little interest in preventing unemployment and aggregate demand from fluctuating. Nor could they really control the domestic money supply. However, the war gave them the tools and motivation for doing so. The high unemployment of the 1930s had created highly destabilizing political struggles in virtually all countries. Most observers linked high unemployment to the attractiveness of fascism and communism. Thus, having spent the better part of a century systematically opening up their interior microeconomies to world market forces, for both political and economic reasons states now wanted to limit the impact of international economic fluctuations on their domestic economies. The domestic lesson of the Depression was that allowing the international market an untrammeled ability to influence domestic production and employment was a recipe for disaster. Allowing the international market to affect the money supply would mean that states had lost control over their internal economy.

This domestic lesson conflicted with the supposed international lessons of the 1920s and 1930s noted in Chapter 8. Keynes summarized those lessons pithily, calling for "the freest possible economic interchange without discriminations, without exchange controls, without economic preferences utilized for political purposes and without all of the manifold economic barriers which had in [his] judgement been so clearly responsible for the present world collapse."[11] Those lessons seemed to indicate that any deviation from liberal principles would throw the international economy into conflict and a downward spiral. It also ran contrary to the needs of firms that had invested in productive capacity too large for their own domestic markets. They needed to export.

Therefore, all the institutions established by the United States in cooperation with Europe had as their mission the promotion of a liberal economic order similar to the pre-World War I order—until that mission came in conflict with the principle of domestic full employment and stable demand. John Ruggie has called this contradiction "embedded liberalism," arguing that a preference for a liberal international monetary and trading order was embedded in a set of institutions ostensibly oriented toward preserving domestic economic stability.[12] Furthermore, the U.S. position on these agencies' missions reflected the unsettled dispute among the three U.S. political factions. These twin constraints on international institutions can be seen clearly in fights over the establishment and mission of the International Monetary Fund and in the failure to establish an International Trade Organization (ITO) and the substitution of the more limited General Agreement on Tariffs and Trade. These fights began at the very first U.S. and British meetings held in 1941 to map out the postwar world, and they continued through to the 1944 Bretton Woods Conference, which formalized plans for the postwar monetary order. Disputes over the ITO continued into the 1940s.

## The International Monetary Fund

In theory at least, the IMF's mission reflected the liberal international lessons of the 1920s and the Depression: the world needed stable, fixed, and realistic exchange rates. As before 1914, currencies would be backed by gold and would be freely exchangeable. Exchange rates would be fixed to prevent the competitive devaluations of the 1930s. The IMF would act as a lender to support those exchange rates when countries ran temporary balance-of-payments deficits. The United States and Britain, the major actors at the 1944 Bretton Woods Conference, put different political spins on this mission, however. After all, given fixed exchange rates, balance could be achieved in one of three ways. Direct import controls in the mode of the 1930s could be used, but the United States and Britain both agreed that this policy had been a mistake in the 1930s. Second, an imbalance of payments meant that a country consumed more than it produced, leading to more imports than exports. Imports (demand) and exports (supply) could be brought into balance by deflating the economy, inducing a recession, and thus lowering demand for imports. Third, balance could be created by increasing domestic supply, lending money to support ongoing economic activity, and thus increasing exports or import substitutes. The United States and Britain disagreed as to which of the last two methods should predominate.

John Maynard Keynes led Britain's delegation to the conference. Consistent with his beliefs, he allowed the domestic lessons of the Depression to determine his views. He put the maintenance of a stable macroeconomy and full employment ahead of maintenance of fixed exchange rates. Instead of local economies adjusting to global pressures, the global economy would adjust to local desires for full employment. Keynes, and to a large extent the rest of the Europeans, wanted the IMF to act as a kind of global central bank. The IMF would create a fiduciary or paper money—money without a gold backing to assure its value—called the bancor. Countries running balance-of-payments deficits could borrow this paper money and use it to pay for exports from countries running balance-of-payments surpluses. By this means, debtor/trade-deficit countries could avoid having to deflate their domestic economy. Countries that were running balance-of-payments surpluses would have to accept this fiduciary money for their exports or use inflationary policies to stimulate their own economies. Keynes also wanted the IMF to have the power to force surplus countries to revalue their currency, which would decrease their ability to export.

Creditor countries thus would have to bear a major part of the cost of stabilizing the global macroeconomy. This stood in stark contrast to the old gold standard, in which outflows of gold and foreign exchange from deficit countries automatically forced deflation. Keynes's system in effect prevented trade-surplus countries from drawing down the gold or money supply in trade-deficit countries.

The United States, on the other hand, favored a mix of policies that reflected the balance among its different political groups. Nationalists opposed funding the IMF on the scale required for it to create a fiduciary currency, and they were skeptical about funding it at all. They favored having deficit countries bear all the costs of coming back into balance through policies that induced local deflation. Internationalists favored a stronger IMF. However, because they realized that the United States would naturally be the world's largest (and perhaps only) creditor/surplus country for quite some time, they also favored limiting the ability of other countries to draw on U.S. resources in the manner Keynes desired. Instead, they were willing to allow deficit countries to use nonmonetary means — temporary discrimination against surplus countries' exports — to bring their international payment position back into balance while borrowing small amounts from the IMF.

The U.S. position largely prevailed. Both sides agreed that exchange rates should be fixed, but any re-/devaluations by more than 1 percent, not Keynes's 5 percent, needed IMF permission. Deficit countries, not surplus countries, were expected to bear the cost of restoring balance through deflation. The IMF was capitalized at $8.8 billion, more than the original $5 billion in the U.S. proposal but much less than Keynes's $26 billion. The IMF could not force surplus nations to change their exchange rates. And, rather than having an automatic right to borrow IMF funds, deficit countries had to seek IMF approval for borrowing in excess of half of their initial contribution to the Fund.

## The International Trade Organization

Where the IMF dealt with monetary issues, the ITO was supposed to deal with trade and investment issues. Like the IMF, the ITO grew out of the international lessons of the 1930s. On the one hand, the efforts of individual countries to boost their exports through devaluation, dumping, and state-controlled bilateral trade and to cut their imports through quantitative restrictions, higher tariffs, and currency controls had proven completely futile. If any created trade surpluses, they did so only by drastically lowering the absolute level of trade. On the other hand, U.S. initiatives beginning with the passage of the Reciprocal Trade Agreements Act (RTAA) in 1934 had shown that mutual accommodation might engender rising exports for all. During the 1930s Cordell Hull used this authority to negotiate over twenty accords covering about half of U.S. trade, facilitating a rough doubling of exports from their 1932 low point.[13]

As with the IMF, while the United States and the British agreed on the need for multilateral control of trade, they had different ideas as to how that control should be exercised. Both sides agreed that, except in agriculture, quantitative restrictions should be prohibited except under extreme balance-of-payments difficulties. Both also agreed that, since more trade probably meant more employment, lower tariffs were desirable. After that, however, conflicts emerged.

The whole thrust of U.S. policy before and during the war had been to open up markets for U.S. goods, particularly markets closed through the French and British imperial systems.[14] The United States wanted across-the-board tariff reductions along most favored nation (MFN) principles. Hence, any nation that lowered tariffs for goods imported from one country would have to lower them for goods imported from all countries that had MFN status with the importing country. Tariff reductions along MFN lines would eliminate imperial preference systems. This would benefit highly competitive U.S. firms.

In contrast, the British wanted to lower tariffs overall, but to retain the Imperial Preference system created at Ottawa in 1932. This system placed higher tariffs on imported goods originating outside the empire, giving imperial producers a competitive advantage, and in some cases specified quotas for nonimperial imports. From their point of view, these minor preferences were much less an obstacle to trade than the absolutely high U.S. tariff levels created by the 1930 Smoot-Hawley Tariff. These averaged 60 percent on the value of imports. In addition, British firms could not compete with U.S. firms in third-party markets.

Because employment and profits lay at the heart of this disagreement, negotiations over the ITO were much more contentious than those over the IMF. Even if people and firms understood the arcane nature of the monetary policy governed by the IMF, its effects were more diffuse than specific barriers to physical exports and imports. Consequently, the ITO talks remained deadlocked, dooming the organization. In a sense, the war had provided a "veil of ignorance"[15] that enabled the United States, Britain, and their allies to compromise over the IMF and the World Bank. Because no one really understood what the postwar environment would be like, it was difficult to calculate precisely the potential losses or gains from any particular institutional arrangement. However, the failure to secure an ITO before the war ended and world trade began to revive allowed both sides to calculate their gains and losses more finely, and thus inhibited a search for compromise.

In Britain, the war had aggravated the noncompetitiveness of British firms.[16] It had also depleted Britain's overseas investments, making merchandise exports even more important for the British trade balance. In the United States, the 1946 elections gave the Republicans, and thus the nationalists, control over Congress. They forced the executive to agree that any tariff reductions negotiated through the ITO would have to be reviewed by a special commission. Tariff reductions that imperiled U.S. industries would be subject to an escape clause permitting the United States to continue its tariff in full force.

A face-saving compromise made it possible to finish writing the ITO's charter in 1947, and 50 countries signed it in Havana in 1948. The ITO was unable to get congressional approval, however. The British waited to see what Congress did. Meanwhile, they continued imperial preference. In the absence of any comprehensive ITO agreement, tariff negotiations continued along the lines laid down by a protocol contained within the ITO charter, called the General Agreement on Tariffs and Trade. While Congress also refused to approve GATT, it proved a durable, if limited, venue for tariff negotiations. All the areas excluded from GATT—nontariff barriers, agriculture, services, and investment flows—have become the most contentious areas in trade negotiations today.

The international organizations set up under U.S. auspices reflected the peculiarities of U.S. domestic politics and the imperatives of mass production. Internationalists overcame nationalists' hesitance about foreign adventures through European participation in institutions to regulate the world economy. The various international organizations therefore relied as much on European participation as on U.S. power. Precisely because those organizations rested on cooperation, however, U.S. power had to be exercised in positive sum ways. The United States could not unilaterally impose solutions without risking a flight from the organizations it had created. At the same time, those international organizations had contradictory missions. They were to prevent a recurrence of the Great Depression by enforcing a liberal economic order, but not at the expense of full employment and continued domestic expansion in the economies participating in those organizations. The specific histories of each of those organizations and their associated "regimes" reflect this tension. Chapter 10 details those tensions as they played out in struggles over the international monetary system, and Chapter 13 as they played out in struggles over trade.

# Notes

1. The peculiarities and advantages of multilaterality are the subject of a special issue—*International Organization* 46, no. 3 (Summer 1992). See also Robert Keohane, *After Hegemony* (Princeton, N.J.: Princeton University Press, 1984); and Frank Costigliola, *Awkward Dominion* (Ithaca, N.Y.: Cornell University Press, 1984).

2. Ira Katznelson and Bruce Pietrykowski, "Rebuilding the American State: Evidence from the 1940s," *Studies in American Political Development* 5 (Fall 1991): 301–339.

3. A short and accessible treatment of conflicts between nationalists and internationalists can be found in Jeffry Frieden, "Sectoral Conflict and U.S. Foreign Economic Policy," *International Organization* 42, no. 1 (Winter 1988): 59–90. More detailed

treatments are Franz Schurmann, *Logic of World Power* (New York: Pantheon, 1947); Thomas Ferguson, "From Normalcy to New Deal," *International Organization* 38, no. 1 (Winter 1984): 41–94; and Peter Gourevitch, *Politics in Hard Times* (Ithaca, N.Y.: Cornell University Press, 1986), ch. 4.

4. Frieden, "Sectoral Conflict," p. 65.

5. William Pullen, *War Debts and U.S. Foreign Policy 1919–1929* (New York: Columbia University Press, 1987).

6. Lynn Eden, "Capitalist Conflict and the State: The Making of United States Military Policy in 1948," pp. 233–261 in Charles Bright and Susan Harding, eds., *Statemaking and Social Movements* (Ann Arbor: University of Michigan Press, 1984).

7. Joel Seidman, *American Labor from Defense to Reconversion* (Chicago: University of Chicago Press, 1953).

8. Or, as Charles Wilson, president of GE during the early postwar period, elegantly described who he thought America's enemies were: "labor at home, Russia abroad." See Stephen Krasner, *Defending the National Interest* (Princeton, N.J.: Princeton University Press, 1978) for arguments that ideology overrode interests.

9. See Michael Piore and Charles Sabel, *Second Industrial Divide* (New York: Basic Books, 1985).

10. Charles Maier, "The Politics of Productivity," in Peter Katzenstein, ed., *Between Power and Plenty* (Madison: University of Wisconsin Press, 1976).

11. Quoted in Richard Gardner, *Sterling-Dollar Diplomacy* (New York: McGraw-Hill, 1969), p. 42.

12. See John Gerard Ruggie, "International Regimes, Transactions and Change: Embedded Liberalism in the Post-War International Economic Order," *International Organization* 36, no. 2 (Spring 1982). Ruggie understates the tension not only between the two imperatives but also among social groups with divergent preferences for those imperatives.

13. Charles Kindleberger, *The World in Depression* (Berkeley: University of California Press, 1973), pp. 233–235.

14. See Lawrence Shoup and William Minter, *Imperial Brain Trust* (New York: Monthly Review Press, 1977) for a somewhat polemical view; also Christopher Thorne, *Allies of a Kind* (New York: Oxford University Press, 1978), which, despite centering on Asian issues, provides a textured account of general policy.

15. John Rawls, *A Theory of Justice* (Cambridge, Mass.: Harvard University Press, 1971). Rawls argued that if people had to design a social system behind a "veil of ignorance" that prevented them from knowing what their position in that social system would be, they would opt for a fairer society.

16. Bradley Smith, *The War's Long Shadow* (New York: Simon and Schuster, 1986).

# CHAPTER 10

## International Money and Domestic Politics

We cannot fight against market forces for long . . . the markets are much too strong. Coordinated central bank intervention can only inspire the markets to be more stable.

*Martin Bangemann*
*(German Finance Minister)*

In 1992 a hotel in the small New Hampshire resort community of Bretton Woods was sold as part of the Resolution Trust Company's fire sale of properties acquired from collapsed savings and loan banks. More than anything else in recent memory, this event symbolized the passing of the post–World War II international economic system. For the 1944 multilateral conference that created the IMF and set exchange rates among global currencies took place in that hotel. The implicit norms and explicit principles embodied in this institutional framework contained two fundamental tensions that ultimately undermined the institutional framework.

First, the norms agreed to at Bretton Woods embodied a fundamental tension between the imperatives of domestic macroeconomic stability and growth, and adherence to a liberal international trading order, that is, between the domestic and international lessons of the Great Depression.[1] Put simply, countries had to balance their international pledge to maintain a constant value for their currency relative to gold against a simultaneous promise to local firms and workers that governments would print as much money as was needed to maintain full employment. As long as international trade and investment flows were fairly small relative to the size of the world's major economies, Bretton Woods could function. Once international trade and particularly capital flows returned to their pre–World War I proportions, however, either domestic policy autonomy or the international monetary system of fixed exchange rates had to disappear. As the pool of liquid capital (i.e., assets) in the international economy grew over time, international capital movements became large enough to swamp countries' efforts to establish independent monetary policy. International forces thus increasingly constrained domestic room for making macroeconomic policy. By the 1990s the international monetary system had gone "back to the future"; it strongly resembled the late-nineteenth-century system in which financial assets dominated reserve holdings and determined whether or not countries would have to react to trade deficits (see Chapters 7 and 8).

The institutions created at Bretton Woods also contained a fundamental tension between their de jure cooperative structure and a de facto fundamental asymmetry between the United States and the rest of the world in terms of vulnerability to international economic shocks. Only the United States had the power to break the rules established at Bretton Woods, and this meant that cooperation ultimately rested on U.S. perceptions of its national interests.[2] As the international monetary system has increasingly gone back to the future, the tension between domestic growth and international liberalism has caused the United States to use its power to change the rules of the game. Put simply, at the peak of U.S. power it behaved most generously. As its power—its insulation from international market forces— has waned, it has behaved more and more predatorially. The United States increasingly acted unilaterally to compensate for the increased domestic costs of its increased international vulnerability and to position U.S. exports more favorably in world markets. By the late 1980s, however, the cost of unilateral monetary policy became apparent to policymakers. At that point, they began serious (but not entirely successful) efforts at multilateral coordination with the other major economies.

At first, these two contradictions in the Bretton Woods system were dormant. At least initially, the U.S. economy was big enough and insulated enough from world markets that it could manage the international monetary system unilaterally without domestic costs. Unlike most other countries, the United States could afford to ignore the domestic consequences of its international transactions. Monetary and fiscal policies could be pitched almost purely at domestic concerns, because imports plus exports represented a small part of the U.S. economy, and because the willingness of other countries to hold dollars meant that the United States could for a time run balance-of-payments deficits without fear of a forced devaluation. Until the 1970s, exports plus imports amounted to less than 10 percent of U.S. gross domestic product (GDP). In contrast, for the major European economies, trade ranged between 30 and 50 percent of GDP. This asymmetry diminished. By the 1980s, U.S. trade amounted to more than 20 percent of its GDP. The U.S. economy also shrank relative to the global economy as the Japanese and European economies recovered from the war.

As the relative vulnerability of these major economies converged, the two contradictions in Bretton Woods undermined efforts to maintain a stable international macroeconomy and exchange rate system. Because the system's stability rested on the strength of the U.S. dollar, it ultimately depended on the strength of the U.S. economy. To the extent that the United States allowed concerns for international economic stability to dominate efforts to support and strengthen its domestic economy, however, the United States undermined the fundamental basis for stability of the international trade and monetary systems. This tension ultimately forced the United States to abandon Bretton Woods.

After 1971 the norms of the Bretton Woods agreement collapsed, and its major institution, the IMF, found a new job (see Chapter 7), but its multilateral framework survived. Paradoxically, multilateralism survived precisely because the countries placed domestic economic concerns ahead of international interests. As Europe in the 1970s and the United States in the 1980s discovered that the scale of international trade and capital movements made domestic monetary, and sometimes fiscal, policy virtually impossible to implement, it became apparent that cooperation was going to be the only way to sustain growth. States sought to replace the failed Bretton Woods system with cooperatively set exchange rates and monetary policies, hoping this would lead to current account balance and growth. This ad hoc mutual accommodation has not been institutionalized, however.

## Three Phases to Monetary Disorder

The international monetary system passed through three distinct phases on its journey toward the past. These phases reflected the tension between domestic and international concerns, and the United States' changing ability to resort to unilateral solutions. From 1945 to 1960 the United States unilaterally ran the international monetary system, and, like Britain in the nineteenth century, functioned as the center of global financial transactions. From 1960 to roughly 1975, the United States continued to act as the source of global liquidity but within the formal framework of the Bretton Woods system. After 1975 the international monetary system evolved a hybrid structure. Countries are using post–World War II institutional forms for preserving cooperation, but they do so in order to accommodate balance-of-payments financing and capital flow patterns that increasingly resemble those that existed in the nineteenth century. Similarly, the reversal in the U.S. position from a surplus/creditor country to a deficit/debtor country has caused a reversal of U.S. policy preferences. So the system has ironically gone back to the future in two ways: it resembles the asset-based monetary system of the late nineteenth century, and the U.S. position on how the system should work has evolved from the deflationary stance it took in IMF negotiations to the more inflationary line Keynes took.

The declining willingness of other countries to hold dollars forced these transitions. Countries held reserves of dollars so that they or their firms could make international payments, for example, when they imported oil. But holding dollars also involved what economists call opportunity costs: the forgone benefits of holding other currencies as well as the risks that the dollar's value might fall in local currency terms. Countries were willing to hold dollars only so long as the risk of a dollar devaluation was minimal and the benefits of holding other currencies were less than those from holding dollars. The three phases through which the international monetary system evolved can be summarized and characterized as follows. In the first phase firms, individuals, and

European and Japanese governments held dollars because they had no alternative; the issue of opportunity costs was moot. At the beginning of the second phase, alternatives to the dollar emerged, but the opportunity costs of holding the dollar were low. As U.S. productivity advantages and thus its competitive edge eroded, and as U.S. inflation rose relative to Europe and Japan, the opportunity costs and risks of holding dollars increased. The dollar came under attack as an international currency as firms and the like fled the dollar for better alternatives. By the beginning of the third phase, the need to hold dollars had disappeared, and opportunity costs fully drove decisions about holding dollars.

## Phase One: 1947 to 1958–60

In phase one, the United States unilaterally ran the world's monetary system. Other countries set their currency's exchange rate by reference to dollars, *not gold*, and held dollars as their reserves. They also let the state control the conversion of local currency into foreign currency and overseas capital investment. The architects of Bretton Woods had anticipated a temporary suspension of currency convertibility and free capital flows during the immediate postwar recovery period. Temporary turned out to mean about 12 years, rather than the five years they had anticipated. The beginning of free currency convertibility marks the end of this period.

The architects' optimism derived from a misjudgment about what was really destabilizing world trade. They thought that once monetary conditions in each country had been stabilized, open trade could resume. However, the vast gap in productivity between the United States and other countries meant that those countries would find it difficult to export to the United States, while cheap, quality U.S. goods would be particularly attractive imports. The only way to earn enough dollars to make their international trade balance would be for states to drive wages and living standards back down to Depression levels. After six years of war and 10 of Depression, however, as well as the confrontation with militant communist labor movements, this approach was politically unfeasible. Europe and Japan needed time not just to rebuild what the war had destroyed but also to assimilate the new American assembly line and continuous-flow technologies to a point where they could actually compete in world markets. Thus, the United States supplied many parts of the world with dollars they otherwise could not have earned, allowing them to reconstruct their economies along U.S. lines without further depressing living standards. Some of this cash represented one-time transfers, like emergency loans to Britain and France or the Marshall Plan. These funds transferred about $26 billion (about $125 billion in 1990 dollars) to Europe. The rest represented ongoing transfers by U.S. overseas military forces and by a flood of U.S. tourists. Europeans used this cash to import critical raw materials, such as oil, and capital goods. U.S. firms also established subsidiaries in Europe, substituting local production for imports of U.S. goods. All three flows turned a U.S. merchandise trade surplus into an overall current account deficit, providing Europe and Japan with funds to import U.S. goods. Unlike the recycling of the U.S. merchandise surplus in the 1920s, these flows did not create new debts and thus did not require Europe and Japan to dramatically increase their exports.

The United States easily reconciled domestic and international goals during this period. European reconstruction with U.S. aid provided a boost to the U.S. economy. Marshall Plan and other aid amounted to a global fiscal stimulus of about 4 percent of U.S. GDP for three years (around 2 percent of global GDP). A Marshall Plan sold for its anticommunist/anti-Soviet merits was one of the few ways to get the nationalist faction in the United States to support Keynesian policies based on increased spending rather than lower taxes. This extra liquidity in the international market boosted U.S. output and exports. It also ensured U.S. security by rebuilding Europe in the face of a plausible Soviet threat. Indeed, U.S. military spending and aid were two of the largest net negative entries in the U.S. balance of payments, running at a fairly consistent $5 billion to $6 billion through the 1950s and 1960s.

During this period, Europeans and others unquestioningly held dollars because no alternative existed. They needed to hold dollars as reserves to cover potential imbalance of payments and to import food and oil from the United States or from U.S.-controlled firms. They also needed those dollars to settle transactions among themselves, even when, as in Europe, institutional clearinghouses like the European Payments Union existed.

Even if necessity did not dictate that Euro-Japanese central banks and individuals hold dollars, the United States' productivity edge and massive reserves created plenty of incentives to do so. Holders of dollars did not have to worry about whether the dollar was sound. With gold reserves of roughly $25 billion in 1948, the United States could more than back its pledge to convert any of the dollars held overseas into gold at $35 per ounce. Even so, why convert? Dollars paid interest, which gold did not; and as U.S. inflation rates were lower than the Euro-Japanese rates, holding dollars provided a useful hedge against local devaluations. The idea that the value of the dollar itself might fall, either passively through inflation or through a U.S. action, seemed unbelievable. Finally, the absolute productivity edge the United States had over Europe (about 2.5:1) and Japan (5:1) before 1960 meant that the United States could probably redeem dollars held overseas by exporting. The only considerations holding back a flood of imports from the United States in the 1950s were Euro-Japanese currency controls, tariffs, and the peculiarities of local markets, as the continuing large U.S. trade surplus on merchandise account demonstrated. So, during this period, a "dollar" standard operated, with most countries' central banks using their holdings of dollars as their financial reserves. Exchange controls meant that few private individuals held dollars, but even they had incentives to hold them rather than trying to exchange them for gold.

## Phase Two: 1960 to 1971 (de facto) or 1975 (de jure)

By the end of the 1950s, the European economies had recovered from the war, and all of them eventually dropped currency controls and, in most cases, capital controls. U.S. multinational firms had helped European producers bridge some of the productivity gap between Europe and the United States. The Japanese (at least formally) abandoned currency controls in 1964, although true capital market liberalization did not occur until the 1980s. During this period the Bretton Woods system operated much as it was intended to—and almost immediately it began to fail under the stress of a major contradiction between domestic and international imperatives.

Robert Triffin, a U.S. economist, best described this contradiction.[3] For the dollar to function well as an international currency, it had to expand roughly in line with the expansion in world trade. Otherwise, the shortage of dollars would cause falling prices in world markets—deflation. (This precisely parallels the monetarists' argument about the need to have the rate of growth of the money supply parallel growth in the real economy.) Deflation would remove world trade as an engine of growth for many economies, and it raised the specter of the deflationary 1930s. World trade was expanding at a rate of 8.5 percent a year during 1961–1973, well in excess of the rate of growth in the global gold supply (about 1 to 2 percent a year). Thus, gold alone could not function as an international money. The dollar could function as an international currency because the United States could print enough dollars to facilitate growing world trade, thus preventing deflation.

The problem was that if the United States printed enough dollars to create international liquidity and put them into circulation by running an imbalance of payments, it would ultimately undermine confidence in the dollar. Because world trade was growing faster than the U.S. economy, printing enough dollars to keep up with global trade meant that the U.S. money supply was expanding faster than its own economy. This could lead to several problems. If the United States ran a balance-of-payments surplus, then U.S. inflation would soon rise above European rates. Alternatively, if the Europeans ran a trade surplus and accepted and held dollars, then they would experience inflation. Finally, there would not be enough goods produced in the U.S. economy for the United States to be able to validate its dollars by exporting goods. Either way, global dollar holdings would soon exceed U.S. gold holdings, and the opportunity costs of holding dollars would outweigh the economic benefits. Influenced by Triffin's analysis, in the 1960s the U.S. Treasury pressured the Europeans to create a new paper gold, Special Drawing Rights (SDRs), to be held by the IMF. This would prevent the United States from being a source of global inflation by substituting an international money of account for the dollar. (Ironically, this represented a partial return to Keynes's original proposal that the International Clearing Union issue an international currency called the bancor.)

The Triffin paradox was latent during the 1950s but emerged with full force during the 1960s. During the 1960s, the United States' productivity advantage declined relative to European and Japanese producers, implying a dwindling U.S. ability to export. Similarly, the absolute gap between European and U.S. manufacturing output disappeared by the mid-1960s. In addition, Euro-American inflation rates steadily converged during the 1960s, thereby highlighting the fact that the dollar was just another paper currency. By 1960, too, dollars held overseas roughly equaled U.S. gold reserves, opening the dollar to speculative attacks. If all foreign-held dollars were cashed in, the United States would have to either stop spending so much overseas or devalue the dollar, because no gold would be left to redeem new dollars accumulating overseas. Finally, in the 1960s, dollars did seem to be accumulating overseas. Partly driven by the Vietnam War, in this period net U.S. overseas military spending and aid amounted to nearly $56 billion. At the same time, U.S. firms invested nearly $28 billion net overseas. U.S. exports of dollars were rising as U.S. merchandise exports were falling, suggesting that at some future time devaluation of the dollar would occur. In fact, in 1961 the Germans and Dutch had revalued their currencies, an implicit devaluation of the dollar.

All these conditions raised the cost to Europeans of holding dollars in their reserves or portfolios. As these factors worsened over the 1960s, speculators' attacks on the dollar produced a slow retreat from the promise of free convertibility of dollars into gold.

The United States and the Europeans generated a series of multilateral responses to the speculative attacks of the 1960s, but these responses continued the fiction that the United States was a different country. The major central banks set up a "gold pool," agreeing to swap gold among themselves to support the dollar at $35 per ounce of gold. The 1962 General Agreement to Borrow, in which central banks agreed to support one another if speculators attacked their currency, supplemented this. Consequently, until 1967, the Euro-Japanese central banks, France excluded, held and sterilized dollars. "Sterilized" means that, after they accepted dollars from their citizens and exchanged them for local currency, they then raised local interest rates to mop up this new emission of local currency. This prevented inflation but raised local interest rates, forcing those central banks to hold dollars without getting any interest on them. Failure to sterilize dollar inflows led to inflation. In 1967 the gold pool failed to prevent a run on the British pound, after which speculators attacked the dollar. In March 1968 the United States unilaterally dropped out of the gold pool and asked the Europeans to replace it with a new two-tiered gold market.

In this new arrangement, central banks agreed to exchange their currencies at the old Bretton Woods par values only among themselves, while in a second private market, gold and currencies would exchange at market rates. Privately, Germany agreed not to exchange its growing pile of dollars for gold. De facto, the two-tier gold market and German promise amounted to a U.S. default on its promise to back up dollars with gold, and, not surprisingly, speculators and the French began shifting out of dollars into other currencies and precious metals.

Despite the two-tier system, a de jure break with gold–dollar convertibility did not occur for another three years. By 1970 U.S. inflation rates had reached the average level in Europe, and the United States ran its first trade deficit in merchandise goods—a sign that its economy had weakened considerably. (See Table 10.1.) The U.S. trade deficit with Japan was particularly troubling; from a surplus in 1965, the U.S. position had rapidly deteriorated. By 1972 the United States ran a $5 billion deficit with Japan out of a total $30 billion deficit. Speculators responded to these various bits of bad news by selling dollars and buying European currency, driving the price of an ounce of gold to $41 and causing a massive outflow of gold from U.S. reserves. So in

TABLE 10.1

Inflation Rates and Industrial Productivity Growth in the United States, EC Countries, and Japan, 1950–1976, Selected Years

| | Inflation Rate | | | Productivity Growth, 1950–76 (annual |
| Country | 1960–65 | 1966–70 | 1971–75 | increase, %) |
|---|---|---|---|---|
| United States | 1.3 | 4.3 | 6.8 | 2.8 |
| Germany | 2.6 | 2.6 | 6.3 | 5.4 |
| France | 3.7 | 4.2 | 8.8 | 5.0 |
| Britain | 3.1 | 4.6 | 13.1 | 2.6 |
| Italy | 4.5 | 2.9 | 11.5 | 4.3 |
| Japan | 5.9 | 5.4 | 11.6 | 8.3 |

SOURCES: OECD, *Historical Statistics*, various issues; Riccardo Parboni, *The Dollar and Its Rivals*, (London: Verso, 1981) p. 93.

August 1971 Nixon unilaterally devalued the dollar by 10 percent, raised tariffs by 10 percent, and made the dollar inconvertible into gold. Nixon delinked the dollar from gold in order to stimulate the domestic economy without suffering a currency crisis.[4] Bretton Woods was dead, although it would take another three and a half years to bury it.

The attack on the dollar during the 1960s reflected the disjuncture between domestic desires to regulate the macroeconomy via the money supply and the international need for a reserve currency with enough liquidity to support trade flows — Triffin's dilemma. Use of the dollar as the international reserve currency created a conflict of interest between the United States and its Euro-Japanese allies over the costs of inflation. The U.S.–European conflict of interest played out as a fight between the United States and the French over the status of the dollar as the international reserve currency.

The French argued that the United States abused its power to print dollars and was living beyond its means. They suggested a return to a pure gold (or gold exchange) standard to prevent this abuse. The French also argued that the inflow of dollars forced European central banks to increase their local money supply and thus created inflation in Europe but without producing an offsetting deflation in the United States.[5] If European central banks tried to sterilize this inflow of dollars by raising interest rates, even more dollars would flow in as speculative capital sought high European interest rates. Thus, for the Europeans, the growing pool of Eurodollars implicit in America's weakening trade position meant a loss of control over monetary policy. The French thus began exchanging their dollars for gold in order to force the United States to rein in the domestic spending the French thought lay at the heart of U.S. trade imbalances.

For their part, the United States argued that use of the dollar as an international currency hurt the United States but was necessary for international economic stability. The Americans suggested that some new international reserve currency—SDRs—be created to reduce the cost to the U.S. economy.

The material basis for this clash lay in the growing pool of capital held as eurocurrencies. The eurocurrency market began as dollars deposited in London banks. Because these deposits fell outside normal domestic banking regulations, banks accepting Eurodollar deposits could lend more cheaply, pay depositors higher interest rates, and still make higher profits. U.S. multinationals, oil exporters, and communist countries afraid the United States would seize dollar deposits lodged in the United States swelled this pool of stateless currencies. Faith in the U.S. dollar fell as the Eurodollar pool—a collection of U.S. IOUs—grew. By 1970, eurocurrency deposits amounted to five times U.S. gold reserves. So if real convertibility had existed after 1968, any run on the dollar would have rapidly exhausted U.S. reserves. By 1990 the eurocurrency market deployed over $4 trillion, about 80 percent of U.S. GNP that year. Eurodollars (and eurocurrency in general) were the physical manifestation of the U.S. inflation and balance-of-payments deficits. Had the United States been able to export more goods, Eurodollars would perforce have come home. In turn, U.S. macroeconomic (i.e., domestic) policies drove the expansion of the pool of Eurodollars.

The seeds of U.S. inflation were planted under President Kennedy, who used tax cuts to stimulate the economy, expecting that this would produce, first, growth, second, new tax revenues, and thus, finally, a balanced budget. (This was more or less what Reagan claimed to expect in 1982.) Johnson and Nixon watered and fertilized Kennedy's deficit by simultaneously expanding the U.S. welfare state and prosecuting the Vietnam War. If the United States had been a truly closed economy, this fiscal stimulus would have caused increased investment in the domestic economy à la Keynes. Productivity might have continued to grow rapidly as businesses sought solutions to the tight labor markets of the 1960s.

But the U.S. economy was not closed. Businesses could take their money and invest anywhere they pleased, including overseas—and they did. Once overseas, they kept their profits in Europe as Eurodollars, for the U.S. tax code did not levy taxes on U.S. firms' profits until they actually repatriated those profits back to the United States. The movement of U.S. firms overseas at the same time the U.S. government wildly overspent its budget (at least by the standards of the time) fundamentally undermined faith in the dollar. Rather than reviving the U.S. economy, these two movements lowered productivity growth and raised inflation, for the slow decline in investment undercut growth in productivity and the domestic capacity to produce goods. In turn, investment overseas worsened the U.S. balance of payments, as U.S. transnational firms began substituting overseas production for U.S. exports.[6] Because U.S. security policy involved stationing hundreds of thousands of military personnel overseas as well as making unrequited transfers of weapons to client states and allies, it also weakened the U.S. balance of payments.

Thus, conflicts between U.S. domestic policy and the international need for liquidity undermined faith in the convertibility of the dollar. Stimulated by the combination of Vietnam War and Great Society spending, U.S. inflation began to creep toward or above European levels. Meanwhile, the outflow of U.S. capital and more important managerial technologies to Europe reduced the productivity gap between Europe and the United States. No reasonable person could expect that holding dollars was a wise investment relative to holding other currencies or goods.

A series of multilateral conferences endorsed Nixon's unilateral recognition of the United States' inability to back up the pool of Eurodollars created by U.S. domestic and security concerns. In December 1971 the G10 (the group of the ten largest capitalist economies) tried to put Bretton Woods back together, affirming the new, post–Nixon devaluation exchange rates and more than doubling the range of exchange rate flexibility in relation to the dollar to 2.25 percent. By 1973, however, as the U.S. dollar fell to 80 percent of its 1970 level, every European country had opted to float its currency versus the dollar, effectively nullifying this agreement. As a result, the signatories to the IMF agreed to amend the IMF's charter to give de jure recognition to the de facto situation: countries now legitimately could float their currencies. Bretton Woods, murdered by Nixon in 1971, was finally buried via the Second Amendment to the IMF's charter in 1975.

## Phase Three: 1971–75 until . . . or, A Tale of Two Yo-Yos

Or was it buried? Although U.S. ability to pursue unilateral domestic policy objectives had eroded, this autonomy could be leveraged if the Europeans could be persuaded to follow U.S. policy initiatives. As the U.S. economy was increasingly affected by international trade and capital flows, multilateral venues for negotiation became important. In 1975, the seven largest market economies (G7) began annual summit meetings to try to coordinate macroeconomic and exchange rate policies. Despite this effort, President Carter and, to a much greater extent, President Reagan each attempted to compel the rest of the world to follow U.S. fiscal and monetary policies driven by U.S. domestic political concerns, rather than compromises with the Euro-Japanese powers. Thus, both the multilateral institutional framework of Bretton Woods and its original conflict over norms rose from the grave.

International money markets sharply constrained Carter's and Reagan's ability to force the other powers to follow the U.S. line. Both Carter and Reagan produced two extreme yo-yo effects in the value of the dollar. By running consistent trade deficits, Carter and especially Reagan increasingly undermined the United States' ability to pursue unilateral policies. When the United States became a nominal net international debtor in 1986, its power became mortgaged to continuing capital inflows, further reducing its ability to pursue an independent domestic monetary and fiscal policy.[7]

Meanwhile, the Europeans had tried to insulate their monetary policies through first the 1972 "Snake" and then the 1979 European Monetary System (EMS). Both of these were efforts to imitate Bretton Woods on a smaller, European Community–wide scale by having fixed exchange rates among European currencies. The first Snake died quickly. A reconstituted Snake emerged in 1975, but collapsed in the face of subtantial U.S. dollar devaluations in the late 1970s. In an eerie replay of the Snake's second collapse, the falling dollar and the costs of German unification in the late 1980s undermined the EMS.

By the end of the 1980s, the United States, Europe, and Japan were searching for a modus vivendi for cooperation, returning to the original multilateral principles of Bretton Woods. The major obstacle that remained was conflict over whose domestic economy would bear the costs of getting the international economy back on track. Ironically, U.S. pursuit of unilateral goals led the United States to press for a return to the very elements Keynes had originally proposed at Bretton Woods. Once the United States became a deficit country, it sought automatic reflation by surplus countries. Meanwhile, like the surplus United States in 1944–1957, surplus countries Japan and Germany sought to avoid responsibility for international reflation in order to pursue domestic macroeconomic stability.

Both academic theorists and politicians thought that the shift to floating rates after 1973 would help countries avoid having to choose between competing international and domestic needs. Floating the currency would decouple decisions about domestic policy from exchange rate pressures. Under fixed exchange rates, a country's attempt to inflate its domestic economy in order to have full employment would put great pressure on its exchange rate and reserves, for speculators would attempt to sell local currency for gold or other stable currencies. In turn, falling reserves would cause deflation, undoing local policy. Theoretically, with floating rates central banks would not be obliged to use their reserves to buy their own currency. Instead, the local currency's exchange rate would fall, providing an additional stimulus to growth as exports presumably increased. The reverse was also true: with floating exchange rates, efforts to control inflation by raising interest rates would lead to a rise in the exchange rate, cheapening imports while reducing exports.

These theoretical hopes about floating rates proved illusory. After 1975, international capital movements began to dwarf the reserve positions of all countries, making it hard to reconcile domestic price equilibrium with balance-of-payments equilibrium. By 1990 the eurocurrency market contained funds equal to U.S. GDP for one year. Efforts to reflate via lower interest rates caused speculative flight away from the relevant currency, *shrinking* the money supply. This also made imports more expensive and aggravated inflation. Efforts to control inflation by raising interest rates caused enormous speculative inflows of capital, putting downward pressure on interest rates. Meanwhile, weakened export competitiveness created trade deficits, requiring even higher interest rates to control the balance-of-payments deficit. Simultaneously, businesses reacted to floating rates by shifting part of their production into their major overseas markets, using direct foreign investment to finesse the problem of exchange rate shifts.

The inability to decouple domestic policy from international capital movements created a need for international policy cooperation by making unilateral action costly. If everyone reflated/deflated at the same time, then exchange rates would remain reasonably stable. If states pursued discordant policies, however, most unilateral efforts to deflate or inflate would cause exchange rate gyrations and damage the initiator's economy. The need for policy cooperation ran afoul of diverging interests, however, so governments in the United States, Germany/Europe, and Japan pursued contrary domestic policy goals during the 1970s and 1980s, producing oscillations in both exchange rates and the world economy.

*Yo-Yo Number One: The Dollar Goes Down*
The period after the 1973 oil shock provided the first test of the putative ability of floating exchange rates to reconcile domestic and international imperatives. The Saudi (and thus OPEC) decision to continue pricing oil in dollars helped preserve a fundamental role for the dollar in world markets. No other currency presented a plausible alternative. The fundamental policy divergence in this environment lay between the United States and Germany. The United States wished to pursue a rapid reflation policy, whereas the Germans wanted to keep down the inflation induced by the oil shock. Roughly the same policy divergence dominated the 1980s, too. Unilateral U.S. reflation in both periods had the same consequences, albeit more violently under Reagan than Carter. Reflation led to faster economic growth in the United States as compared with Europe, and thus initially strengthened the U.S. dollar. As the dollar rose, making U.S. exports weaker, both Carter and Reagan tried to drive the dollar's relative value down in order to use exports to sustain domestic economic expansion.

The Carter government's effort to reflate the U.S. economy after the 1973–75 recession induced by the oil shock started the first global yo-yo in the dollar's exchange rate by widening the U.S. trade deficit and thus flooding the world with U.S. dollars. In terms of exchange rates, Carter's policy raised the dollar back to 100 percent of its 1971 level from the roughly 80 percent of 1973. The dollar then slid to 72 percent of its 1971 level by 1980, thereby producing yo-yo number one. Carter's policy caused GNP growth rates well in excess of the European average in the second half of the 1970s. On average, the major European economies grew about 3 percent per year in real terms after the 1973–75 recession, and the United States by about 4.5 percent.

The Carter administration's policy tools—mostly fiscal deficits but also lower interest rates—caused growing U.S. inflation and a flight from the dollar. By 1980 U.S. inflation had doubled to 13.5 percent, and the trade balance had gone from the surpluses of 1975–76 to deficits averaging an unprecedented $30 billion per year. Speculators noticed these trends, and by 1978 they fled the weakening dollar, driving it down to 72 percent of its 1971 value by 1980. This yo-yo in the dollar's value, more than twice the 10 percent devaluation Nixon had ordered in 1971 and in both directions, disrupted European and Japanese efforts to use exports to the United States to restart their own economies and their efforts at monetary stability.

The European currency Snake, an effort to stabilize exchange rates inside Europe around the German deutsche mark, collapsed as currencies appreciated at different rates against the dollar and as European countries pursued different domestic policies. The deutsche mark experienced the most extreme appreciation, rising nearly 50 percent from 1976 to 1979. To maintain parity with the mark, the weaker economies would have had to appreciate their currencies to a point that would threaten their growth. Thus, one by one, countries dropped out of the Snake during the 1970s, putting domestic concerns ahead of exchange rate stability.

From the Europeans' point of view, the problem continued to lie in the United States' efforts to have its domestic cake while dining out on international credit. The United States refused to accept the costs of the first oil shock by allowing the price of domestic oil and natural gas to rise to market levels. Instead, it controlled domestic prices, leading to even greater imports of uncontrolled foreign oil. Ford's and Carter's attempts to pull the economy out of the 1973–75 recession relied on excessive credit creation in the U.S. economy. As long as the United States gave artificial boosts to demand, it would run balance-of-payments deficits and have higher inflation.

From the United States' point of view, the problem lay in Euro-Japanese free riding: these governments refused to reflate their economies. By reflating alone, the United States risked higher inflation rates and trade deficits than did the other major economies, which was what put downward pressure on the dollar. At the same time, the United States also helped pull the other economies out of their recession by increasing their exports. So it was that the United States thought those economies should also bear part of the risk of increasing inflation. Conversely, the United States also accused the Europeans of "dirty floating" — of deliberately manipulating their currencies to keep the dollar's value from falling. Carter was willing to cooperate with the Europeans and, if necessary, to intervene in foreign exchange markets to bring currencies back to what his administration thought were equilibrium exchange rates.

At the 1978 Bonn G7 conference, the Americans, the Japanese, and the Europeans tried to hammer out their differences on reflation and worked out a basic deal.[8] The United States agreed to tighten monetary policy and to decontrol oil prices — that is, to accept the decline in national income that had been caused by the oil shock. Paul Volcker, an advocate of low(er) inflation, replaced Arthur Miller as chair of the Federal Reserve Board in 1979. The Germans and Japanese agreed that, like the United States, they would serve as the "locomotives" to pull the world economy out of recession, lowering their domestic interest rates and reflating their economies through fiscal deficits.

All parties more or less kept their promises. Despite this agreement and partial cooperation, the perceived consequences of the Bonn summit undercut future efforts at cooperation. The 1979 oil shock delayed U.S. decontrol of oil prices. Meanwhile, European and Japanese central bankers felt that their efforts at reflation only caused growing budget and trade deficits and higher inflation in their own countries. Japan's inflation doubled to 8 percent, and it had a current account deficit of 1 percent of GNP in 1979 and 1980. Germany's inflation rose to 6 percent, the fiscal deficit hit 5 percent of GNP, and it ran its first trade deficit since the 1950s. In each country, the government's net debt position roughly doubled as a percentage of GDP, causing net interest payments and thus fiscal deficits to rise. These domestic costs made the Germans and Japanese particularly insistent that the United States not abuse its asymmetrical power and that it sort out its domestic problems before they would act to coordinate macroeconomic policy again.

### Yo-Yo Number Two: The Dollar Goes Up

Under Reagan, the United States again resorted to unilateral action for domestic economic and political reasons. After 1979 Volcker raised real interest rates to unprecedented levels in an effort to choke off inflation. This action combined with the 1979 oil shock (this one inspired by the Iranian revolution) to plunge the world back into recession. High interest rates, however, caused the dollar to climb back to and past its 1973 levels, starting a second yo-yo as the dollar rose to 130 percent of its trade-weighted 1971 value in 1985. Domestic political concerns made the Reagan administration unwilling to abandon the mix of fiscal and monetary policies it had adopted in 1981 simply in order to harmonize policy with the Europeans and Japanese. Reagan pursued very tight monetary policies in order to stop inflation, which both the Japanese and Germans agreed with. The United States and the Euro-Japanese, however, diverged on fiscal policy as a tool for reflation. For domestic political reasons, the Reagan administration preferred to cut taxes immediately but to put off spending cuts until sometime in the future. The tax cuts of 1981, designed to cement the Republican party's 1980 electoral coalition, caused enormous fiscal deficits.

Germany and Japan preferred precisely the opposite policy mix: they wanted first to bring down spending slowly, and then to loosen both monetary and fiscal policy to reflate their economies. The high levels of public debt and fiscal deficits inherited from the 1978 locomotive effort made them deeply suspicious of the Reagan approach. Thus, no agreement could be reached at the 1982 Versailles G7 summit, and the United States pursued its preferred, domestically driven policy mix.

Reagan's enormous and rising fiscal deficit successfully reflated the domestic economy, but domestic reflation combined with a rising dollar made it harder to export and much much easier to import. This situation created an unstable situation in which interest rates kept the value of the dollar higher than the evolving trade deficit would have permitted. This suited the Europeans and Japanese, whose economies reflated on the basis of U.S. demand. From 1980 to 1985, external demand generated one-third of Japanese GDP growth and three-fourths of German GDP growth. This free ride on the expanding U.S. trade deficit may have suited the fiscally and monetarily conservative finance ministries and central banks in these countries, but it placed them in a dangerous situation: they had no control over long-term macroeconomic policy as long as the United States pursued a go-it-alone strategy, but the reverse was not as true. If they went it alone, they could not hope to influence U.S. policy. The United States drove growth in the world economy, and because it did, it could potentially choose to slow growth as well. With the dollar at unsustainably high levels in 1985, both Japan and Germany had to fear the consequences of a free fall in the dollar and the U.S. economy. So the

U.S. still held the cards, even though its trumps had already been played. If the United States could negotiate a deal with one or the other of the major economies, then it could distribute the benefits of U.S. reflation differentially.

In 1985 and 1986 the Reagan administration opted for both strategies. Thus, the Reagan administration combined efforts to divide and conquer with efforts to get monetary cooperation. In its divide-and-conquer efforts, the Reagan administration tried to play the Japanese card against the Europeans and the French card against the Germans (and especially the Bundesbank) in hopes of getting a pact with everyone. Even so, U.S. domestic political and economic pressures still drove policy. The domestic sources of the Reagan policy shift lay in the erosion of the manufacturing sector because of the high dollar. The high dollar had cost the U.S. manufacturing sector about 1 million jobs, and even in the highly efficient agricultural sector it had led to import penetration in markets like wheat. The ballooning of the trade deficit from $11.2 billion to $168.6 billion (both in 1982 dollars) came not just from extra imports but from the displacement of U.S. exports and domestic production by foreign producers. Capacity utilization in U.S. manufacturing *fell* from 1984 to 1986, despite economic recovery.[9]

Real U.S. interest rates (measured by the long-term Treasury bond net of inflation) had nearly hit 9 percent in 1985 before falling somewhat to 7 percent. The Reagan administration could no longer pretend that the trade and exchange rate issues were not connected, and Federal Reserve Chair Volcker feared high interest rates might choke off growth. So the United States started looking for ways to lower interest rates and the dollar's value against other currencies. To do so it had to have the cooperation of the other major central banks. Otherwise, the dollar might fall precipitously. From the point of view of the Japanese and the Germans, as well, the time to talk had come. A precipitous fall in the dollar's relative value would hurt both their externally driven economies. Hence, market pressures pushed all three countries to come together at the Plaza Hotel in New York in September 1985, after the dollar had already fallen about 10 percent from its early 1985 peak. At the Plaza a deal was cut to lower the dollar about 10 percent relative to other currencies, and to lower interest rates if the United States cut its budget deficit.

In 1986, the year after Reagan signed the Gramm-Rudman-Hollings deficit reduction act into law (December 12, 1985), the Japanese and Germans made a 100-basis-point (i.e., 1.0 percentage point) and 50-basis-point (i.e., .5-percent-age-point) reduction in their official discount rates, respectively. This permitted a 50-basis-point (i.e., .5-percentage-point) reduction in the U.S. discount rate.[10] (The discount rate is the interest rate that the central banks charge private banks, and it can be lowered or raised to expand or contract the money supply.) After the Plaza meeting, the G5 central banks systematically intervened to slow the fall of the dollar, particularly when it fell more than the 10 percent originally anticipated. As it turned out, the dollar slid by about 40 percent against the yen and the deutsche mark during 1985–1987. Japan and Germany ran larger fiscal deficits, and after 1985 domestic growth picked up in both countries.

Along with the cooperative Plaza accord, the United States tried to divide and conquer its competitors by playing the French against the Germans. The French disliked the very high interest rates imposed by the German Bundesbank on the rest of Europe via the EMS. To weaken the Bundesbank, the French preferred relatively firm exchange rate signals as triggers for intervention by central banks in the five largest economies. These automatic signals would constrain the Bundesbank's ability to exert deflationary pressure in the EMS. The price the United States asked, however, proved too high for the French: a serious effort to liberalize trade in agriculture at the upcoming Uruguay Round of the GATT talks (see Chapter 13).

Unable to move the Europeans, the United States pursued a separate deal with the Japanese, most prominently in the 1986 Baker-Miyazawa accord to lower the U.S. and Japanese discount rates simultaneously. During 1986 the Fed's discount rate fell from 7.0 percent to 5.5 percent, while the Bank of Japan cuts its discount rate from 4 percent to 3 percent. The Baker-Miyazawa deal of 1986 foreshadowed a series of bilateral alliances against Europe. Slow European growth, the falling dollar, and U.S.–Japanese cooperation then forced the Germans to lower their discount rate. As at Bonn in 1978, the Japanese insisted on a quid pro quo. In return for a promised 6-trillion-yen increase in spending and further liberalization of financial markets, the Japanese insisted that the United States stick to its Gramm-Rudman budget reduction targets.

Just as in the late 1970s under Carter, the Plaza and Baker-Miyazawa deals sent the dollar into a two-year decline that generated domestic pressures to set a floor under the dollar in Europe and Japan. As the yen rose, small and medium-sized Japanese businesses found it impossible to export. As providers of a big chunk of campaign financing for the ruling Liberal Democratic party, they screamed for relief from *endaka* (high yen). In Europe, declining exports forced two EMS realignments, which in effect devalued the French franc. These pressures forced non-U.S. central banks to support the dollar in 1987; about 75 percent of the capital inflow into the United States that year came from central bank interventions buying dollars. U.S. reliance on this official inflow compelled the United States to come to the table once more; domestic pressure brought everyone else. In 1987 at the Louvre, the G5 and G7 countries tried once more to coordinate monetary policy.

Once more, cooperation proved elusive. United by their common situation of being net foreign debtor and trade-deficit countries after 1988, the United States and France tried to get the others to agree to specific exchange rate levels that would trigger automatic intervention.[11] They also tried to get everyone to agree to a common set of macroeconomic indicators that would signal a need for reflation or deflation. The two creditor countries, Germany and Japan, steadfastly refused to be bound by automatic triggers and a definite set of indicators. They wanted to preserve the greatest possible policy autonomy. Consequently, the G5 central banks and states could not agree on anything more than vague target ranges for intervention. As a result, from 1988 through 1992 the dollar oscillated above and below those target ranges, indicating that the Louvre accord had had only limited success in cementing central bank coordination.

## Winners and Losers

U.S. policy produced winners and losers in the international economy. First and foremost, the United States served its own interests, using devaluation of the dollar to increase the international competitiveness of firms exporting from the United States. Table 10.2 shows how the two great devaluations of the dollar led to lower unit labor costs in the United States relative to the other two major economies. Second, in monetary policy coordination (and as we will see in trade policy, too), a tacit U.S.–Japanese alliance against the Europeans eventually emerged. The basis for the U.S.–Japanese alliance lay again in an asymmetry in the world economy. Japan has a disproportionate stake in the U.S. economy. Roughly one-third of Japanese exports went to the United States, and even more, if disguised exports from Japanese subsidiaries in East Asia are included. In contrast, only about 10 percent of German exports went to the United States and about 3 percent to Japan. The exports of other European countries hovered around those figures. The Japanese had more at stake if U.S. monetary policy and a high dollar were to push U.S. trade policy in a protectionist direction. The reverse was also true: the United States could use an increasingly protectionist Congress to extort cooperation from Japan. Such threats served less well with the Europeans.

U.S.–Japanese cooperation diverted the bulk of growth and the benefits of growth in the 1980s to these two countries rather than to Europe. Over the 1980s both the United States and Japan grew faster than any of the European Community economies.[12] From 1983 to 1989 U.S. GDP grew at an annual average rate of 3.8 percent and Japanese GDP 4.4 percent, but European (EC) GDP only 2.7 percent. Differences in job creation tell a similar story. Overall, the United States added about 15 million jobs (though often low-quality jobs) during the 1980s; Japan moved to a situation of extreme labor shortages; but Europe lost about 2 million jobs, and unemployment continued to hover around 10 percent. U.S. manufacturing output rose 47 percent from 1982 to 1990, and Japanese output by 54 percent. In Europe, British output rose by only 30 percent, German by 22 percent, and French by 11 percent. U.S. manufacturing productivity grew 37 percent from 1982 to 1990, compared to

TABLE 10.2

Percent Change and Level of Relative Unit Labor Costs in the United States, Japan, and Germany, 1970–87, Selected Years

| Country | Percent Change[a] | | | Level[b] (1980 = 100) | | |
|---|---|---|---|---|---|---|
| | 1970–74 | 1976–78 | 1984–87 | 1974 | 1978 | 1987 |
| United States | −28.0 | −9.0 | −28.0 | 107.0 | 96.0 | 87.9 |
| Japan | 37.0 | 20.0 | 37.0 | 114.0 | 134.0 | 135.1 |
| Germany | 13.0 | 9.0 | 13.0 | 102.0 | 101.0 | 108.0 |

[a]Negative numbers indicate improved competitiveness.
[b]Lower numbers indicate improved competitiveness.
SOURCE: OECD, *Economic Outlook No. 42*, December 1987 (Paris: OECD, 1987) p. 70.

38 percent for the Japanese. In contrast, German productivity grew only 26 percent.[13]

As in the 1970s, the Europeans tried to protect themselves by setting up a zone of currency stability centered in Germany. With intra-European Community trade accounting for more than half of any given country's exports and imports, currency volatility inside Europe would have been costly and economically unbearable. The European Monetary System, which came into effect in March 1979, revived and strengthened the old currency Snake of the 1970s. EMS was a smaller version of Bretton Woods: fixed exchange rates relative to a weighted pool of EC currencies (instead of gold); a 2.25 percent band for stronger currencies and a 6 percent band for weaker ones; and mandatory intervention by central banks. Like Bretton Woods, it did not endure severe conflicts between external monetary stability and internal growth.

During the expanding economy of the 1980s, EMS countries found it relatively easy to track the deutsche mark. Even Britain eventually ceded some of its prized sovereignty and autonomy to join EMS. During the early 1990s, however, Germany raised interest rates to cope with the inflation created by reunification, while the rest of the Europeans sought some relief from the recession of 1990–92. EMS unraveled under the pressure of diverging domestic economic policies. Rising German interest rates forced interest rates up in other EMS countries, driving them deeper into recession. In the fall of 1992, a series of devaluations occurred as countries sought relief from German interest rates, triggering a major realignment in August 1993.[14] By mid-1993, the future of monetary integration seemed uncertain, with monetary union trapped at an unstable point halfway between complete flexibility and complete integration, and with no signs that domestic policy would again converge enough to make fixed exchange rates work.

# The Present Structure:
# Back to the Future

## Keynes's Revenge

"Where you stand depends on where you sit," according to most observers of bureaucratic politics. The same is true for international monetary policy. A creditor country in 1944, the United States adamantly refused to be automatically responsible for helping reflate deficit countries. Keynes and the Europeans, anticipating future deficits, wanted some kind of automatic mechanism to force surplus countries to help reflate deficit countries.

Once Reaganomics turned the United States into a deficit country, the United States consistently proposed plans for some kind of automatic target zone in which central bank intervention would drive up the value of the currencies of surplus countries. That is, the United States sought an automatic mechanism with rigid trigger zones to make surplus countries share the burden of reflation, just as Keynes had. In contrast, surplus Germany and Japan refused to be bound by automatic triggers.

In some ways, the United States is now being haunted by its initial veto of Keynes's proposed International Clearing Union. Neither a binding agreement nor the pressure of norms makes surplus countries reflate. Rather, the old norm that deficit countries must balance their trade by cutting back on domestic consumption will probably prevail. So during the 1990s the United States will finally have to bear the cost of setting its economy right alone, by reducing domestic consumption.

## A Return to an Asset-Based Monetary System

The irony of the situation described above is dwarfed by a larger one. By 1990 the international monetary system had come to resemble the asset-based exchange system of the nineteenth century. Although the current system is not a gold standard system, it does function much like the asset-based international money of the late nineteenth century. In the nineteenth century, capital flows overwhelmed the rudimentary or nonexisting central banks of the peripheral agricultural exporters, including the United States. As in the nineteenth century, international capital movements in the late twentieth century have become so large as to make isolated domestic monetary policy impossible except in a very limited way for the big three economies.

International stocks and flows of assets have become enormous when compared with those in the period 1929–1970; they have returned to levels typical of the late 1800s. In 1980 the stock of international bank lending totaled about 4 percent of the combined GDP of the OECD countries, and the stock of internationally issued bonds totaled about 3 percent. By 1991 these had respectively risen to 44 percent and 10 percent of aggregate OECD GDP. By way of rough comparison, the outstanding stock of overseas investment in 1914 amounted to about 42 percent of the GDP of the largest industrial countries.[15] For the three major economies today, gross international sales and purchases of stocks and bonds had risen from negligible levels in 1970 to 93 percent of GDP for the United States, 119 percent for Japan, and 58 percent for Germany.[16] As in the late 1890s, money can be moved internationally simply by selling assets in one place and buying them in another. Short of reimposing capital controls, central banks are powerless to halt this process.

In the nineteenth century, the emergence of an asset-based monetary system had positive and negative consequences. Positively, it meant that large imbalances of payments could be sustained for extremely long periods of time, if both capital and confidence were available. Negatively, however, if both capital and confidence evaporated, a country could be drastically and immediately deflated, as with Argentina or Australia during the 1890s.

Today most small countries face precisely the situation the agricultural periphery faced in the 1890s, and the larger economies face a weaker version. Volatile asset transactions can cause uncontrollable expansions and contractions in the domestic monetary supply. As in the nineteenth century, this can have positive consequences. The U.S. trade deficit was sustained well past the point anyone would have predicted, precisely because this large pool of international capital was available. But, as in the nineteenth century, a sharp reduction in this capital inflow could have catastrophic consequences. For a single economy, it could mean a sharp downturn in economic activity. If that economy happens to be the United States, it could mean a weakening of overall world growth, as Chapter 15 will argue.

## Notes

1. John Ruggie, "International Regimes, Transactions and Change," *International Organization* 36, no. 2 (1982).
2. See Joanne Gowa, *Closing the Gold Window* (Ithaca, N.Y.: Cornell University Press, 1983); David Calleo, *Imperious Economy* (Cambridge, Mass.: Harvard University Press, 1982); and John Odell, *U.S. International Monetary Policy* (Princeton, N.J.: Princeton University Press, 1982).
3. Robert Triffin, *Gold and the Dollar Crisis: The Future of Convertibility* (New Haven, Conn.: Yale University Press, 1960).
4. For a detailed account, see Gowa, *Closing the Gold Window*.
5. See, for example, Jacques Rueff, *The Age of Inflation* (Chicago: Regnery, 1964), and, retrospectively, Riccardo Parboni, *The Dollar and Its Rivals* (London: Verso, 1981).
6. Robert Gilpin, *U.S. Power and the Multinational Corporation* (New York: Basic Books, 1975).
7. In reality, the United States probably did not become a net debtor until around 1989 or 1990. Because the Department of Commerce calculated the U.S. overseas asset position on the basis of book (original) value until 1991, it tended to understate the value of U.S. overseas holdings from the 1960s and 1970s. Nonetheless, reworking of the figures at current values still shows that the United States was a net debtor by 1990.
8. Robert Putnam and Nicholas Bayne, *Hanging Together: Cooperation and Conflict in the Seven-Power Summits* (Cambridge, Mass.: Harvard University Press, 1987).
9. I. M. Destler and C. Randal Henning, *Dollar Politics: Exchange Rate Policymaking in the United States* (Washington, D.C.: Institute for International Economics, 1989), p. 35.
10. The Japanese discount rate went from 5 to 4 percent, the German from 4 to 3.5 percent, and the U.S. from 7.5 to 7 percent.
11. See OECD, *Economic Outlook No. 51*, June 1992 (Paris: OECD, 1992), p. 148, for data on net asset position.
12. Data from OECD, *OECD Current Outlook No. 50* (Paris: OECD, 1992) and various OECD *Surveys* of specific economies.
13. *New York Times* May 27, 1992; *The Economist*, July 3, 1993, pp. 5–19.
14. See *The Economist*, October 3, 1992, pp. 81–82; *The Economist*, October 10, 1992, p. 97.
15. This figure is derived by dividing the outstanding stock of international debt in 1914, about £7.7 billion, by the aggregate 1914 GDP of the United States, Western Europe, Canada, Australia, Argentina, and New Zealand, about £18.4 billion. This group is roughly comparable to today's OECD.
16. *The Economist*, September 19, 1992.

# CHAPTER 11

## Transnational Firms: The United States versus Europe, Japan versus the United States

> What impressed Europeans about American plants in Europe and the United States [in the 1920s and 1930s] was mass production, standardization, and scientific management; in the 1960s Europeans were remarking that American superiority was based on technological and managerial advantage [and] that this expertise was being exported via direct investment.
>
> *Mira Wilkins*

The sharp reduction in world trade flows in the 1930s and 1940s, and the slowness with which countries reopened their markets to global trade after World War II created enormous barriers to exports. The ability of U.S. firms to manage the assembly line and market on a continental scale gave them significant competitive advantages. But European states lagged behind the United States in reopening their domestic markets. Many U.S. manufacturing firms chose to shift a part of their production overseas into those relatively closed markets, becoming transnational corporations (TNCs). In contrast to most nineteenth-century manufacturing firms, which manufactured within one national economy and exported finished products to other countries, TNCs dispersed their production, service, and sales operations into their major overseas markets. They replaced exports with production in former export markets. Eventually, they integrated their operations globally.

These new, mostly U.S.–based TNCs that proliferated before and after World War II re-created the threat of displacement competition that had been posed to European industry by the British industrial revolution.[1] Like the flood of cheap British textiles, the intrusion of TNCs into the domestic markets of other countries called forth responses that created competitive local firms. As in the nineteenth century, host states, which controlled the country into which direct foreign investment (DFI) flowed, played an active role in fostering local industry in the face of foreign competition. Host states' responses and local firms' learning and imitation helped competitive laggards catch up to firms using best practice technologies in manufacturing and, to a lesser extent, services. Once these firms caught up with transnational U.S. firms (or, in the case of many Japanese firms, surpassed them), they, too, began to transnationalize their operations in order to maximize the return on their particular managerial or technological advantages. By the end of the 1980s, direct foreign investment had created three rough regional blocs, characterized by high levels of bilateral trade and investment flows, and centered on the United States, Japan, and the European Community (EC).[2] The dominant economy (-ies) in each bloc also received substantial investment flows from the dominant economy (-ies) in the other blocs. TNCs established (or tried to establish) themselves in each of the three major blocs.

This regionalization in turn caused a profound change in the nature of international trade. As world markets gradually reopened during the 1960s and 1970s, TNCs were able to integrate their production flows on a global scale. By the end of the 1980s, roughly half of the trade of developed countries occurred *within* firms as part of their administration of globally oriented production plans.

The rise of these new TNCs thus shifted international investment flows away from portfolio investment and toward DFI, in which the investor retains control of daily operations.[3] It also accelerated the diffusion of hard and soft best practice manufacturing technologies. Simultaneously, states evolved industrial policy in response to the displacement threat TNCs posed to local firms and in response to the difficulties TNCs posed for states' ability to control their local macroeconomy. Finally, by increasing intrafirm international trade, the rise of TNCs dispersed manufacturing activities globally, creating a manufacturing analogue to the agricultural von Thünen rings of the nineteenth century. This chapter will look primarily at the first two consequences, leaving a discussion of the consequences for trade to Chapter 13.

## The Old Transnationals

In some sense, transnational firms have always existed; consider the Dutch East India Company described in Chapter 1. These transnationals were simply one way of moving capital internationally in order to capture resources—usually raw materials and climate-specific agricultural products—that are not present in the home economy. Before 1900, agricultural products were the biggest attraction for this kind of investment; after 1900, oil supplanted agricultural products.[4]

These earlier transnationals were not really transnational (or multinational in the sense of operating in a range of different countries) in either political or economic terms. They actually tended to operate in a kind of stateless space, even though their operations were far-flung and global. Most of these early transnationals connected European economies with colonial or quasi-colonial economies. When they dealt with local or host states, they were often simply dealing with extensions of their metropolitan state. For example, firms like Royal Dutch Shell or Unilever operated primarily in Dutch and British colonies. Therefore, these transnationals rarely crossed national boundaries; they often operated within a single legal space. In East Asia and the Middle East, the gradual extension of European state power secured various forms of *extraterritoriality* for transnationals, allowing them the right to operate under their domestic law rather than local law.

. Nor were the early transnationals particularly transnational economically. Most of them engaged in the extraction of raw materials that could not be produced back in their home economies. They exported these raw materials back to the metropolis for further processing. The maritime-based connection between urban metropolis and the raw materials periphery was closer and more organic than the low level of integration between the maritime-oriented economy in the metropolis and its own interior microeconomies.

A few firms used cheap labor to produce manufactured goods with the status of commodities, such as low-quality textiles and garments in Asia. These manufactured goods were then exported to neighboring markets and occasionally back to the metropolis. In such cases, Ricardian comparative advantages dictated the kind of investment and economic activity, and as a result home states found little to object to. Indeed, by cheapening the cost of imported raw materials and foods, these investments helped to position manufactured exports more competitively in international markets. In any case, most of these international capital movements took the form of portfolio investment, so it would have been difficult to channel the capital to domestic firms anyway. TNCs did not seem to have any major negative economic impact on the home economy.

On the other hand, considerable conflict arose between host countries and transnationals extracting raw materials. As Stephen Hymer colorfully put it, "These [long-distance merchant] firms [and] the mining and plantation enterprises in the production sector . . . were like dinosaurs, large in bulk, but small in brain, feeding on the lush vegetation of the new worlds (the planters and miners in America were literally *Tyrannosaurus rex*)." [5] Put more plainly, the basic conflict between hosts and extraction TNCs was about who would capture the rent inherent in production of relatively scarce raw materials. Rents inhere to all nonrenewable raw materials and often to many renewable ones because by definition their replacement cost is higher than the cost of extraction; otherwise, substitutes would be used immediately. This rent can be captured by either the host or the TNC, or it can be shared between them. During the period of direct colonization, TNCs captured the entire rent because the "host" government existed to support TNC operations. Even with nominally independent states, corrupt governments and the absence of any bargaining skills meant that hosts appropriated little, if any, of this rent and that what they captured in turn was personally appropriated by politicians.

After decolonization, a bargaining situation emerged. TNCs controlled technology and investment capital that were otherwise unavailable to potential hosts. Hosts, on the other hand, controlled access to their raw materials. The distribution of rents between host and TNC depended on the relative scarcity of the raw material in question, the relative scarcity of investment capital, and the relative scarcity of extraction technologies (that is, the difficulty hosts faced in trying to learn or buy extraction technologies). In general, the scarcer the raw material was relative to demand, the more plentiful capital and the easier technological transfer, the greater were the opportunities for hosts to maximize their share of rents, and, if the reverse, the greater were the TNCs' ability to maximize their share of the rents. Whatever the initial bargain struck between TNCs and hosts, bargaining power inevitably shifted toward the host. This became known as the obsolescing bargain because, over time, bargaining power usually shifted toward the host, and thus the terms of the agreement became less acceptable to it, that is, obsolete.[6]

Bargaining power shifted toward the host for three reasons. First, once a TNC commits itself to investing and actually builds production facilities, it must operate the facility to recoup its investment. So TNC bargaining power based on threats to relocate evaporate after the TNC invests. Second, over time hosts become familiar with extraction technologies. Finally, accrued rent itself can be used as capital, lessening reliance on external sources of capital. Thus, analysts of the obsolescing bargain typically speak of cycles in which TNCs bargain for a large share of the rent, commit to local production, and then find that hosts demand revision of the bargain in the host's favor. As the bargain obsolesces, hosts extract more of the rent through export taxes, social security contributions, bribes, and so on.

Constant interaction between hosts and TNCs has increased the sophistication of the strategies used to capture rents. TNCs initially captured the entire rent. Once hosts became independent, particularly in the 1960s, they sought to recapture the rent by nationalizing the actual extraction facility. They thought that nationalization would confer control over the rent. In fact, TNCs simply retreated back into their processing and distribution networks and used control over these downstream activities to continue extracting rents. Hosts then tried to form cartels so as to present TNC processors with a united front. The Organization of Petroleum Exporting Countries (OPEC) was virtually the only successful example of such a cartel.

Most of the cartels foundered because, among other reasons, many raw material deposits occurred in *developed* countries in which the issue of rent was less salient. With more diverse economic structures, these developed countries had little reason to make common cause with LDCs.[7] Investment patterns also reinforced this division after 1973. Roughly 80 percent of new investment in raw materials extraction from 1973 to 1980 went to three politically safe countries: Australia, Canada, and the United States. In addition, higher prices caused consumers to downsize, economizing on raw materials inputs and using substitutes. Another factor causing the cartels to founder was the Japanese attempt to foster global overcapacity in some raw materials to drive down prices.[8] All of these forces created pressure on LDC cartel members to cheat by selling more than their cartel-set quota allowed.

## The New Transnationals

After World War II, this older pattern of TNC investment and its resulting conflicts was displaced by the rapid global expansion of U.S. manufacturing firms. Whereas absolute scarcities of raw materials had driven the older form of DFI, two different logics drove the new DFI. First, firms wanted access to markets that were otherwise closed for political reasons. Second, just as a gradient of land rental costs underlay the emergence of von Thünen zones for agriculture, manufacturing firms sought to disperse their production rationally along a gradient based on skill levels at different wages.

The proliferation of the new type of manufacturing TNC after World War II thus broke with past patterns. These mostly U.S. firms invested primarily in other developed countries, not in the raw materials or agricultural periphery. Investment in developed countries accounts for about three-fourths of DFI since World War II. Related to this geographical shift was the investment shift from extraction to manufacturing. By the 1980s only about one-quarter of DFI was for raw materials extraction, while about half was for manufacturing and another quarter for services.[9] Moreover, these new manufacturing TNCs mostly invested in leading-sector products and production processes. On the other hand, the risk that TNCs might lose their technological advantages through diffusion was much greater than with raw materials extraction in LDCs.

## How Can Firms Transnationalize?

The problems these changes created can best be seen by first asking how firms can transnationalize. After all, from the standpoint of formal international trade theory, DFI should not happen; in a world of perfect markets, TNCs should not exist.[10] According to international trade theory based on factor costs and comparative advantage, if a foreign company is capable of producing a product locally, using local labor and resources, then a local company should be able to outcompete that firm and drive it from the market. Local companies, after all, don't have to bear the costs of being foreign — of not being integrated into local supplier and marketing networks, of not being politically connected, of losing economies of scale, of bearing the cost of communications and transportation between dispersed operations. In economists' language, transaction costs are higher for foreigners. With lower transaction costs, local companies should be more profitable, and thus able to displace foreign interlopers from their own domestic market. Alternatively, the costs of being foreign should motivate would-be investors to choose portfolio investment rather than direct investment, and should permit local managers and firms to deal with the peculiarities of local markets. What does international trade theory miss here?

The fact that local firms cannot compete and that TNCs do invest directly indicates that TNCs must have some enormous competitive advantage and/or motivation. Three complementary theories suffice to explain the TNCs' competitive advantages and motivations. These argue that as oligopolies seeking market dominance these firms were pushed to transnationalize; that the natural evolution of production processes and markets along a typical product cycle motivated transnationalization and provided a competitive advantage; and that the asymmetrical nature of markets for information (including technology) makes it more rational for some firms to transnationalize production than to sell or license technology. The oligopolistic rent-seeking model arguments are associated with Stephen Hymer and Charles Kindleberger; the product cycle model with Raymond Vernon; and the transaction cost approach with Oliver Williamson and D. J. Teece.[11]

Hymer argues that the institutional nature of the firm spurs it to expand overseas. U.S. firms compete in oligopolistic markets, he states, using tightly held technology with potentially large economies of scale and in an environment in which the costs of gathering information about the future are high. Because firms compete in oligopolistic markets, they seek to preempt competitors in the existing product lines. Their ability to preempt competition rests on technological advantages and market access. Their technological advantage declines over time, as products run through a natural cycle, the so-called product life cycle. As this advantage erodes, production technology becomes more standardized, making it possible for firms in export markets to begin competing with the original, innovating firm. At this point, the innovator invests overseas to preempt competition.

How do technological advantages erode over the product cycle? Vernon's product cycle model argues that products and production processes move through four distinct stages (see Figure 11.1). When a product is innovated, its market is unsure and small, and the optimal production technologies are unknown. Consequently, it is a luxury good, produced in small lots by skilled labor using general-purpose machines and at a fairly high cost. Competitive advantage rests on novelty and scarcity, which make high production costs less important. By the second stage, production technologies and the market are fairly certain, allowing the introduction of some dedicated machinery. This reduces production costs and allows the market to expand into the middle class domestically. It also makes possible exports to markets with similar income and consumption structures. These exports alert firms in the importing country that a market for these goods exists, but they cannot as yet acquire the technology to produce similar goods *competitively*. Much knowledge about production is embodied in workers' experience as tacit or firm-specific knowledge.

By the third stage, continued expansion of the market combined with more experience has allowed for extensive standardization of production. The good is mass produced using dedicated special-purpose machinery and mostly unskilled labor. This special-purpose machinery replaces much of the workers' tacit knowledge, and so allows importing countries to use tariff and other barriers to encourage their firms to begin production, since the technical challenge is much smaller. These barriers also stimulate the original producer to jump over the tariff barrier (if legally possible). The original producer hopes to preempt foreign competitors, or to limit their ability to use verdoorn effects to catch up (or surpass) it. Thus, the search for continued oligopoly rents and the threat of market closure motivate the original producer to invest overseas, shifting the locus of production.

The original producer(s) continues to have a competitive advantage relative to upstart firms, but this advantage erodes as those firms acquire greater tacit knowledge through contact with the original producer (which by virtue

*Figure 11.1 Product Cycle Model*

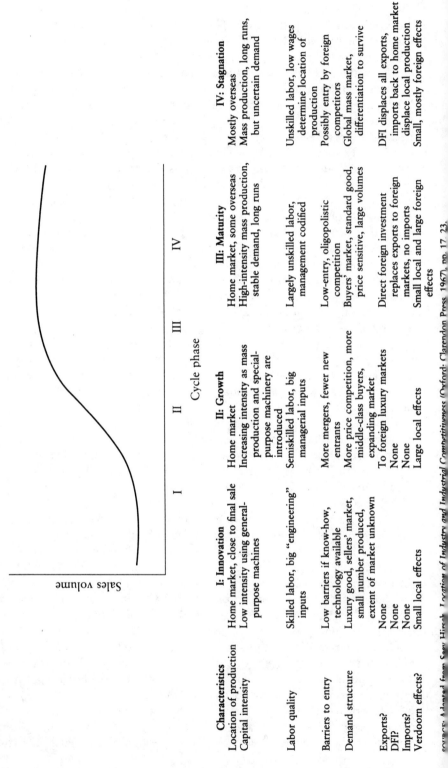

| Characteristics | I: Innovation | II: Growth | III: Maturity | IV: Stagnation |
|---|---|---|---|---|
| Location of production | Home market, close to final sale | Home market | Home market, some overseas | Mostly overseas |
| Capital intensity | Low intensity using general-purpose machines | Increasing intensity as mass production and special-purpose machinery are introduced | High-intensity mass production, stable demand, long runs | Mass production, long runs, but uncertain demand |
| Labor quality | Skilled labor, big "engineering" inputs | Semiskilled labor, big managerial inputs | Largely unskilled labor, management codified | Unskilled labor, low wages determine location of production |
| Barriers to entry | Low barriers if know-how, technology available | More mergers, fewer new entrants | Low-entry, oligopolistic competition | Possibly entry by foreign competitors |
| Demand structure | Luxury good, sellers' market, small number produced, extent of market unknown | More price competition, more middle-class buyers, expanding market | Buyers' market, standard good, price sensitive, large volumes | Global mass market, differentiation to survive |
| Exports? | None | To foreign luxury markets | Direct foreign investment replaces exports to foreign markets, no imports | DFI displaces all exports, imports back to home market |
| DFI? | None | None | | |
| Imports? | None | None | | displace local production |
| Verdoorn effects? | Small local effects | Large local effects | Small local and large foreign effects | Small, mostly foreign effects |

SOURCE: Adapted from Seev Hirsch, *Location of Industry and Industrial Competitiveness* (Oxford: Clarendon Press, 1967, pp. 17-23).

of having begun local production is now much closer and can be observed) and through verdoorn effects. By the fourth stage, the product is fully mature, and, because market growth in the home country has leveled off, more and more production is shifted to overseas production sites. Wage costs become a crucial source of competitive advantage since the production process is well understood. Both the original producer and its imitators search for cheap labor.

The significance of tacit knowledge in the product cycle has been used to explain why firms with technological advantages prefer to invest overseas, rather than simply licensing technology and taking a minority stake in a local producer. Williamson and Teece, for example, maintain that the transaction costs involved in selling knowledge, particularly tacit knowledge, are extremely high. Buyers cannot evaluate the value of such knowledge until they receive it, but once sellers show a potential buyer the information, why should that buyer pay for it? Potential buyers therefore offer sellers a much lower price than sellers will accept. Rather than selling knowledge cheaply, innovators accept the costs of investing overseas once export markets are closed by tariff barriers.

TNCs' explicit and tacit technological advantages and their motivation to preempt competition show not only why TNCs can go overseas and compete, but also why host states often fear this kind of investment. The same technological edge permitting DFI also means that TNCs might very well displace local firms.

## Investment in Developed Countries

Because TNC investment took place largely in developed countries, the kind of struggle that took place around those investments differed from that in LDCs. Host states feared that TNCs would deny potential verdoorn effects to local producers by taking away part of their market and thus potential increases in output. In turn, this would cause economic or technological stagnation in their domestic economy. Most TNCs were in high-tech industries in the sense that they possessed some hard technology (e.g., U.S. electronics and computer firms) or soft technology (e.g., U.S. automobile firms) that local producers did not have. By dominating the Schumpeterian growth sectors, TNCs would deprive local firms of the opportunity to enter those sectors. In turn, this displacement threatened to create macroeconomic problems for host states.

States attempting macroeconomic stabilization—the domestic lesson of the Depression—feared that TNCs would undercut their ability to make macroeconomic policy. Because TNCs disposed of revenues that were not only greater than those of virtually all domestic firms, but sometimes also the entire host country, they weakened states' ability to control the growth and composition of local economic activity. (See Table 11.1.) TNCs might choose to increase or decrease investment for reasons totally unrelated to local macroeconomic policy, and their ability to draw on offshore capital markets made them indifferent to the changes in local interest rates states used to regulate the

TABLE 11.1

## Relative Size of TNCs to Countries (ranked by 1991 GDP or annual sales, $million)

| | | | |
|---|---|---|---|
| United States | 5,392.2 | Philippines | 43.9 |
| Japan | 2,942.9 | Samsung Group (South Korea) | 43.7 |
| West Germany | 1,488.2 | Nissan Motors | 42.9 |
| France | 1,190.8 | New Zealand | 42.8 |
| Italy | 1,090.8 | Ireland | 42.5 |
| Britain | 975.2 | Malaysia | 42.4 |
| Canada | 570.2 | Algeria | 42.2 |
| Spain | 491.2 | Unilever | 41.3 |
| Brazil | 414.1 | Columbia | 41.1 |
| P.R. of China | 364.9 | ENI (France) | 41.0 |
| Australia | 296.3 | Dupont | 38.0 |
| Netherlands | 279.2 | Texaco | 37.6 |
| India | 254.5 | Chevron | 36.8 |
| Mexico | 237.8 | Peru | 36.6 |
| South Korea | 236.4 | ELF Aquitaine (France) | 36.3 |
| Sweden | 228.1 | Nestlé | 35.6 |
| Switzerland | 224.9 | Pakistan | 35.5 |
| Belgium | 192.4 | Nigeria | 34.8 |
| Austria | 157.4 | Romania | 34.7 |
| Finland | 137.3 | Singapore | 34.6 |
| Denmark | 131.0 | Egypt | 33.2 |
| General Motors | 123.8 | Toshiba | 33.2 |
| Indonesia | 107.3 | Hungary | 32.9 |
| Norway | 105.8 | Honda Motor | 30.6 |
| Royal Dutch Shell | 103.8 | Philips Electric | 30.2 |
| Exxon | 103.2 | Renault | 29.4 |
| Turkey | 96.5 | Chrysler | 29.4 |
| Argentina | 93.3 | Boeing | 29.3 |
| South Africa | 90.7 | Asea Brown Boveri | 28.9 |
| Ford | 89.0 | Hoechst | 28.5 |
| Saudi Arabia | 80.9 | Peugeot Group | 28.4 |
| Thailand | 80.2 | Alcatel Alsthom (France) | 28.4 |
| Toyota Motor | 78.1 | United Arab Emirates | 28.3 |
| IBM | 65.4 | BASF | 28.1 |
| IRI (Italy) | 64.1 | Chile | 27.8 |
| General Electric | 60.2 | Procter & Gamble | 27.4 |
| Hong Kong | 59.7 | NEC | 26.7 |
| British Petroleum | 58.4 | Sony | 26.6 |
| Greece | 57.9 | Amoco | 25.6 |
| Daimler Benz | 57.3 | Bayer | 25.6 |
| Mobil | 56.9 | Daewoo (South Korea) | 25.4 |
| Portugal | 56.8 | Total (France) | 25.4 |
| Hitachi | 56.1 | Morocco | 25.2 |
| Israel | 53.2 | PDVSA (Venezuela) | 24.0 |
| Matsushita | 48.6 | Mitsubishi Electric | 24.0 |
| Venezuela | 48.3 | Kuwait | 23.5 |
| Philip Morris | 48.1 | Nippon Steel | 23.1 |
| Fiat | 46.8 | Bangladesh | 22.9 |
| Volkswagen | 46.4 | Thyssen | 22.5 |
| Siemens | 44.9 | Imperial Chemical | 22.3 |

SOURCES: World Bank, *World Development Report* (New York: Oxford University Press, 1992), pp. 221–223; *Fortune*, July 27, 1992, p. 179.

macroeconomy. Moreover, TNCs' economic activity could create new sectors, expand old ones, or displace existing producers. Shifts in the sectoral composition of the economy also change the kinds of social and political groups in that economy, destroying old or creating new political actors. Thus, TNCs could change the political and economic environment in which a given state operated.

TNCs often occupied a strategic position in the local economy. The old resource-based TNCs, particularly the oil companies, controlled access to a crucial raw material used elsewhere. Most new TNCs produced goods that were related to the new leading sectors of the 1930s and 1960s cluster. These goods combined a multitude of manufactured components, whose value existed only to the extent that they could be combined into a commodity package. Consider cars, which contain radios, glass, textiles, plastics, electronics, tires, and a variety of machined, stamped, and forged metal products. In the motor vehicle – petroleum industrial complex, upstream commodity flows tended to converge on and downstream flows to emanate from a small number of bottleneck firms. The new TNCs tended to control the key bottleneck processing step. Thus, they threatened to dominate all the subsidiary and supporting industries that clustered around the leading sector, because they could exert monopsony (single-buyer) pressures on upstream sellers and monopoly on downstream buyers.

For example, in the automotive industry, thousands of small component-producing firms supplied only a handful of assemblers. Ford USA, for example, had about 3,000 parts suppliers in the 1970s and could pit them against one another. In contrast, the suppliers faced only three and a half firms in the U.S. market in the 1970s: Ford, GM, and Chrysler, as well as American Motors and VW (which together equaled about half a firm). An enormous percentage of the economy thus flowed through a small number of assemblers. In the United States and Europe, the auto industry accounted for about one-seventh to one-sixth of GDP. The U.S. big three routinely set prices with an eye toward their rate-of-return targets rather than market conditions. Host states feared that the TNCs would similarly exploit local component firms and consumers.

Finally, the new-style TNCs changed the nature of trade from open market exchanges between firms and consumers located in different countries to a flow of goods and services inside a single company, albeit internationally. This change also undermined macroeconomic stability. Market signals alone no longer sufficed to stimulate/restrict exports and imports when a country ran trade deficits. Corporate planning—administration—structured trade flows.

Host states, however, could deploy various weapons against TNCs. Because these new-style TNCs invested in other developed countries, they had to operate within foreign and varied legal regimes backed by reasonably competent states. These states could manifest their hostility to TNCs through policies favoring local producers. At the same time, states' efforts to protect local industry could magnify the threat of displacement. Protection created a dilemma for host states. If states allowed foreign firms to directly invest in their economies, this would increase the possibility that foreign firms might monopolize the stimuli for income and productivity growth. On the other hand, if states banned foreign investment, their local firms might never assimilate the hard and soft technologies that gave TNCs their competitive advantage.

In the nineteenth century, states faced with displacement-causing trade could use protection to engender local industry. Migrating entrepreneurs did not pose a threat because they, together with their technologies, tended to be assimilated into the local economy. Emigrés soon became indistinguishable from local capitalists. After World War II, however, TNCs replaced these migrant entrepreneurs. Unlike those entrepreneurs, TNCs retained a corporate identity and base of operations in some other nation. European and other states thus had to generate new strategies for late development. These strategies used nontariff barriers and various kinds of subsidy to support local industry.

Post–World War II intracore transnational investment underwent two distinct waves. In the first, U.S. firms invaded the world, but primarily Europe. In the second wave, first European and then Japanese firms invaded the United States, particularly during the Reagan administration's great fire sale of U.S. assets in the mid-1980s. How did these conflicts play out first between U.S. TNCs and European firms and states, and then between Japanese TNCs and U.S. and European firms and states?

## America versus Europe

In 1967 Jean-Jacques Servan-Schreiber, a French journalist, wrote a call to economic arms for France and Europe. *Le Défi américain* (The American Challenge) called for a wide range of state initiatives to remedy the competitive edge U.S. firms held over European firms. Without these initiatives, Servan-Schreiber claimed, "fifteen years from now the world's third largest industrial power, just after the United States and [the Soviet Union], may not be Europe, but *American industry in Europe*."[12] Servan-Schreiber was wrong about two things: a little more than 15 years later, the second largest industrial power in the world was Japan, and barely a decade after that there was no Soviet Union. Why couldn't European firms at first outcompete U.S. firms on their own home court? Why didn't U.S. firms later swamp the Europeans?

Servan-Schreiber did, however, correctly identify the source of the American challenge to European industry: U.S. firms managed mass production much better than did their European competitors. Until European firms assimilated the soft technologies associated with the American art of management, they risked being displaced from their own home markets by U.S. TNCs. In the long term, by occupying the dynamic and high-profit sectors of the economy, TNCs threatened to choke off locally controlled growth and to denationalize part of the local pool of investment capital. In the 1960s, U.S. firms in Europe produced 80 percent of Western Europe's computers, 24 percent of its motor vehicles, 15 percent of its synthetic rubber, and 10 percent of its petrochemicals. Squeezed out of dynamic sectors, local firms faced stagnant profits. Meanwhile, rational holders of liquid capital would lend to dynamic U.S. TNCs. More than half of the capital invested by U.S.

TNCs in Europe, for example, came from local sources, including the Euro-dollar market; only about 10 percent represented actual capital transferred from the United States.[13]

Because of their superior production systems, U.S. firms had greater profits and economies of scale than their European competitors. Collectively, the twenty largest U.S. firms, for example, had annual revenues equal to or greater than any of the largest European economies in the 1960s. In computers and electronics, the new leading sector, the disparity was even greater. IBM invested more in the development of the System 360 computer unveiled in 1964 than Siemens, then the largest European computer firm, generated in annual revenues in the years the System 360 was developed.

Thus, from the point of view of the European states, U.S. DFI contained the dangers and opportunities noted above. Allowing DFI to occur meant allowing a well-constructed Trojan horse inside the national economic fortress, exposing local economic sectors. Those sectors directly competing with or linked to the TNC risked losing growth and market share to the invader. Letting TNCs in, however, created an opportunity to observe the carpentry secrets that allowed the horse to be constructed in the first place. If those tricks and secrets could be learned and mastered, then local firms could counterattack and regain both domestic and international market share. European responses to the invasion of U.S. car firms from 1920 through the 1960s reflect these different dangers and opportunities.

## U.S. Firms in Europe

U.S. car firms transnationalized early in their industrial history, more or less along the lines predicted by product cycle theory. Because of transportation costs, during stage two, U.S. firms mostly exported *parts*, in the form of completely-knocked-down car kits (CKDs), which were then assembled in the major markets. Ford had set up assembly plants in Canada, Argentina, Brazil, and Britain before 1918. Continental Europe was the next logical step, since U.S. car firms already exported both CKDs and assembled cars there, and since both Ford and GM already assembled cars in Britain.

These assembly plants were the bridgehead for a shift of the complete production process to Europe and Britain (stage three) during the 1930s. Local efforts to protect domestic industry induced direct investment. During the 1920s European states tried to control the market share of U.S. firms in two ways. First, they imposed high and sometimes prohibitive tariffs. Thirty-three-percent tariffs in Britain, higher tariffs and import quotas in France, and foreign currency shortages in Germany began to price Ford and GM products out of the European market. Second, states imposed high taxes based on engine displacement. This move favored local producers of small cars; the unassembled cars exported as parts by U.S. firms were large cars. Meanwhile, some of the more nimble European firms adopted some of Ford's assembly-line techniques, further eroding the U.S. firms' price advantages even in the large-car segment. As a result, by the end of the 1920s, U.S. firms had to transnationalize into the European market to protect their market and profit shares from the combination of state intervention and European catch-up.

GM led the way, mostly because it took the easy route of buying up existing firms like Vauxhall (UK) in 1925 and Opel (Germany) in 1929. The French and Italian states prohibited GM from buying local firms. GM strategically picked off the most up-to-date competitor in each country. Opel, for example, had the most modern machine tool stock of the German firms and had gone farthest in introducing a basic assembly line.[14] In contrast, Ford set up greenfield plants—new plants in open fields—in Britain and Germany in 1931 and France in 1934, transferring its production processes intact rather than having to deal with existing practices at a (relatively) backward European firm. As with GM, the Italian state rejected Ford's efforts to begin full-scale production.

## The European Response

Britain, France, and Germany responded to the evolution of the threat from imports to transnational production in distinctly different ways, depending on whether their states focused more on the opportunities or on the dangers inherent in DFI. Britain focused mostly on opportunities and disregarded the dangers, and France mostly on the dangers and not the opportunities, while Germany kept a wary eye on both. The outcome was distinctly bad for British industry, less so for French, and least so for German.

The British state permitted unrestricted DFI by U.S. car firms. The British hoped that U.S. managerial practices would diffuse to Britain's backward industrial sector. Diffusion did indeed occur, but slowly. Disregarding minor niche marketers of luxury cars, U.S. firms simply displaced inefficient British rivals. By the 1970s, U.S. firms accounted for over 50 percent of British car production. Because these firms had global planning horizons and investment options, they began systematically disinvesting from Britain in the 1970s in the face of persistent labor unrest and foreign exchange crises.

Britain then found it could not regenerate an automobile sector without more foreign investment inasmuch as local managerial talent and organizations did not exist. Instead, imports expanded to meet expanding British demand for cars. Consequently, the state invited in a second wave of TNCs, this time Japanese firms like Honda, Nissan, and Toyota. All three sought access to the highly protected European Community market. Aside from Honda, which sought a strategic alliance with Rover, this wave of Japanese firms threatened a rerun of Britain's experience with the U.S. TNCs. However, by the end of the 1980s British industry seemed to be slowly absorbing superior Japanese production practices.[15]

In France the danger of displacement occupied the state to the exclusion of learning induced by the demonstration effect. As late as 1927, the average French car absorbed 300 person-days of labor from raw materials to finished product, compared to 70 person-days in the United States.[16] By raising tariffs to nearly prohibitive levels, by setting quotas for imports, and by preventing anyone but Ford from entering the market via DFI (and then quite late), it preserved about three-fourths of the market for French producers. After the war, France nationalized Renault and provided extensive support to Peugeot, helping it to absorb the smaller French firms as they failed. Pressured by their state, French producers assimilated U.S. manufacturing practices.[17] The state continued to use tariffs and import quotas to restrict the competitive threat from U.S. and Japanese firms, and also blocked any DFI.

By the 1980s France was a net exporter of cars, with about one-quarter of the European market and one of the largest national car industries in Europe. However, the absence of competition within the French market weakened the ability of French firms to compete with stronger firms in the overall world market. French firms had barely assimilated U.S. production methods when even better Japanese car-assembly practices rendered the gain nugatory. The French continue to resist the full force of market pressures from Japanese car firms, including those that have transnationalized into Britain. For example, they tried to get the European Community to classify Japanese cars built in Britain as imports because they had only 80 percent EC content, and delayed market liberalization under the Single European Act (Europe 1992) for the auto industry.

Germany chose a middle path. During the 1930s the Nazi government had tolerated but disliked Ford's and GM/Opel's dominance (over 50 percent) of the mass market, creating state-owned Volkswagen to challenge the U.S. pair. Given its status as an occupied country after the war, it could hardly refuse reentry by the U.S. producers in the same way France did, but it could try to restructure its industry to gain maximum benefits from their presence. The state encouraged each local firm to concentrate on different parts of the market. German firms competed with the U.S. firms and, to a lesser extent, each other, forcing them to attain world market levels of competition and productivity. The quasi-luxury firms had an easier time doing this. VW had the harder task, but with overt and covert state aid it prospered. It added U.S. levels of assembly-line productivity to German-style attention to details, remaining one of the few European firms, aside from luxury producers, that could export in large volumes to the United States.

## The European Attempt to Catch Up

How did the Europeans catch up? Practically, they didn't. By the 1970s, European cars still cost about 30 to 60 percent more than similar U.S.-built cars, reflecting an equivalent productivity disadvantage.[18] But the way in which the industry avoided complete displacement mimicked earlier catchup patterns. As in the nineteenth century, state intervention basically bought time for local entrepreneurs, preserving space in the local market so that they could experience verdoorn effects. Then it was up to local producers to become competitive. In the process of catching up, local producers generated novel innovations that ultimately brought them up to or past the competitive position of their rivals. In the nineteenth century, German and U.S. iron and steel producers had used scale economies to catch up with Britain's smaller plants and then taken advantage of their more plastic labor forces to introduce high-productivity electrical machinery and surpass the British.

In the automobile industry in Europe, local firms benefited from the proximity of U.S. TNCs. U.S. firms trained local workers and managers who later cycled through locally owned firms. Similarly, the demands of U.S. firms on local component producers forced them to introduce high-volume, U.S.-style assembly-line techniques in order to win contracts for parts. To this method the Europeans added a hard technological edge and better design skills. Their fragmented market forced them to make their cars distinctive. They used advances in design (front-wheel drive, econo-boxes, styling, lifetime service contracts) and in hard technologies (antilock brakes, electronic ignition) to set their cars apart from those of other local competitors. This fragmentation of the market placed the transplanted U.S. firms at a disadvantage. While they had vast experience in high-volume assembly-line production, U.S. firms had less experience producing and selling into highly differentiated markets. Thus, they gave up part of their advantage to come into the European market, while transferring part of their advantage to local competitors via imitation. Ironically, some of the stronger European firms had an easier time transnationalizing into third-party LDC markets because their experience with low-income, fragmented markets gave them a competitive edge.

Finally, because protection forced U.S. TNCs to produce locally, both the local components producers and the national (but partly TNC) car industry experienced far higher levels of growth than did the U.S. industry. From 1950 to 1973, U.S. car production grew from just under 7 million units to just under 11 million units, a 60 percent increase. But average production since the 1950s has hovered around 9 million units. European car production, including U.S. TNCs, jumped from 1.1 million units in 1950 to just over 11.4 million units by 1973, with fairly rapid and steady growth, and then edged up to about 13 million units through the 1980s. Consequently, from 1950 to 1970 the European industry experienced extremely rapid increases in output and extremely rapid productivity growth. Figure 11.2 shows the differences in output and world market share.

# Japan versus America (and Europe?)

Servan-Schreiber had the satisfaction of being flattered by a hundred imitators about 20 years later, when a veritable deluge of books appeared in the United States on the theme of *le défi japonais*. Much less clearly than Servan-Schreiber had done, these works identified the source of Japanese competitive advantage in Japan's superiority in the management of mass production. Japanese investment in the United States raised the same fears as it had in Europe in the 1950s. U.S. firms face competitive displacement—ask any of the nearly 150,000 workers laid off by GM during the 1980s and 1990s as its market share slid from about 50 percent to 35 percent. Similarly, Japanese (and European) investment raised fears that the United States was losing control of domestic economic management.

Just like the U.S. auto firms vis-à-vis the Europeans, Japanese electronics and automobile producers possessed an overwhelming managerial advantage (see Chapter 14). (Technologically, neither their products nor their production

**Figure 11.2** *Share of World Auto Production by Location of Production, 1946–1990, Selected Years*

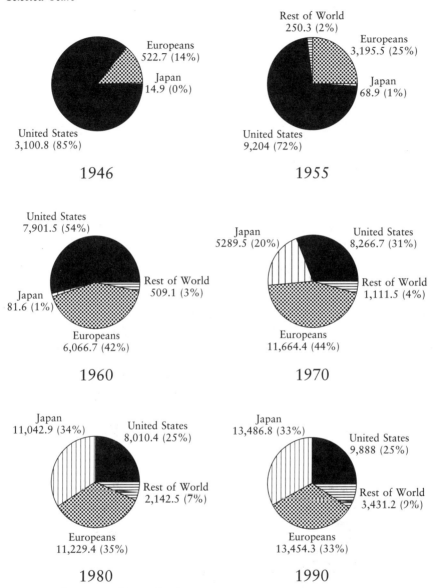

1946        1955

1960        1970

1980        1990

SOURCE: *Ward's Automotive News*, various issues.

machinery were particularly advanced until the late 1980s.) Their managerial advantage allowed them to export into the U.S. and European markets,
sweeping aside other small-car producers. By 1980 Japan had about 20 percent
of the U.S. market and just over 10 percent of the entire European car market
(although as much as 40 percent of the market in small, non-automobile-pro-
ducing countries like Denmark).

Just as in the past, the United States and European states tried to protect their domestic producers. Because the strictures of GATT prevented them from raising tariffs to any great extent, they resorted to the great and by then time-honored method of subverting GATT: the voluntary export restraint (VER) agreement. Italy benefited from a pre-GATT accord limiting the Japanese to no more than 3,000 sales per year in Italy. In 1977, reflecting the different temperament of their states, the French threatened the Japanese with a severe response should the Japanese take more than 3 percent of their domestic market, while the British worked out a gentlemen's agreement under which the Japanese held themselves to about 10 percent of the market. In 1981 the United States worked out a VER limiting Japanese exports to 1.85 million units per year, which induced the rest of the Europeans to impose similar VERs for fear of being inundated with diverted Japanese exports. Like high tariffs and quotas in the 1920s and 1930s, VERs forced the Japanese to transnationalize their operations into their major developed country markets. Honda was first, followed by Nissan and Toyota. Mitsubishi (15 percent ownership by Chrysler), Mazda (25 percent ownership by Ford), and the minor firms (GM has equity stakes in Daihatsu and Isuzu) then set up joint ventures with their respective U.S. partners. In Europe Honda negotiated a joint venture with Rover, while Nissan and again, after some delay, Toyota set up assembly plants in Britain and Spain. These plants gave them access to the entire European market under existing European Community rules.

As in Europe with U.S. firms, the shift from imports to local TNC production aggravated the potential threat. Imports could be controlled by quotas, but what about transplants? By 1991 Japanese transplants in the United States accounted for two-fifths of Japan's U.S. sales, and the plants had not yet reached full operating capacity. In Europe the Japanese threat was still over the horizon, as it mostly affected firms selling into the British market, but the threat of higher future sales was clear. Perhaps these problems could be controlled by internal quotas. Just as the French tried to count Japanese transplant production as imports, so some U.S. car executives called for including transplants' production in Japan's overall quota. But transplants employed local workers, bought from local suppliers, and so were able to lobby local politicians to prevent the imposition of internal market quotas. Honda's factory complex in Ohio employs over 10,000 workers with an annual payroll of over $350 million.

Just as European firms learned from transplanted U.S. firms, so U.S. firms began to learn from Japanese firms. Strategic alliances (Ford–Mazda and Chrysler–Mitsubishi) confronted the U.S. partner with undeniable evidence of problems in their design, assembly, and component buying practices. Those firms began shifting to Japanese-style practices. Ford, for example, adopted Japanese-style labor practices in its Taurus/Sable plant in Atlanta. Japanese levels of quality and productivity emerged; Atlanta reputedly is the most productive plant in the United States and even more productive than the average Japanese plant in Japan. Ford also tried to cut back its supplier network by 25 percent in order to create strategic alliances with the best suppliers and to shift part of the design work onto them, mimicking Japanese *keiretsu* structures (see Chapter 14).

Just as with U.S. firms in Europe, the Japanese invaders lost some of their original sources of superiority when they entered the U.S. market. Toyota's ability to do just-in-time production, for example, derives in large part from the proximity of its supplier firms, most of which are located literally next door to its main assembly plant in Japan. By shifting production to the United States, Toyota has been forced to ship components halfway around the world, thus undercutting this advantage. To re-create their just-in-time inventory systems, Japanese TNCs will have to develop a local (i.e., U.S.) components industry that is up to their quality and delivery standards. By imposing their standards on local firms, they force those components firms to attain Japanese levels of productivity and quality. This helps the U.S. assemblers create their own just-in-time systems. As in Europe, locals learn how to improve from proximity to a TNC competitor, while those TNC competitors lose part of their edge by transplanting themselves.

The trend toward more managed trade (see Chapter 13) has accelerated the speed at which this assimilation occurs. The reality or threat that states might restrict market access through quotas or subsidies to local firms has prompted existing and would-be TNCs to enter into an enormous range of strategic alliances.[19] These alliances facilitate a more rapid transfer of managerial and technical knowledge than that discussed above.

So just as in Europe, the situation is likely to equilibrate, with the Japanese taking a specific market share while local, but improved, firms retain the bulk of the market. Direct verdoorn effects are unlikely to be present in a stagnant U.S. market. However, a kind of indirect verdoorn effect is likely to occur. The rate of reduction in defects in U.S. cars has been much more rapid since the mid-1980s than in Japanese cars. The heart of the Japanese productive system is now diffusing through the nonautomotive parts of the U.S. economy, which on average is already more productive than the Japanese economy.[20] The ultimate question is whether U.S. firms, unlike British firms in the 1890s and 1900s, will be able to understand, adopt, and adapt the new techniques.

# Notes

1. See Mira Wilkins, *The Maturing of Multinational Enterprise: American Business Abroad 1914–1970* (Cambridge, Mass.: Harvard University Press, 1974).

2. United Nations Centre on Transnational Corporations, *World Investment Report 1991: The Triad in Foreign Direct Investment* (New York: United Nations, 1991), pp. 31–66.

3. DFI is sometimes called FDI (foreign direct investment). There is no difference between the two.

4. In 1990, 16 of the 100 biggest TNCs (and four of the 10 largest) were involved in petroleum extraction, and another two were food processors.

5. Stephen Hymer, "The Multinational Corporation and the Law of Uneven

Development," in Jagdish Bhagwati, ed., *Economics and World Order* (New York: Macmillan, 1972), p. 115.

6. For a general overview, see Charles Kindleberger, *Six Lectures on Direct Foreign Investment* (New Haven, Conn.: Yale University Press, 1969); on the obsolescing bargain, see Raymond Vernon, *Sovereignty at Bay* (New York: Basic Books, 1971), pp. 46–59.

7. See Jeanne Laux and Maureen Molot, *State Capitalism: Public Enterprise in Canada* (Ithaca, N.Y.: Cornell University Press, 1988); G. Crough and E. L. Wheelwright, *Australia: a Client State—Sold Off!* (New York: Penguin Books, 1982). For a general consideration of raw materials cartels, see Stephen Krasner, "Oil Is the Exception," *Foreign Policy* 14 (Spring 1974): 68–90.

8. Terutomo Ozawa, *Multinationalism, Japanese Style* (Princeton, N.J.: Princeton University Press, 1980), ch. 3.

9. Wilkins, *Maturing of Multinational Enterprise*; UNCTC, *Transnational Corporations in World Development* (New York: United Nations, 1988), pp. 76, 86.

10. Charles Kindleberger, "A Theory of Direct Foreign Investment," in *Six Lectures on Direct Investment*.

11. Stephen Hymer, "The Multinational Corporation"; Kindleberger, "A Theory of Direct Foreign Investment"; Vernon, *Sovereignty at Bay*; Oliver Williamson, *Economic Institutions of Capitalism* (New York: Free Press, 1985), especially ch. 11; D. J. Teece, "Technology Transfer by Multinational Firms," *Economic Journal* 87 (June 1977): 242–261; D. J. Teece, "Economies of Scope and the Scope of the Enterprise," *Journal of Economic Behavior and Organization* 1, no. 3 (September 1980): 223–245; and Theodore Moran, "Foreign Expansion as an Institutional Necessity," *World Politics* (April 1973): 369–386.

12. Jean-Jacques Servan-Schreiber, *The American Challenge* (New York: Avon, 1969), p. 35; emphasis in the original.

13. Ibid., p. 14. The rest came from retained earnings.

14. James M. Laux, *The Automobile Revolution* (Chapel Hill, N.C.: University of North Carolina Press, 1982).

15. See "Down but Not Out: A Survey of the British Economy," *The Economist*, October 24, 1992, *passim*.

16. Laux, *The Automobile Revolution*, p. 102.

17. Ibid., chs. 6 and 10.

18. See James Womack, Daniel Jones, and Daniel Roos, *The Machine That Changed the World* (New York: Rawson Associates, 1992); and Alan Altschuler et al., *Future of the Automobile* (Cambridge, Mass.: MIT Press, 1985). Daniel Jones, "Motor Cars: A Maturing Industry?" in Geoffrey Shepard, François Duchene, and Christopher Saunders, *Europe's Industries: Public and Private Strategies for Change* (Ithaca, N.Y.: Cornell University Press, 1983), pp. 114–115.

19. Robert Reich, *The Work of Nations* (New York: Alfred A. Knopf, 1991); Peter Cowhey and Jonathan Aronson, *Changing the World Economy: Consequences of Corporate Alliances* (New York: Council on Foreign Relations, 1992).

20. "Toyota Plant Is Font of Ideas for U.S.," *New York Times* May 5, 1992, p. A1. Twenty thousand U.S. engineers and managers have apparently visited Toyota's Georgetown, Kentucky, plant since 1988. On the U.S. productivity edge, see the *New York Times* October 13, 1992, summary of a McKinsey Global Institute report.

# CHAPTER 12

---

# Industrialization in the Old Agricultural Periphery: The Rise of the Newly Industrialized Countries

The First Industrial Revolution was built on laissez-faire, the Second on infant industry protection. In Late Industrialization, the foundation is the subsidy [from the state]—which includes both protection and financial incentives.

*Alice Amsden*

A transfer of income from the richest 20 percent to the poorest 80 percent would probably increase the demand for food, but not the demand for automobiles. The result of a sudden redistribution would be merely to generate inflation in the food producing sector and excess capacity in the car sector.

*Mario Henrique Simonsen*
*(Brazilian Finance Minister)*

Once upon a time, in an era now far, far away, it was fashionable to talk about the Third World. The concept of Third World was peculiar in all respects. It was a residual category into which to lump all the countries that did not fall into the camp of the First World (the developed market economies confronting communist regimes) or the Second World (the communists, whether developed or not), regardless of the degree of similarity or dissimilarity of those countries. As a number, it implied a rough (and unfortunately accurate) level of importance in the world economy. (The preunification West German economy, after all, was about half again as large as the combined economies of Latin America and the Caribbean.) The Third World included countries as diverse and unlike as Brazil and the Maldive Islands, Togo and Taiwan, Kuwait and Indonesia. The opacity and uselessness of the Third World as a concept made its survival remarkable.

In the 1970s and 1980s, the newly industrializing countries (NICs) developed manufacturing muscle and income growth, while other Third World countries experienced a relative and in some cases an absolute regression in living standards. This signalled the disintegration of the Third World in both a practical and a conceptual sense.[1] If the grouping had once made sense as a classification for most agricultural exporters, by the 1970s it did not. By then, many so-called Third World countries had become exporters of manufactured goods. By then, too, some people were beginning to talk of a Fourth World made up of the poorest of the poor, with per capita incomes under $200. The suicide of the Second World in 1989–91 confirmed this disintegration of the Third World; how can you have a Third World without a Second?

## Decomposing the Third World

The Second World's death revealed an underlying truth hidden by the murky label Third World. The Third World was a collection of countries with disparate, sometimes desperate, strategies for confronting the key economic problem raised by the emergence of the assembly line, the motor vehicle, and the Keynesian revolution after World Wars I and II. What happens to and in the global agricultural periphery when dissolution of the last European microeconomies reorients European economies inward? Europe's adoption of the motor vehicle made it possible for Europeans to rely on domestic food sources; the right's political weakness and thus reliance on rural votes after the war made self-sufficiency a reality through subsidies. Eventually, the European Community's Common Agricultural Policy turned self-sufficiency into subsidized exports.

Second, increased industrialization and income levels in Europe and America meant that the proportion of income spent on food and thus food imports declined steadily (Engel's Law). Because total population in the industrial countries continued to grow, so did peripheral exports, but very slowly. The Argentinean Raul Prebisch argued that the slower growth of demand for agricultural goods relative to manufactured goods caused declining terms of trade and thus economic stagnation in the periphery.[2] As peripheral terms of trade declined from roughly 1953 to 1973, it also became harder for them to import manufactured goods in the volumes to which they had become accustomed.

Thus, as the old Ricardian strategies looked less and less useful, theorists like Prebisch called for a strategic shift from agriculture to manufacturing, that is, a shift to Kaldorian strategies trying to take advantage of Verdoorn's law. This shift was successful in an aggregate sense. From 1960 on, what the World Bank likes to call less developed countries had, as a whole, a growth rate usually twice as high as the Organization for Economic Cooperation and Development countries as a whole. These higher growth rates reflected a shift out of agriculture and into manufacturing in general, a shift that can be seen in the LDCs' changing export mix. The proportion of manufactured goods in LDC nonoil exports rose from only 10 percent in 1955 to 65 percent in 1986. Meanwhile, foods and nonfood agriculturals (NFAs) fell from 77 to 29 percent and minerals from 29 to 6 percent.[3]

This aggregate success conceals quite divergent individual performances. This increase mostly reflected the astounding success of about eight countries — or, to be precise, five countries, two islands, and one province with disputed ownership. By the end of the 1980s Taiwan, South Korea, Hong Kong, and Singapore accounted for one-half of all LDC manufactured goods exports. Brazil, Mexico, Argentina and Colombia accounted for another quarter.

# Late Development in the Agricultural Periphery

The LDCs' varying success at industrializing reflected their varying ability to master the problems Alexander Gerschenkron identified as inherent in late industrialization (see Chapter 4). The essential precondition for success was a relatively strong and autonomous state: could it control or influence society enough to impose and consistently carry through a development strategy? A state capable of guiding an industrialization strategy had to choose among a variety of possible responses to the following problems:

~ Where would the initial capital investment come from, and what institutional form should be used to concentrate and invest that capital — exploitation of local agriculture, borrowing abroad, multinational investment, or self-reliance? private local banks, state banks, or foreign banks? large firms or small firms?

~ What sector(s) should policy target for growth; agriculture or industry? and, within industry, heavy (capital goods) or light (consumer goods) industry?

~ (related to the above problems): Could TNCs be used as engines of growth without an LDC's losing the effects of learning by doing?

~ What should the country's trade goal be — a closed economy with import substitution or a gradually opening economy using import substitution to create export capable industry? Equally important, who should receive subsidization and how?

~ How should labor be controlled — through repression or incorporation? Given the increasing importance of human capital, who should train labor and management — the state or private firms?

A mix of historical and geographic circumstances sharply circumscribed these options. Any given country's geographical location and colonial history largely determined its natural markets. In the nineteenth century, when only Britain plausibly provided an external motor for growth, this condition did not matter. In the twentieth century, however, the three biggest economic powers — the United States, Japan, and the European Community — grew at different rates and provided markets for different sorts of goods. Virtually all countries had to rely on external capital because only Taiwan and South Korea really succeeded in using their agricultural sector as an initial source of capital (see the discussion of East Asia later in this chapter). This combination of constraints created four basic models for industrialization, listed in decreasing order of their success: an export-oriented, partly debt-financed East Asian model linked to both Japan and the United States; a debt- and TNC-financed, import-substitution-oriented Latin American model linked to the United States alone; an export-oriented, TNC-financed southern European model linked to Western Europe; and an import-substitution-oriented, debt-financed Eastern European model linked to Western Europe.

The following discussion omits more than a few countries for the following reasons. After 1955, sub-Saharan Africa was preoccupied with efforts to satisfy the *precondition* for Gerschenkronian late development efforts: create a state.[4] With a few exceptions, the old externally imposed Ricardian strategies continued, leading for the most part to declining incomes. Most borrowing took the form of concessional loans from development agencies and was directed toward state-building projects.

India tried a self-reliant, low-debt strategy. China initially attempted the same thing but is now shifting toward the generic East Asian model, with explosive growth in the regions closest to Hong Kong and Taiwan. If China maintains growth rates of 8 to 12 percent per year for the next two decades, it will become one of the world's five largest economies.

The Maghreb countries adopted and adapted southern Europe's model. The Mideast countries adopted an oil-led strategy with ambiguous results; the exception was Iran's abortive adaptation of the Latin American model. Meanwhile, a whole host of countries simply fell by the wayside because their economies were too small to support any world-market-competitive manufacturing. There are 30 countries (mostly small islands and archipelagoes) with populations under 1 million and a further 29 countries with under 5 million. Although an industrial economy is not impossible under those conditions, full-scale *late industrialization* probably is. The absence of a large domestic market makes it difficult for local entrepreneurs to get started and to learn in a relatively protected environment. The obvious exceptions—Singapore with a population of 3 million and Hong Kong with about 6 million—benefitted from their location.

The discussion in the next section contrasts a generic Latin American model, looking at Brazil, Mexico, and Argentina, a generic East Asian model, looking at Taiwan and South Korea, and a stylized discussion of Eastern European industrialization. While detailed, it will help clarify differences and similarities in origin and outcome in these different strategic paths. One caveat is in order here. As noted above, the first two sets of countries chosen are mostly the success stories. Therefore, while the discussion may at times seem to imply failure or wrongheaded choices, the reader should keep in mind the vast array of countries that would like to have the problems of these countries.

## The Latin American Path

Latin American industrialization occurred in three distinct waves. In each wave some countries dropped out of the race for reasons of scale or incompetent execution of their chosen strategy. Each wave involved a different level of industrialization and a different key entrepreneurial actor, but the level of state involvement increased with each wave. The first wave involved import substitution in light industry (consumer nondurables) largely through private efforts, as well as the creation of a rudimentary capital goods industry under the aegis of the state. In the second wave, transnationals developed a consumer durables industry that again was oriented toward the domestic market, while the state continued to expand the capital goods sector. In the third wave, the state borrowed abroad to finance capital goods deepening and consolidation of an export-oriented consumer durables industry in an effort to displace the TNCs. Since only Mexico, Brazil, and, to a much lesser extent, Argentina made it to the third wave, the discussion will concentrate on these countries.[5]

## Wave One: Consumer Nondurables

The first wave of industrialization in Latin America, around the turn of the century, was a natural consequence of these countries' original Ricardian strategies and resembled similar contemporary industrial spurts in Eastern Europe, Australasia, India, and Japan. Local industrial entrepreneurs benefitted from a kind of natural protection from external competition. Many basic goods were nontradables at this point because of high transportation costs: beer and basic food processing, construction materials, and, because of local tastes, some textiles. Producing and processing local agricultural output also spurred milling, machinery repairs, and sometimes machinery building. The low capital requirements for market entry facilitated this wave of industrialization. By 1914, in both Brazil and Argentina, local firms had captured about 50 percent of the local textile and garment market. In all countries, production centered on the most dynamic agricultural export or mining area: São Paulo in Brazil, Santa Fe province in Argentina, and Monterrey in Mexico.

The Great Depression forced a consolidation of this wave of industrialization by adding overt protection and a conscious development strategy to the natural industrialization promoted by the old Ricardian strategy. The Depression hit Latin America much harder than other peripheral areas, Argentina excepted. When export revenues declined and as Mexico and Brazil refused to pay interest on their foreign debts, the state in all three countries intervened to create state-owned metals and petroleum industries, often expropriating foreign producers in the process, while also creating a basic administrative capacity to structure the market for industrial goods. All three states created labor unions that controlled an otherwise volatile labor force. Because of U.S. concern to assure security in its own hemisphere while fighting a two-front war, both Brazil and Mexico managed to extract relatively high levels of resource and technical transfers from the United States during World War II, as well as considerable assistance in building professional military and civil bureaucracies. In conjunction with this aid, Brazil's foreign debt was substantially written down and Mexico received a favorable rescheduling agreement. After the war, this aid prepared these two states to vault ahead of Argentina, which they had lagged behind throughout the nineteenth century.

In Mexico the great state builder Lázaro Cárdenas nationalized the oil industry and railroads and established a state steel industry. He expanded the powers of the central bank, and he created the basis for substantial state control over finance through the Nacional Financiera (Nafinsa) bank and other banks specializing in rural and export lending. Nafinsa was used to expand indigenous heavy industry. Nafinsa's control over the allocation of

U.S. wartime aid in the 1940s strengthened its hold on industrial capital formation. Like German banks in the nineteenth century, Nafinsa took equity positions in many of the companies it funded, and by the 1950s the state would control between one-third and one-half of all investment. By the end of the 1940s Mexico produced most of its consumer nondurable consumption. Politically, Cárdenas forged durable alliances between the state and small business and between workers and peasants, incorporating those unions into the political party that continues to rule Mexico today, the Partido Revolucionario Institucional (PRI). PRI controlled and channeled demands to the state upward and state action downward.

In Brazil, Getúlio Vargas also rebuilt the Brazilian state, trying to centralize and professionalize power. Like Cárdenas, he nationalized railroads and oil, and he established state-run steel mills and coal/iron ore mines. By 1949 virtually all consumer nondurables and about half of capital goods consumption were locally produced. Like Cárdenas, Vargas established a strong state bank, the National Bank for Economic Development (BNDES in Portuguese), to control industrial finance. By the 1950s the state controlled 25 percent of investment, and by 1960 half of investment. Vargas repressed peasant revolts and unionized urban workers from above but failed to institutionalize his rule in a dominant political party such as PRI. GDP growth averaged 4.5 percent per year in the 1930s, led by a 6.1 percent expansion in industrial output.[6]

Argentina did not turn away from a Ricardian strategy until the Peronist governments of the 1940s, because Argentina was able to negotiate a bilateral trade deal with Britain in 1933, precisely when the other two countries shifted strategies. Once Juan Perón came to power in 1943, Argentina followed in the footsteps of the other two, nationalizing the oil industry, repatriating ownership of the railroads, and setting up a range of state-owned, primarily military industries. In the absence of U.S. aid, and in the face of well-developed local capital markets, the Argentine state's hold over industrial investment was weaker than in Mexico or Brazil. Still, the state Institution for the Promotion of Trade (IAPI) used its control over foreign exchange to channel investment to a range of state-owned or -favored industries. The absence of indigenous iron and coal fields hindered the creation of a basic metal industry. While Perón also tied labor unions to the state, those unions predated Perón and consequently were much stronger than their counterparts in Mexico or Brazil. This heightened class conflict in Argentina and led to considerable political instability.[7]

## Wave Two: Consumer Durables and Capital Goods

After World War II, a second wave of industrialization occurred in consumer durables, particularly autos, but with TNCs as the major actor in each country.[8] Each state tried to use TNCs as an engine of growth for the local economy and as a transmission belt to carry new technologies to local firms. These three states passed domestic content laws that forced TNCs to locate manufacturing production, and not just final assembly of parts manufactured elsewhere, inside the local economy. These three states hoped to create a local parts and components industry that later could move upstream into final assembly. The TNCs had various motives for cooperation. U.S. TNCs saw local manufacturing as a way to stem the postwar erosion of their dominant market share; Europeans saw DFI as a way to gain global economies of scale.

Brazil passed its first automobile local content laws in 1955 and 1956, setting 80 percent and 95 percent content requirements for trucks and cars, respectively, while limiting the number of TNCs that could enter the country. Foreign exchange controls, devaluations, and high tariffs supplemented this policy, encouraging the new local parts producers to turn to the local capital goods industry for tooling and metals. The car industry expanded on the basis of local demand, particularly after the 1964 military coup encouraged a redistribution of income toward the top 20 percent of the population. Brazilian car production soared from fewer than 50,000 units in the 1950s to over 1 million units by 1978, all within a relatively concentrated industry. This expansion pulled the rest of the economy along with it; car production constituted a greater proportion of economic activity in Brazil than in the United States! Productivity in the car industry roughly doubled in the ten years after the 1964 coup, as the industry benefited from verdoorn effects. Somewhat unexpectedly, from the point of view of the state, TNCs' suppliers themselves went transnational and followed their assembler into the Brazilian market. By the end of the 1970s, locally owned firms accounted for only half of component production.

Argentina also passed a domestic content law in 1959, but the large number of producers (up to 15 at times) in a relatively stagnant and highly protected market created enormous inefficiencies. In Brazil the average production run per model was about 13,500 units in 1978, but in Argentina it was only 2,850, which made Argentinean-produced cars cost roughly twice world market prices.[9] The lack of standardization also meant that component imports stayed high. The more severe class conflict than in either Brazil or Mexico discouraged further investment by TNCs, particularly after the violent 1969 Cordobazo strikes, which centered in the auto factories. Production fluctuated between 100,000 and 200,000 units. Relations with TNCs were worse than in Brazil, for some of the TNCs were very exploitative. For example, Kaiser Automobile, a new and ultimately failed entrant into the postwar U.S. market, shipped an outdated and worn-out plant from the United States to capitalize its Argentine subsidiary in the 1950s. Given that Kaiser could not compete in the United States, it was hard to see how it could compete in export markets by combining obsolete equipment with less productive Argentine labor, with even lower economies of scale than in the United States, and with higher transportation costs to foreign markets.

Mexico was the last to adopt local content legislation, waiting until 1962. Like Brazil, it limited the number of permitted models to maximize economies of scale. Unlike Brazil and Argentina, it pursued a different strategy to preserve locally owned assembly. The state fostered a dual structure, allowing in foreign assemblers but requiring component producers to have majority local ownership and requiring that engines be locally produced. This forced would-be

TNC component firms to enter joint ventures with Mexican firms. Production rose to over 400,000 units by 1980. Like Brazil, it also experienced rapidly rising growth and productivity rates, especially during the late 1980s, when TNC producers anticipated a unified North American Free Trade Zone.

All three countries ran into difficulties with their TNC-led strategies that echoed the fears generated by U.S. transnational investment in Europe. Although each state had tried to induce TNC investment with a mix of carrots and sticks (subsidies and domestic content laws), each state found that TNCs were content to live behind tariff walls without making any effort to bring local production to world market standards. Even in the most efficient LDC car producers in the 1970s, Brazil and Mexico, production costs were one-third to one-half above costs in TNCs' home factories. The TNCs also had no desire to export cars or other products, such as petrochemicals, drugs, and tires, and they had a high propensity to import the machinery they used. This induced the state to shift gears in the 1970s, when rising oil prices increased the need to export.

TNCs also dominated the strategic points in the production chain. Latin American countries feared denationalization of their economies, much as the Europeans had, but with much greater cause for alarm. The Europeans, after all, did have some dynamic, export-capable industrial firms; the Latin American countries did not. By 1970 foreign firms dominated the automotive, chemical, and machinery industries. TNCs controlled 40 percent of Mexican manufacturing production and 36 percent of the 400 largest Mexican firms, as well as 20 percent of the 400 largest Brazilian firms, accounting for nearly half of capital invested in manufacturing.[10] TNC control was magnified because TNCs tended to buy out the most dynamic existing local firms rather than starting up a new subsidiary. Finally, TNCs' pursuit of global economies of scale made them big importers of capital goods and sometimes parts, without generating any offsetting exports. All three Latin states therefore decided to ditch the TNC-led strategy. Instead, they would borrow directly in international capital markets to create locally controlled state and/or private industry.

## Wave Three: Debt-Financed Industrial Deepening

The basic problem with the TNC-led strategy was TNCs' failure to continue investing once the domestic market was saturated. By the early 1960s, for example, Brazil produced 99 percent of its consumer goods, 91 percent of intermediate goods, and 87 percent of capital goods.[11] Import substitution had exhausted itself as a growth strategy. Because the market served by import substitution was so limited, verdoorn effects could not pull local industry up to a world market standard of competitiveness, and continued protection for local producers sheltered them from the need to get there. Local firms generally were too small, too risk averse, and too unprofessionally managed to undertake either exports or the assimilation of new technologies. The inability to export manufactured goods hampered further industrialization and vice versa. The Latin states turned to overseas borrowing to overcome these limitations. Foreign capital could substitute for exports until a new range of export-competitive industries was developed; it could help further expand the domestic market, generating additional verdoorn effects; and foreign capital acquired as loan capital seemed free of the deleterious consequences of capital controlled by foreign TNCs. Retrospective analyses of this debt-led strategy have been critical because of the debt crises of the 1980s, but these strategies were both reasonable and reasonably successful, particularly with regard to the two largest Latin economies. Mexico and Brazil together account for about 40 percent of all LDC foreign commercial debt. There, relatively well-disciplined states executed reasonable debt-led development plans.

Brazil had the largest, most ambitious, and most successful of the Latin debt-led strategies. The state's strategy revolved around the creation and/or expansion of a wide range of state-owned firms in heavy industry. These would consciously contract with local suppliers for their inputs, and so their growth would spur the development of a wider industrial economy. By 1978 the state had both enveloped the local private sector and displaced TNCs as the engine of growth.[12] The state supplied nearly all of the private sector's capital investment via BNDES, while state firms absorbed half of the private sector's output. At the same time, between 65 and 75 percent of capital goods consumption came from state firms making capital goods. Thus, as the expanding state firms pulled local industry forward, this in turn helped state firms expand.

As a result, TNC's share of local Brazilian assets and markets shrank relatively. From 1969 to 1984 TNCs' share of local assets fell from 27 to 9 percent, while state firms' share rose from 28 to 50 percent and local firms' share stayed about the same. All of this growth rested on borrowed money: from 1970 to 1980 public foreign debt increased from under $5 billion to over $50 billion.

This strategy proved reasonably successful. From 1965 to 1980 Brazilian GDP tripled in real terms, led by industrial production, which quadrupled. After Mexico defaulted in 1982, the flow of capital to Brazil also ceased, paralyzing new investment. The entire economy went into a deep recession, from which it recovered only in the 1990s. Nonetheless, the investment wave of the 1970s positioned Brazil as a successful exporter of manufactured goods such as small aircraft, cars and car components, armaments, and, of course, textiles and shoes. Brazil's export surplus boomed from less than $1 billion in 1982 to $13.1 billion in 1984. Part of this expansion reflected an abrupt decrease in imports, but part also reflected a jump in exports. By 1989, 75 percent of exports were manufactures.

In Mexico the state began systematically reducing the influence of TNCs after 1970. A 1973 law decreased opportunities for TNC investment. Instead, the state channelled an enormous amount of borrowed money through Nafinsa, expanding foreign public debt from $6.8 billion in 1972 to $58.1 billion in 1982, and doubling its investments absolutely during the 1970s. Most of this investment went to state-owned or -controlled firms, particularly the state oil monopoly PEMEX, which absorbed 40 percent of government borrowing by 1979. The number of state firms increased ninefold during the 1970s, increasing the public share of GDP to 45 percent by 1979. The fiscal deficit also expanded to 15 percent of GDP, causing the current account deficit to grow to $12.5 billion in 1982.

Unfortunately, Mexico's export capacity was tied too closely to its oil giant, PEMEX, which by the end of the 1970s was generating about half of Mexican exports. Declining oil prices and rising interest rates after the 1980 recession destroyed Mexico's ability to continue servicing its enormous debt. Like Brazil's, Mexico's public foreign debt had gone from less than $5 billion to nearly $75 billion in 10 years. Mexico had to go to Washington for a bailout, triggering a general shutdown of lending to LDCs during the 1980s.

Mexico weathered the 1980s better than Brazil in the sense that it experienced a smaller drop in per capita GDP. Its stable government controlled inflation and its proximity to the United States encouraged a wave of investment in maquiladoras—a kind of export processing zone—along the border, particularly in the car industry. Thus, by the end of the 1980s Mexico was exporting more cars to the United States than Brazil was, despite having a smaller industry, and nearly 2.5 million engines. Automotive-related exports accounted for nearly 30 percent of Mexico's nonoil manufactured exports by 1990.

In Argentina borrowing went more toward propping up existing consumption levels and the military than toward any development strategy, particularly after a succession of military governments dismantled the institutional apparatus constructed by Perón. Not surprisingly, Argentina experienced the least growth of these three Latin NICs during the 1970s and the largest fall in per capita GDP during the 1980s, despite (and because of) about $50 billion in debt. Unlike the case in the other two countries, TNCs continued to dominate Argentine industry.

The key weakness in all of the Latin debt-led strategies was the long gestation period between the contracting of foreign debt and the creation of export competence in manufactures (see Chapter 7). As late as the middle of the 1970s, over two-thirds of Brazilian, Mexican, and Argentine exports were still primary products. This allowed debt to accumulate for some time before generating offsetting export revenues from goods with rising rather than flat demand. The volume of capital goods these three countries could import was restricted by the limits on agricultural exports. Gambling on a rosy post–1979 oil shock scenario, these states also deliberately exposed themselves to a considerable risk: they borrowed heavily in the short term from 1979 to 1982 in the hopes of a quick global recovery. When that recovery did not materialize, they found themselves unable to roll over their debt and without mature export industries.

## Eastern Europe

Eastern Europe is the equivalent of Latin America with commissars (who are now gone). That is, Eastern Europe followed the same kinds of Ricardian strategies as did Latin American countries, except that Eastern Europe's natural market was industrial Germany, not Britain. Consequently—and not-withstanding the creation of heavy industry during the period of Soviet domination—Eastern Europe faces the same kinds of problems in shifting to Kaldorian strategies and industrializing that Latin American countries did after World War II. Eastern European countries also have to (re-)build states; at this juncture it is impossible to tell whether this will make industrialization easier or harder than in postwar Latin America.

Industrialization in Eastern Europe proceeded in three waves, as in Latin America, but only the first wave was identical to that in Latin America. In the second and third waves, the local state played an even greater part in industrialization in Eastern Europe than in Latin America, but with somewhat unfortunate consequences. During the Depression and the war, Germany also proved a more difficult and exploitative partner than was the United States in its relations to Brazil and Mexico. Eastern European countries also tried to exclude TNCs while taking advantage of technology transfer by TNCs, but all they got for their trouble was their own version of Argentina's disaster with Kaiser Automotive, buying obsolete technologies from uncompetitive firms.

## Wave One: Consumer Nondurables

The first wave of Eastern European industrialization occurred exactly as in Latin America. Agricultural exports created rising local incomes, which in turn spurred local light industry during the pre–World War I period. In Hungary, for example, agricultural exports rose 300 percent from 1874 to 1914, spurring investment in milling and in food processing, in local textile production, and in construction. As in Latin America, not all areas benefited equally from this wave of industrialization. Bohemia and eastern Poland did best. Bohemia (now the Czech Republic) developed into the Austro-Hungarian empire's major source of railroad equipment and textiles. The eastern part of modern Poland (at that time the westernmost part of the Russian empire) also industrialized during this period, producing textiles and machinery for agricultural exporters in the Ukraine and other parts of the Russian empire.

As in Latin America, the Depression consolidated this early wave of light industrialization. With their agricultural exports falling 40 percent in volume terms from 1929 to 1932, the Eastern European countries faced the same choice as Latin America between bankrupt Ricardian strategies and a shift to Kaldorian strategies. But because of German policies and the weakness of their mostly new states, none made as complete a shift as Brazil or Mexico did in the 1930s. Yugoslavia and Hungary were busy creating states for themselves from the leftover bits of the Austrian imperial administration. Bulgaria and Romania were seduced by German willingness to pay above-market prices for their agricultural exports. They watched their credit balances swell in German banks, but they never collected on these debts. They did develop textile industries.

The more industrially oriented economies in Central Europe moved into rudimentary capital goods and heavy industry. Czechoslovakia, for example, began producing cars in this period. Poland introduced the most ambitious industrialization plan, using its control over all trade to channel investment to state industries. By the start of World War II, the Polish state owned 100 percent of munitions and armaments production, 80 percent of chemicals, 50 percent of metals, and over 90 percent of air and rail transportation.

Unlike Mexico and Brazil vis-à-vis the United States, however, Eastern Europe did not benefit from its association with Germany or get aid from Germany before or during the war. Rather, the opposite was the case. Germany made deliberate efforts to assure itself a flow of raw materials during the 1930s and 1940s. By 1934 it had constructed a set of bilateral treaties with each Eastern European economy (save Czechoslovakia) in which Germany exchanged its manufactures for raw materials. This arrangement forced them back into a Ricardian mold. Nominally, the Germans paid very good prices for their raw materials imports, but practically all this meant was that Eastern Europeans accumulated credit balances, which they would never use, in Germany. During the war the Germans simply took what they needed, buying on even more spurious credit. In any case, the war leveled most of Eastern Europe.

## Wave Two: Stalinist Heavy Industrialization

The second wave of industrialization in Eastern Europe took place under Soviet-style socialism. During this phase the Eastern European economies (re-)created heavy industry. In many ways heavy industry is ideally suited to a command economy, since economies of scale predominate over economies of scope and since capacity utilization is important for macroeconomic efficiency. As in Latin America, the state sponsored this investment, adding heavy industry to the light industry created before the war by private entrepreneurs. Unlike Latin America, the state then socialized light industry and in some places agriculture as well.

Like Latin America (albeit about 10 years later, the time required for reconstruction), the state also tried to encourage TNCs to help develop a local automotive industry. But where the major Latin states initially countenanced TNC ownership of assembly plants, the socialist Eastern European states did not, for ideological reasons. Consequently, they tried to get the benefits of TNC technology transfer without the hazards of admitting TNCs to the local economy. But the absence of competition meant that production practices settled into inefficient patterns.

In order to wrest technology away from TNCs without actually letting TNCs operate inside their economies, the Eastern European states tried to emulate the strategy used by LDC host states confronting raw materials TNCs. But this strategy failed miserably. In raw materials extraction, picking on the weakest firms meant that the host got the best financial deal and confronted a firm with the least amount of vertical integration and thus the least market power. Such TNCs were happy simply to gain access to raw materials sources, and hosts thus captured a large share of the rent from resource extraction.

When Eastern European states picked on the weakest of the European car firms to get the best deal, they got the weakest technology. These TNCs had an incentive to transfer technology, for this allowed them to amortize the development and sometimes production costs for that technology over a larger market. As a result, the technology the Eastern Europeans got was not competitive. So Eastern Europe simply re-created Argentina's experience with Kaiser, buying uncompetitive and obsolete technology. Poland, Yugoslavia, and the Soviet Union all obtained licenses and machinery to produce Fiat's 124 and 127 models; Romania licensed a Citroën model. All these were obsolete models being phased out by their respective firms. The Eastern Europeans planned to sell these cars back into Western Europe as "new used cars," that is, as unused versions of an older car. (In contrast, Czechoslovakia and the German Democratic Republic [East Germany] rehabilitated their prewar car industries, and in the case of the Czechs ended up with the best car industry of any of the Eastern European economies.)

The Eastern Europeans essentially bartered with the TNCs, buying machinery and factories by promising to pay the car firms back with finished goods. Despite being good Marxists all, the Eastern Europeans did not realize that hard technologies alone do not constitute the means of production. The means of production also include the relations of production, or soft technologies that enable physical machinery to be used productively. The Eastern Europeans bought machinery from the TNCs without also getting the practical knowledge they needed in order to make the machines run well.

The melding of Italian and French car technology with Eastern European production practices produced cars that could barely compete against *used* used cars in the Western European or U.S. market. The Romanian-built Citroën, for example, never achieved the minimum quality standards that PSA (Citroën's parent) demanded for sales in Western Europe. Moreover, the Eastern Europeans were never able to operate their factories at maximum capacity, which limited potential exports. From 1973 to 1979, all five Eastern European car producers (including Czech Skoda) had increased their sales in Western Europe by about 90,000 units off an existing base of about 50,000 units.[13] The contrast with South Korean car producer Hyundai is telling. Hyundai alone achieved sales volumes of over 200,000 units in the U.S. market, which is slightly smaller than the European market, in three years. And it did so by selling cars with quality and styling levels found in new cars.

## Wave Three: Borrowed Money and Collapse

Like Latin America in the 1970s, the Eastern Europeans also embarked on a borrowing spree. Much of the borrowing went to subsidize living standards rather than for productive investment. However, even productively invested funds were not used efficiently. The persistent inability to increase production and maintain quality standards created in the 1980s the same kind of crippling debt crisis that Latin America faced. Indeed, the crisis started earlier in Eastern Europe, with Poland's quasi-default in 1980 and with Yugoslavian and Romanian debt reschedulings in 1981.

The current period resembles the 1920s. States are trying to construct themselves out of the rubble of the old administration, while simultaneously creating legal regimes for investment and production. Like Latin America in the aftermath of the 1980s debt crisis, they have been inviting in TNCs in an effort to rehabilitate both their consumer durables and nondurables sectors. Bringing in the TNCs will give the Eastern European economies access to TNCs' tacit knowledge, particularly as European TNCs create a Mexico — a zone of low-wage labor for labor-intensive parts of the production process — in selected parts of Eastern Europe. As in Latin America, however, the bulk of this investment will go to the most stable and productive economies. Of the $11 billion of direct investment in Eastern Europe as of 1992, over 40 percent was in Hungary, and another 20 percent was in the Czech Republic.[14]

## East Asia

Industrialization in Taiwan and South Korea has many of the institutional pieces found in Latin America and Eastern Europe. As in Latin America, the state played a major role in the industrialization process. The state started many basic industries, and state or state-controlled banks channeled investment funds to the private manufacturing sector. The state also controlled access to the domestic market, using tariffs and quotas to exclude imports and capital controls to limit TNC access. And the state systematically repressed labor.

At the same time, the arrangement of the pieces, their situation in a different colonial legacy and in a different postcolonial environment, created enormous differences. Not surprisingly, industrialization in Taiwan and South Korea closely resembled the earlier pattern of industrialization in Japan. As in Japan, the state funded the early stages of heavy industrialization with capital drawn from intensive and deliberate exploitation of the agricultural sector. As in Japan, industrialization occurred from below. The state used exports of consumer nondurables to provide a market for a protected capital goods sector. These consumer goods were in market niches that developed country producers were willing either to abandon or in fact to shift to East Asia through subcontracting.

The two East Asian states also balanced the costs and benefits of association with TNCs differently than the Latin states did. They allowed TNCs to produce in enclaves within their economies or to subcontract to local producers, but only for export. This shielded domestic producers from direct competition with TNCs while allowing domestic producers to observe how TNCs produced world market competitive goods. The East Asian states also subsidized manufactured exports in order to boost production volumes and thus capture verdoorn effects. In short, after 1960, Taiwan and South Korea aggressively and singlemindedly pursued Kaldorian growth strategies.

These states could do so because they differed considerably from the Latin American and Eastern European states. State-building was much less problematic than in Latin America or Eastern Europe. The U.S. military created disciplined militaries for these two states, as they were front-line allies confronting communist regimes on the Asian mainland. Thus, these two states were highly autonomous, built first and foremost around highly independent militaries. Furthermore, these states did not face a well-organized and politically entrenched landlord class, because the U.S.-run decolonization removed Japanese landlords after World War II. Decolonization similarly removed any comprador bourgeoisie interested only in commercial operations and not in industrial production. Finally, Taiwan and South Korea received massive amounts of U.S. aid, which at least initially rendered their states less dependent on local social groups.

## Wave One: Agriculture, Capital Investment, and Consumer Nondurables

Japanese colonization reoriented the Taiwanese and South Korean economies toward agricultural exports—mostly rice but also sugar for the Japanese market. As in Latin America, industrialization began as a consequence of rising rural income. The Japanese state encouraged productivity increases in its colonies through the application of flat land taxes, just as it had done back home. In Taiwan, for example, from 1895 to 1945 per capita income in agriculture doubled as productivity rose. This also allowed extremely high rents, which captured about half the crop for landlords and the state. World War II and U.S. occupation opened the door to thorough land reform in each society.

The United States installed the Kuomintang (KMT) in power on Taiwan and redistributed Japanese-held land to former tenants. Pressured by the United States, the KMT rapidly implemented a further land reform, which was essentially complete by 1953. The fact that the KMT was an outside force with few connections to local landlords made this a fairly painless exercise for the KMT, though not for local landlords. In contrast, the U.S.-installed South Korean state, dominated by local landlords, dragged its heels until 1950. Then the invading North Korean army started land reform by shooting large numbers of landlords. After the war, under U.S. pressure, the South Korean state finished the job in a more peaceful fashion by 1958.

Land reform positioned both states to capture rents that landlords had previously consumed or invested in more land. *The state's ability to divert agricultural rents directly to industrial investment constitutes East Asia's first big divergence from Latin America.* The two states did this through taxes, control over the extension of credit to peasants, and some judicious price fixing. Both states created state monopolies for the purchase and export of rice and the domestic sale of fertilizer. They lowered rice purchase prices and raised fertilizer sale prices. In both countries, the state captured about 35 percent of total agricultural production. The state exported part of this production and used its foreign exchange earnings to buy capital equipment for a range of state-owned heavy industries such as cement, steel, fertilizer, electricity, and chemicals. The KMT on Taiwan performed this transfer process best, tripling the outflow of capital from agriculture as compared to the outflow under the earlier Japanese colonial administration, and providing about one-third of gross domestic investment during the 1950s. Because of South Korea's later land reform and postwar reconstruction, it was more dependent on U.S. aid for capital formation during the 1950s. Roughly 80 percent of Korean investment then came from U.S. aid.

Other than the successful squeezing of agriculture, this first wave of industrialization (from 1945 to, say, 1965) closely resembled that in Latin America. Private entrepreneurs using family savings capitalized light industry while the state created heavy industry. Agricultural exports (rice, sugar, and the ubiquitous bamboo shoots and mandarin oranges) paid for capital goods imports. In Latin America the problem at this point had been to move past light industry into consumer durables, while still trying to finance capital goods imports with limited agricultural exports. Taiwan and South Korea again diverged critically from Latin America at this point. They used the TNCs more cautiously, and they used *manufactured*, not agricultural, exports to finance further imports of capital goods. *This shift to manufactured goods exports is the second decisive difference between the Latin American and East Asian industrial trajectories.*

## Wave Two: Simultaneous Import Substitution and Export Expansion

The essence of industrialization strategies in Taiwan and South Korea was as follows: use TNCs to generate more exports, and teach local consumer non-durables firms how to manufacture efficiently to world market standards; use rising exports of consumer nondurables to accelerate the expansion of a highly protected capital goods industry. As these capital goods and heavy industrial suppliers to the expanding nondurables sector themselves grew, verdoorn effects would make them more competitive. In turn, they too would be freed from protection and forced or induced to export. Eventually, the entire economy would be freed from protection and would be export competitive. At the heart of this strategy lay an institutional innovation: the export processing zone (EPZ or FTZ, Free Trade Zone). These zones concentrated on producing the three *T*'s: toys, textiles, and trash (e.g., cheap shoes, hibachis, inflatable swimming pools), and so on.

The Taiwanese and Korean EPZs imitated Hong Kong, which by virtue of its geography (an island), demography (too many people), and resource base (none) had become a completely open economy surviving by manufacturing low-end consumer nondurables, including and especially garments and junky trinkets. In 1965 Singapore went over to this model, and Taiwan created its own EPZ. Korea created its first EPZ in 1970. Any TNC could come to an EPZ and find cheap and willing labor (mostly peasant women earning extra income for their hard-pressed farm families), could bring in goods to be worked up without any tariffs, and could take worked-up goods out without any taxes.

Three environmental conditions helped make the EPZ-led strategy successful. First, the TNCs had an interest in finding low-wage but productive labor to do the labor-intensive processing steps in their production chain (see Chapter 13). This was particularly true for Japanese firms.[15] Provisions in the

United States and other developed countries' tax and tariff code which levied tax only on the value-added overseas for reimported goods encouraged this global dispersion. Second, the progressive lowering of tariffs following the Kennedy Round (1964–67) of GATT negotiations facilitated a rapid rise in global trade. Finally, during the war in Vietnam the United States bought significant volumes of exports from both Taiwan and Korea, helping to ease the balance-of-payments constraint during the beginning of the EPZ-led strategy.

Taiwan (and later Korea) benefited from the EPZ in many ways. Even the small wage earned by the EPZ's labor force represented a net addition to Taiwan's ability to import capital goods. Moreover, many TNCs subcontracted work to local firms, enabling them to gain access to world markets, to learn about the outside world's quality standards, and to produce at large volumes and thus improve productivity. Finally, when these local firms and many TNCs bought locally produced capital goods, such as machine tools, this expanded demand created in the EPZ to the domestic market, producing verdoorn effects in the capital goods and local use consumer nondurables sectors. TNCs in the EPZ were contractually bound to export what they produced, preserving the maximum possible market for local firms.

Both states used additional measures to spur exports and thus production volumes. Both states used control over the banking system to allocate capital only to firms that met export targets. Firms willingly exported at a loss to get access to capital; once they succeeded in exporting, they naturally tried to lower their losses and eventually found themselves profiting from exports. Therefore, state policy subverted market pressures that might have kept production volumes, and thus long-term productivity growth, low. Once firms were competitive, the state exposed them to world market competition and moved protection further upstream to producers of more sophisticated goods or of capital goods and inputs. Exactly this process occurred in Japan before World War II; consumer nondurable exports drove heavy industrialization. In contrast, protection was only rarely removed in Latin America, and so firms had less incentive to become productive and competitive.

## Wave Three: Now What?

During the 1970s Korea and Taiwan began to diverge. For political reasons the KMT government in Taiwan wanted to keep the Taiwanese-owned firms that did most of the subcontracting and exporting small. It avoided borrowing and stayed out of the production of consumer durables for export. Taiwan remained an economy specializing in subcontracting and recently, the export of low-end capital goods to other would-be industrializers from the bottom up, especially China. In the short term this strategy has been successful; Taiwan had the world's largest accumulation of foreign reserves by 1990. At the same time, this decision has forced it to gamble on a strategy of leaping over heavy industry into high-tech light industry, like computers, scientific equipment, and light machine tools.

In contrast, Korea opted to borrow heavily overseas to capitalize a range of heavy industries that could only be run by gigantic corporations. Like the Latin American borrowers, this strategy gambled that new export industries would mature in time to service debt, and as in Latin America this proved false. However, South Korea's existing expertise in light consumer goods gave it enough exports to weather the early 1980s more easily than the Latin Americans did. By the mid-1980s the consumer durables investments had matured, and Korea was exporting cars to the United States. Rapid expansion of these exports—the value of Korean car exports zoomed to nearly $1 billion by 1985—then created verdoorn effects that made Korean car producers about as efficient as the average U.S. car maker.

Although Korea and Taiwan still have some distance to go before they become fully developed industrial economies, both clearly possess enough internal dynamism to continue growing. Korea had per capita GDP growth rates of over 7 percent per year from 1965 to 1990. The problem will be to sustain rapid growth long enough not only to catch up with, say, Spain's income levels, but also to leap past them to the level of, say, Britain. For Taiwan the problem in particular is the creation of sophisticated light industry. For Korea the problem is that the gigantic corporations that house industrial expertise may be *too* bureaucratic to function in a world with rapidly changing tastes and technology. The danger for both is that they will continue to produce at the low end of the product spectrum in terms of quality and technology, absorbing products and industries cast off from Japan and the United States. The opportunity that presents itself for both is to use these to vault into middle-range products and industries.

## LDC Industrialization in Perspective

LDC industrialization shows strong parallels with earlier efforts at late industrialization using Kaldorian strategies. It has also led to a decomposition of the old agricultural periphery. Some economies have vaulted out of the agricultural periphery and into a kind of industrial periphery characterized by the production of low-value-added manufactured goods. A few others have vaulted twice and now produce relatively sophisticated consumer durables. The majority, however, remain agricultural producers and exporters.

Industrialization among the NICs was very Gerschenkronian. State involvement in the later waves was extremely high, and the most successful NICs experienced very rapid growth. In the most successful NICs, the state dominated the allocation of investment funds through state-owned banks and in some cases became directly involved in industrial production. States had to overcome the natural risk aversion of local entrepreneurs facing entrenched competitors in world markets. The more the state was oriented toward a Kaldorian strategy, the greater the success.

States' social bases also affected industrialization significantly. The Brazilian state's inability to override the immediate interests of local elites created one of the world's most skewed distributions of income, with the bottom 20 percent of the population receiving only 3 percent of GNP. Although Brazil has the world's tenth largest economy, its local industry faced a constricted domestic market. However, this is a question of nuance in an otherwise successful process of industrialization. Brazil and Mexico since the 1940s and Taiwan and South Korea since the 1950s all have averaged real growth rates of 6 to 7 percent annually.

Finally, luck — timing, strategic location, and externally induced destruction of local social groups — was very important. The two East Asian states began industrializing just as world trade was experiencing rapid growth. TNCs stood ready to facilitate exports by at least a few low-wage suppliers. These conditions made the apparent rewards of an outward-looking export orientation very high. In contrast, the Latin American and Eastern European states began industrializing during periods in which the potential rewards for export-oriented policies were quite low. The Depression caused an absolute reduction in global income and trade — not a very congenial environment for novice manufactured goods exporters, particularly since there were few true TNCs.

Brazil and Mexico's strategic importance during World War II and Korea and Taiwan's importance during the Cold War enabled all four to extract significant amounts of U.S. financial and technical aid. Not least in importance, U.S. efforts to create professional militaries in these countries substantially aided the efficiency of their states' later industrialization drives. Finally, the U.S.-inspired elimination of landlords in Taiwan and South Korea helped remove potential obstacles to industrialization drives initially financed out of agriculture.

As noted earlier, the process of industrialization in the old agricultural periphery has been very uneven geographically, with half of manufactured goods export capacity concentrated in four Asian countries and much of the rest in four Latin American countries. The fact that success has eluded most countries shows once more the difficulty late industrializers face and how competitive markets tend to create divergences among economies. By definition, some firms, sectors, and countries will prove more competitive than others, and thus some will drop out of the race.

The importance of domestic factors such as highly autonomous states and early land reform suggests that in the short run the general success of the NICs cannot be repeated. The NICs emerged from among a set of countries that had domestic markets large enough to support a modicum of heavy industry and consumer durables production, states competent and stable enough to promote industrialization, and a local pool of investment capital large enough to get things started. The failures (e.g., Iran) are now out of the race. The countries that never entered the race will have to find some way of surviving on the basis of continued agricultural exports in order to develop far enough to contemplate a shift to a Kaldorian strategy.

In the larger picture, the emergence of the NICs signaled an end to the process of global deindustrialization through displacement competition that had started with the British industrial revolution. The industrial revolution in northwest Europe and North America decreased the share of global manufacturing outside those areas from about two-thirds of world manufacturing in

1800 to about 7 percent during 1900–50. By 1980 the Third World's share was back to about 14 percent.[16] In all likelihood this share will continue to rise, although it will be concentrated in a few winners, particularly in East Asia.

Nonetheless, a clear qualitative difference divides the industrial activity occurring in the former agricultural periphery from that occurring in the mature industrial economies. Most manufacturing in the old agricultural periphery involves the production of commodity-like manufactures, ranging from undifferentiated garments to almost undifferentiated cars. We could argue that a new set of von Thünen zones is emerging, arranged on the basis of relative productivity and knowledge intensity in manufacturing. High-relative-productivity, knowledge-intensive manufacturing takes place in the town, while low-relative-productivity, non-knowledge-intensive manufacturing feeds the town with basic industrial commodities. Chapter 13 will look at this phenomenon in the context of changing patterns of trade.

## Notes

1. Out of 79 developing countries with populations over 1 million for which the World Bank provides data, 23 experienced declining per capita GDP from 1965 to 1990. Fifteen of these were in sub-Saharan Africa. World Bank, *World Development Report 1992* (New York: Oxford University Press, 1992), pp. 218–219.

2. Raul Prebisch, *The Economic Development of Latin America and Its Principal Problems* (New York: United Nations, 1950).

3. International Monetary Fund, *Direction of Trade Statistics* (Washington, D.C.: IMF, various years).

4. See Robert Klitgaard, *Tropical Gangsters* (New York: Basic Books, 1990) for an accessible, informative, and tragicomic account of development and economic stabilization efforts in Equatorial Guinea. Equally useful, if more serious, accounts are Robert Bates, *Markets and States in Tropical Africa* (Berkeley: University of California Press, 1981); Thomas Callaghy, *State-Society Struggle: Zaire in Comparative Perspective* (New York: Columbia University Press, 1984); and Robert Fatton, *Predatory States* (Boulder, Colo.: Westview, 1992).

5. For all its faults, Fernando Cardoso and Henrique Faletto, *Dependency and Development in Latin America* (Berkeley: University of California Press, 1979), particularly chs. 3–5, provides a good analysis of the diverging, path-dependent trajectories of development in the different Latin American economies.

6. Angus Maddison, *Two Crises* (Paris: OECD, 1985), p. 25.

7. Carlos Waisman, *Reversal of Development in Argentina* (Princeton, N.J.: Princeton University Press, 1987).

8. The single best study of this is Rhys Jenkins, *Transnational Corporations and Industrial Transformation in Latin America* (London: Macmillan, 1984). See also Douglas Bennett and Kenneth Sharpe, *Transnational Corporations versus the State: The Political Economy of the Mexican Auto Industry* (Princeton, N.J.: Princeton University Press, 1985); and Richard Kronish and Kenneth Mericle, eds., *The Political Economy of the Latin American Motor Vehicle Industry* (Cambridge, Mass.: MIT Press, 1984).

9. Jenkins, *Transnational Corporations*, pp. 62–64.

10. Ibid., pp. 32–34; UNCTC, *World Investment Report: The Triad in Foreign Direct Investment* (New York: United Nations, 1991), pp. 99–102.

11. Werner Baer et al., "Structural Changes in Brazil's Industrial Economy 1960–1980," *World Development* 15, no. 2 (1987): 275–286.

12. See Peter Evans, *Dependent Development: The Alliance of State, Multinational and Local Capital in Brazil* (Princeton, N.J.: Princeton University Press, 1979) for the classic critical study.

13. Alan Altschuler et al., *The Future of the Automobile* (Cambridge, Mass.: MIT Press, 1984), pp. 178–179.

14. John Parker, "Rejoined: A Survey of Eastern Europe," *The Economist*, March 13, 1993, p. 10.

15. See Terutomo Ozawa, *Multinationalism, Japanese Style* (Princeton, N.J.: Princeton University Press, 1979) for an analysis of the state policies and market conditions that propelled Japanese firms to Taiwan and Korea.

16. Paul Bairoch, "International Industrialization Levels from 1750–1980," *Journal of European Economic History* 11, no. 2 (Fall 1982): 275.

CHAPTER 13

# Trade, Protection, and Renewed Von Thünenization

Like the postwar international monetary system, world trade patterns moved back to the future between 1945 and the 1990s, reflecting two different processes. First, although the dynamics differed, in both agricultural and industrial production new von Thünen rings emerged. In agriculture, competing urban/industrial uses and rising industrial populations continued to displace cultivation outward. In addition, late-twentieth-century industry dispersed. Firms searched for ways to match wage levels to skill levels, but found this difficult to do within any given industrial economy. As a general rule, postwar labor legislation had homogenized wage levels with individual economies. Thus, industry in some sense mimicked the dispersion of nineteenth-century agriculture; nineteenth-century agriculture went searching for cheap land and twentieth-century industry for cheap(-er) labor. Nineteenth-century agriculture dispersed to find land without peasants and landlords; twentieth-century manufacturing dispersed to find labor without unions and embedded work practices that limited productivity gains.

Second, markets alone did not push this dispersal of industrial activity. States intervened in trade patterns in contradictory ways. On the one hand, states participated in multilateral negotiations to remove Depression-era tariff barriers and bilateral deals. On the other hand, states sought creative ways to make sure that market outcomes in this liberalized trade would still help local firms more than foreign competitors. Like the legal framework surrounding the international monetary system, the legal framework states used to regulate international trade after World War II reflected the contradictory lessons of the Great Depression. A belief in the benefits of international free trade (and pressure for free trade from competitive producers) conflicted with a determination to protect domestic employment and production from external shocks (and pressure for protection from producers uncertain about their competitiveness).

Market pressures on firms to disperse production interacted with the states' creative efforts at protection to create industrial von Thünen rings. As Chapter 9 noted, agreement on a legal framework governing trade did *not* emerge before the end of World War II. Efforts to reach a comprehensive accord, embodied in the International Trade Organization (ITO), failed. Instead, after 1948 an ad hoc, "temporary" (but as it turned out, "permanent") accord called the General Agreement on Tariffs and Trade (GATT) governed trade. Although GATT facilitated a gradual reduction in tariff barriers and a rapid expansion of world trade, it also contained numerous qualifications, exemptions, and escape hatches. Because of these exemptions, and because the liberalization of trade was gradual, the situation after World War II in many ways resembled that prevailing in the nineteenth century *before* Britain liberalized trade in most agricultural products. Extant barriers to trade created enormous but unfulfilled pressures to disperse production.

Competitive manufacturing firms responded to those opportunities by gradually dispersing their production globally, much as individual farmers and mercantile capital dispersed agricultural production in the nineteenth century. Chapters 11 and 12 already discussed part of this process, leaving a discussion of trade effects until this chapter. As Chapter 11 noted, the rise of transnational corporations (TNCs) meant that a large proportion of international trade took place *across borders but within one firm*. Twentieth-century food processing firms also abetted a dispersion of agricultural production. In turn, the threat of imports produced by those newly dispersed producers caused other producers to seek novel forms of protection, forms that GATT could not control. This protection in turn only induced more dispersion; the interaction of protection and trade liberalization drove global dispersion of production.

This chapter looks first at the legal regime governing trade, after which it addresses each of the problems described above. It shows how agricultural dispersal is still following a typical von Thünen pattern and how TNCs have begun to disperse manufacturing along von Thünen lines as well (but with labor costs relative to skill and productivity rather than land rents as the driving force). In both cases, protectionist responses to dispersal took new forms to get around an international legal regime superficially designed to prevent protection. Finally, it shows how protectionist policies have had paradoxical effects, often worsening the competitive pressures on the very producers states are trying to protect in the first place, and generating new von Thünen rings — more dispersion — more rapidly.

## States and the Postwar Trade Regime

### The Effort to Create an International Trade Organization

Like the legal structure enveloping international monetary relations, the legal structure governing trade reflected a tension between the international and domestic lessons of the Depression. Individual states' efforts to create trade surpluses by closing local markets to imports had led to collective disaster in the 1930s, as world trade declined by over two-thirds during 1929–32. Even the United States saw exports fall not only absolutely but as a percentage of GNP. The 1930s protectionist surge hurt many major U.S. industries, and they pushed for freer trade after the war. In Europe they had counterparts that also pushed for lower trade barriers.[1]

This international lesson spurred efforts to construct a trade regime paralleling the money regime constructed at Bretton Woods. Twenty-three countries met in Geneva in 1947 to construct the International Trade Organization; in 1948 over 50 countries signed the ITO's charter in Havana.[2] The ITO provided comprehensive supervision of all aspects of world trade, including foreign investment flows, agricultural goods, and other commodities like oil. Like Keynes's proposed International Clearing Union (ICU), it had strong disciplinary powers, which it could use against countries setting up barriers to trade. But whereas Keynes's ICU was stillborn, the ITO was aborted.

The domestic lessons of the Depression aborted the ITO. Domestically, these lessons signaled the economic and political importance of stabilizing incomes and employment. The Depression shifted control over agriculture into the hands of virtually every state in the world.[3] The Depression and the war also left a residue of high tariffs and state control over imports. In recovering Europe, states naturally gave priority to imports of food, fuels, and essential capital goods over other goods. Thus, while competitive industries in many countries were willing to support efforts to get the ITO, they faced stubborn opposition from larger groups benefiting from protection. Britain wanted to retain its preferential tariff. Agricultural countries poised to industrialize, like Australia, Argentina, and India, thought the ITO would strangle their industry in its infancy. Even the smaller European countries, for whom trade was essential, worried about a powerful ITO.[4]

Free traders in the United States wanted even more free trade than the ITO aimed at, while protectionists feared any intrusion into the normal political process surrounding U.S. trade policymaking. Constitutionally, Congress has control over trade. In 1934, seeking to undo some of the damage of Smoot-Hawley and hoping to expand exports, Congress had passed the Reciprocal Trade Agreements Act. But Congress certainly did not intend to delegate authority to anonymous international bureaucrats at the ITO rather than a president subject to political pressures and horse-trading.[5] Congress refused to ratify the ITO in 1948. Instead, one component of the original ITO proposal, GATT, emerged as an ad hoc solution to the problem of how to regulate trade. GATT's weakness was reflected in its small staffing and uncertain legal status. By 1990 it had grown to only 350 people compared with several thousand each for the IMF and IBRD; the U.S. Congress habitually declared that appropriations to support GATT did not imply congressional ratification of GATT's authority or rulings.

## The General Agreement on Tariffs and Trade

GATT quite literally embodied a set of compromises between the domestic and international lessons of the Depression. Nominally, parties to the agreement consented to enforce three principles in settling trade disputes and in regulating trade practices:

~ Transparency and trade barrier reduction: all nontariff barriers should be replaced with tariffs, and all tariffs should be lowered. Quotas, dumping, and subsidies were prohibited.

~ Nondiscrimination: all signatories agreed to give most favored nation status to other signatories. Any favorable trade conditions granted to one party had to be generalized to all signatories so that everyone would have the same exact treatment. Customs unions or free trade areas with lower trade barriers were permitted, however.

~ Reciprocity: multilateral talks arranged mutual tariff reductions.

These principles informed seven rounds of tariff reduction negotiations, which succeeded in lowering the average tariff on manufactured goods from 40 percent in 1947 to about 5 percent today.

This reduction in tariffs seemed to spark an unprecedented expansion in world trade. From 1950 to 1975 the volume of trade grew twice as fast as gross product in the OECD; despite global economic disorder during 1975–85, trade still grew faster. By 1990 total world trade amounted to about $3.75 trillion, equivalent to roughly 70 percent of U.S. GDP or 20 percent of gross world product. This meant that world trade by 1990 was approaching the same global proportion it held in the early 1900s.

Unlike the very broad ITO, however, GATT basically covered only manufactured goods, and the areas it neglected grew in importance after the war. Moreover, GATT contained several escape hatches that allowed states to depart from its principles even with regard to manufactured goods. Meanwhile, at U.S. insistence, agriculture was excluded from GATT in 1955. By 1990 agricultural trade had shrunk from its pre–World War I predominance to about 10 percent of world trade, reflecting rapidly growing trade in services and manufactured goods. Agriculture still constituted a major portion of exports for most developing countries and some developed countries. Trade in services, which was fairly small in the 1940s, was also omitted from GATT. By 1990, however, trade in services amounted to about 20 percent of world trade. Both agriculture and services were major U.S. exports, and represented two areas where the United States had a trade surplus and Japan and Germany large deficits.[6] Finally, under Article 19, the serious injury clause, states were permitted to impose trade restrictions if the rate of growth of imports threatened to create large-scale unemployment in a particular sector. These restrictions had to be temporary, however. All of these delimitations in GATT became the source of serious increases in protection over time, and in turn protection spurred more dispersion. How? Let us look at agriculture first.

## Agriculture under GATT

The rapid postwar expansion of urban population in northwestern Europe, in the U.S. industrial heartland, and, as we have just seen, in parts of the old agricultural periphery increased demand for foods and nonfood agriculturals (NFAs) while raising the implied rent on agricultural land near cities. Consequently, agricultural production continued to expand in terms of both volume and geography. The old von Thünen logic should have forced a reduction in the production of grains, meats, and nonfresh dairy products in some parts of the United States and in Europe, and of most foods in Japan. Production should have continued to shift outward to the Southern Hemisphere dominions and into new lands made accessible by better, cheaper transportation and refrigeration.

To a certain extent it did. Increased demand for beef and cotton in the United States and the industrialization of the U.S. South pushed production of low-quality beef (for fast food chains) and cotton southward. Cotton acreage quadrupled in Central America, and low-quality beef production doubled, in turn displacing traditional subsistence agriculture (and many peasants). By 1970 grazing areas accounted for 43 percent of land in agricultural use in Central America; and by 1980 for about two-thirds.[7] As in nineteenth-century Ireland, this displacement provoked violent peasant resistance.

A new set of rings also grew over the nineteenth-century set of von Thünen rings. These new rings involved production of *nontraditional* fresh fruits and vegetables and flowers in Southern Hemisphere and tropical locations. Tropical areas had exported fruits like bananas (in value terms the single largest fruit export in the world at $2 billion in 1988) and pineapples since the late nineteenth century.[8] In the 1970s and especially the 1980s, Northern Hemisphere fruits and vegetables also began to be cultivated in new locations. As in the nineteenth century, more lucrative urban uses for land, especially suburbanization in the United States, absorbed food-producing areas or raised the opportunity costs of retaining land in farm use. While land resources declined, demand for fresh foods grew as health consciousness grew and tastes became "yuppified" in the 1980s.

Consumers wanted fresh fruits and vegetables year-round, and geographical dispersion made this possible. Southern Hemisphere growers of traditional Northern Hemisphere fruits like oranges (Brazil and Australia), apples (Brazil, Australia, and New Zealand), and grapes (Chile) could supply Northern Hemisphere consumers during the traditional off-season. Similarly, producers of vegetables and fruits in Northern Hemisphere tropical climates—for example, Mexican (or Israeli or Moroccan) tomato, strawberry, and cucumber growers—could extend the growing season at either end. As in the nineteenth century, all the competitive producers had reasonably stable governments promoting export production.

Meanwhile, technological changes facilitated the profitable dispersal of agriculture. Just as refrigeration/freezing permitted Southern Hemisphere producers to export meat in the nineteenth century, so the declining cost and increasing reliability of refrigerated transport opened up tropical and Southern Hemisphere areas for products that until then had been grown only in proximity to cities.[9] Traditional TNCs in agriculture (e.g., the banana-exporting firms in Central America) and former nontransnationalized food processors (e.g., Campbell's) diversified into these new crops. They supplied cloned and thus standardized varieties of foods/seeds, and they used their control over refrigerated transportation to dominate the flow of goods from new supply areas to industrial country markets.[10]

The new agricultural zones grew up around and in response to growing industrial centers. Not unexpectedly, each of the three major industrial nations drew foods primarily from nearby regions, with, for example, Mexico and Central America supplying the United States and Canada, and Mediterranean countries supplying northern Europe.[11] However, preference systems based on former colonial empires, like the European Community's African–Caribbean-Pacific (ACP) system, which gave countries in those areas preferential tariffs and quotas, meant that some odd trade patterns emerged.

Despite this continued dispersion of agricultural production, import quotas and production subsidies in all the industrial countries encouraged local overproduction of uncompetitive, high-cost, traditional agricultural goods.[12] Developed country farmers used their political muscle to maintain and extend the import controls and price floors created in the 1930s. Although food imports were getting cheaper, protecting against them was not. All told, agricultural protection cost OECD states and consumers $260 billion in 1990, versus a total international agricultural trade of about $330 billion.

The EC, through its Common Agricultural Policy (CAP), was the most egregious offender in terms of the volume of food produced and the total amount spent on protection. CAP consistently consumed over half of the EC's budget, and provided about half of EC farmers' income. For this Europeans gained the privilege of frying French lamb, at about seven times the landed cost of New Zealand lamb, in German butter, at about three times the landed cost of New Zealand butter. (New Zealand is the world's low-cost producer for those commodities.) At the same time, New Zealand's export quotas to the EC were being steadily reduced.

Japan's smaller population and economy meant it spent less than the EC, about $30 billion, but this smaller amount provided about two-thirds of farmers' income. In Japan, rice sells at between six and 10 times, and beef at four times, world market prices. With very little arable land in proportion to its large industrial population, but with its ruling party dependent on rural votes and money to win elections, Japan found itself in the peculiar position of being the world's largest food importer at the same time that it had the world's strictest controls over food imports.

The United States' efficient agriculture (the U.S. Department of Agriculture runs one of the world's most successful industrial policies) meant that subsidies provided less than a third of farmers' income. Still, the United States' huge agriculture consumed about $30 billion in subsidies annually. Unlike the other two major industrial areas, the United States was directly hurt by developed country agricultural protection; in turn, its own policies largely harmed LDC producers. For example, Japanese quotas meant that the United States was unable to sell as much citrus fruit and beef as it could in the absence of quotas. The quotas that protect U.S. sugar producers keep out cheaper LDC sugar and maintain the U.S. price of sugar well above world market prices. From the United States' point of view, however, at least the Japanese did not export subsidized food into the world market. The EC did.

Production subsidies naturally encouraged farmers to overproduce. By the early 1980s, the EC had achieved self-sufficiency in major food commodities and had begun to build up enormous stockpiles of uncompetitive wheat, butter, and meat. From 1980 to 1991 it spent nearly $100 billion to dump these stockpiles into world markets.[13] This dumping hurt existing, competitive producers in the United States and Australasia. In 1985 the United States responded with a two-pronged strategy designed to divide competitive from uncompetitive EC farmers and net losers from net winners in Europe's agricultural subsidy game, in order to conquer its European adversaries in agricultural trade. The stick in the strategy was the Export Enhancement Program (EEP), which subsidized U.S. sales of wheat to third-party markets in the late 1980s. The EEP forced the EC to provide even larger export subsidies. In 1988 Britain (a net loser from agricultural subsidies) forced the EC to put production caps in place, and thus limit subsidies, for the first time.

Meanwhile, reversing its post–World War II stand, the United States, along with other competitive agricultural exporters (collectively known as the Cairns Group), proposed reform of agricultural trade policy at the Uruguay Round of GATT talks.[14] This reversal made the conflict between GATT as a set of principles and domestic political interests completely clear. Econometric analysis suggested that competitive food exporters stood to gain about $100 billion if all restraints on agricultural trade disappeared, while, of course, the uncompetitive states would save themselves the cost of subsidies. In the face of one to two hundred billion compelling arguments, why has it been so hard to remove protection in agriculture?

The specifics of the negotiations show the persistent power of domestic farm lobbies. The Reagan administration never missed a chance to use the same policy idea twice, so, just as it had in arms control negotiations, in 1985 it proposed a zero-option for agricultural subsidies: by A.D. 2000 everyone would remove all subsidies. The EC completely rejected this proposal (as did uncompetitive sections of the U.S. agricultural community). The United States then gravitated toward the position of the Cairns Group, which involved converting all forms of subsidy into tariffs and then gradually lowering those tariffs. At this point, the Europeans wavered over accepting the principle that rural income support should be disconnected from production subsidies, which would help end overproduction. European stubbornness forced several extensions of the Uruguay Round. Finally, in 1992 the Europeans proposed 29 percent cuts in subsidies but no real shift away from production subsidies as a concept. The United States felt this would simply prolong the problem of overproduction and trade fights. With negotiations deadlocked at the end of 1992, the United States used a dispute over U.S. soybean exports to impose selective punitive tariff increases in order to create a free trade community among the EC's *competitive* farmers. It slapped 200 percent tariffs on French and German white wines and British wheat gluten—all competitive products —to get the EC to cut subsidies for uncompetitive oilseeds. The EC made minor concessions to keep the talks moving forward. But the French, who had the most to lose from eliminating or reducing the CAP, fiercely resisted, threatening to veto any EC concessions to the United States.

So the situation in the early 1990s resembles that of the late 1800s in all but two countervailing respects. Unlike in the 1800s, agricultural trade is managed. Import quotas are doled out to the most politically powerful foreign providers, regardless of economic rationality. Thus, for example, when the United States pressured Japan to liberalize beef imports in 1990, Japan increased its imports of U.S. beef by reducing Australia's quota for the Japanese market. However, also unlike the situation in the 1880s, GATT provides an institutional arena in which negotiations to reduce protection can occur. Which of these tendencies will prevail is uncertain.

As in the previous century, the continued creation of more competitive agricultural production zones put enormous pressure on existing producers to upgrade or exit. As in the 1800s, most states chose to protect agriculture. As in the earlier period, this sheltering prolonged adjustment in rural areas and intensified institutional and other interests bound to continued protection. For example, continued protection of Japanese agriculture has contributed to Japan's outrageously high land prices.[15] These land prices have become built into the price of stock shares (since companies own land); into the structure of lending (land provides at least 30 percent of the collateral backing bank loans); and into people's expectations about retirement (via their ability to reverse amortize their landholdings). Removing protection and all the various tax breaks that make it rational to hold land in agricultural use in Japan now would cause a collapse in land prices. Thus, the vested interests created by protection extend outward from agriculture into other sectors as well.

The global consequences of agricultural protection are large and negative. (Chapter 15 expands on this subject.) If agricultural trade were liberalized, the developing countries, most of which are heavily in debt, would gain about $25 to 30 billion in additional export income as their exports of traditional and nontraditional agricultural products rose. This additional income is roughly equivalent to 20 percent of their aggregate current debt service burden; if they had that income, they could service their debt more easily. Similarly, it is also roughly equal to their aggregate 1991 current account deficit; if they had that income, they would not be accumulating debt. Although, as Chapter 12 noted, aggregate accounting about the LDCs makes less sense than ever, these numbers do indicate that the weakest economies suffer the most from protection. Thus, agricultural protection is not just a matter of expensive butter in France. *Subsidies for rich (and uncompetitive) farmers in the industrialized countries mean more poverty in LDCs.*

## The Von Thünenization of Industry

In a peculiar way, some manufacturing sectors have also begun to demonstrate a von Thünen–like dispersion of production. Just as agricultural stay-behinds faced competition from migrants in the nineteenth century, twentieth-century industrial stay-behinds came under increasing competitive pressure from migrants, and like nineteenth-century stay-behinds, they also resorted to protection to stave off their decline. However, protection actually accelerated the decline of the stay-behinds. Protection induced more rapid technical advancement in the new production areas, ratchetting up the competitive threat to established industry in the protected sector or economy. So dispersion and protection interacted, with each pushing increases in the other.

Why did manufacturing production disperse, and what kinds of production dispersed? In general, two different processes were at work. One pulled industry out to poorer regions in developed countries and then to LDCs, and the other pushed it. The first process reflected efforts by some poorer regions and LDC states to industrialize in sectors at the end of the product cycle, where technologies were very well understood and thus more easily transferred than in sectors in which tacit knowledge or extremely highly skilled labor was needed. The second process reflected firms' efforts to rationalize their wage structure, matching wage hierarchies to skill levels and thus, they hoped, marginal product. These firms usually were TNCs. The first process has been treated in Chapter 12. By looking at the second process, we can also understand what kinds of industries would-be LDCs were successful at pulling in.

We can paint a more detailed picture of what kind of firms and production processes were dispersed by looking first at wage levels and then at the nature of the production process. In general, we will learn that the least skill-intensive sectors, producing undifferentiated commodities, have fled more skill-intensive areas not because of rents on land but because of rents on labor. A finer-grained analysis is also revealing.

In general, firms try to follow the advice of Charles Babbage, an English mathematician of the nineteenth century. He suggested that firms break up production processes into skilled and unskilled tasks.[16] Rather than paying a skilled worker (who could command a relatively high wage) to perform a mix of these tasks, skilled workers could be detailed to do tasks requiring skills, and unskilled workers tasks not requiring skills. Workers could then be paid wages that matched their marginal productivity.

In the postwar era, however, diffusion of the assembly line and its related unionism raised wages in the industrial countries; unions succeeded in raising the share of wages in the total value produced. They also raised indirect wages across the entire economy by making demands for more and better public services. Finally, unions also succeeded in compressing the wage structure, raising wages for the unskilled and semiskilled workers who constituted the bulk of union membership. Unionization and tight labor markets defeated firms' efforts to "babbage-ize" production and wage levels, and thus to maximize their profits. To babbage-ize production, firms had to go outside their national economies to find nonunion labor and states that did not support welfare programs.

If a search for low wages explains why firms might *want* to disperse production, it does not explain why this search took precedence over other pressures or, equally important, whether they *can* do so. Not all production processes are amenable to geographic dispersion. It is pointless to have a skilled worker install antilock brake systems in a car and then ship that car somewhere else to have an unskilled worker install windows. In contrast, cloth can be woven and cut using expensive machines requiring skilled operators, and then shipped elsewhere for assembly into garments by (relatively) unskilled sewing machine operators. In general, the more tightly coupled production processes are, the nearer in time and space each step in the process has to be for things to get put together right, and the less likely it is that a process will be dispersed. Conversely, the less tightly coupled production processes are, the easier it is to disperse production.

Low-value-added and labor-intensive industries in the industrial countries started the dispersion of production. They faced the greatest wage pressures, for they no longer could compete with the wages offered by higher-value-added, assembly-line-based industries. The textiles and garment industry was the largest of the migratory industries characterized by high labor intensity and low levels of coupling in the production process. Because of the low level of capitalization needed to enter this industry, many local firms in LDCs could start production. Yet because they often lacked the design, merchandising skills, and market access of developed country firms or retailers, LDC producers typically acted as subcontractors for those firms.

In higher-value-added mass production industries (e.g., cars), rising wages for unskilled workers motivated a search for places to assemble low-value-added components using cheaper labor. At first, only component production was dispersed, with components shipped back to assembly sites in high-wage areas. Eventually, however, even cheaper cars, once their entire production process had been routinized and debugged, could be shipped to low-wage areas as well, because virtually all skills had been incorporated into special-purpose machinery (recall the product cycle model in Chapter 11).

Finally, in heavy industry such as steel, both cheaper labor costs and cheaper raw materials made it possible for LDC states to buy off-the-shelf technology from existing steel producers or equipment makers. LDC states, rather than private firms, typically built these mills. The high level of capitalization needed to build a mill put it out of the reach of most LDC firms, unless, like Hyundai's Pohang steel subsidiary, those firms had access to subsidized capital from their state.

Next we will look at the interaction of dispersion, trade, and protection in the textile and automotive industries; what happened in steel essentially duplicated the processes there.

### Textiles and Garments

In all three major economies, the United States, Germany, and Japan, textiles and especially garment producers went south both literally and figuratively in search of cheaper labor. The industry split into its somewhat higher-value-added, mechanized, tightly coupled textile branch (the spinning of fibers and weaving of fabrics) and its low-value-added, uncoupled assembly of garments from fabrics. For Germany and Japan, which lacked extensive internal souths, this required the transnationalization of production. Garment producers went first to southern Germany and then to low-wage Mediterranean countries like Yugoslavia and Tunisia. For its part, Japan went to rural Japan and then to the Asian newly industrialized countries (NICs) — Hong Kong, Singapore, Taiwan, and South Korea. U.S. firms at first had the good fortune to find the south inside their own country in non-union low-wage states like the Carolinas, Arkansas, and Georgia. U.S. producers migrated south soon after World War

TABLE 13.1

## Economic Significance of Textiles and Garments Production in Industrialized and Developing Countries, 1963 and 1980

| Industry | Industrialized Countries | | Developing Countries | |
|---|---|---|---|---|
| | 1963 | 1980 | 1963 | 1980 |
| Textiles (as a % of total manufacturing) | | | | |
| Production | 6.30 | 4.40 | 19.30 | 11.50 |
| Employment | 9.90 | 7.20 | 28.30 | 24.0 |
| Relative value added[a] | 0.64 | 0.61 | 0.68 | 0.48 |
| Garments (as a % of total manufacturing) | | | | |
| Production | 4.00 | 2.80 | 5.90 | 4.50 |
| Employment | 8.00 | 5.70 | 10.90 | 10.90 |
| Relative value added | 0.50 | 0.49 | 0.54 | 0.41 |

[a]Relative value added is production divided by employment. Thus, 1 = average for all manufacturing; > 1 is above average; < 1 is below average.
SOURCE: GATT, *Textiles and Clothing in the World Economy* (Geneva: GATT, 1984).

II, because U.S. wages were then the highest in the world. Producers in the other two countries did not begin to move until the 1960s, when economic recovery from World War II and the baby busts caused by war casualties created local labor shortages. (Table 13.1 indicates value added relative to all manufacturing as well as the economic importance of textiles and garments, and Table 13.2 presents data on the sources of garment imports.)

This movement put severe strains on firms, since transnationalization cost money. In particular, search and relocation costs were high. In Germany and Japan, joint state–industry organizations facilitated the orderly relocation of the industry, finding sites, providing subsidized capital, and negotiating with host governments. In the southern United States host governments facilitated an orderly relocation through their industrial policies. Despite this aid, the U.S. industry felt itself to be under extreme competitive pressure. The industry was also shifting out of cotton fabrics into synthetics, which was a higher-value-added good for the industry. This shift also took capital needed for the relocation south. Hence, the U.S. textiles and garment industry began to demand protection. The response it got from the federal government set the pattern for virtually all protectionist responses in manufacturing sectors there-

TABLE 13.2

## Sources of Industrial Country Garment Imports, 1963, 1973, and 1982 (percentages)

| Region | 1963 | 1973 | 1982 |
|---|---|---|---|
| Other industrial countries | 77 | 54 | 39 |
| Developing countries | 21 | 41 | 54 |
| Former CMEA and People's Republic of China | 2 | 5 | 7 |

SOURCE: GATT, *Textiles and Clothing in the World Economy* (Geneva: GATT, 1984).

after. It also unwittingly intensified the long-run competitive threat the industry faced.

In 1955, in response to rising imports of Japanese cotton textiles and garments, the U.S. industry made its first postwar demand for protection. Imports then amounted to only 2 percent of consumption. In 1957 the United States asked the Japanese to voluntarily restrain their exports, which they did. This first voluntary export restraint (VER) set the new pattern for protection. Nominally, VERs abided by GATT's rules. The Japanese, after all, could not be condemned if of their own free will they set a quantitative limit on their exports, while, since the United States ostensibly had done nothing, it could not be condemned for violating the principles of transparency and nondiscrimination. Practically, however, VERs violated the spirit of GATT.

Japanese producers responded to the VER rationally. The VER limited *Japanese* exports to *cotton* textiles. So Japanese firms, aided by their state, began shifting cotton textile production to the Asian NICs, especially Hong Kong, while moving up the value-added ladder into synthetics at home. Then they could export *synthetics* from Japan and *cottons* from the NICs, making an end run around the VER. Competitive pressures reappeared, and in more product lines. Threatened U.S. producers appealed to Congress for more protection. In 1961 President Kennedy needed to win congressional approval to launch what turned out to be the single greatest round of GATT tariff reductions. Congress exacted a new, expanded VER, the 1962 Long-Term Agreement (LTA), as the price for approval. The new VER expanded voluntary restraint to the NICs. Producers again responded rationally. Since the LTA VER limited NICs cotton exports, they began weaving fabric blends with 51 percent polyester content, which qualified these as synthetics. (Table 13.3 shows the protection-induced shift in fiber content.) Between 1960 and 1970 imports of cotton textiles doubled in the United States, but imports of synthetics grew 10 times. The NICs and Japan also began diverting exports to Europe. The Europeans rushed to sign their own bilateral deals with the major exporters.

Both despite and because of this proliferation of protection, textile and

TABLE 13.3

### Fiber Content of Textile Production, World and East Asia, 1959–1983, Selected Years (percentages)[a]

|  | 1959–61 | | 1969–71 | | 1981–83 | |
|---|---|---|---|---|---|---|
|  | S | C | S | C | S | C |
| World | 22 | 68 | 38 | 55 | 51 | 45 |
| Japan | 19 | 58 | 41 | 37 | 54 | 35 |
| South Korea | 2 | 92 | 42 | 54 | 70 | 26 |
| Taiwan | 6 | 90 | 27 | 70 | 78 | 21 |

[a] S = synthetics; C = cotton. Percentages may not total 100 because of wool and other natural fibers.
SOURCE: Kim Anderson, "China and the Multi-Fibre Arrangement," in Carl Hamilton, ed., *Textiles Trade and the Developing Countries* (Washington, D.C.: World Bank, 1990), p. 151.

garment exports from the NICs exploded during the 1960s. Taiwanese garment exports, for example, rose over 40 percent per year from 1965 to 1971. By the end of the 1960s, U.S. synthetics producers were calling for protection. The United States negotiated yet another VER with the Japanese and the NICs that now included all fibers, not just cotton. Rather than let the United States divert the Asian steamroller into their market, the Europeans pushed for a catch-all multi-fiber arrangement (MFA), signed in 1973 and since then renewed every few years. The MFA allowed the industrial countries to negotiate detailed bilateral quotas for exports from developing countries. This agreement slowed but did not stop the flood of exports, particularly in garments. (See Table 13-2.)

Domestic employment losses from imports continue to keep pressure for protection high. In the major industrial countries, employment losses from the downsizing of textiles and garments accounted for between 10 and 20 percent of unemployment by the end of the 1970s. Not all of this unemployment was attributable to imports, but blaming them was easy enough.

By the 1980s the industry had seemingly stabilized along lines that might have been predictable in the 1950s. The higher-value-added textile segment of the industry had increased its capital intensity and productivity. In the United States, for example, the textiles industry (spinning and weaving) doubled its capital intensity between 1950 and 1980, enabling it to become a major and competitive exporter. Meanwhile, the labor-intensive garment industry had gone even further south into the Caribbean basin, searching for cheaper labor. Consequently, U.S. "imports" of garments grew more in the 1980s than in any other decade, as textiles firms subcontracted low-skill assembly to export processing zones in the Caribbean and elsewhere.

As with agriculture, the Uruguay Round proposed to liberalize trade in textiles and garments, freeing it from levels of planning and state intervention characteristic of the old Eastern Europe. Like agriculture, residual uncompetitive producers in the industrial countries continue to block any reasonable deal. Protection in textiles and garments created completely irrational outcomes from the point of view of firms wishing to stem competitive pressures. By enforcing quantitative restrictions on imports from specific countries, the industry forced a more rapid movement into higher-value-added products and a more rapid geographical diffusion of textiles and garment production technologies than might otherwise have occurred.

### Automobiles

A similar process of dispersion and protection occurred in automobile production, with three differences. First, unlike the textiles and garment production chain, where the intermediate good (fabric) was amenable to capital-intensive, high-value production, and assembly of the final good was labor intensive, in autos generally intermediate components were labor-intensive, low-value-added goods and final assembly was capital intensive. Second, a more important dividing line than that between component production and final assembly lay between firms using the older assembly-line paradigm created by the U.S. firms in the 1920s and 1930s and firms that used the newer Japanese-style zero-defect, just-in-time production paradigm, so-called lean production. (Chapter 14 goes into this divide in much more detail.) Third, the capital intensity of automobile manufacturing and the importance of soft management technologies created very high barriers to entry. This meant that unlike textiles and garments, where LDC producers could jump into the market, TNCs largely dominated the dispersion of production.

Pressures for protection and free trade played an important but more limited role in this process than with textiles and garments. An invisible form of protection had shielded the U.S. market from major car imports until the 1970s. The U.S. car market was oriented toward large cars. Over 90 percent of the cars sold in the United States had engine displacements of over 2 liters in 1970, compared with only 30 percent in Europe and less than 1 percent in Japan.[17] Exporters had little to offer the U.S. mass market until the oil shocks of the 1970s suddenly caused consumers to downsize. U.S. firms then faced serious competition from high-quality Japanese and European cars.

At the end of the 1970s Chrysler faced bankruptcy, and all three domestic manufacturers suffered enormous financial losses during the 1980–81 recession as the Japanese market share rose over 21 percent. In response, President Reagan negotiated a VER with Japan, capping car imports at 1.7 million units. Pressured by U.S. autoworker and other unions, Congress also briefly considered domestic content legislation in 1982 and 1983, but this would have hurt the U.S. firms, for they had already dispersed component production to, for example, Mexico and assembly to Canada. Thus, a solid coalition favoring this more severe (but in some ways more rational) form of protection did not emerge.

Just as with textiles and garments, Japanese producers responded quite rationally to quantitative limits. They shifted from the smallest and cheapest cars to larger and more expensive cars, loading their cars with nonnegotiable options. Despite only incremental growth in their market share, their total sales *value* continued to grow. The VER forced firms like Honda to turn simple but good cars like the small Accord hatchback of 1980 into the complex BMW-killer Acura Integra. In due time, Toyota and Nissan also evolved prestige lines like Lexus and Infiniti.

As with textiles and garments, VERs also forced Japanese firms to transnationalize their production. Honda again led the way, expanding its existing motorcycle factory in Ohio into a production complex capable of producing more than 250,000 low-end vehicles, and starting production in Canada. Every other Japanese firm followed, going to the United States, Canada, or Mexico. By 1992 the Japanese firms had installed capacity equal to 20 percent of the U.S. market, threatening to displace both their own exports (which by 1991 had fallen in volume terms below the old VER limit) and U.S. firms' production. The Japanese then found themselves threatened by renewed calls from U.S. auto firms for domestic content legislation during the 1990–92 recession. In turn, the Japanese firms began bringing over their component suppliers, placing additional pressure on the U.S. industry.

As with textiles and garments, the Japanese competitive threat also forced U.S. car firms to disperse the labor-intensive, low-value-added parts of their production process. Because car *assembly* is tightly coupled in the U.S. production paradigm (the production of most components *and* final assembly is tightly coupled in just-in-time production), car firms dispersed component production first. As with textiles and garments, they sent component production south. And, as with textiles and garments, U.S. firms started this process by first going to their own local south. Employment in transportation equipment manufacturing industries grew rapidly in the Sunbelt states after 1950. This shift was less about high wages than about escaping union work rules that firms felt inhibited productivity. Thus, the even lower wages to be found across the border in Mexico were not attractive enough to motivate a wholesale shift in production locale until the 1970s.

During the late 1960s and early 1970s, car firms in the United States and Europe experienced extremely high levels of labor militancy. A new generation of workers, undisciplined by the Depression and wartime training, entered the factories, demanding better wages and more interesting, humaner work. At the same time, U.S. automakers faced an unusually competitive threat as Japanese cars began entering the U.S. market. The U.S. companies thought Japan's competitive edge lay in lower wages. Although they were wrong about that (see Chapter 14), they began looking for low-wage sites to which to shift work. Korea and Taiwan, with wages at around $4 per hour, not the $20 U.S. autoworkers got, suddenly looked much more attractive. Both GM and Ford began sourcing cars, respectively, from Daewoo Motors and Kia Motors.[18] Mexico, where hourly wages were $2 to $3, looked even better, was closer, and did not involve deals with other firms.

For its part Mexico made itself attractive by expanding its *maquila* program in 1983. The *maquila* program, started in the 1960s, was a Mexican version of the Taiwanese export processing zone, but one that encompassed the entire border area, not just a specific city. In 1983 Mexico liberalized the rules governing *maquiladoras*. The number of *maquiladoras* and their employees roughly doubled in the 1980s to 1,200 factories with about 330,000 employees. Roughly one-quarter of value added in the *maquiladoras* was automobile related, making it the second largest sector after the entire electrical/electronics goods group; automobile-related *maquiladoras* employed about one-sixth of total *maquiladora* labor. About 60 percent of those exports in 1986 were low-technology components.[19] Mexican law governing DFI in automobiles also required that engines—whose assembly is labor intensive—be wholly sourced within Mexico.

The combination of the liberalized *maquila* law, continued engine-building requirements, and U.S. automakers' desire to escape U.S. unions led to an explosion of production in Mexico and exports to the United States. By the end of the 1980s, automobiles and auto parts provided 28 percent of Mexico's nonoil manufactured exports, and Chrysler was Mexico's second largest exporter after PEMEX. Export of whole engines led the way, jumping from 320,301 units worth $212 million in 1982 to 1,050,000 units worth over $1.3 billion in 1989. Car exports grew off a smaller base, from 14,428 units in 1981 to 195,994 (of which two-thirds went to the United States) in 1989.[20] All of these exports were small cars; larger, more expensive cars continued to be produced in the major industrial centers. When we look at the kind of production Ford dispersed to Mexico, we will understand why.

Ford relocated production of the Mercury Tracer (the Escort's twin) to a plant in Mexico. Because the Escort/Tracer line is essentially a re-skinned Mazda 323 ("Protege"), this plant could be built off the shelf as a duplicate of Mazda's own plant.[21] The Mazda 323 had been in production for over a decade and all the bugs in its design and production process had been worked out. Consequently, even though the Mexican workers were relatively unskilled compared to Japanese and U.S. workers, Ford could use them. This Mexican labor did not need to know how to figure out the ad hoc solutions to the production problems that always crop up with new models; those problems had already been eliminated. Working with an established model, this Mexican labor produced cars with labor inputs and defect levels that rivalled those of Japanese producers.

In contrast, Ford retained production of more expensive, more sophisticated models like the Taurus and Probe in U.S. plants. These cars had more complicated components and trim features whose assembly could not be automated; U.S. workers retained the "tricks" that had been built into the machines operated by Mexicans. And Ford continues to launch new models in the United States, where more experienced production teams can figure out solutions to the myriad of things that go wrong in the first few years of production.

Producers in the other major industrial countries mimicked the U.S. pattern. In Europe first component production and then assembly was shifted to low-wage Spain and Portugal, and is now being dispersed into even cheaper Eastern Europe. Picked by Ford, GM, and Volkswagen, Spain now produces as many cars as Britain, but as Nissan, Honda, and Toyota expand production, Britain may again surpass Spain. Nissan plans to shift production of the subcompact Sentra to Mexico in order to free up production space at its Smyrna, Tennessee, plant for a compact car. The Japanese continue to produce their prestige models in Japan, leaving production of Corollas and Altimas to what they regard as lazy and illiterate Americans and Britons.

---

## Outcomes

The most important outcome of the brief cases described earlier is the transnationalization of production. Firms dispersed their production globally to avoid being locked out of major markets, and, when possible, to take advantage of variations in wages. While transnationalization remained an overwhelmingly U.S. phenomenon, the rest of the big economies raced to catch up. Table 13.4 provides data on the stock of DFI that each major industrial economy had in the other two (conflating the EC economies into one), and on the rate of growth of investment. These numbers show that the tightest connections existed between the U.S. and European economies, with a strong Japanese presence in both of those economies but a much weaker presence by

TABLE 13.4

## Transnationalization in the Triad Economies, 1988

| To | Stock of Investment ($billion) | | | Annual Rate of Growth of Investment, 1980–88 (%) | | |
|---|---|---|---|---|---|---|
| | United States | EC | Japan | United States | EC | Japan |
| *From* United States | — | 131.1 | 17.9 | — | 6.3 | 14.1 |
| *From* EC | 193.9 | — | 1.7 | 19.3 | — | 19.8 |
| *From* Japan | 53.4 | 12.5 | — | 35.5 | 22.3 | — |

SOURCE: United Nations Centre on Transnational Corporations, *World Investment Report* (New York: United Nations, 1991), p. 40.

them in Japan. Undoubtedly, this reflects a variety of barriers to inward investment in Japan.[22] It also shows the surge in Japanese firms' DFI everywhere during the 1980s.

This transnationalization of production created continental/hemispheric, industrial von Thünen zones.[23] On an aggregate basis, firms transnationalizing into LDCs mostly went into nearby areas with low wages and stable, acquiescent governments. The biggest exception was investment by U.S. firms into the four Asian NICs, but trans-Pacific transport became increasingly cheaper after World War II and by the 1960s all four countries had very stable states. Figure 13-1 presents data on the clustering of investment by firms from the three dominant economies. Not surprisingly, U.S. investments predominantly went to Latin America; European investments went to Africa and western Asia; and Japanese investments to East Asia.

This transnationalization–*cum*–von Thünenization also affected trade flows considerably. By the end of the 1980s, the majority of world trade was being conducted by TNCs shipping goods from one subsidiary to another. These flows reflected three patterns: the shipment of intermediate goods back and forth between high-wage, high-skill zones and low-wage, low-skill zones; the shipment of finished goods between different markets where TNCs had concentrated production of different goods; and traditional exports of finished goods from a manufacturing base to final markets. By the beginning of the 1980s, U.S. and Japanese TNCs alone accounted for about 28 percent of world exports of manufactured goods. In the U.S. economy itself, the world's largest open economy, TNCs controlled a fairly consistent 54 percent of U.S. exports during the 1980s, with U.S.-based firms accounting for about three-fifths of that and intrafirm transfers also accounting for about three-fifths. TNCs also controlled a fairly consistent 54 percent of imports, with U.S. firms again accounting for about three-fifths of that amount. However, TNC intrafirm transfers accounted for about 80 percent of TNC-controlled imports into the United States.[24]

The protectionist pressures described in this chapter created a strong imperative for TNCs to disperse themselves into each of the three major regional trading areas. TNCs that did so not only sheltered themselves against foreign exchange rate volatility—which, as Chapter 10 discussed, was quite

**Figure 13.1** *Regionalization of DFI Holdings in LDCs, 1988[a]*

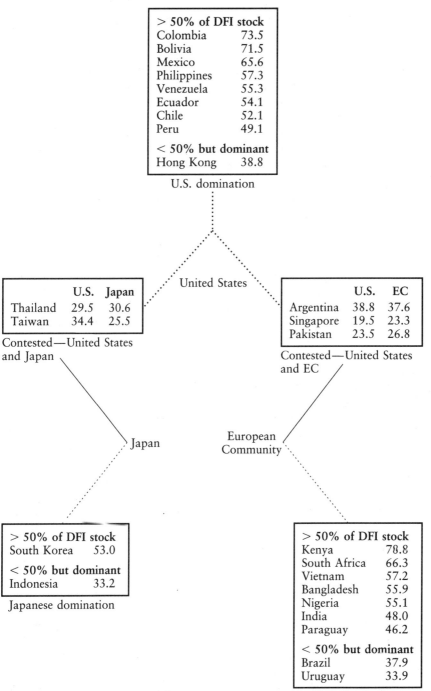

> 50% of DFI stock
| | |
|---|---|
| Colombia | 73.5 |
| Bolivia | 71.5 |
| Mexico | 65.6 |
| Philippines | 57.3 |
| Venezuela | 55.3 |
| Ecuador | 54.1 |
| Chile | 52.1 |
| Peru | 49.1 |

< 50% but dominant
| | |
|---|---|
| Hong Kong | 38.8 |

U.S. domination

United States

| | U.S. | Japan |
|---|---|---|
| Thailand | 29.5 | 30.6 |
| Taiwan | 34.4 | 25.5 |

Contested—United States
and Japan

| | U.S. | EC |
|---|---|---|
| Argentina | 38.8 | 37.6 |
| Singapore | 19.5 | 23.3 |
| Pakistan | 23.5 | 26.8 |

Contested—United States
and EC

Japan

European
Community

> 50% of DFI stock
| | |
|---|---|
| South Korea | 53.0 |

< 50% but dominant
| | |
|---|---|
| Indonesia | 33.2 |

Japanese domination

> 50% of DFI stock
| | |
|---|---|
| Kenya | 78.8 |
| South Africa | 66.3 |
| Vietnam | 57.2 |
| Bangladesh | 55.9 |
| Nigeria | 55.1 |
| India | 48.0 |
| Paraguay | 46.2 |

< 50% but dominant
| | |
|---|---|
| Brazil | 37.9 |
| Uruguay | 33.9 |

E.C. domination

[a]Numbers indicate percentage of inward DFI held by dominant country in host country.
SOURCE: UNCTC, *World Investment Report, 1991*, p. 54.

high during the 1980s — but also found that they could use their new host states to pressure third-party markets for access. Honda Motor, for example, was the largest exporter of cars from the United States to non–North American markets. These exports reflected a global rationalization of Honda's production, with Honda using relatively less skilled U.S. labor to produce its midrange Accord sedans for export back to Japan, while it used its well-tested high-quality Japanese production facilities to produce Acuras for export to the United States. Honda also exported U.S.-built Accords to Taiwan and Europe. Honda could piggyback its export efforts onto general U.S. pressure on Taiwan and Europe to open their markets.

## Back to the Future in Trade

The brief cases described in this chapter show the paradoxical swings between protection and free trade. GATT permitted more free trade, but as it did so it generated powerful protectionist pressures as producers threatened by competitive imports used political, rather than economic, talent to protect their market share. With GATT blocking the use of tariffs, states responded to those political pressures by using quantitative limits, like VERs, or countervailing duties to slow the flow of imports. This then triggered dispersion. VERs drove former exporters to transnationalize into their major markets; transnationalization made local producers disperse in search of cheap labor or back into the exporters' economy. Dispersion and transnationalization fractured the old protectionist coalition.[25]

Uncompetitive producers remained protectionist, but as some formerly protectionist firms became competitive, dispersed their own production, and did joint ventures with the "invaders," their motivations for supporting protection declined. Instead, they began to support free trade — meaning the ability to arrange global flows of goods as they wished. Often, however, this free trade meant a new free trade area that incorporated the places to which they had dispersed production but excluded the sources of invader-controlled imports. Thus, U.S. auto firms have been major supporters of the North American Free Trade Agreement (NAFTA) because it would allow a free flow of goods within North America. U.S. firms have significantly dispersed their operations across the United States, Canada, and Mexico. In contrast, the flow of goods by U.S. auto firms between their U.S. and European operations are fairly small. Similarly, big European TNCs appear to have been a driving force behind the Single European Act (SEA), which would have created a barrierless EC-wide internal market.[26] Those Euro-TNCs largely operate within Europe.

Thus, control over trade showed completely opposite trends through the 1970s and 1980s. By the end of the 1980s, tariffs were down to insignificant levels, but about 20 percent of industrial country imports were subject to VERs and quantitative restrictions. When we add to this restriction other restrictions on trade, such as countertrade (bilateral exchanges) and negotiated offsets, roughly half of world trade was managed, a level of protection approximating that in the 1930s.[27] Yet at the same time major new free trade agreements were being completed, and the most ambitious GATT round ever, an effort essentially to expand GATT back into an ITO, began in 1986 and had made reasonable progress by 1992. Fears that NAFTA, the SEA, and the enmeshment of Japan in East Asia's economies would lead to the emergence of three large and rival blocs, each dominated by its own currency and resisting imports from the other bloc, were offset by the fact that trade between these blocs is growing faster than trade inside them. For example, during the 1980s North American trade with the Asian NICs nearly tripled, a far faster rate of growth than for U.S. trade with either Canada or Mexico. Meanwhile, Japanese trade with the United States doubled, an increase faster than its growth rates for nearly all its Asian partners.

Thus, trade, like money, showed a distinct movement back to the future. The period between 1914 and 1950, with its marked reduction in world trade and inward reorientation for most major economies, represented a distinct divergence from nineteenth-century patterns. Then world trade had averaged around 50 percent growth per decade.[28] The situation immediately following World War II represented a quite unusual period in which reconstruction, with tight control over trade and capital flows, coincided with an orientation by producers toward their domestic market. After the 1950s, trade began to grow explosively again. This rapid increase in trade facilitated the reemergence of market pressures to disperse agriculture toward low-land-cost areas and, ultimately, as labor shortages and militancy emerged in core countries, to disperse industrial production toward low-wage areas with disciplined labor as well.

In this context, tariff reduction under GATT had the same effects as railroads and steamships in the late 1800s. As in the late 1800s, domestic producers suddenly faced competitive pressure and market penetration from more distant and more competitive producers. As in the late 1800s, too, firms reacted by demanding protection, and trade continued to grow as most industries adjusted to changes in best practice manufacturing and agriculture. After a decade of protection, for example, the U.S. steel industry doubled its labor productivity.[29] (Granted, it imported Japanese technology to do so, but this is what adjustment is about: one copies from the leader.) As industries continue to adjust, the successful firms in each industry will probably drop out of domestic protectionist coalitions. Similarly, the rising proportion of intrafirm, intrasectoral but cross-national trade will prevent any massive increase in protection as in the 1930s. The result will probably be a rolling protection, temporarily shielding declining sectors, while incremental movement toward liberalizing highly regulated sectors occurs.

The only flies in this ointment are sectors in which transnationalization is quite difficult or in which the state is a major buyer. Thus, agriculture, where most farmers are completely immobile, continues to be a major opponent to trade liberalization. Similarly, LDC firms, struggling simply to survive as they confront industrial country TNCs larger than their own home economy, and with virtually no hope of transnationalizing, oppose continued liberalization. Big-ticket infrastructure purchases — for example, civilian transport aircraft and telecommunications systems — remain highly politicized and subsidized.[30] The two greatest obstacles to successful completion of the 1986 GATT Uruguay Round remaining by 1993 were countries with uncompetitive agriculture and countries with infant and rudimentary service industries. The most aggressive instances of state support for manufactured exports came in aviation and telecommunications. We could say virtually the same thing about trade in 1900, if we substituted rudimentary manufacturing industries for service industries and railroad systems for aircraft.

## Notes

1. A lovely account of U.S.–European ties that, unfortunately, focuses too much on personalities can be found in Kees van der Pijl, *Making of an Atlantic Ruling Class* (London: Verso, 1982).

2. Richard Gardner, *Sterling-Dollar Diplomacy* (New York: McGraw-Hill, 1969).

3. See Paul de Hevesy, *World Wheat Planning and Economic Planning in General* (New York: Oxford University Press, 1940) for a detailed survey of intervention in grain and other markets, as well as a plea for a less political form of planning.

4. See Gardner, *Sterling-Dollar Diplomacy.*

5. This continues to be a worry: a variety of social and environmental groups ran a full-page ad in the *Washington Post*, December 14, 1992, p. A20, claiming that the Uruguay GATT Round was a threat to U.S. democracy because it transferred power over trade, labor, health, and environmental legislation to "a secretive foreign bureaucracy in Geneva."

6. *The Economist*, May 9, 1992, p. 128.

7. James Dunkerley, *Power in the Isthmus* (London: Verso, 1988), p. 193.

8. K.C. Buckley, "The World Market in Fresh Fruit and Vegetables, Wine and Tropical Beverages: Government Intervention and Multilateral Policy Reform," U.S. Department of Agriculture Report AGES9057, 1990.

9. These transportation improvements also enlarged the supply of vegetables from distant sources within countries; thus, California could supply, for instance, half of U.S. broccoli consumption.

10. William Friedland, "The Global Fresh Fruit and Vegetable System: An Industrial Organization Analysis," Working Paper no. 4, Focused Research Activity on Agroecology and Sustainable Agriculture, University of California, Santa Cruz, 1992.

11. N. Islam, *Horticultural Exports of Developing Countries* (Washington, D.C.: International Food Policy Research Institute, 1990).

12. Except where noted, all data in this section are from OECD, *Agricultural Policies, Markets and Trade: Monitoring and Outlook* (Paris: OECD, various years); for individual countries, see the OECD's country surveys, *National Policies and Agricultural Trade* (country name).

13. EEC, *The Agricultural Situation in the Community* (Brussels, 1991).

14. The best source for the early set of negotiations is Dale Hathaway, *Agriculture and the GATT: Rewriting the Rules* (Washington, D.C.: Institute for International Economics, 1987); on the Cairns Group, see Richard Higgott and Andrew Cooper, "Middle Power Leadership and Coalition Building: Australia, the Cairns Groups and the Uruguay Round of Trade Negotiations," *International Organization* 44, no. 4 (Autumn 1990): 589–632.

15. Edward Carr, "Survey: Agriculture," *The Economist*, December 12, 1992, p. 10.

**16.** For an analysis that overstates the importance of the Babbage principle in the global dispersion of industry, see Folker Froebel, Jurgen Heinrichs, and Otto Kreye, *New International Division of Labour* (New York: Cambridge University Press, 1980).

**17.** James Dunn, "Automobiles in International Trade: Regime Change or Persistence?" *International Organization* 41, no. 2 (Spring 1987): 225–252.

**18.** Daewoo Motor is a 50–50 joint venture between GM and Daewoo Industries; Ford owns 10 percent of Kia, with Mazda holding an additional 8 percent.

**19.** Organization for Economic Cooperation and Development, *Foreign Direct Investment and Industrial Development in Mexico* (Paris: OECD, 1990), pp. 63–65, 126.

**20.** Ibid., pp. 112–115.

**21.** This paragraph draws on ibid. and on Harley Shaiken, "Universal Motors Assembly and Stamping Plant: Transferring High-Tech Production to Mexico," *Columbia Journal of World Business*, 26, no. 2 (Summer 1991): 124–137.

**22.** Dennis Encarnation, *Rivals beyond Trade* (Ithaca, N.Y.: Cornell University Press, 1992).

**23.** For an interesting analysis that applies the product cycle model, rather than a von Thünen logic, to northeast Asia but comes up with the same conclusions, see Bruce Cumings, "Political Economy of North-East Asia," *International Organization* 38, no. 1 (Winter 1984): 1–40.

**24.** United Nations Centre on Transnational Corporations, *Transnational Corporations and World Development* (New York: United Nations, 1988), p. 97; U.S. Department of Commerce, *Direct Investment Abroad* and *Direct Investment in the United States* (Washington, D.C.: Government Printing Office, various dates).

**25.** Helen Milner, *Resisting Protectionism* (Princeton, N.J.: Princeton University Press, 1988).

**26.** Wayne Sandholtz and John Zysman, "1992: Recasting the European Bargain," *World Politics* 42, no. 1 (Fall 1989): 1–30.

**27.** H. Richard Friman, *Patchwork Protectionism* (Ithaca, N.Y.: Cornell University Press, 1990), pp. 1–2. See also Joseph Greico, *Cooperation among Nations: Europe, America and Non-Tariff Barriers to Trade* (Ithaca, N.Y.: Cornell University Press, 1990).

**28.** Peter Katzenstein, "International Interdependence," *International Organization* 28, no. 4 (1975): 1024.

**29.** *The Economist,* May 16, 1992, p. 98.

**30.** See, for example, Laura Tyson, *Who's Bashing Whom?* (Berkeley: Institute for International Economics, 1992).

# CHAPTER 14

## U.S. Hegemony:
## Declining from Below?

If the most efficient way for the U.S. to get steel from the Japanese is to produce tapes of *Dallas* and sell them to the Japanese, then producing tapes of *Dallas* is our basic industry.

*Herbert Stein*

Just as production innovations in the United States and Germany undercut the basis for British hegemony in the 1890s, innovations in Japan undercut U.S. hegemony in the 1970s and 1980s. This and the next chapter mirror Chapter 8, discussing first the institutional innovations propelling the Japanese forward at the level of production and then how these innovations affected international finance. In the 1880s and 1890s the U.S. and German economies outcompeted the British economy by professionalizing management, cartelizing competition, electrifying production, and taylorizing work. As late developers, U.S. and German producers had to find some kind of competitive edge. They successfully took advantage of their rapidly growing domestic markets and their weakly unionized and thus fairly plastic labor forces to create new production processes.

In the 1950s Japanese firms, particularly automobile firms, confronted an environment that forced them to create a similar range of innovations: at the level of firm organization, the *keiretsu*; at the level of production processes, *kanban* (just-in-time inventory); and at the level of the worker, responsible multiskilled workers via *kaizen* (continuous improvement) and total quality management. In the 1960s and 1970s these innovations—the three *k*'s— diffused to other parts of the Japanese economy. In those sectors the Japanese found themselves able to outcompete producers in all of the world's major markets (when they were allowed to do so). These sectors encompassed most of the high-growth, assembly-line-based sectors of the post–World War II period: ground transportation and industries based on the internal combustion engine, obviously, but also consumer electronics, electric tools, the standardized parts of the machine tool industry, and parts of the semiconductor and computer industry.

Can the Japanese propel themselves to hegemony on the basis of these product innovations? At this point, it appears that their innovations are *not* the basis for the kind of rise to hegemony that the United States managed after World Wars I and II. As the United States did with metals production in the 1890s, the Japanese have perfected an existing production system, allowing them to outcompete the existing hegemon in an existing product line. However, the Japanese do not yet have the overwhelming productive superiority that the United States obtained by innovating the assembly line, which established a whole new area for economic activity. Even before the devastation of World War II, which left the United States with about 40 or 50 percent of gross world product, the United States had about 45 percent in 1929 of world manufacturing output. The Japanese today have only about 13 percent of gross world product, which is about three-fifths of the United States' gross national product (GNP). In contrast, by 1914 German GNP equaled Britain's by 1914, and U.S. GNP was three times Britain's.[1]

## Defects in the U.S. – Style Assembly Line

### Inventory as Production Process

Japanese advances on the assembly line cannot be understood without first understanding the defects they remedied. The U.S. version of the assembly line was extremely productive, but the outcomes of struggles between management and labor built in inefficiencies. Before the 1970s these problems were irrelevant, because the assembly line and the integrated, multidivisional firm gave U.S. firms an enormous competitive edge over non-assembly-line-based small firms outside the United States, and because the U.S. market was fairly sheltered from international competition. As Chapter 11 noted, however, assembly-line technologies diffused, and the 1973 oil shock exposed not only the automobile but also other industries to international competition. The Japanese fine-tuned the assembly line and by doing so were able to run demand-driven rather than supply-driven assembly lines, posing a competitive threat to U.S. firms.

The U.S.–style assembly line had three problems. The assembly line was very unresponsive to changes in demand, there was a huge incentive to keep the line flowing regardless of the quality of production, and workers were very alienated from the production process. All of these problems can be summed up as a problem in balancing the line, that is, making sure that parts flowed and workers worked in precisely the right rhythms to assure that no bottlenecks disrupted production. All three derived from management's fear that production might be interrupted, particularly by workers. Thus, all these problems could be traced to management's willingness to accept the costs of fixing defects *after* cars were assembled rather than accepting what they perceived as the larger costs of interrupting production to fix defects *during* production by allowing workers greater autonomy.

The assembly line used expensive machines designed to perform a limited range of operations, for example, milling holes in a certain kind of engine. Each factory required a large number of specialized and thus costly machines. Maximizing economic return on these machines meant maximizing the number of units produced, spreading the cost of the machines over the largest possible number of units of output. In the United States this was done by producing cars ahead of demand in large factories that were often designed to produce a single model of car. Changing from one model to another meant shutting down a factory to reorganize the flow of parts and subassemblies, to change welding rigs, and to change the dies on stamp presses.[2] Shutting down cost the firm money, because these machines — and thus the firm's investment — sat idle.

Because assembly lines were profitable only if they were run continuously (thus maximizing output), management had a huge incentive to prevent any interruption to the production process. Interruptions could arise for two reasons. First, the absence of the right number and kind of parts or workers at any given step in the assembly process forced a shutdown. For example, if workers ran out of engine valves, obviously it was pointless to continue producing engines. These engines would not run without the valves, and the valves could not be put in later.

In the United States, management compensated for the danger of parts or labor shortages by holding large amounts of both as buffer inventory. These buffers provided management with insurance against defective or missing parts. Because management tried very hard to make jobs as simple and repetitive as possible, they could easily substitute a buffer worker for a defective, that is, absent worker.

This approach was expensive. Excess inventory and labor tied up money that could have been invested elsewhere (or on which firms were paying interest). The typical U.S. car firm held between two weeks' and two months' worth of inventory depending on the part. Holding inventory also encouraged sloppiness. Firms could tolerate defective parts coming from their own subsidiaries or from subcontractors because excessive inventory assured that enough good parts could always be found. High levels of inventory also meant that firms had to use workers to move parts from storage areas to work sites; all this handling damaged a predictable number of parts and added to the labor costs of production.

Firms also ignored defects created by the improper assembly of defect-free parts. If workers botched an assembly operation, they simply let the car or subassembly continue moving down the line. Other workers would rectify the error later. This was a disguised way of holding extra inventory. Cars could not be sold until the defects were fixed. Extra labor, in the form of specialized quality control workers, had to examine each car for defects.

## Taylorization of Workers

Management's fear of production interruptions prevented them from giving any discretion to line workers. Instead, they taylorized work, assigning each worker one specific task that typically involved a series of simple motions done over and over. Management basically wanted workers to behave like robots, programmed by a separate white-collar engineering staff and supervised by foremen who "fixed" broken robots by yelling at them. This hostile environment generated an equally hostile response from workers and their unions.[3] Workers' unions tried to prevent job fragmentation from turning into work intensification by insisting on very rigid job categories and descriptions. Welders could not paint, painters could not weld, and neither could do the work of an electrician or a machinist. Thus, GM's old Fremont, California, plant ended up with over 200 job classifications.

Because management did not trust workers, it did not bother to ask workers to suggest better ways to put together the products workers assembled; instead, management relied on degreed engineers to figure out improvements. This had a very high and somewhat unmeasurable cost, because all the knowledge workers gained by putting together cars every day was lost to the company. Indeed, workers actively resisted transferring that knowledge to management, fearing that it would lead to speeding up the assembly line. Instead, engineers had to find out how to make things more efficiently, but without being able to ask the people who had a very intimate knowledge of what was wrong and right about current designs and current production practices.

Because workers were treated like robots, they behaved like robots, and so they lost interest in trying to produce high-quality products. This lack of interest had no effect on how they were treated by management, on their wage (which was linked to their job description), or on the pace at which parts came down the line. This problem also affected white-collar workers, because the idea that thinking about work and actually doing it could be divided extended into the lower levels of management and design work.

Because blue-collar workers were not allowed to think, U.S. firms had to hire someone to think for them. The result was a proliferation of white-collar workers doing minor engineering tasks, quality control, and various coordination activities, as well as an increase in skilled workers who did routine maintenance. U.S. car firms typically employed 12 to 30 percent more supervisory white-collar workers than did Japanese car firms, spread out over perhaps twice as many levels of management. Japanese firms used their supervisory labor savings to hire more engineering staff; this, combined with their flatter hierarchies, enabled them to generate new models more rapidly.[4]

Conflict between workers and management tended to freeze production processes in place. The great prewar gains in productivity gave way to incremental gains. Workers had no incentive to cooperate with management efforts to redesign production processes. Management, confronted with slow growth in total U.S. sales and with no way to export from the United States to Europe, had no incentive to take on workers and risk major strikes. Instead, like British metals producers in the 1890s, they fixed things at the margins.

## Bureaucratization of Multidivisional Firms

The multidivisional structure of U.S. firms led to two very different ways of organizing the flow of parts among different companies. Companies were either completely inside the multidivisional firm, coordinated via bureaucratic mechanisms, or they were completely outside the firm and coordinated via arm's length, market-based contracts.

U.S. firms used high levels of vertical integration, requiring their subsidiaries to produce inputs or to consume outputs from other parts of the firm according to fairly rigid central plans. Integration, however, insulated subsidiaries from competitive pressures and also distorted investment choices, because internally produced goods had administered prices whose final profitability could not really be known. Subsidiaries had enormous incentives for overinvestment and were protected from the costs of their inefficiency. GM represented the extreme version of this kind of firm, producing over 70 percent of its parts in-house.

U.S. firms also bought parts from outside subcontractors, but they deliberately pitted these subcontractors against one another and threatened to take the work back in-house in order to drive the prices of parts down. This subjected subcontractors to market pressures, but those same market pressures assured that subcontractors had no incentives to invest in long-term quality control or in design staff. Because they could lose their contract at any moment, they could not be sure of amortizing this investment. Nor did they receive enough information from the big car firms to restructure their production processes or to redesign parts in advance of model changes.

The noncompetitive structure of the U.S. automobile market aggravated both sources of inefficiency by removing pressures to find more efficient ways to produce.[5] The big three automakers — GM, Ford, and Chrysler — operated a cozy, high-profit oligopoly. From 1946 to 1973 GM had an after-tax net profit of 20 percent on its assets, compared with the 9 percent average in all U.S. manufacturing. It did so by simply setting the retail price of its cars at a level that assured this high rate of return. The other two followed GM's price leadership.[6] Because U.S. market and consumer demand were overwhelmingly oriented toward large cars, the U.S. firms' oligopoly did not face a major competitive threat from foreign producers. For a while, Volkswagen's 1.3 liter – engine "Bug" successfully catered to the small segment of the U.S. market that wanted small cars. However, the big three used their enormous profits from sales of big cars to subsidize sales of their small cars, driving the foreign share back down. The ability of U.S. firms to cross-subsidize small cars did not encourage them to search for more efficient ways to meet the import threat at the low end. When the two oil shocks shifted U.S. demand toward small cars, the U.S. firms were caught off guard, particularly by the Japanese. But if the Japanese were lucky — because of the oil shocks — they were also smart. What did the Japanese do differently, and why?

---

## Remedies in the Japanese Assembly Line

### *Kanban* and Balancing the Line

U.S. firms balanced their assembly lines by producing ahead of demand, by buffering inventory and labor, and by trying to impose minute top-down control over workers' actions. Despite the obvious advantages of the U.S.

assembly line, three factors constrained Japanese firms from adopting U.S. production techniques simply out of admiration. First, the postwar Japanese market was too small to make supply-driven, economy-of-scale–oriented production possible. Second, capital was extremely short in postwar Japan, making inventory extremely expensive to hold. Third, Japanese workers made different demands on management than did U.S. workers, leading to different kinds of wage and supervisory arrangements.

Because Japanese firms didn't have the luxury of simply imitating the U.S. version of assembly-line production, they innovated a range of different managerial techniques to overcome the balancing problem. These techniques are summed up in the Japanese words *kanban* and *kaizen*, words that encompass a range of concepts. *Kanban* refers in English to the three zeros: zero buffering of inventory (sometimes called just-in-time inventory), zero buffering of labor (sometimes called 97 percent manning), and zero defects. *Kaizen* refers to continuous improvement of the three *p*'s: production, products, and producers. Although the Japanese borrowed liberally from U.S. thinking about these subjects, especially Edward Deming's work on total quality management, the incentive to adopt and adapt came out of the competitive environment Japanese firms faced.[7]

The entire Japanese car market amounted to perhaps 50,000 units in 1950 (about two days' production in the United States) and had risen to only 250,000 units by 1959. This was smaller than the average U.S. car factory, a factory, moreover, often devoted to the production of *one* model. Even worse for Japanese car producers, rural and urban transportation/hauling needs diverged more than in the United States, forcing greater diversity in models. Even if Japanese firms could have afforded to invest in product-specific machinery, they could not hope to produce in advance of demand to maximize throughput. The market simply was too small. Instead, they tried to produce in response to demand, scheduling production only when they had enough orders to make it rational to temporarily reorganize their assembly lines around the production of a specific model and learning how to make such reorganizations in record time.

Capital was extremely scarce in postwar Japan. Firms could not afford to tie up precious capital in inventory simply to buffer against defective parts. Instead, they looked for ways to produce only what was needed. The *kanban* (zero buffering) system emerged from this situation. As a system of inventory control, *kanban* is deceptively simple. *Kanban* literally means "card" and refers to parts cards located at each station on the assembly line. When the level of inventory at a given station fell to about a two-hour supply, the worker there simply attached this card to a moving clothesline. A parts orderer would take the card off and call the relevant parts producer, who would then make just enough parts to restore inventories to about a four-hour supply. Then the parts would be rushed to the main assembly plant and unloaded next to the relevant assembly point. Ideally, the parts would arrive just as the assembler put the last part into the car moving down the line. Practically, this proved impossible to achieve, but as long as inventory was kept down to a fraction of a day rather than weeks or months everyone was happy.

A similar and equally simple system was used to zero buffer labor. Above each workstation were a set of traffic lights, or *andon*. Workers controlled the lights, setting the light to green if everything was OK; to yellow to indicate that they were stressed and needed help or that something might go wrong; and, finally, to red to shut down the line in order to prevent defective subassemblies or cars from being produced. A red light would draw assistance from foremen and other workers. The *andon* light system was a beautiful way of showing management precisely where production flows were unbalanced, where subassemblies had to be redesigned for easier and defect-free assembly, or where excess labor existed.

Counterintuitively, management loved to see yellow lights on everywhere at all times, not green ones. Green lights showed management places where they had too much labor; this meant that a labor buffer existed and should be pared down. Toyota, for example, typically manned its lines with 97 percent of their rated labor requirement. Red lights located serious problems for management, which could then allocate engineering talent to solving that problem. Yellow lights told management that everything was working as efficiently as possible, with no buffered labor and with few difficulties in putting assemblies together. The car producers also tried to lay out their assembly lines in a horseshoe shape, making it possible for workers to do two different jobs at once by standing in the middle of the horseshoe. This method economized on space—land was expensive in postwar Japan—and maximized the amount of time workers actually spent working. The U.S. United Auto Workers Union estimated that where its workers typically worked about 45 seconds out of any given minute, Japanese workers were working 55 seconds.[8]

Zero buffering of parts had a more profound consequence than simply saving money on inventory holdings. Zero buffering could only work in conjunction with a zero defects policy. Having very few parts on hand implied a risk of shutting down the line if parts were defective and could not be replaced immediately. Thus, zero buffering of parts implies zero defects in the components being assembled; parts had to be made right the first time. By putting pressure on components producers to produce and deliver defect-free parts, it also put pressure on them to introduce *kanban* and *kaizen* principles into their own production.

## Kaizen and Multiskilled Workers

All three *kanban* zeros took time to work out in practice, but as a system they tended to locate and eliminate waste at all points in the assembly process. By eliminating waste, they eliminated drags on the assembly line. This allowed for *kaizen*, or continuous improvement, a way of overcoming the problems U.S. firms faced in getting their workers to be efficient. Unlike the U.S. system, in which management distrusted workers and tried to impose a rigid top-down control, the Japanese system gave basic responsibility for production to work teams, even to the extent of allowing workers to shut down the line by switching the *andon* light to red. This was once unthinkable in the United States. Why could Japanese firms allow workers this authority?

As in the United States, and contrary to most myth-making about the cooperative Confucian Japanese work ethic, relations between management and labor in Japan historically were quite tense.[9] This was especially true in the late 1940s and early 1950s, when workers and unions launched a campaign to seize control of the production process and of factories. Like similar struggles in the 1930s in the United States, this campaign generated a set of institutionalized compromises. Led by good Marxists, Japanese workers wanted wages to be linked to need, not to specific jobs. This turned into a wage whose largest component was based on seniority (the *nenko* wage), since older (male) workers were more likely to have families to support.

Japanese workers also demanded job security. They forced employers to expand the system of lifetime employment that employers created for skilled workers during the 1920s to all production workers directly hired by the firm.[10] Lest the reader get the impression that workers got everything they desired, management and the state broke the U.S.–style industrywide unions, leaving only unions inside each firm, so-called enterprise unions. Thus, Japan's lifetime blue-collar employees have a relationship to their firm that most closely resembles that of U.S. white-collar employees.

Immune from layoffs, lifetime employees represented a fixed cost that management had to utilize as productively as possible. Thus, management had an incentive to increase the utility of employees to the firm by constantly training them and upgrading their skills. That way workers could be shifted around the assembly line in response to yellow and red lights, could adapt to assembly lines that themselves were constantly changing as production volumes grew and new models were introduced, and could produce higher quality cars. Multiskilling helped to zero buffer labor, because the typical worker could perform maintenance tasks while workers waited for the next assembly. It also helped to zero buffer parts, because their training gave them enough of an all-round view of the system to spot waste and to figure out ways of assembling things more easily.

Workers' suggestions provide most of the information needed to eliminate defects by re-engineering parts to make them easier to assemble. (All of this intelligent behavior was wasted in U.S. firms until they began imitating the Japanese in the 1980s.) Workers had an incentive to cooperate with management because multiskilling made work more interesting, and because enterprise unions and lifetime employment tied each individual worker's fate/income to the fate/income of his firm. Since they typically worked in teams and received part of their wage as a bonus tied to individual and team productivity, they also faced intense social pressure to cooperate. This white-collar-like relationship allows Japanese firms to get by with only half as many administrative layers as a comparable U.S. car firm, because many of the tasks relegated upward to white-collar workers in the United States are done by blue-collar workers in Japan.

## *Keiretsu* and the Organization of Entrepreneurship

U.S.-style multidivisional firms sourced parts from either completely integrated subsidiaries or disintegrated subcontractors. In contrast, the Japanese developed a new entrepreneurial system of partially disintegrated firms, building on the ruins of their prewar form of organization, the *zaibatsu*. The *zaibatsu* were more centralized versions of the business empires created in Germany by banks, and as in Germany they reflected a need to centralize capital during late industrialization. Japanese banks created and controlled a vast range of subsidiaries. Every bank tried to enter new sectors of the economy as they emerged, extending *zaibatsu* control as the economy grew. The banks' multiple interests cushioned them against instability in the market. Like *kanban* and *kaizen*, *keiretsu* emerged from the circumstances of the 1940s and 1950s.

After the war, the U.S. occupation authorities tried to break up the *zaibatsu*. They introduced legislation prohibiting banks from holding more than 5 percent of any company's equity. Instead, the *zaibatsu* simply decentralized into *keiretsu* by having all their former subsidiaries purchase small amounts of stock in one another. If the former *zaibatsu* looked like a cone, with the controlling bank at its apex, the new *keiretsu* looked like spider webs, with an enormous number of small connections linking together the fates of a large number of nominally independent firms. As the automobile firms grew, they created similar kinds of *keiretsu* based on their supplier networks.[11]

The *keiretsu* structure extended all the way out to the smallest firms. Toyota, for example, sourced parts from about 220 primary subcontractors, who in turn dealt with about 5,000 secondary subcontractors, who dealt with over 30,000 tertiary subcontractors. (The typical car has about 10,000 discrete parts). Eighty percent of these producers were located near Toyota's main assembly plants, facilitating just-in-time parts delivery.[12] In many cases Toyota had a substantial equity stake in those firms; for example, it owns about 40 percent of the electrical parts giant Nippondenso and 40 percent of Aishin Keikinzoku, a components producer.

*Keiretsu* provide the advantages of independent subcontractors and vertically integrated subsidiaries without their disadvantages. Because component suppliers are not directly owned and controlled by the car assembly firms, they have an incentive to search for other markets, which keeps them competitive and helps them to innovate. However, because the assembler firms typically have a large equity stake in the component firms, component firms could be sure that they have a long-term relationship with their major customer. Thus, they have incentives to cooperate in parts design, to make long-term investments in better production machinery, and to integrate their production with the assembler's production to facilitate *kanban* practices. In conjunction with *kaizen*, *keiretsu* also helped speed up the design process for cars, allowing Japanese producers to generate and produce a new model in an average of four years as compared with a six-year average for U.S. and European makers. Because of their ties to subcontractors, the assembly firms are willing to provide advance information on proposed models, allowing subcontractors to begin their own design and engineering work before those plans were finalized.

*Keiretsu* also help minimize risk. During the period in which capital was in short supply and allocated, *keiretsu* could combine small amounts of capital from their large number of firms to finance ventures in new sectors of the economy (e.g., computers in the late 1970s) or to finance risky and expensive development projects like new car models. These days *keiretsu* permit coordination across an even larger number of firms than even the largest U.S. car firm can manage. Where GM produces about 70 percent of its parts in-house, the large Japanese firms acquire about 80 percent of their parts from inside their *keiretsu*, but without the administrative headaches GM has. The assembler firm does not have to manage the component producers as a part of its own hierarchy.

Although *keiretsu* structures muted competition among a given set of firms, it did not mute competition among producers in specific industrial sectors. Because each *keiretsu* attempted to enter each major industrial sector, competition was quite fierce. During the 1960s and 1970s, when Japanese auto firms made their greatest productivity and output increases, between seven and nine firms competed over domestic market share, compared with the three present in the U.S. market. The three largest Japanese firms combined never achieved the dominance that GM had with its consistent 45 percent share of the U.S. market.[13]

*Kaizen* and *kanban* were essentially improvements on ideas, such as the seniority system and total quality control, that had first been generated in the United States. Similarly, *keiretsu* were an improvement on the multidivisional firm. The multidivisional firm allowed a company to reduce risk and to allocate capital into new areas, related to its original business, thus gaining economies of scope. *Keiretsu* permitted the same thing, but over a wider range of activity and without losing efficiency from bureaucratization created by mandatory internal purchases and sales from/to subsidiaries.

## "All Together Now"

*Kanban*, *kaizen*, and *keiretsu* rapidly increased the productivity of Japanese car firms to the point where they could compete head on against U.S. firms. In the 1960s Japanese car firms were less efficient than U.S. firms, taking 50 percent more hours of labor to produce all components and assemble them. Continual efforts to improve the production process reduced the number of hours to U.S. levels by 1976. By 1980 the Japanese had created a roughly 30 percent advantage in labor input.[14] Consequently, in 1981, Honda, *which lacked economies of scale*, could land a Civic in Portland, Oregon, for a total cost of about $4,500, while a Detroit-built GM Chevette in Detroit cost $6,000. And the Civic was a better car, because Honda could use its labor savings to install all manner of refinements in an otherwise basic car that was already more reliable than its U.S.–built competitors. Not surprisingly, with this kind of advantage, Japanese exports had taken 25 percent of the U.S. market by the mid-1980s, and, if the production of their U.S. subsidiaries is included, about 33 percent by the early 1990s. Table 14.1 compares labor productivity, measured by the number of person-hours of labor required to assemble a car, and defect rates in 1989.

The inherent efficiencies of the Japanese version of the assembly line combined with verdoorn effects as Japan's own automobile production doubled to over 11 million units between 1970 and 1980, making it the world's largest car producer. This rapid growth also made it impossible for Japanese

TABLE 14.1

## Comparison of Labor Productivity and Defect Rates among Car Manufacturers, 1989

| Owner | Location | Assembly Hours | Defects per 100 Cars | Inventory (days, 8 selected parts) |
|---|---|---|---|---|
| Japanese | Japan | 16.8 | 60 | 0.2 |
| Japanese | N. America | 21.2 | 65 | 1.6 |
| U.S. | N. America | 25.1 | 82 | 2.9 |
| European | Europe | 36.2 | 97 | 2.0 |

SOURCE: James Womack, Daniel Jones, and Daniel Roos, *The Machine That Changed the World* (New York: Dawson Associates, 1992), pp. 92–93.

producers ever to codify their production systems; they had to continually search for new ways to do things. Consequently, they were also forced to search for ever more efficient ways of doing things.

In contrast, U.S. production floated around 8 million units, and thus U.S. firms' share of world production fell from 57 percent in 1960 to 36 percent in 1990. (See Table 14.2; Figure 11.1 [p. 246] provides an additional comparison by the *location* of production.) As with British metals producers in the late nineteenth century, stagnation in the absolute number of units they produced hindered U.S. efforts to figure out how to react to the Japanese threat. U.S. producers had already codified their production systems during the 30-year period in which the U.S. car market stabilized at around 10 million units. (As we saw in Chapter 13, this codification did allow U.S. firms to transplant production to low-skill zones such as Mexico.) The introduction of voluntary export restraints on Japanese cars in 1981 motivated those firms to transplant production to the United States, just as U.S. and German firms had gone multinational into Britain in the 1900s. And just as U.S. and German firms then squeezed the British out of their own domestic market, those Japanese trans-

TABLE 14.2

## Relative Share of World Car Market by Ownership of Company, 1970–1990, Selected Years[a]

| Country | 1970 | 1975 | 1980 | 1985 | 1990 |
|---|---|---|---|---|---|
| Japan | 22.4 | 26.0 | 33.7 | 32.1 | 37.3 |
| Big Three[b] | 14.6 | 19.0 | 21.7 | 19.2 | 24.2 |
| Rest | 7.8 | 7.0 | 12.0 | 12.9 | 15.1 |
| U.S. Big Three | 47.0 | 44.2 | 33.3 | 41.3 | 36.0 |
| European | 30.7 | 29.9 | 33.1 | 26.7 | 24.8 |

[a]Totals may not add to 100 because of rounding.
[b]Toyota, Nissan, Honda.
SOURCE: DRI International, *World Automotive Forecast*, various issues.

plants showed every sign of squeezing American-based multinationals out of their core domestic market.

Despite this situation, and unlike British firms, U.S. firms proved adept at trying to incorporate the innovations that gave Japanese firms their competitive edge. By 1992 U.S. firms had made substantial advances. GM had generated the new Saturn division, in which teams produced small cars using some *kanban* and *kaizen* principles. Saturn competed directly with cars like the Corolla and Civic, which had once been the core of the Japanese threat. Ford had increased its overall productivity to near Japanese levels through the introduction of U.S. versions of the three *k*'s and a strategic alliance with Mazda. The alliance with Mazda gave Ford an open window on Japanese production advantages. For its new LH models (e.g., the Intrepid), Chrysler had made a major investment in a new Japanese-style plant, with loading bays located near assembly points to facilitate *kanban* inventory control, and a determination to hold no more than 8 hours of inventory and to use team work principles. In 1992, U.S. automakers regained about 2 percent of the market from the Japanese, partly because of correct perceptions that the quality gap between comparable U.S. and Japanese models had shrunk, and partly because the recession made consumers more price sensitive (see Figure 14.1).

Meanwhile, the growth of Japanese firms has begun to level off. As Chapter 11 argued, their transnationalization into the U.S. market is likely to rob them of some of their competitive advantages. The days when the car industry could draw the best blue-collar workers out of the labor force and assure their loyalty through lifetime employment and rapidly rising wages are gone. Today younger Japanese workers try to avoid jobs characterized by the three *d*'s: dirty, dangerous, and dull. The dispersion of production abroad actually led to the unprecedented closing of a Japanese factory by Nissan in 1993.

*Figure 14.1  U.S. Car and Light Truck Market Share by Producer, 1992*

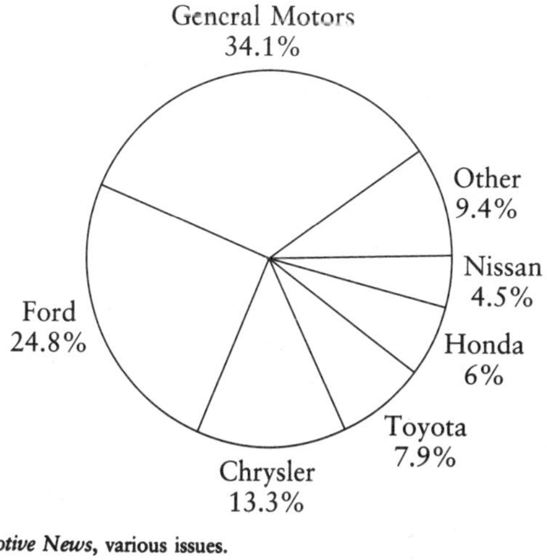

SOURCE: *Ward's Automotive News*, various issues.

## What Now? High-Tech Industries

Just like U.S. and German producers in the 1890s relative to British ones, Japanese producers have outclassed U.S. producers in the mass production industries that made up the core of the old growth cluster. What about the new set of leading sectors, however? Ultimately, U.S. supremacy and the German threat to Britain rested on their ability to generate a whole new set of leading-sector industries that the British could not. Japanese producers have posed a similar threat to U.S. producers in the high-technology—that is, leading-sector—industries of the 1980s and 1990s, but the Japanese challenge still falls short of that generated by U.S. and German producers in the nineteenth century.

The latest growth cluster is made up of information processing industries. The new source of energy, at least until photovoltaic generation of electricity becomes economically viable, is the saving of energy through the use of instant electronic transfers between data processing devices, preferably using wireless technologies like satellites and microwaves. Faxes, for example, permit information transfers without having to physically move a document. Similarly, it is now possible to download specifications and to manufacture goods at a distance without having to transfer blueprints, tooling, and other physical goods. The key technology in this cluster is the integrated circuit (IC) in its various forms, like memory chips (DRAMs), application-specific chips (ASICs), and microprocessor units (MPUs). The storage capacity of ICs has doubled every three years, from roughly 1 kilobit (1k) for DRAMs in 1972 to 4 megabits (4m) in 1990. Currently, 16m and 64m DRAMs are in the pilot stages of production. This advance has permitted a 28 percent per year decline in the cost of processing information since the 1960s, roughly *seven* times the rate of decline in the cost of cotton textiles during 1780–1815.[15]

Much like the internal combustion engine, ICs supply the motor that drives a wide range of goods, including the now ubiquitous personal computer. This hard innovation has facilitated a change in soft technologies of the production process, away from mass production using dedicated machine tools and toward a more flexible production process using more general-purpose tools. The totemic worker in this new production process is the "white-collarized" skilled worker, who is paid for acting responsibly and applying his or her skills to the generation of newer products, produced more rapidly and efficiently. Just coming over the horizon are allied processes based on information transformation, including biotechnologies, optoelectronics, and a wide variety of entertainments (e.g., high-definition TV [HDTV]). Given the importance and dynamism of this cluster, the competitive balance among U.S., Japanese, and European producers clearly affects the United States' overall position in the global economy. If it can't sustain and retain its lead, it ends up looking like Britain.

U.S. firms made the major innovations in this cluster. Defense and space contracts funded much of the research effort prior to innovation, and government contracts helped push IC production far enough down the learning curve during the 1960s to make ICs commercially viable for civilian computing uses.

Cheap processing capacity led to explosive growth, with new start-up firms becoming industrial giants in the space of a decade. For example, Intel started in a garage and now dominates microprocessor production, and Microsoft, with a few thousand employees, has a market capitalization greater than the ailing GM. Other new companies used these technologies to displace older, less adaptable firms. Wal-Mart's use of electronic point-of-sale information to control its inventories allowed it to displace Sears as America's largest retailer by 1990.

With the largest collection of innovating and end-use firms, as well as the world's largest final market for computing, the United States naturally dominated this cluster well into the 1970s. At the end of the 1970s U.S. firms had 70 percent of the $15 billion world market for ICs, the Japanese had only 15 percent, and European and other producers shared the rest. By the mid-1980s, however, Japanese firms had displaced U.S. producers as the dominant makers of memory chips (DRAMs) and had taken a roughly equal share of the total world market. In 1972 the 10 largest producers of ICs were U.S. firms; by 1987 seven of the top 10 were Japanese firms. What happened?

The Japanese combined the strengths of *kaizen, kanban,* and *keiretsu* with judicious amounts of state-run industrial policy. This allowed them to catch up to and temporarily displace U.S. producers. The Japanese already had a large and growing end-market for ICs: their consumer electronics industry. Consumer electronics accounted for about 50 percent of IC consumption in Japan, compared with only 15 to 20 percent in the United States. This industry combined many elements of mass production with strong consumer desires for differentiated goods. The three *k*'s permitted the six big Japanese electronics producers to continually vary their models while still gaining economies of scale. All these electronics producers wanted to have in-house capacity to produce ICs, which were becoming an integral part of consumer electronics.

The Japanese state also wanted IC production. Its strategists in the Ministry for International Trade and Industry (MITI) had targeted information industries as early as the 1960s. When the 1973 oil shock made the future of Japan's energy-intensive basic industry look quite shaky, they targeted ICs as well. As with all late developers, they sheltered the domestic market from foreign competition, forcing U.S. producers to license their patents, delaying U.S. DFI into the Japanese market, and using government purchases to stimulate local production.

The basic problem was not so much an absence of demand as of supply, and the basic problem with local production was that local firms could not fabricate chips efficiently. MITI consolidated state and private R&D programs in ICs into one program in 1975, the so-called Very Large Scale Integrated Circuit (VLSIC) program. It allocated $250 to $350 million in funding over four years, with half coming from the government and half from the six large firms. Roughly one-third of the funds were spent buying most advanced U.S. IC manufacturing and quality-testing equipment. This equipment was reverse engineered, thereby permitting Japanese firms to learn how to make their own equipment. With their own equipment, the Japanese could make export-quality ICs, and they entered the market for 16k DRAMs in the late 1970s, surprising U.S. producers and capturing about two-fifths of the market. Japanese attention to quality—*kaizen*—proved their major advantage. By 1981 Japanese firms had captured 70 percent of the market for 64K DRAMs.

Even so, the Japanese did not fully displace U.S. producers, and U.S. firms' strengths and their relationship to the extensive government-sponsored public R&D system allowed them to regain their competitive edge. Japan's particular strengths had allowed its firms to catch up to U.S. producers only in certain areas. Put simply, wherever manufacturing qua manufacturing was important and technology reasonably standard, Japanese firms tended to prevail; wherever technology was in flux and innovation and market responsiveness were important, U.S. firms tended to prevail.[16] Japanese firms tended to dominate the production of highly standardized ICs, like DRAMs, and of the components that went into, for example, personal computers, but they did not dominate MPU production or the design and assembly of the various sorts of PCs.

Japanese weaknesses apparently stemmed from some of the very factors that gave them their competitive edge when they engaged in catchup activities.[17] While *kaizen* permitted, indeed encouraged, the constant incremental improvements needed for catching up, it hindered the kind of radical breakthroughs on which technological leadership ultimately rested. Japanese state policy encouraged collaborative research among firms trying to catch up to established leaders; the firms' common interest in catching up gave the state a common goal around which to organize their research.[18] In new areas, however, firms had fewer common interests, and their *keiretsu*-driven struggle for market share made them wary of disclosing their strengths in those new areas.

Meanwhile, Japan lacked the kind of publicly supported basic R&D infrastructure that the U.S. has provided since the 1862 Morrill Land Grant College Act. The most dynamic U.S. firms and industries have emerged from precisely this infrastructure. WordPerfect's parent corporation emerged from a computer science department at Brigham Young University funded by the National Science Foundation; biotechnology firms from biomedical complexes in the San Francisco bay area, Boston, Philadelphia, and other college towns; and the aerospace industry from continuous Defense Department funding. Japanese inability to jump into new technologies made them vulnerable to challenges from other countries playing catchup. South Korea's giant electronics firms, for example, seriously eroded Japan's control over standardized DRAMs by 1992, taking about 25 percent of the world market. Korea's Samsung seems likely to beat Japanese producers to the market with 16m and 64m DRAMs.[19]

Telling examples of Japanese firms' particular weaknesses are their eroding dominance in personal and especially laptop computers and the potential obsolescence of their HDTV program. They should excel in personal computers, for they require small, reliable components and have high economies of scale and steep learning curves. Moreover, Japanese firms dominate several of its key technologies, like LCD screens and disk drives. By 1992, however, a set of small, highly innovative, risk-taking U.S. firms had regained market dominance. Because U.S. firms design the software and MPUs that run PCs, they determine technical standards. U.S. firms were able to adapt to Japanese-style rapid product development, but Japanese firms had a harder time developing world-class standards and behaving responsively to rapid changes in the marketing and servicing of PCs. Consequently, by 1991, Japanese firms' share of final sales of PCs in the United States had declined to only 6.4 percent.[20] Meanwhile, U.S. firms' share of the Japanese PC market was rising.

HDTV reveals the Japanese state's weaknesses in organizing R&D.[21] In the 1970s, MITI, the Ministry of Post and Telegraph, and the national television company launched a much heralded cooperative R&D program with industry in HDTV, leading to the development of the MUSE broadcasting standard and its related equipment. MUSE reflected the limited data processing capacity of the early 1980s. Consequently, MUSE was a mixture of digital and analog technologies, using analog technology to save on data processing time. A more adventuresome approach would have aimed for full digitization. By the end of the 1980s, processing power made it possible to design fully digitized HDTV technology; an American firm did so, making Japan's MUSE standard and equipment instantly obsolete. (It did not, however, eliminate Japanese firms' manufacturing expertise or the knowledge they acquired from trying to create MUSE.)

U.S. and Japanese firms thus reached a kind of dynamic equilibrium by the beginning of the 1990s. This equilibrium took its institutional form in a series of strategic alliances between technologically dynamic U.S. firms and high-quality Japanese manufacturers.[22] The alliance between Sony and Apple Computer in the early 1980s foreshadowed these alliances. In that alliance, Sony contributed its manufacturing wizardry, including its ability to miniaturize electronic circuitry (for example, the 3.5-inch floppy diskette drive), while Apple contributed its design and software skills (for example, Macintosh's icon-based menu software). For firms from both countries, these alliances guaranteed the political clout needed to insulate trade from overt protectionist pressures and covert, *keiretsu*-generated resistance to buying outside the group. It also signaled a joint U.S.–Japanese manufacturing assault on the highly protected European market that paralleled the emerging U.S.–Japanese financial alliance (see Chapter 10).

# From the Bottom Up, From the Top Down

Despite catchup activity, residual U.S. strengths, and the inherent limitations of the Japanese model, the U.S. hegemonic position seriously eroded over the 1980s. The inherent strengths of the three *k*'s — *kanban, kaizen,* and *keiretsu* — are nowhere more clear than in Japanese firms' responses to U.S. macroeconomic and trade policy. Because the United States was unable to influence the investment patterns of U.S. firms directly, and because the Reagan administration's hostility to labor precluded any significant effort to create a new compromise like that worked out in the 1930s, U.S. policymakers used a mixture of extraordinary devaluations of the dollar and voluntary export restraints to stem the Japanese onslaughts of the 1970s and 1980s. (See Chapters 10 and 13.) From 1970 to 1973 the yen rose 36 percent against the dollar, the largest rise in the currency of any developed country in those years; from 1976 to 1978 the yen appreciated 41 percent; and from 1985 to 1987 it appreciated nearly 100 percent.[23] Despite these three *endaka*—high yen shocks—Japanese firms were able to continue exporting profitably to the U.S. market. The three *k*'s permitted Japanese firms to diversify in the face of VERs and to shift their product mix up-market into less price-sensitive goods— for example, the Lexus, Infiniti, and Acura cars, and smaller yet better camcorders.

Ultimately, this export drive combined with U.S. macroeconomic policy choices to erode U.S. hegemony from above. Japanese strength from below was a precondition for the erosion from above, but U.S. policy choices hastened the erosion of U.S. dominance. The next chapter compares the erosion of the U.S. position with that of the British in the pre– and post–World War I periods. Unlike this chapter, which looked at this process from the bottom up, the next looks at it from the top down, examining international financial structures.

---

## Notes

1. Paul Kennedy, *Rise and Fall of the Great Powers* (New York: Random House, 1987), p. 330; World Bank, *World Development Report* (New York: Oxford University Press, 1992), p. 223. See Michael Dertouzos et al., *Made in America* (Cambridge, Mass.: MIT Press, 1989) and its companion volumes, *Working Papers of the MIT Commission on Industrial Productivity in America* (Cambridge, Mass.: MIT Press, 1989), 2 vols.

2. Stamp presses make body panels and the like out of flat sheet metal; dies are the molds that actually give the metal its new form. The press stamps the die(s) over the flat sheet metal.

3. The most enjoyable study of this environment is a lovely bit of admittedly biased ethnography; see Ben Hamper, *Rivethead* (New York: Warner Books, 1992). For more formal studies, see Richard Edwards, *Contested Terrain* (New York: Basic Books, 1973), which looks at large U.S. manufacturing firms; Michael Burawoy, *Manufacturing Consent* (Chicago: University of Chicago Press, 1979), which looks at the machine tool industry; and Ronald Dore, *British Factory—Japanese Factory* (Berkeley: University of California Press, 1973), which provides a comparative perspective. Charles Sabel, *Work and Politics* (Cambridge: Cambridge University Press, 1982) and William Lazonick, *Competitive Advantage on the Shop Floor* (Cambridge, Mass.: Harvard University Press, 1990) provide different synthetic looks across a range of industries.

4. Victor Pucik, "White Collar Human Resource Management: A Comparison of the U.S. and Japanese Automobile Industries," *Columbia Journal of World Business* 19, no. 3 (Fall 1984): 87–94; Raphael Kaplinski, "Restructuring the Capitalist Labour Process," *Cambridge Journal of Economics* 12, no. 34 (1988): 451–470; James Womack, Daniel Jones, and Daniel Roos, *The Machine That Changed the World* (New York: Dawson Associates, 1992).

5. See David Halberstam, *The Reckoning* (New York: Avon Books, 1986), for a fine analysis of Detroit's mind-set.

6. Lawrence J. White, "The Automobile Industry," in Walter Adams, ed., *Structure of American Industry* (New York: Macmillan, 1982), pp. 153–155, 168.

7. See Halberstam, *The Reckoning*, chs. 14–17, Michael Cusumano, *Japanese*

*Automobile Industry* (Cambridge, Mass.: Harvard University Press, 1985), and Womack et al., *Machine That Changed the World,* for accounts of technological and managerial borrowing.

8. If Hamper's *Rivethead* is to be believed, the UAW estimate is a generous one. He reports that workers routinely doubled up on jobs; that is, one man worked two jobs while the other slept or did not show up for work.

9. See Dore, *British Factory—Japanese Factory;* David Cole, *Japanese Blue Collar* (Berkeley: University of California Press, 1971); and Andrew Gordon, *The Evolution of Labor Relations in Japanese Heavy Industry, 1853–1945* (Cambridge, Mass.: Harvard University Press, 1985).

10. Lifetime employment did not fully bind workers to firms. Workers still quit and were fired, but separation rates were roughly half those in U.S. manufacturing; see Cole, *Japanese Blue Collar,* pp. 113–127, and Ronald Dore, *Japan at Work: Markets, Management and Flexibility* (Paris: OECD, 1989). Temporary workers, who constitute about a tenth of the manufacturing labor force, also did not get a lifetime guarantee.

11. The *keiretsu* structure is not unique to Japan. Similar organizational forms can be found in Germany, the United States, and Britain. Nowhere else, however, save in South Korea, is the *keiretsu* form so pervasive. South Korean *chaebol* are an uneasy mixture of *zaibatsu* and *keiretsu.*

12. Richard Florida and Martin Kenney, "Beyond Mass Production: Production and the Labor Process in Japan," *Politics and Society* 16, no. 1 (1988): 121–158.

13. However, as the big four Japanese firms—Toyota, Nissan, Honda, and Mitsubishi—achieved global economies of scale in the 1980s, the five small firms— Toyo Kogyo (Mazda), Fuji Motor (Subaru), Daihatsu, Suzuki, and Isuzu—all found their competitive position and market share rapidly eroding. Each had to make an alliance to survive: Mazda with Ford; Fuji with Nissan; Isuzu, Daihatsu, and Suzuki with GM; and Daihatsu also with Toyota. The Japanese industry is likely headed for a period of consolidation like that in the United States in the 1940s and 1950s, when the minor auto firms collapsed into American Motors and the U.S. big three attained their dominant position.

14. Alan Altschuler et al., *Future of the Automobile* (Cambridge, Mass.: MIT Press, 1986), pp. 145–162, especially p. 160. William Abernathy, Kim Cole, and Alan Kantrow, *Industrial Renaissance* (New York: Basic Books, 1983), pp. 58–59, 61, suggests that the Japanese labor input advantage in small-car assembly ranged between 1.2 to 1 and 2.4 to 1. For a comprehensive analysis of the differences between and among U.S.-, European-, and Japanese-style production that extends the analysis to topics omitted here, such as design, marketing, and service, see Womack et al., *Machine That Changed the World.*

15. Kenneth Flamm, *Targeting the Computer* (Washington D.C.: Brookings Institution, 1987), p. 9.

16. But see Steven Cohen and John Zysman, *Manufacturing Matters* (New York: Basic Books, 1987) and Richard Florida and Martin Kenney, *Breakthrough Illusion* (New York: Basic Books, 1990) for arguments that manufacturing per se is critical.

17. Herbert Kitschelt, "Industrial Governance Structures, Innovation Strategies and the Case of Japan," *International Organization* 45, no. 4 (Autumn 1991): 454–493, provides an explanation, based in organizational theory, for the difference in competencies between the United States and Japan. A similar but less pessimistic interpretation can be found in Christopher Freeman, "Japan: A New National System of Innovation?" pp. 330–348 in Giovanni Dosi et al., *Technical Change and Economic Theory* (London: Pinter, 1988). Steven Collins, "Chips, Genes and the State: The Political Economy of Science and Technology in the United States and Japan," University of

Virginia, Ph.D. diss., 1994, blends both theoretical explanations in an empirical study of those two sectors.

18. Daniel Okimoto, *Between MITI and Market* (Stanford, Calif.: Stanford University Press, 1989).

19. *New York Times*, December 17, 1992, pp. D1, D5.

20. *New York Times*, November 24, 1992, pp. D1, D4.

21. Gregory Noble, "The Politics of HDTV in Japan," paper presented to the American Political Science Association Annual Meeting, September 1992, photocopy.

22. See Peter Cowhey and Jonathan Aronson, *Managing the World Economy: Consequences of Corporate Alliances* (New York: Council on Foreign Relations, 1993).

23. World Bank, *World Tables*, vol. I (Baltimore: Johns Hopkins University Press, 1983), pp. 238–239.

CHAPTER 15

# U.S. Hegemony: Declining from the Top Down?

For the world economy to be stabilized, there needs to be a stabilizer—one stabilizer.

*Charles Kindleberger*

Is American hegemony declining? And if so what are the likely consequences of this decline? In the 1890s and in the 1970s, Britain and the United States, respectively, lost ground relative to newer, more dynamic economies. Hegemony eroded from the bottom up. Yet this erosion left a residue of financial and market power standing. Both countries had massive stocks of overseas assets (and thus earnings), and both could exercise market power because they had the largest single import market in the world. Both in the 1920s and the 1980s, however, these financial and market advantages also eroded.

In the 1920s the decline of British hegemony and the United States' reluctance to take up the reins certainly contributed to the Great Depression.[1] Today's situation resembles the 1920s in several important respects, but it would be alarmist to argue that another great depression is around the corner. The key similarity between the 1920s and the 1980s is that in each case, the hegemon's efforts to deal with a global debt crisis eroded its hegemonic advantages at the level of the international economy. In each period the hegemon allowed its current account position to deteriorate to permit its debtors to service their debt. In both periods, the hegemon partly financed this deterioration by borrowing from a new, more dynamic economy, in order to avoid having to make hard choices between allocating costs among either its financial or productive sector, and about decreasing its citizens' personal consumption. In each period, this short-term solution unraveled after about a decade, leading to a global financial crisis.

Unfortunately, the underlying and perhaps proximate causes for instability today look very similar to those in the 1920s. Recall the stylized model from Chapter 8. That model posited an international economic system with three types of countries: a large developed country that is also a large net creditor; several other, and often smaller, developed countries that are only marginally

321

net creditors or perhaps even marginal net debtors; and a large group of highly indebted developed and less developed countries that are mostly primary product exporters. Their debts forced the developed and the LDC agricultural periphery either to run large trade (goods and services) surpluses with developed countries in general or to attract new lending to cover cumulating deficits on the investment income side of their accounts. Other indebted developed countries must also run trade surpluses with the creditor country in order to prevent their own net investment income deficit from cumulating into more debt. Neither group can run a surplus with the other since this would simply aggravate one group's position. Economic stability requires the large creditor country to run a current account deficit, and thus boost exports from debtor countries, or to finance debtors' ongoing current account deficits directly. If the large creditor does neither, the trade system will tend to contract as countries try to maximize their merchandise surplus by restricting their own imports. Crisis in this stylized system comes if the major creditor country (or most of the minor creditors) no longer provides credit directly as loans or indirectly by accepting increased imports. Then all other countries will immediately be forced to reduce their imports. The more abrupt the contraction of lending, the more abrupt the efforts to constrict imports.

## Debt Structures Today

As in the 1920s, two interconnected debt problems exist. First, both the agricultural periphery and most of the newly industrializing countries (NICs) carry high and unsustainable levels of debt. Second, high levels of debt in the developed country markets for peripheral and NIC exports preclude the kinds of current account deficits needed to amortize the developed country's debt. Let us start with developed country debt first, reflecting a continued U.S. perspective on the problem.

### Debtors

Developed country debt largely arose from efforts to sustain existing living standards in the face of the dual oil shocks and economic instability of the 1970s, and then from an orgy of deficit financing during the early 1980s. This deficit spending created public debt, particularly in Europe. States borrowed domestically at first, and when local supplies of cash ran out they turned to foreign lenders. The weakest economies experienced an almost immediate flowthrough of deficit spending into extra imports and rising foreign debt. By 1990, for example, Australia owed over U.S. $100 billion, making it absolutely the world's third largest overseas debtor, behind the United States and Brazil, and with a foreign debt to GDP ratio equivalent to Brazil's. Belgium and Italy ran up *net* government debts exceeding their GDP by the end of the 1980s, though mostly from domestic sources.[2]

As in the 1920s, these indebted developed countries could not cover their investment income deficits with each other, leaving only exports to either

LDCs or NICs, borrowing from creditor countries, or exports to creditors. But, pressured by the International Monetary Fund to maximize their trade surplus, most LDCs and NICs behaved exactly as their 1920s counterparts did under pressure from the Bank of England. They erected a phenomenal array of import controls and undertook massive devaluations during the late 1980s. The sustained decline in oil prices removed OPEC as a major importer.

Instead, during the 1980s most developed countries chose to finance their current account deficits by borrowing from the few net creditors left in the system, namely, Japan and Germany, with Britain and the Netherlands a distant third and fourth. For example, from 1988 to 1990 the OECD–European countries ran an annual average current account surplus of about $7 billion with the rest of the world. But Germany alone was running a surplus of $55 billion, implying a $48 billion net deficit for the rest of OECD-Europe.[3] OECD-Europe thus borrowed heavily from Germany to make ends meet. This ploy worked until 1991, at which time developed country external debt had risen to post–World War II highs and the pool of capital suddenly evaporated in the heat of German reunification.

The sources of debt among the developing countries closely parallel those in the 1920s, as do their problems. Like the big pre-1914 debtors, all the major LDC debtors pursued deliberate policies of developmental borrowing even before the 1979–80 oil shock. (See Chapter 12.) The success of these debt-funded development strategies led to debt servicing difficulties after the oil shock. This borrowing created an oversupply of exported *manufactured* commodities, and terms of trade for LDC exporters fell.[4] Unlike the interwar period, this terms of trade decline encompassed LDC manufactured exports, too.

Thus, even a country with a highly diversified export base, like Brazil, experienced a terms of trade decline of 45 percent from 1977 to 1985. This decline began *before* the second oil shock and was magnified by it, and roughly parallels the overall decline for all LDCs.[5] Like the sudden change in postwar demand patterns in the 1920s, the 1970–80 oil shock aggravated the NIC's terms of trade decline. As in the 1920s, debtors needed to finance their growing debt service by either borrowing new money from creditors or by generating export surpluses with those countries. But, as in the interwar period, rising levels of external debt and rising levels of protectionism in most developed countries eliminated them as an outlet for goods, except for the United States. The alternative sources of capital and outlets for goods, Germany and Japan, were not as promising as might be thought.

## The United States in the 1980s

During the 1980s the United States played the same role Britain had played in the 1920s, but the United States had more economic breathing room than 1920s Britain. Like Britain in the 1920s, the United States tried to organize a flow of new lending to the debtors after Mexico nearly defaulted in August 1982. The fiscal bureaucracies of the U.S. government, using the International Monetary Fund as their instrument, coerced U.S. and other banks into refinancing LDC debt as a condition of those banks' receiving such interest payments as LDCs could make.[6] As in Britain in the 1920s, this outflow matched neither past outflows nor the demand for new lending. In fact, the outflow of interest, commissions, and occasionally principal from LDCs often exceeded new capital inflows.[7] Net capital outflows from debtors meant that they had to export, for all overseas interest payments ultimately take the form of exported goods. (See also Chapter 7.)

At the same time that U.S. macroeconomic policy during the 1980s created and/or exacerbated the international debt crisis, it also reinforced the tendency to import rather than lend. The Federal Reserve kept interest rates at historic highs, driving the dollar's exchange rate value to historic highs (160 percent of its March 1973 value) as international capital flowed into the United States.[8] Meanwhile, Reagan lowered taxes while roughly doubling defense spending in nominal terms. Not surprisingly, people holding fistfuls of overvalued dollars rushed to spend them on cheap imports, particularly because many U.S. goods had gotten a reputation for shoddiness during the 1970s. Yuppies gobbled up Italian shoes, French wines, German cars, and big Japanese TV sets; plain old working people bought out K-Marts full of cheap clothes, furniture, and microwave ovens.

High interest rates also hampered investment. In 1920s Britain, falling investment rates worsened an ongoing competitive decline vis-à-vis other advanced industrial economies. By the end of the 1980s, the United States by some measures invested slightly less in *absolute* terms than the Japanese did (in their smaller economy), while consuming about 97 percent of GNP. This low rate of investment both reflected and caused continued uncompetitiveness. Firms asked why they should invest if they could not compete, and by not investing they guaranteed that they would not become competitive.

So like Britain, the United States acted as a market rather than as a lender of last resort. Alone among the creditor countries at the beginning of the 1980s, the United States consistently ran current account deficits. While the United States protected its domestic market during this period, and indeed set the pattern for protection elsewhere, the U.S. market remained relatively open compared to other developed country markets. Even in the highly protected and politicized textiles and garment sector, U.S. imports nearly doubled in real terms during the 1980s. Like 1920s Britain, in the 1980s the Treasury and Federal Reserve made defeating inflation a priority over increasing exports. Just as British exporters struggled with an overvalued pound in the 1920s, U.S. interest rates led to an overvalued U.S. dollar that crippled exporters and made imports cheap. High interest rates also put enormous pressure on debtors to import less and export more.

Whatever the domestic origins of the rising U.S. trade deficit of the 1980s in macroeconomic policy, in policymaking coalitions or factory-floor realities, its consequences at the level of the international economy are clear. The United States allowed debtor LDCs (and, during the period of the overvalued dollar in the mid-1980s, debtor European countries) to run the current account surpluses they needed in order to service debt. In 1987 the United States absorbed 22 percent of the world's manufactured exports, up from 11 percent in 1975. Moreover, the United States also absorbed over 50 percent of NIC exports of manufactures. In contrast, despite an economy half the size of the United States, Japan in 1987 absorbed only 4 percent of world manufactured exports, up from 2 percent in 1975.[9]

Since this point runs counter to the prevailing image of Japan as the major source of the U.S. trade deficit in the 1980s, it is worth some repetition: *the enormous U.S. trade deficits of the 1980s owe much more to "extra" imports from and especially "lost" exports to indebted LDCs than they do to expanded imports of Japanese goods.* The United States had a cumulative current account deficit of $998,097,000,000 — nearly $1 trillion — from 1980 to 1989. Deficits with LDCs account for 47 percent of this total, while the bilateral deficit with Japan accounts for only 38 percent.[10] Lest this seem a comparison of apples and oranges, it should be noted that the LDCs as a group had an aggregate GDP slightly *smaller* than Japan's by the end of the decade. Logically, then, they should account for a smaller proportion of the deficit as well. While U.S. exports to Japan grew during the 1980s, both absolutely and relative to total U.S. exports, exports to LDCs fell absolutely and relatively.

Like Britain's deteriorating trade position in the 1920s, the U.S. current account deficit kept countries from resorting to even harsher nonmarket measures of balancing. Unfortunately, just as in the 1920s, this U.S. trade deficit could not continue indefinitely. When Britain ran out of cash at the end of the 1920s, it retreated into an economic space small enough for it to manage with its diminished resources, its empire. Similarly, by the end of the 1980s the United States was unable to continue financing global trade and was retreating to a much smaller zone of influence in the Western Hemisphere via the North American Free Trade Agreement with Canada and Mexico.

By serving as a market of last resort during the 1980s, the United States staved off LDC and perhaps some developed country default, but it also undermined its ability to continue functioning as either a lender or a market of last resort. U.S. foreign and domestic economic policy during the 1980s literally liquidated U.S. leadership. Although the United States began the 1980s as a large net creditor, it owed as much as $375 billion net at the end of 1990.[11] As in the 1920s, when the United States financed Britain's liquidation of its hegemony, the United States, too, had a financier through the 1980s.

## Japan in the 1980s

Here conventional wisdom is right: during the 1980s the Japanese played a role similar to that which the United States played in the 1920s — financing the U.S. current account deficit and keeping things going during the 1980s. From 1983 to 1989 the Japanese lent nearly $600 billion overseas. (The Germans lent not quite $240 billion, but most of it went to Europe to cover non-German Europe's persistent current account deficit.) Like U.S. lending in the 1920s, most Japanese lending occurred as portfolio investment.

Just as the United States in the 1920s sparked overseas lending, Japan took the lead in the 1980s. Japan's sweeping liberalization of its financial system in the early 1980s opened pipelines for a vast private capital outflow.

Like 1920s U.S. lenders, Japanese private lenders shied away from uncredit-worthy LDCs. Instead, as the 1920s United States financed Britain and Europe, the Japanese chose to finance the United States, indirectly allowing it to provide a market for shaky LDC debtors. Like the United States in the interwar period, the 1980s Japanese lent hesitantly, and mostly to other nearby creditors, and they do not yet appear fully committed to making the internal political and economic changes necessary to keep the international economy functioning. As with the United States in the 1920s, this behavior provided only a short-term solution to the debt problem, for it allowed LDCs to continue piling up debt while the United States' ability to absorb exports declined, exposing the world economy to the risk of an end to Japanese lending.

Like 1920s U.S. lending, Japanese lending began to ebb at the end of the 1980s. (In 1992, Japan had a small net capital *inflow*.) As in the United States in 1929, saturated markets and worried central bankers put a brake on Japan's investment and speculative sprees. Both supply and demand factors in 1990–91 curtailed the outflow of Japanese investment. Japanese lending in the 1980s was fueled in equal parts by expansion in its monetary base, by property and stock market speculation triggered by this monetary base expansion and the high profits Japanese firms earned in export markets, and by the devaluation of dollar-denominated assets after 1986. From 1983 to 1987 banking assets rose 80 percent in Japan, driven by a similar rise in land prices.

On the demand side, both the dollar's steep slide relative to the yen and the U.S. recession of 1990–92 along with related crises in commercial real estate reduced the enormous U.S. appetite for Japanese funds and Japanese willingness to invest in the United States. Most Japanese investment went into U.S. Treasury bonds and real estate. A rash of books like *Yen!* and *The Gnomes of Tokyo* and novels like *Rising Sun* predicted that rapidly expanding Japanese influence would create a stranglehold on America's future.[12] A better title might have been *The Innocents Abroad* (if we reverse some of Twain's political ironies). Far from being all-powerful, Japanese portfolio investors lost enormous amounts of money to American sellers with good timing. The value of the dollar fell by half against the yen from 1985 to 1988. As a result, Japanese purchasers of dollar-denominated bonds and stock had a *negative* net return of about 25 percent. Lenders to purchasers, and direct purchasers of expensive Hawaiian, Californian, and New York real estate also saw their collateral and investments lose value when U.S. property markets collapsed after 1990.

On the supply side, much of the money Japanese banks and other private investors lent overseas involved the export of capital created by the explosion of stock and property market values in Japan after 1985. From 1982 to 1989 Japanese land and stock prices more than tripled. Since 1990, however, both property and stock values have tumbled, as Japanese monetary policy has eerily tracked U.S. policy in the 1920s. From 1987 to 1990 the Japanese money supply measured broadly (M2) increased at roughly 10 percent per annum, compared to roughly 2 percent in the United States in those same years. Like the U.S. Federal Reserve in 1928, the Bank of Japan significantly tightened monetary policy in late 1990 to deflate the speculative boom, dropping money supply growth to 1.8 percent in 1991 and zero in 1992.[13] Japan's central bank succeeded in deflating the boom, perhaps too much so. By 1993 the Nikkei stock index stood at 50 percent of its 1989 peak (and, while it never started raining stockbrokers in Tokyo, scandals did force brokerage presidents to resign). Property values fell 20 percent, perhaps on their way toward the 30 percent total fall that would bring land values back to their historic level in relation to GDP.

Falling stock and especially property prices undermined the ability of Japanese banks to lend either at home or abroad. About 40 percent of lending in Japan is directly collateralized by property; falling values force banks to call in loans or slow loan growth. Meanwhile, nonbank financial institutions, heavily involved in property speculation, have been collapsing alongside declining property prices. Even if property prices do not continue falling, as many fear they will, new international banking standards mean that the current drop in property and stock values seriously undercut the ability of Japanese banks to continue lending overseas.[14] In 1987 the G10 countries agreed to bind their banks by a set of capital adequacy standards.[15] These new standards require banks to have risk-adjusted capital to assets (loans) ratios of 8 percent by 1993. Under these accounting rules, Japanese banks were allowed to count 45 percent of unrealized capital gains on stocks and property toward these ratios. At pre-crash values, most Japanese banks easily met the new capital ratio requirements, but by 1992 none came close to meeting the new standard.[16]

If Japan is unable to act as a lender of last resort, might it act as a market of last resort, replacing the United States in this role? Imports did grow 37 percent in volume terms from 1985 to 1988, but the yen appreciated over 100 percent versus the dollar during those same years. Exports from the United States and other dollar-denominated exporters, particularly the Asian NICs, did not increase in a similar proportion. After 1985, Japanese imports of goods from the Asian NICs rose by 20 percent per annum, albeit off of a low base. However, as was true of the U.S. market in the 1920s, structural and political realities essentially close today's Japanese market to imports.

Like the introduction of the assembly line in the 1920s United States, Japanese just-in-time manufacturing and systems for continuous improvement (the three *k*'s) makes many sectors import-resistant simply on the basis of differential productivity. In the most glaring example, the best Japanese car factories produce about 80 percent more vehicles per employee, have 70 percent fewer defects per vehicle, and use about 30 percent fewer labor hours to make a vehicle than the average car factory in the rest of the world.[17] In many other sectors, particularly agriculture, extreme levels of protection prevent Japan from functioning as a market of last resort. More subtle forms of protection also close the market—for example, the tendency to buy from *keiretsu* partners, and the veto that small shopkeepers exercise over the building of stores by large, discount-oriented merchandisers.

Until other countries close the productivity gap between themselves and Japan, they will find it difficult to do the kind of intraindustry trade that is typical of U.S.–European trade. And until the structure of Japanese politics changes to better reflect consumer/worker interests, Japan will not import as much as is needed to create growth in other economies. Without these two reforms, Japan could only function as a lender, not as a market of last resort, during the 1980s, just as the United States lent rather than imported in the 1920s.

And just as in the 1920s United States, political and economic considerations suggest that Japan is unlikely to become a major importer, a market of last resort, in the short run. First, politically powerful sectors of the economy would block any major changes. The small and medium-sized businesses most vulnerable to overseas competition were heavily invested in stock and property markets and are unlikely to countenance more competition from NICs or liberalization of agricultural trade, particularly as the economy slid into recession in early 1992.

Second, even for the larger, export-oriented businesses that presumably have the most to gain from liberalization, liberalization of Japanese import markets has *ambiguous* consequences. Like U.S. firms in the late 1920s, Japanese firms took advantage of their rising stock market to issue equity and undertake massive new investments in fixed productive capital. They invested almost $3 trillion in new production processes from 1986 to 1991, believing that market growth and competitive pressures demanded this kind of investment. When recession hit in 1991–92, Japanese firms were stuck with expensive new plants and no way to amortize the cost, just as U.S. firms ended up with massive overcapacity in the 1930s. In the semiconductor industry, which today occupies roughly the same place in Japan as the auto industry did in the United States in 1929, the investment boom in 1988–90 created excess capacity equal to between 30 and 50 percent of projected consumption. Overcapacity increased Japanese firms' desire to protect their domestic market while pouring excess production into world markets.

The financial costs of liberalizing agricultural markets also preclude major political initiatives by large Japanese firms, because it would further erode their banks' ability to lend, as well as devaluing some of their own assets. Although liberalization could help prevent protectionism in some export markets, the resulting fall in Japanese land values — estimated at 50 percent off the 1989 peak should agricultural trade be completely liberalized — would further undermine the ability of Japanese banks to expand abroad. As a group, large firms are thus likely to split over the issue of liberalization. Politically powerful farmers obviously oppose any liberalization of agricultural markets. After European farmers, Japanese farmers were the second biggest obstacle to completion of the Uruguay GATT Round from 1990 to 1992.

Still, there are historical precedents for the kind of major change we are talking about here. The British accepted precisely these kinds of economic costs in the 1840s when they liberalized agricultural trade. Land prices in Britain fell by 60 percent from 1875 to 1910 in the face of rising grain imports.[18] And a coalition favoring a more open U.S. market emerged from World War II and the Depression. Yet these changes suggest just how difficult change is. In Britain the preexisting fusion of landed capital with industrial capital, fear of industrial unrest, and the Irish famine made repeal of the Corn

Laws possible. It took the disaster of the 1930s to shake open U.S. politics and to create political space for even a limited domestic willingness to contemplate lower protection and international monetary coordination. Even then not much happened until World War II. Should we expect the Japanese to be any more adventuresome than their British or American predecessors?

# Introduction to the Missing Part III

What trends are likely to shape the future? Will a new hegemonic power emerge? And if not, will the global economy slide into the same kind of pit as in the 1930s? Let us try to answer the last, easiest, question first.

## Toward a New Depression?

Several things suggest that the situation is not as bad as 1930. First, the institutionalized deficit and welfare spending created in reaction to the 1930s Depression should prevent the kind of free fall in aggregate demand that crippled U.S. firms and then world trade after 1929. Second, while global trade talks have stalled, negotiations at least continue. Third, Japanese politics are changing, albeit slowly. Finally, while the United States is certainly a net debtor, it is probably not as big a debtor in terms of debt to GDP as the statistics suggest. So even being pessimistic, we have a few more years to try muddling through before the situation gets desperate. However, as the discussion of hegemony and long-term trends will suggest, the most likely scenario for the future is not a replay of the 1930s but of the late nineteenth century. That, too, was a period of intense competition, of falling prices for industrial goods, and of state efforts to protect declining sectors — particularly agriculture — and promote high-tech "sunrise industries" like electricity generation, open hearth steel making, and bicycles. It was also a period during which British control of the world economy first seemed to be receding in the face of sustained challenges from other rapidly industrializing countries.[19]

## A Three-Way Struggle for Hegemony?

What about hegemony? Clearly, the only contenders are the European Community (EC), the United States, and Japan, which, respectively, accounted for 27.9, 24.2, and 13.2 percent of gross world product in 1992. Excluding intra-EC trade, these three areas accounted for half of global trade. In addition, they had the strongest firms, for their TNCs controlled 80 percent of direct foreign investment as of 1989.[20]

The discussion below will concentrate on three areas:

~ Market size: the larger the market, the more powerful the von Thünen effects on agricultural and industrial production in surrounding regions.

~ Penetration of the local market by TNCs: the greater the degree to which the local market is penetrated by foreign TNCs, the more

TABLE 15.1

## Direct Foreign Investment in and by the Three
## Dominant Economies, Late 1980s

| | Stock (1988) | | Flows (annual avg., 1985–89) | |
|---|---|---|---|---|
| Area | Outward | Inward | Outward | Inward |
| EC | | | | |
| $billion | 332 | 239 | 39 | 19 |
| % world total | 34 | 23 | 37 | 19 |
| United States | | | | |
| $billion | 345 | 329 | 18 | 46 |
| % world total | 35 | 31 | 17 | 46 |
| Japan | | | | |
| $billion | 111 | 10 | 24 | — |
| % world total | 11 | 1 | 23 | — |
| World total[a,b] | 974 | 1059 | 105 | 100 |

[a]Excludes intra-EC DFI.
[b]Figures unequal because of reporting errors and omissions.
SOURCE: United Nations Centre on Transnational Corporations, World Investment Report 1991 (New York: United Nations, 1992), p. 32.

likely it is that local firms will not experience verdoorn effects. (Tables 13.4 [p. 296] and 15.1 and Figure 13.1 [p. 297] provide some comparative data on TNC investment.)

~ Potential sources of internal and external political instability.

An assessment of each region's strengths and weaknesses in these three areas suggests that, in regard to hegemony, the world economy is again going back to the future.

### Europe

Europe today is in a rough, if unhappy, economic equilibrium with a slow-growth trajectory. Although German unification stopped capital outflows from Germany, it also allowed European debtors to export more to Germany, servicing their debt. High German interest rates will probably continue to throttle growth in the rest of the EC, but the currency realignments of 1992–93 kept growth in the larger EC economies from being completely choked off. During the 1980s Western Europe added about 3.5 million jobs — about one for every six added in the United States. The 1990s will probably see a similar low-growth trend as firms substitute cheaper Eastern European labor, particularly in the inner tier of countries (the former East Germany, the new Czech republic, and a reviving Poland and Hungary) for expensive Western European labor. Slow employment growth suggests that the EC market will not grow as fast as the Japanese or even the aggregate U.S. market, making the EC less important as a growth pole for other countries.

In the short run, the EC, if unified, remains the world's largest market, even if the non-EC developed economies opt for only partial integration. But this "if" is a big one, not because the EC is likely to unravel, but because unification through the Single European Act (Europe 1992) has run into three rather prosaic sources of opposition. First, neither currency union nor the Maastricht Treaty, which was to confirm this union and the single market, seems to have widespread popular support. Second, the near collapse of the European Monetary System in 1992–93 suggested that individual European states were unwilling to sacrifice local growth and employment to the long-term benefits of harmonizing tax rates and of converging inflation rates, fiscal deficits, and government debt, and that speculators understood this. Finally, as the November 1992 GATT crisis over soybean subsidies showed, various uncompetitive agricultural interests were willing to risk intra-EC discord to continue receiving protection.

These continued divisions suggest that sanguine predictions that the EC will emerge as the dominant economy are farfetched.[21] In fact, Europe will continue to Americanize. Northern Europe's universal welfare states were once the key to factory floor peace and high quality, if not always high productivity. Currently, however, these welfare states are evolving, though at different speeds, toward a smaller, American, market-style model. Meanwhile, Europe faces a worse version of the problems the United States has had with Latin American immigration. North Africans and Eastern Europeans have been flooding in, provoking nationalist reactions and spurring the growth of right-wing parties. Finally, Europe's eastern flank will probably continue to be a zone of instability which, judging by their nonreaction to the disintegration of Yugoslavia, the EC will be able neither to preempt nor to cope with.

Rather than emerging as the dominant economy, Europe seems more likely to become even more than now an economic colony of powerful U.S. and Japanese transnational corporations. Established U.S. TNCs dramatically boosted their investment in the EC, with annual increases of 24.3 percent in the flow of inward investment from 1985 to 1989 (including reinvested earnings). Japanese TNCs also flooded the EC during the late 1980s; their annual investment rose 46 percent during 1985–89.[22] Both seem determined to use their investments as "Trojan horses." Production in any one region or nation within the EC gives them access to the entire market. However, because the EC nations have different attitudes toward and needs for inward investment, both U.S. and Japanese TNCs can extract the best possible terms for investment and generate local political champions for their cause. The investment of Japanese automobile TNCs in Britain is exemplary in this regard. It helped boost British exports and employment during the bleak 1980s, when manufacturing was melting away in other sectors. Consequently, Margaret Thatcher used her famous handbag to hit the French when they raised trade barriers to British-built Japanese cars.

Similarly, Europe's industrial programs in high-tech industries reveal more about their weaknesses in this regard than their strength. The Europeans have allowed U.S. TNCs based in Europe to participate, which means that those U.S. firms will gain as much as the remaining indigenous European firms. (But not necessarily the Japanese: when Fujitsu bought the British computer firm

ICL, ICL was booted out of JESSI, the EC's semiconductor project.) The salience of U.S. and Japanese TNCs in Europe's major industries means that any European success will also reward the United States and Japan. The reverse is not as certain, particularly given Europe's weak ties to the dynamic Asian economies.

In short, Europe appears divided against itself, threatened from within by U.S. and Japanese TNCs and from without by an arc of instability extending from Oran to Murmansk.

*Japan*

In the long term, the Japanese may very well construct the capacity they need to challenge seriously the United States as a major import market, particularly because the world's fastest growing economies are in Japan's backyard—the Asian NICs and China. Japanese domestic investment levels absolutely exceeded U.S. investment levels through the late 1980s and early 1990s, with the Japanese investing more than twice as much per capita as the United States. If GDP growth rates return to their pre–1990–92 recession trends, the Japanese economy will be about three-fourths the size of the United States by the year 2000, positioning it for a serious challenge. Chinese growth—and continued Russian stagnation and fragmentation—will also decrease the United States' leverage over Japan on defense issues. Chinese growth also fuels growth in greater East Asia by drawing in imports of simple capital goods from the four Asian NICs, who in turn get more complex machinery largely from Japan.

Reciprocally, the Japanese seem willing to continue shedding their obsolete industries to the Asian NICs, who in turn have been shedding their own obsolete industries to China. This activity creates strong trade ties. If these Asian outlets for Japanese capital and goods exports and sources for Japanese imports collectively overtake the United States, which currently is Japan's largest trading partner, then the forces that currently impel the Japanese to seek accommodation with the United States will erode.

Of the three major markets, the Japanese market remains the least penetrated by TNCs from the other two countries. (See Tables 13.3 and 15.1.) In contrast, Japanese direct foreign investment grew relatively more rapidly during the 1980s than either U.S. or EC DFI, jumping from 10 percent of U.S. outward flows in 1980 to about 160 percent. Most of this Japanese DFI went to the United States. As stated in Chapter 14, however, this has led to an equilibration of U.S. and Japanese firms' abilities, with the Japanese losing some of their edge and the United States picking up Japanese methods.

Japanese hegemony also requires that the Japanese desire to act as hegemon. As in 1920s America, the very good times that preceded the crash dissuaded Japanese domestic interests from any need to change their positions on international trade. Domestic politics—willingness—is just as important in creating leadership as a country's structural position in the world economy —ability. Turning Japan into a market on the same scale as the EC or the United States, let alone a larger market, would require a domestic political coalition willing and able to implement far-reaching domestic and international policies of restructuring in Japan. It is not clear that the seven-party coalition government that emerged in 1993 can do this. Because change will cause a massive redistribution of power and income among different groups in Japan, it will probably take a catastrophe on the scale of 1929–32 to generate change.

In the short term at least, the Japanese are still somewhat hostage to U.S. economic fortunes. Most analysts point to Japan's financial stake, but its trade stake is equally important. In quantitative terms, the United States is Japan's major export market, and in qualitative terms the United States remains Japan's most *sophisticated* market. Hungry Taiwanese and South Korean firms would like to grab Japanese industries before they are obsolete, rather than wait for Japan to pass them on in its own good time. If Japanese firms are to stay ahead, they need the U.S. market as a testing ground and as a spur to innovation. This Japanese dependence on the U.S. market has its most obvious political expression in the Structural Impediments Initiative talks started in 1989 between the United States and Japan. These talks were designed to remedy what each side thought were the greatest causes of trade friction in their partner. (The Japanese put the U.S. budget deficit on the table.) The United States raised high Japanese land prices as an issue in these talks. The fact that the Japanese would allow this issue to be put on the table, even though lower land prices have enormous political and economic repercussions, shows the degree to which they feel they must conciliate the United States in order to head off pressures for protection in the United States.

In short, Japan is just as unlikely to emerge as the dominant economic power as the EC. Its internal political rigidities make it difficult for it to outflank the United States. Europe is hostile to Japan on economic issues, and the reciprocal of diffuse European ties to Asia is diffuse Asian ties to Europe. As Chapter 14 argued, Japan's soft technological edge is eroding faster than it is gaining on the United States' hard technological edge.

### The United States

But Japanese and EC weakness does not constitute U.S. strength. At best, the United States will continue to be *primus inter pares* among these three economic powers. Financially, the U.S. position resembles that of 1920s Britain, but on the productive side of the economy the United States possesses many competitive and growing industries in the new growth cluster, which 1920s Britain did not. Unlike Britain, the United States has a huge, perhaps crippling budget deficit. But U.S. domestic and foreign debt is denominated in dollars, whereas Britain's foreign debt in the 1920s was not denominated in pounds. This gives the United States much more leverage over the Japanese than the British had over the 1920s United States.

On average, the United States seems to be in the same position Britain was in the 1890s. In fact, the best analogy for the U.S. position is that it is playing the role of Britain in an 1890s-type world without any America looming over its western horizon. In terms of size, Japan in the 1990s is not America in the 1890s. The U.S. economy is still significantly larger than the Japanese economy, whether one uses nominal or purchasing parity-adjusted exchange rates; the reverse was true for Britain and the United States from 1890 to 1930.

Japan's competitive edge is not as broad as the U.S. edge was in the 1930s. Although Japan seems to possess a collection of dynamic industries capable of challenging their U.S. counterparts, the broad mass of U.S. manufacturing remains 25 percent more productive than Japanese manufacturing.[23] The same was true for Britain vis-à-vis Germany in the 1890s. Like Japan, Germany used protection to propel a handful of industries to international competitiveness, but that protection hindered other industries' efforts to become competitive. British agriculture and consumer goods industries were more efficient than their German counterparts at the end of the nineteenth century. Britain's problem was that its industry was cut off at the pass in terms of most of the new growth sectors, but U.S. firms are adapting and assimilating Japanese practices while also generating new technologies.

Vis-à-vis the Europeans, the United States seems to be in the same position the British were in relation to the French in the 1890s. Franco-British relations were actually fairly tense then, reflecting a series of colonial crises. At the same time, they had a common interest in containing the rising threat to the East posed by Germany (read, in modern terms, Japan).

Like Britain in the 1890s, the United States remains at the center of the world economy in terms of trade and investment flows.[24] The financial and trade ties between Europe and Asia remain smaller than those linking the United States to Asia and to Europe. Japan's *total* trade, imports plus exports, with the OECD countries of Europe—a rough stand-in for the enlarged EC everyone expects by A.D. 2000—was less than its exports to the United States in 1988. OECD-Europe's total trade with Japan was smaller than its exports to the United States.[25] For both rivals the United States, and by extension North America, remains the key external market.

So the real question is how America's financial weakness but continued economic strength will interact. Now a net debtor, the United States will have to run trade surpluses to service its foreign debt. Indeed, U.S. exports increased faster than those of any other developed country's during the late 1980s in volume terms, allowing the United States to displace Germany as the world's largest exporter in 1991. Because the North American Free Trade Agreement creates the world's largest market, European and Japanese TNCs are likely to replace their home country exports with U.S.-sourced exports to Latin America. Conversely, European and Japanese TNC activity in Canada and Latin America will help generate additional U.S. exports to those areas. Honda's export of U.S.-built Accords to Japan and other Asian countries signals this shift in miniature. The combination of high productivity and relatively low wages in the United States makes it an ideal export platform in the 1990s; macroeconomic realities mandate increased U.S. exports. So the United States is likely to experience export-driven growth.

The United States' major weaknesses are political. Its difficulties mirror those of Japan and Europe but are not as severe. If Japan's political rigidities prevent it from adopting a greater international role, the United States' political rigidities have made it difficult to resolve the fiscal deficit. Whereas the entire structure of Japanese politics would be threatened by the adoption of that greater role, the same is not as true about U.S. efforts to cope with the deficit. Elections do matter, at least more than they do in Japan, providing mandates for change.[26] And while the United States, like Europe, has regional rivalries and many conflicting interests, it already has a common currency, common law, common market, and common military.

In short, and at least in the short term, the United States is positioned to benefit more from any revival of the world economy than the other two economies. In this respect, it greatly resembles late Victorian Britain. Its future is in its own hands; options do exist.[27]

## Long-Term Trends

As the introduction to Part I noted, this book argues that since the 1500s the expansion of the international market has gone hand in hand with an expansion of state efforts to construct viable domestic economies to serve as a secure revenue base. The outward geographic expansion of a dynamic world market from northwest Europe has been complemented by its expansion inward, as state policy supporting transportation innovations broke down barriers between the microeconomies of Europe. States faced a difficult choice in this process. Shutting out the world market most likely meant stagnation, because only a successful and selective use of world export markets could generate verdoorn effects and thus create world market competitiveness. Hooking into those international market forces — most particularly the import demand of whatever was then the world's largest economy — meant exposing the local economy to market pressures to disperse agricultural and industrial production along von Thünen lines. This dispersal would not necessarily lead to development, and it could cause considerable political dislocations as entire sectors shifted location. In the late nineteenth century, states used tariff protection to mitigate those market pressures as more and more of their local economy came into contact with the world market.

As Karl Polanyi has argued, the dislocations brought about by World War I and the Great Depression — when the market seemingly ran amok — spurred states to even greater efforts to shield their newly vulnerable economies.[28] These efforts and World War II *temporarily* reversed the trends toward greater world market pressures on local producers. With the post–1945 restoration of political and economic stability, however, those market pressures have reasserted themselves, generating new pressures for the dispersal of agricultural and industrial production. As in the late nineteenth century, states have tried to mitigate those pressures, this time using nontariff barriers and selective industrial policies. Also as in the late nineteenth century, these can only buffer local producers from world market forces, that is, from the restructuring of local production to cater to the most powerful source of demand. And as in previous centuries, those world market forces will continue to generate significant degrees of inequality. Every von Thünen city generates its own von Thünen periphery. Population pressures, state capacity, and luck determine whether or not those peripheries can develop.

With that in mind, it seems likely that the future will look much like the past — but like the past of the late nineteenth century, not that of the early twentieth century. As the British might say: "World market forces rule—OK?" The days of stable lifelong employment in large, bureaucratic corporations with secure domestic markets are gone. The erosion of America's competitive advantage in assembly-line production means that U.S. domestic policies can no longer determine the shape world market forces take, just as the rise of Britain's industrial rivals eliminated British capacity to project its domestic political choices into the world market. The rest of Part III, as my old calculus textbooks used to say, is left to the reader as an exercise. After all, you will be living it.

## Notes

1. Charles Kindleberger, *World in Depression* (Berkeley: University of California Press, 1986), p. 304. For an amusing critique of Kindleberger and hegemonic stability theory, see Isabelle Grunwald, "Exploring the 'Myth' of Hegemonic Stability," *International Organization* 44, no. 4 (1990): 432–477.

2. OECD, *Economic Outlook No. 51* (Paris: OECD, June 1992), p. 116.

3. OECD, *Economic Outlook No. 47* (Paris: OECD, June 1990), p. 31.

4. Terms of trade are the ratio of prices received for exports to prices paid for imports. Falling terms of trade imply that a country has to export increased volumes of goods to import a given volume of goods.

5. Eliana Cardoso and Albert Fishlow, "Macroeconomics of Brazilian External Debt," in Jeffrey Sachs, ed., *Developing Country Debt and the World Economy* (Chicago: University of Chicago Press, 1989), p. 98.

6. Philip Wellons, *Passing the Buck: Banks, Government and Third World Debt* (Cambridge, Mass.: Harvard University Press, 1987).

7. William Cline, *Mobilizing Bank Lending to Debtor Countries* (Washington, D.C.: Institute for International Economics, 1987).

8. This capital inflow should not be interpreted as investment; most of it went into paper assets such as Treasury bonds, into real estate, or into the purchase of existing private stocks and bonds. By and large, it did not create new productive assets.

9. OECD, *Economic Outlook No. 42* (Paris: OECD, December 1987), pp. 70–71.

10. OECD, *Monthly Statistics of Foreign Trade* (Paris: OECD, various dates).

11. This figure, based on *market valuation* of assets, was released by the Department of Commerce in May 1991. Earlier data based on book values suggested a net liability of $675 billion at year-end 1989; *The Economist*, December 15, 1990, p. 100. Current figures are undoubtedly higher.

12. Daniel Burstein, *Yen: Japan's New Financial Empire and Its Threat to America* (New York: Simon and Schuster, 1988); Jim Powell, *Gnomes of Tokyo* (New York: Dodd Mead, 1988); Michael Crichton, *Rising Sun* (New York: Alfred A. Knopf, 1992). For a timely corrective, see Bill Emmott, *The Sun Also Sets* (New York: Times Books, 1989).

13. *The Economist*, October 31, 1992, p. 75.

14. Well-publicized state economic stimulus packages—including one $80 billion construction spree—announced in late 1992 temporarily rescued the stock market when the Nikkei index appeared ready to fall below 13,000 (33 percent of the 1989 peak). A fall below 13,000 would have pushed many banks to the brink of insolvency. It was not clear whether these packages would bring property and stock value back to 1990, let alone 1989, levels. In 1993 Japan announced a new $115 billion stimulus package.

15. Ethan Kapstein, "Resolving the Regulator's Dilemma: International Coordination of Banking Regulations," *International Organization* 43, no. 2 (Spring 1989): 323.

16. *The Economist*, February 8, 1992, p. 82.

17. Paul Anderson and Mark Snowdon, "Globalization: Implications for the Automotive Industry," *EIU International Motor Business*, (London: Economist Intelligence Unit, January 1990), pp. 96–97.

18. Avner Offer, *The First World War: An Agrarian Interpretation* (Cambridge: Cambridge University Press, 1989), p. 103.

19. Aaron Friedberg, *Weary Titan: Britain and the Experience of Relative Decline*, (Princeton, N.J.: Princeton University Press, 1988).

20. World Bank, *World Development Report* (New York: Oxford University Press, 1992), pp. 222–223; United Nations Centre on Transnational Corporations, *World Investment Report 1991* (New York: United Nations, 1991), p. 36.

21. Lester Thurow, *Head to Head: The Coming Economic Battle among Japan, Europe and America* (New York: William Morrow, 1992).

22. United Nations Centre on Transnational Corporations, *World Investment Report 1991* (New York: United Nations, 1991), p. 40.

23. *New York Times*, October 13, 1992, pp. D1, D19. In 1989 the average full-time worker in the United States produced $49,600 of goods and services, compared to $47,000 in France, $44,200 in Germany, $38,200 in Japan, and $37,100 in Britain.

24. For a polemic, see Susan and Martin Tolchin, *Selling Our Security* (New York: Alfred A. Knopf, 1992). For more reasoned analyses, see Edward Graham and Paul Krugman, *Foreign Direct Investment in the United States* (Washington, D.C.: Institute for International Economics, 1989); and Dennis Encarnation, *Rivals Beyond Trade* (Ithaca, N.Y.: Cornell University Press, 1992).

25. OECD, *Monthly Statistics of Foreign Trade* (Paris: OECD, 1990).

26. For an argument about the tendency in Japan to postpone change, see Kent Calder, *Crisis and Compensation: Public Policy and Political Stability in Japan* (Princeton, N.J.: Princeton University Press, 1988). Karel von Wolferen, *Enigma of Japanese Power: People and Politics in a Stateless Nation* (New York: Alfred A. Knopf, 1989) provides an extreme version of the argument for stasis.

27. From a voluminous literature, see Paul Kennedy, *Rise and Fall of the Great Powers* (New York: Random House, 1987); Joseph Nye, *Bound to Lead* (New York: Basic Books, 1990); Henry Nau, *Myth of America's Decline* (New York: Oxford University Press, 1990). Much of this debate is misplaced, since it focuses on the relative costs of maintaining *military* dominance versus a now disintegrated Soviet Union. Bruce Cumings presents a more supple and subtle analysis in "Power and Plenty in Northeast Asia," *World Policy Journal* 5, no. 1 (Winter 1987–88): 79–107, and in "Origins and Development of the Northeast Asian Political Economy," *International Organization* 38, no. 1 (Winter 1984): 1–40.

28. Karl Polanyi, *The Great Transformation* (Boston: Beacon Press, 1957).

# Index

absolute private property rights, emergence
  of modern state and, 19–20, 45
addictive substances, Indian Ocean trade and,
  32, 39
Aden, 32
AEG, 100, 176
aerospace industry, U.S. R&D and, 314, 316
Africa
  development of, 262
  labor supply in, 127–28
  southern, 132, 136
  investment in, 153, 155
African slaves. See slavery
agricultural exports. See also agricultural
  periphery
  effects on local population of, 58, 115,
    117, 127
  profitability of, 150–52
agricultural machinery, industrialization and,
  143
agricultural periphery, 54, 56–60. See also
  developing countries; late
  industrialization; newly industrialized
  countries; Third World; and specific
  countries
  British hegemony and, 132–33, 145–46
  crisis of 1890s and, 140–43
  debt and, 266–68, 271–72, 322–33
  dominions, 132–33, 140–43, 145
  ecology and, 113–14, 120
  emergence of, 58–61
  expansion of, 110–14, 150–51
  exports by, effects on local population of,
    58, 115, 117, 127
  family farming and, 142
  in interwar period, 188–93
  Ireland as, 114–17
  labor supply and, 112, 117–28
  Ricardian development of, 130–46
    colonial states, 131
    dominions, 136–40
    failure of, 140–43
    state intervention and, 130, 135
  spatial inequality and, 47
  temperate zone, 132–33
  tropics, 144–45

in U.S., 133, 135–36
  World War I and, 189–90
agricultural products, transportation of
  emergence of modern state and, 12–14
  evolution of spatial inequality and, 50–60
agricultural revolution, in northwest Europe,
  52–53, 87–88
agricultural subsidies, 285–87
agricultural workers
  coerced labor, 48, 58–60
  indentured laborers, 123, 127–28
  late industrialization and, 90–91
  slaves, 34, 117–26
    as last-resort labor supply, 117–19
    manumission and, 122–23
    transition to wage labor and, 117–19,
      127–28
agriculture. See also headings starting with
  agricultural
  convertible husbandry, 52
  crop rotation, 52, 88
  East Asian industrialization and, 273–74
  fallowed land and, 56
  family farming, 142
  under GATT, 283–87
  Great Depression and, 282
  industrialization and, 88, 95
  in Japan, 101–2
  limits imposed by
    emergence of modern state and, 11–15,
      50–60
    late industrialization and, 91
  non-food agricultures (NFAs), 50. See also
    cotton; wool
  postwar, 283–87
  research and, 174
  seed-to-yield ratios and, 50, 88
  in 16th-century Europe, 12–15
  technological innovations and, 87–88
    diffusion of, 52–88
    evolution of spatial inequality and, 50–53
  tenant farmers in, 49
  trade liberalization and, 299–300
Amboina, 37
Americas. See also specific topics
  gold and silver from, 15, 26–27

338

# About the Author

HERMAN SCHWARTZ is assistant professor of government at the University of Virginia. He most recently published *In the Dominions of Debt: Historical Perspectives on Dependent Development* (Ithaca, N.Y.: Cornell University Press, 1989). He has received Fulbright and NEH fellowships. His current project looks at the reorganization of the state in Australia, Denmark, New Zealand, and Sweden in the 1980s.